D1327274

Khrushchev
Speaks

Khrushchev Speaks

SELECTED SPEECHES, ARTICLES, AND PRESS CONFERENCES, 1949–1961

Edited, with Commentary, by Thomas P. Whitney

Ann Arbor: The University of Michigan Press

Library of Congress Catalog Card No. 63-8075
Published in the United States of America by
The University of Michigan Press and simultaneously
in Toronto, Canada, by Ambassador Books Limited
Manufactured in the United States of America
by Vail-Ballou Press, Inc., Binghamton, N.Y.

Preface

By any standards Nikita S. Khrushchev is one of the more remarkable and fascinating statesmen of our times. Some of his utterances are basic source documents for study of current history, international affairs, and the international Communist movement. Others are not so important in themselves as they are interesting in the light they throw on the personality and attitudes of this man who has such tremendous opportunity to influence the course of events relating to the basic issue of the era—peace or a new World War. There are many uses which a collection of significant and revealing Khrushchev statements can have—in the area of education and outside it. This is the first more or less comprehensive Khrushchev anthology to appear anywhere which gives a broad selection of his works in their complete, uncut texts covering a lengthy period of his political activity. The editor hopes it may be useful as auxiliary reading for college and university courses in various social studies. He hopes it may have utility to students of Soviet affairs, journalists, diplomats, and others as a convenient reference work. He also hopes, since the anthology comprises a dramatic whole, taking Khrushchev, through the medium of his own utterances, right from the moment he returned to Moscow at the time of Stalin's seventieth birthday in 1949 to take up duties as a secretary of the Central Committee up till the conclusion of the 22nd Party Congress which ended with the decree removing Stalin's bier from Lenin's Mausoleum, that some readers may even read the book through from beginning to end as a story.

The editor wishes to express his gratitude to *The Current Digest of the Soviet Press* and Leo Gruliow, its editor, for invaluable assistance in the form of permission to use nine translations (as credited in the footnotes) from the *Current Digest* of Khrushchev speeches and documents. Gratitude is also expressed to E. P. Dutton for permission to use the translation of Khrushchev's 1958 speech on the Berlin problem contained in the volume, *For Victory in Peaceful Competition with Capitalism,* to Mr. Gene Sosin and President Howland Sargeant of the American Committee for Liberation for assistance in locating texts and translations of several documents, to the Press Department of the Soviet Embassy for other translations, and to the *New York Times Magazine* for permission to reprint an article written by the editor.

Thomas P. Whitney

Contents

Introduction

*The Tireless Voice of the Kremlin**

Stalin deeply impressed on the world the image of a Communist dictator as a mysterious, strong, silent man who hid behind Kremlin walls and hurled his rare and terrifying pronunciamentos like thunderbolts from the heights of Olympus.

In contrast with Stalin, Nikita Khrushchev, ebullient, accessible, jovial, talkative, scatters his verbal wealth about him with the greatest of generosity, not to say prodigality.

"In life one cell must die and another take its place, but life goes on . . ." commented Khrushchev at a foreign embassy reception on the dismissal of Marshal Zhukov as Defense Minister in late 1957. Can one possibly imagine Stalin talking thus in public about a rival whom he had removed from his path? But Khrushchev appears to be willing to talk in public about anything and everything.

This plenitude of eloquence by Khrushchev is, contrary to popular impression inside the Soviet Union and out, not an entirely post-Stalin development. Khrushchev was the same talkative—though a more cautious—character when Stalin was alive. In those days readers of the paper *Moscow Bolshevik,* perusing accounts of party meetings in the nation's capital, would time and again come across the laconic statement: "The First Secretary of the Moscow City and Regional Party Committee, N. S. Khrushchev, spoke." Period.

The difference nowadays is not so much that he talks more, but that he talks more in public, that the Soviet press publishes most of his speeches, and, of course, that he speaks with greater freedom and authority. He became the voice of the Kremlin—and his words carried

* *New York Times Magazine,* Nov. 10, 1957. Reprinted with permission of *The New York Times Magazine*. Revised for this volume by the author.

far indeed. Khrushchevisms became a part of international language:

"Those who wait for the Soviet Union to abandon communism will wait until a shrimp learns to whistle."

"The time will come, my little doves, when we will see whose system is better."

"The imperialists call us Stalinists. Well, when it comes to fighting imperialism, we are all Stalinists."

Khrushchev is the grass-roots politician, the back-slapper, the baby-kisser, the extrovert who loves to be seen and heard by people. He enjoys his job. He's at home in a cornfield, at a diplomatic reception or on the rostrum of the great palace of the Kremlin. He expresses himself when he talks both as a personality and a politician. And he loves to depict himself—because he likes the role and because it is good political technique—as a man of the people.

"We—working people, from among workers, collective farmers, the laboring intelligentsia—cannot be people with lily-white hands and think that farming is, so to speak, dirty work."

"A leader must know his business. Here you have correctly talked about a certain Secretary of a District Party Committee who doesn't know how long a hen sits before the eggs hatch. The Comrade is like that intellectual who said: 'Ugh, it smells of cows,' and held his nose, but at the same time eats veal even though he doesn't know where calves come from."

"Soon after the war I went to the village where I was born and called on my cousin. She had an orchard. I said to her: 'You have wonderful apple trees.' She replied: 'I'm cutting them down this fall.' I asked 'Why?' She answered: 'I'll have to pay big taxes. It's not profitable to have an orchard.' I told J. V. Stalin about this conversation and informed him that collective farmers are cutting down their orchards. And he told me that I was a *narodnik* [a peasant-oriented Socialist], that I possessed a peasant approach, that I had lost my proletarian class touch."

Here we see Khrushchev portraying himself deftly not only as a man of the soil who understands peasant problems but also as a character of backbone who stood up to Stalin and told him about the real state of affairs in the countryside. The Khrushchev technique of telling the public through little anecdotes what kind of person he is—or, rather, what kind he wants them to think he is—comes out all the time in his speeches. In one famous passage in which he discussed the unexemplary state of plumbing in a Urals hotel where he stayed for a few days, he mentioned that, after all, he had been a plumber himself.

Somehow, in many of the Khrushchev speeches touches also occur to show how, as a true son of the people, he has a somewhat sardonic contempt for eggheads. When, for instance, Soviet scientists rejected organic-mineral fertilizer mixtures advocated by that other son of the people, the controversial agronomist T. D. Lysenko, Khrushchev declared:

"Can one really thus decide scientific controversies? That's like the anecdote in which it was decided that the girl who gave birth to a baby should nevertheless still be called a virgin."

And when Soviet agricultural economists told him it would be impossible to carry out his project of catching up with the United States in milk, butter and meat production in three or four years' time he took occasion to ridicule them in an address, telling how they "took up their little pencils" and figured everything out, forgetting "what forces have accumulated in our people." So, he said, "let them blush."

This is also an excellent example of Khrushchevian demagogy. It was the much-ridiculed agricultural economists with their "little pencils" who turned out to be right in the end and Khrushchev who turned out to be mistaken. The much-heralded Khrushchev plan to catch up with America in meat, milk, and butter production is not mentioned any longer in the Soviet Union. And in fact in 1962 in order to try to stimulate the lagging output in these items the Soviet government was forced to raise prices charged in retail outlets to consumers for them by nearly one-third—with the result that in some Russian cities price demonstrations and riots took place.

Never is Khrushchev more vivid than when he is dealing with his enemies.

On Malenkov, Molotov and company: "We had some black sheep in a good flock. They thought they would seize power but you know how it ended. We took the black sheep by the tail and threw them out."

On capitalists: "Whether they like it or not they must die. It is like a pregnant woman who is about to give birth. You can't tell her to put it off. She has to give birth. It is a natural phenomenon. It is the same with the death of capitalism. Of course, we will contribute what we can."

Khrushchevian oratory indeed runs the gamut of the emotions.

Defiant: "If you believe that the capitalist system can accomplish something, enter the competition. The truth is on the side of the people. Apart from that, we do not depend on your hate or your love. We go our way. Victory is ours!"

Conciliatory: "We said, and say, to representatives of capitalist countries, 'Let's compete, let's coexist peacefully, even if it's without love and by necessity, but coexist we must since capitalist and Socialist countries are on one planet. . . . Indeed, it sometimes happens that people marry not for love and then live their whole lives together. So let's coexist peacefully, living on one planet.' "

Threatening: "This should also be kept in mind by the statesmen of the United States, since in our time, when rocket developments are rapid, no distance will protect any country from the effects of atomic and hydrogen weapons."

Exuberant: "Life is short. Live it up. See all you can. Hear all you can and go all you can."

Warning: "We say: good gentlemen, watch the edge and don't fall in. Walk around it but don't stick your nose in."

Candid: "Now there are richer countries in the world than we Socialist countries. That is, they are richer than we today."

Practical: "Now I ask you, would it be bad if we spread our Marxist-Leninist teachings with a piece of butter? I say that, with a good bread spread like that, Marxism-Leninism would be even more tasty. And with good housing, with a better and more abundant life, with good schools, we will win all the peoples for socialism and communism."

Sardonic: "To me it makes no difference whether I am involved in the explosion of a 'clean' or a 'dirty' atomic bomb because both would kill me."

Biblical: "Mister Capitalists, think about the healing of your own souls before you talk about healing others. Heal yourselves and meanwhile we will worry about ourselves."

Proverbial: "Now the ardent defenders of capitalism will write on this all sorts of fables. They'll think up something. Well, let them yelp. The folk saying goes: 'The dog barks and the wind carries it away.' "

Inspirational: "There will come a time when our descendants, studying the heroic history of our deeds, will say: 'They did a great thing.' The people will wonder at how the workers of semi-literate Russia heading the working class went out to storm capitalism. . . ."

Khrushchev is no Demosthenes of inspired delivery. He reads off the long and boring speeches prepared for him by uninspired ghost writers with no flash of fire, his only gesture a repetitious punching of the air with his finger. But when he speaks extemporaneously—and almost all his original phrases come from such extemporaneous talks or from his own asides from his prepared addresses—he is a different man and his vigorous character can emerge.

He has a gift for dialogue and repartee. When put on a hot spot in Engand, for instance, he snapped back with the quotation: "You may call me a pot but don't put me on a stove."

Occasionally in give and take, however, when he has felt himself cornered, he has lost his temper and exploded. One such instance, a famous one, occurred in England when he was asked by leaders of the Labour Party about the fate of some 200 Social Democrats behind the Iron Curtain and replied angrily that there were none in Russia and that he had no concern with such people in other countries. This remark, accompanied by other anti-Socialist fireworks before a Socialist audience hardly increased his popularity with the European Socialists he was wooing at the time.

But Khrushchev appears to be irrepressible. His occasional *faux pas* have not caused him to shut up. And there is much in him that is rather refreshing.

Often enough it has happened that Soviet officialdom has been forced to revise or "censor" some of Khrushchev's more forthright or less judicious remarks. "I have seen the slaves of capitalism—and they live well!" Khrushchev declared in the house of American farmer Roswell Garst, in Iowa in September 1959, when he visited there—but to the best knowledge of the writer this statement was never reported in the Soviet press. There is even one case on record—Khrushchev's speech delivered in 1958 in Moscow after returning from a visit to Hungary—when comparison of the original radio text of his remarks as delivered by Khrushchev himself with the subsequent text published in the Soviet press shows hardly more than a dozen sentences in a lengthy address left intact and unchanged from Khrushchev's actual delivery of them.

His originality does, of course, have to be judged in the context of the fact that, as the only man, generally speaking, in Soviet politics who can afford to be original, he has a great advantage over any Soviet competitors. Also it might be added that much of his seemingly original material has been lifted from the rich store of Russian folk proverbs and literature.

The superficial side of the Khrushchev personality, his public face, which we have been discussing, is one thing, and the man's inner character another. One can observe the former and only guess at the latter—paying particular attention to what he has actually done and how he has done it.

For those few people in this world who read all of Khrushchev's speeches in full, and not just selected quotations, the impressive thing is not the yards and yards of monotonous Marxist-Leninist jargon which they, of course, contain, nor the frequent and amusing asides to be found there, but his wide-ranging curiosity and his encyclopedic knowledge in areas of particular interest—especially agriculture.

Even allowing for good briefing by his assistants, Khrushchev demonstrates a worthy grasp of facts and figures—on crop yields, regional problems, agricultural technology, and farmers' taxation and income. One cannot help but think that this leader of what is still, despite industrialization, a nation in large part peasant in make-up owes, in some appreciable part, his rise to leadership to his comprehension of peasant problems and psychology.

And yet this knowledge of the peasant and agriculture has not enabled Khrushchev to solve definitively Russia's farm problems. They have remained acute—and so far as can be seen are likely to remain so for an indefinite future.

There have been occasions on which Khrushchev has been portrayed in individual organs of the Western press as a drunken clown. This is highly misleading. Khrushchev's own speeches, articles, and press conferences show him to be a statesman possessed of a quick, active, and able mind—a man who in difficult situations has on occasion manifested both great self-control and remarkable histrionic ability at projection of a personality image. His personal and political record demonstrates that he has determination, stubbornness in pursuit of his aims, independence of character, and considerable political skill. If during the course of his rise to power Khrushchev's jovial effervescence and sometimes seemingly loose tongue now and then led rivals and enemies to underestimate him this at times turned out to be the worse for them.

One cannot, of course, foresee at this point whether Khrushchev's political talents will be adequate to enable him to hold his position as the recognized Soviet Communist party spokesman and leader until such time as he may choose to retire of his own volition—or until illness or death ends his stay in office. His position, after all, is difficult. And this is particularly true in the light of the divisions and divergencies in the world communist movement, in particular the conflict between the leadership of communist China and that of the Soviet Union, a conflict reflected in divisions within the Soviet party itself. He will need all his abilities.

However that may be, two things are relatively certain: In the first place, so long as Nikita Khrushchev does hold his position of leadership of the Soviet Communist party he will continue to have much to say.

In the second place, Khrushchev's public statements, which constitute in themselves a chronicle of recent Soviet affairs, will always be primary sources of Soviet history and useful keys to the understanding of modern Russia.

1949:
Stalin's Seventieth Birthday

The year of 1949 was packed with significant events for the Soviet Union and the international Communist movement. It saw the explosion in September of the first Soviet atomic bomb. It ushered in, with the proclamation in Peking on October 1 of the formation of the Chinese People's Republic, the triumph of Chinese Communism. At about the same time, meanwhile, the Russians were setting up the Soviet puppet state of the German Democratic Republic in East Germany and thereby laying the foundation for an eventual new Berlin crisis in the more distant future to succeed the one overcome only earlier that same year with the lifting by the Russians of the Berlin blockade.

The year 1949 was also marked by ominous developments in Soviet cultural and scientific life signalling that turn to aggravated and even hysterical xenophobia so characteristic of Russia during the last several years of the reign of Joseph Stalin. For a few months in the early part of the year, for example, there raged a ferocious antisemitic campaign against "homeless cosmopolitans"—a campaign which resulted in the liquidation of many prominent writers and critics of Jewish origin and in the ostracism from the arts and cultural world of many more. It was in 1948 that Stalin had formally installed the semi-charlatan prophet of "Michurinist biology," Trofim D. Lysenko, as an absolute dictator over the biological sciences in the Soviet Union with license to persecute anyone who did not agree with his thoroughly discredited thesis of heredity of acquired characteristics, any Soviet scientist who dared to express belief in the long-established relationship of genes and chromosomes to heredity. And in 1949 the campaign to propagate "Michurinist" biology was in full swing. It was in 1949 that the parallel Soviet campaign to claim all important inventions and scientific discoveries of history—and to discredit Western "bourgeois" science and technology—reached its frenetic heights.

In internal politics within the topmost levels of the Soviet leadership the year 1949 was a period of intense activity among Joseph Stalin's immediate lieutenants, his "comrades-in-arms" as they styled themselves, would-be heirs of his vast power.

In the summer of 1948 the leading spokesman of the Soviet Communist Party under Stalin, a man second in authority only to Stalin, Andrei Zhdanov, had died. This had the effect of throwing open competition among Zhdanov's colleagues for succession to his influence and position—and setting the stage for clandestine intrigues around and involving Stalin himself. Among the intriguers were the prominent Soviet political figures, Georgi Malenkov, then a leading secretary, under Stalin, of the Central Committee of the Soviet Communist Party, and also the powerful Georgian so closely associated with the Soviet police and security apparatus, Lavrenty Beria. The authority of both of these men, at the time evidently close political allies, had been considerably diminished by the rapid rise of Zhdanov in the immediate postwar period—and their opportunities were greatly enhanced by his disappearance from the scene.

Exactly what took place within the Kremlin clique in that period may never be known in full—but the results, many of which were kept in deepest secret for years, were startling. In early 1949 one of the most powerful men of the Kremlin, Politburo member and chief of the State Planning Commission, Nikolai A. Voznesensky, was arrested on Stalin's orders. Preceding and following this arrest there was taking place a general purge of persons in high positions in Moscow and particularly in Leningrad who had been close to the late Andrei Zhdanov. Among those arrested was the secretary of the central committee in charge of overseeing the work of security organs, A. A. Kuznetsov. Also arrested were the Communist party chief of Leningrad Popkov, the premier of the Russian Republic Rodionov, and many other prominent executives. Subsequently during this year, under Stalin's own supervision, was the assembly—the fabrication, as it is now described by no less an authority than Khrushchev himself—of materials for the so-called Leningrad Case, a "trial" which resulted in the execution for treason of Voznesensky and many others accused along with him. All of this, it must be emphasized, except merely the bare facts of removal of Voznesensky and others from their positions of authority, was being kept secret from the Soviet public.

So this was 1949: the first Soviet atomic bomb explosion still reverberating with its tremendous implications; the triumph of Communism in China; secret intrigue and silent purge in the Kremlin. These and other developments of the year set the scene for the biggest public celebration of Soviet postwar years—the seventieth birthday of Generalissimo Joseph Stalin on December 21, 1949.

It was for this occasion that each of the members of the Politburo of the Central Committee of the Soviet Communist Party wrote an article of eulogy to be published in the newspaper, *Pravda,* praising Stalin.

One of those articles was written by Nikita S. Khrushchev—and it constitutes the first of Khrushchev's works selected for inclusion in this particular volume. It should be read while keeping in mind the fact that Stalin, particularly during the latter years of his life, demanded from all those about him incessant paeans of praise to himself and for all his works. It was impossible to be a member of the leadership of the Soviet Communist Party and the Soviet government without giving frequent voice to such lavish praise of Stalin.

December 1949 marked not only Joseph Stalin's seventieth birthday—but also the return of Nikita Khrushchev to the political scene in Moscow.

Khrushchev had been an eminent member of the topmost level of the Soviet leadership under Stalin for many years before this. He had risen to prominence in the mid-1930's when he was made the head of the Communist Party organizations of the city and province of Moscow. In January 1938, however, he was sent by Stalin and the Party to Kiev in order to take charge of the Communist Party of the second most populous of the Soviet republics—the Ukraine. From that time on for not quite twelve years he was living and working in the Ukraine—the only member of the topmost level of the leadership to be living outside the Moscow area. In this situation Khrushchev from 1938 right on till December 1949 was not on the "inside" of things in Moscow, in the Kremlin, in Stalin's immediate entourage.

Khrushchev's return to Moscow in December 1949 where he took up duties as one of the secretaries, under Stalin, of the Central Committee of the Party, and simultaneously returned to his old duties as head of the Party organizations of the city and province of Moscow, was probably dictated by several considerations. In the first place there was evident need to add new and experienced talent to the Party secretariat—the executive arm of the Party and the actual central executive arm of government of the country—in the wake of the death of Zhdanov and the purge of his friends. In the second place Stalin probably had his own personal considerations in making the appointment. It was never his habit to allow any one particular person or faction in his entourage to become too powerful. The death of Zhdanov and the purge of Zhdanov's friends, along with other developments of the period, had certainly had the result of concentrating enormous power in the hands of Georgi Malenkov and Lavrenty Beria, and Stalin, no doubt acutely conscious of this, presumably was looking for someone independent of the Malenkov-Beria axis whom he could bring into the center of things in order to have the possibility of playing his favorite game of setting one faction in the leadership against another. He settled on Khrushchev.

So as it happens, Khrushchev's eulogy to Stalin, reprinted here, coincides almost exactly in date with Khrushchev's re-entry, by virtue of his permanent return to Moscow, into what one might call "the great Kremlin sweepstakes." In its own way it is a particularly interesting pronouncement for that memorable occasion:

STALINIST FRIENDSHIP OF PEOPLES—GUARANTEE OF OUR MOTHERLAND'S INVINCIBILITY *

All peoples of the Soviet Union and progressive mankind throughout the world are observing a precious date—the seventieth birthday of our inspired leader and teacher, Josef Vissarionovich Stalin. Millions of persons turn to Comrade Stalin with the most profound feelings of love and devotion because he, together with Lenin, formed the great party of the Bolsheviks and our socialist state, because he

* This article was published over the signature "N. Khrushchev" in *Pravda,* Dec. 21, 1949, page 9. The English translation is based on the condensed translation of this document published and copyrighted by *The Current Digest of the Soviet Press,* Vol. I, Issue 52, pp. 30–31, with the passages missing from this condensation translated [within brackets] by Thomas P. Whitney. *The Current Digest of the Soviet Press* is published weekly by the Joint Committee on Slavic Studies, appointed by the American Council of Learned Societies and the Social Science Research Council. It is edited by Leo Gruliow.

enriched Marxist-Leninist theory and raised it to a new, higher level. [Comrade Stalin, the brilliant leader and teacher of our party, defended and developed the Leninist theory of the victory of socialism in one country. Armed with this theory, the Bolshevik party, under the leadership of Comrade Stalin, rallied the peoples of our country and led them to the triumph of socialism. The victory of socialism found its expression in the new constitution, which has justly been called by the peoples of the U.S.S.R. the Stalinist Constitution.]

The despised enemies of our people have more than once attempted to shatter the unity of the Bolshevist party, to ruin Soviet rule. A great service of Comrade Stalin is that he, in mortal combat with the enemies of the people—Mensheviks, S.R.s,* Trotskyites, Zinovievites, Bukharinites, bourgeois nationalists—upheld the purity of Lenin's teaching, the unity and iron solidarity of our party's ranks. [Led by the great Stalin, the party of Bolsheviks guided with confidence the peoples of our country along the Leninist-Stalinist path to communism.]

Soviet citizens link all their achievements in the struggle for communism, in rebuilding a multinational socialist state, with the name of the immortal Lenin, with the name of the great continuer of Lenin's cause—Comrade Stalin. Comrade Stalin's name is the banner of all victories of the Soviet people, the banner of struggle for the workers of the entire world against capitalist slavery and national oppression, for peace and socialism.

Prepared for and executed under the leadership of Lenin and Stalin, the great October socialist revolution shattered and destroyed forever the chains of social slavery and national oppression. Relying on Lenin's and Stalin's teaching, our party has in fact effected a proletarian solution of the national question, has established equal rights for all peoples and nations of our country and has created the great friendship of peoples which is a source of our motherland's strength and might. Herein lies Comrade Stalin's tremendous and invaluable service. He is the true friend and comrade-in-arms of the great Lenin.

From the very first days after the victory of the great October socialist revolution, Comrade Stalin, as the outstanding leader of the national policy of the Party and the Soviet state, did much to rally all nationalities of former Tsarist Russia in the formation of national

* [Socialist Revolutionaries, members of a non-Marxist Russian party.]

Soviet republics and regions and in the creation of friendship among peoples.

The first All-Soviet Congress of Soviets, Dec. 30, 1922, adopted, on Comrade Stalin's report, the historic resolution on forming the Union of Soviet Socialist Republics. The U.S.S.R. guaranteed the sovereignty and equality of all national republics, their collaboration and mutual aid in military, economic and cultural respects.

"Where the military union of the Soviet republics during the Civil War years enabled us to beat off armed interference by our enemies," said Comrade Stalin, "and the diplomatic union of these republics during the period of Genoa and The Hague alleviated our struggle against the Entente's diplomatic pressure, so the unification of the Soviet republics in a single allied state will without doubt create such a form of universal military-economic collaboration as will basically abet the economic success of the Soviet republics. It will convert them into a citadel against attempts by international capitalism" (J. Stalin, *Works* [Russian edition], Vol. V, p. 144).

The formation of the Union of Soviet Socialist Republics was a major victory of our party's Leninist-Stalinist national policy and had a decisive influence on the further strengthening of the Soviet state and of its defense capacity. [The creation of the U.S.S.R. was a classical solution indeed of the national question and an establishment of genuine friendship of peoples on the basis of Soviet power and socialism and opened broad perspectives for the development of statehood, economics, and culture of every Soviet republic.

Lenin and Stalin stood by the cradle of every Soviet republic, defended it against threatening dangers, helped in a fatherly way its growth and strengthening. If today all the republics of the Soviet Union stand before the world in the flowering of their material and spiritual forces, for these they are obliged to the brilliant teaching of Lenin-Stalin, to the wise leadership of Comrade Stalin. That is why all the peoples of our country with unusual warmth and a feeling of filial love call the great Stalin their dear father, our great leader, and their brilliant teacher.]

After the victory of the great October socialist revolution a national revival of all the formerly oppressed nations of our country began. New socialist nations arose and developed on the ruins of the old order. [On the basis of the historical experiment of completing the first multinational socialist state in the world, Comrade Stalin developed and enriched Marxist-Leninist thought on the national question.]

The new socialist nations, Comrade Stalin teaches, were developed and formed on the basis of the old bourgeois nations, by means of a radical transformation, in the spirit of socialism, after capitalism had been overthrown in Russia and the bourgeoisie and its nationalist parties had been eliminated and the Soviet order established. [In his work, "The National Question and Leninism," Comrade Stalin wrote: ". . . The destruction of national oppression led to the national renaissance of previously oppressed nations of our country, to the growth of their national culture, to the strengthening of friendly international ties between peoples of our country and to the establishment of cooperation between them in the cause of Socialist construction.

"It is necessary to remember that these reborn nations are no longer old, bourgeois nations, led by the bourgeoisie, but new, Socialist nations arising from the ruins of the old nations and led by the internationalist party of the working masses" (J. Stalin, Vol. 11, p. 353).]

All the fraternal peoples of our country see with a feeling of national pride the great transformation they have brought about in the composition of the U.S.S.R. under the leadership of the party of Lenin and Stalin and relying on Stalinist friendship of peoples.

This is clearly seen in the example of the Soviet Ukraine, as in any other republic of the Soviet Union. On the eve of the war, the socialist industry of the Ukraine produced almost twice as much as did the industry of all pre-revolutionary Russia, and 11 times as much as the industry of the Ukraine in 1913.

Only with the aid of the entire Soviet Union were rapid development of machine building, the high degree of mechanization in the Donets Coal Basin, and provision in a relatively short time of a large number of Marten ovens and rolling mills possible. The Ukraine alone would have been incapable of equipping such giants of socialist industry as the Lenin Dnieper Power Station, the Stalin Machine Building Works at Novo-Kramatorsk, the Kharkov Tractor Works and others. [Thanks to the successful carrying out of the Stalin period of industrialization, our country has become a first-class industrial power.]

Basic changes also took place in agriculture. On the basis of the triumph of the Stalinist policy of collectivizing agriculture, the most numerous exploiting class, the kulaks, was eliminated. Bondage to kulaks and village poverty disappeared. The widespread use of machinery and agrotechnics in collective farm production have considerably lessened the labor of the peasants and have increased harvests.

Collective farms of the Ukraine and other fraternal republics are increasing their total harvest of wheat and other crops from year to year and are fulfilling their obligations to the state ahead of schedule. The incomes of collective farms and their workers are steadily growing. The path of a prosperous, cultured and joyful life has opened up before collective farm peasantry.

A culture that is socialist in content and national in form is being successfully developed. Universal compulsory primary education in the native language has been established in the republic. General secondary education in the cities and workers' settlements and seven-year education in villages are being realized. In the 29,768 primary, secondary and seven-year schools of the Ukraine, 6,544,000 children are taught. The Ukraine has been transformed into a republic of 100 per cent literacy. There has been a significant growth in the network of higher educational institutions and scientific and cultural-educational institutions in the republic. The 157 higher educational establishments and the 560 technicums have 335,000 students at present. An Academy of Sciences, an Academy of Architecture, 480 research institutes and establishments, dozens of theaters and tens of thousands of clubs, palaces of culture and libraries have been established.

The life of every national republic of the Soviet Union is rich in examples of such cultural progress. [The Bolshevik party, carrying out the directions of Comrade Stalin, brilliantly solved the problem of creation in our republics of culturally and technically educated cadres of personnel for all branches of industry and agriculture, leaders of the cultural fronts, the education of cadres of party, economic, and trade union officials.]

The working class is growing from year to year. More than 1,000,000 technically trained young workers have been drawn into Ukraine industry since the war alone. They are graduates of the republic's schools, vocational schools and railroad schools. There are about 35,000 specialists with higher and secondary education in Ukraine agriculture. [During the postwar years in the Ukraine there have been prepared more than 2 million workers trained in machine operation, agrotechnics, and animal husbandry.]

The Bolshevist party has trained an army of 700,000 Soviet intellectuals, Party members, Soviet officials, engineers, agronomists, teachers, doctors and other specialists in the Ukraine. The formation of national cadres in the Ukraine, as in all other fraternal republics, is proof of the depth and scope of the cultural revolution which has taken place in our country under Comrade Stalin's leadership.

Like a careful gardener, Comrade Stalin cultivates and trains this personnel in a spirit of ardent Soviet patriotism. He has taught and is teaching them the Bolshevist mode of work and sharp implacability toward the slightest manifestation of alien bourgeois ideology, toward the ideology of bourgeois nationalism, rootless cosmopolitanism and servility before decadent bourgeois culture.

For centuries the Ukrainian, Belorussian and Moldavian peoples dreamed of joining their lands into united national states. But thanks only to Comrade Stalin's fraternal solicitude for the fate of these peoples, founded on the friendship of the peoples of our country and helped by the great Russian people, were these treasured dreams and aspirations of the people realized. All the Ukrainian, Belorussian and Moldavian lands are now joined together in united Soviet national states.

For all these successes, the Ukrainian people, like all peoples of the Soviet Union, are indebted to the Bolshevist party and to the leader of the Party and the people, the great Stalin. [Carrying out the brilliant program outlined by the great Stalin for the gradual transformation from socialism to communism, the peoples of our multinational motherland are incessantly strengthening their fraternal co-operation and mutual aid. In our Stalinist economic plans there are combined the interests of further strengthening of the power of our great motherland as a whole and the interests of each republic individually.

The Stalinist friendship of the peoples of the U.S.S.R. is a guarantee of prospering and invincibility of our motherland. In the person of the Soviet Union, as a multinational socialist state, the peoples of all the Soviet republics see the firm basis of their independence and prosperity. In the Stalinist friendship of the peoples they find their strength and power. ". . . so long as this friendship shall exist," teaches Comrade Stalin, "the peoples of our country will be free and invincible. No one, neither internal nor foreign enemies, is frightening to us so long as this friendship shall live and prosper."]

The power of Stalinist friendship of peoples was manifested with particular force during the years of the great patriotic war. [The Soviet multinational state emerged with honor from this severe trial.] All attempts by our enemies to disunite the peoples of the Soviet Union, to undermine the friendship of peoples and establish a regime of imperialist slavery in our country failed. ["The friendship of the peoples of our country has withstood all the difficulties and trials of war and has become yet more tempered in the common struggle of all Soviet people against the Fascist invaders" (J. Stalin).

Thanks only to the Bolshevik party which, under the leadership of Comrade Stalin, rallied all the peoples of our country in a powerful, invincible camp, thanks only to the great Soviet Union were the Ukraine, Belorussia, Moldavia, and other Soviet republics temporarily occupied by the enemy able to get rid of Fascist slavery.

Russians, Ukrainians, Belorussians, Georgians, and the sons and daughters of all the peoples of our country, motivated by the enthusiastic feeling of love for the motherland, for the great Stalin, fought shoulder to shoulder at the front and in the rear for victory over the enemy.]

One can never forget how Comrade Stalin prepared reconstruction projects, unprecedented in their scope, for Soviet land liberated from the enemy. Our advancing troops were still far from this or that district of the Ukraine, Belorussia, Moldavia or the Smolensk area when Comrade Stalin had already worked out plans for reconstruction work in these areas. [He daily interested himself in, and verified what was being done in order to develop more quickly the reconstruction of cities destroyed by the enemy, of enterprises, collective farms, and demanded the speeding up of the dispatching to liberated areas of industrial equipment, tractors, and agricultural equipment and seed for collective farms.] Comrade Stalin is the organizer of the aid shown by the fraternal peoples of the U.S.S.R. and the country as a whole to republics which suffered from the occupation. [Without this help, the workers of the republics and regions which underwent temporary occupation could not have even dreamed about those quick tempos of reconstruction and development of their economy and culture of the postwar period.

In the brotherly friendship of the peoples of the U.S.S.R., successfully building communism, all the peoples of the world see for themselves a great example, and are convinced of the fact that the Soviet

Stalinist path of solution of the national question is the only correct one.]

Guided by the Bolshevist party and the great Stalin, the peoples of the Soviet Union are showing the working people of the whole world the path to liberation from the social and national yoke, the path to true freedom and happiness.

Thanks to the Soviet Union and thanks to Comrade Stalin, the peoples of Hungary, Rumania, Poland, Czechoslovakia, Bulgaria and Albania stand on the path of construction of socialism. Under the leadership of fraternal Communist and Workers' parties and relying on the Leninist-Stalinist principle of proletarian internationalism, they have succeeded in strengthening their freedom and independence.

The successes and gains of the Stalinist friendship of peoples of the U.S.S.R. inspire the oppressed peoples of colonial and dependent countries in the struggle for freedom and independence, against the imperialists. The victory of the Chinese people's revolution and the formation of the Chinese People's Republic is a triumph of the all-conquering ideas of Lenin and Stalin.

Loyalty to the great cause of Lenin and Stalin, to the cause of internationalism, is determined and verified by the attitude toward the Soviet Union, which stands at the head of all forces of democracy and socialism. Treachery toward the Soviet Union and treachery toward proletarian internationalism inevitably lead into the camp of nationalism, fascism and imperialist reaction. An example of this is the Tito-Rankovic band of murderers and spies, which completed the transition from nationalism to fascism and converted itself into the direct agent of imperialism, became its weapon in the struggle against socialism and democracy.

The freedom-loving peoples of the world and all progressive mankind brand with shame these betrayers and traitors. They rally still more closely around the great, invincible banner of Lenin and Stalin, for the decisive struggle against the enemies of the Soviet Union, the enemies of proletarian internationalism. [On the day of the seventieth birthday of Comrade Stalin, all the Soviet peoples give to their dear teacher and leader an oath—incessantly to strengthen the Lenin-Stalin friendship of the peoples as the indestructible basis for happiness and prosperity of our country, as the powerful guarantee of its national independence and statehood, the guarantee of the further prosperity of the Soviet Union and of every Soviet Republic entering into its composition.]

Today the peoples of the great Soviet Union and all advanced progressive mankind greet our own Comrade Stalin, inspirer of the indissoluble friendship of peoples wholeheartedly. [Glory to our dear father, our wise teacher, to the brilliant leader of the party of the Soviet people and of the workers of the entire world, Comrade Stalin!]

1950:
Reorganization of Agriculture

The year 1950 stands out for one particular event in the area of world affairs and international relations which had heavy and lasting impact on life in a number of countries—in particular the Soviet Union, Communist China, and the United States. On June 25 the armed forces of the Soviet puppet state of North Korea, acting no doubt on orders from Moscow, attacked South Korea and thereby began the Korean War. This inaugurated an era of the most acute hostility between the United States and Russia, led to the large-scale buildup of arms industries and armed forces in both countries, and resulted in a type of tension in internal political life in both nations characterized, though in very different ways and degrees, by political hysteria and witch-hunting. Thus in Russia the antiforeign, particularly antiwestern, trends of the previous period were further accentuated and deliberate efforts were made by the government to whip up hate among the Soviet populace against America.

At the same time the self-assurance of the Stalinist leadership of the country in its ability to accomplish economic miracles found expression in various projects. This self-confidence had received a tremendous fillip in 1949 as a result of success in manufacturing an atom bomb and also, of equal importance, in the accomplishment of a very substantial degree of recovery from war damage and losses in industry.

It was in 1950 that there were promulgated decrees announcing one after another the so-called "great Stalinist construction projects," including such vast undertakings as the Volga-Don Canal, the great hydroelectric projects at Kuibyshev and Stalingrad, the ill-fated

Turkmenian Canal, and some others. These had their propaganda aspects—being intended to show that the Soviet Union was engaged in "peaceful construction" at the same time as the "imperialists" were engaged in the "Korean aggression." And they also illustrated the Soviet, especially Stalinist, obsession with the supercolossal, the gigantic. Beyond this they showed too, since most of them were actual and practical projects, that the Soviet Union had indeed matured in its economic capabilities and might.

The same psychology which led to the "great Stalinist construction projects" and the same tendency toward the big, the gigantic, carried over also into Soviet agriculture. And this is where the new secretary of the Central Committee of the Communist Party and simultaneous chieftain of the Communist Party organizations of Moscow city and province, Nikita S. Khrushchev, was manifesting great activity.

When Khrushchev had come to Moscow in December 1949 to take up his new duties he had evidently been told by Stalin to investigate the situation in agriculture and make recommendations. Agriculture has always been an acute problem in Soviet Russia, always a thorn in the side of the Communist Party, always an area of relative failure. And in the years immediately following the war the crisis was particularly profound.

The Politburo member who in the war years and afterward up to 1950 had been the principal Party spokesman on agricultural questions was A. A. Andreyev.

In early 1950, shortly after Khrushchev's arrival in the Kremlin, Andreyev was publicly attacked in *Pravda.* The occasion for the attack was a discussion of the question of whether stress should be placed in the organization of work on collective farms on teams or "links" —smaller units—or on brigades—the larger units. Taking a particular situation in Kursk Province—Nikita Khrushchev's home province, as it happened—as jumping off point *Pravda* editorially came to the conclusion that stress must be put on brigades, that it had been previously incorrectly placed on teams or "links," and that the fault for this lay on Politburo member Andreyev.

The particular article marked the end of Andreyev's leadership over Soviet agriculture and led to a precipitate decline in his authority from which he never recovered. It likewise marked the emergence of Khrushchev into the forefront of public attention as the Party's new spokesman on farm problems.

This new position and authority of Khrushchev became fully apparent shortly after the criticism of Andreyev and the team or "link" system when *Pravda* published on April 25 an article by Khrushchev calling for the merger in Moscow province of small collective farms so as to form fewer but larger farm units. The Khrushchev article launched, as things turned out, a nationwide campaign for merger of small farms into larger farms which resulted in a reduction of the total number of collective farms in the country from over 250,000 to well under 100,000 in the course of little more than a year. The average farm area was correspondingly greatly increased.

Khrushchev who had previously been able to apply some of his ideas on changes in the structure of collective farm agriculture in the Ukraine when he was Party chieftain there endeavored to apply them on a nationwide scale.

Khrushchev's *Pravda* article of April 25, 1950, is printed here as the second item in this collection of Khrushchev documents:

ON SOME QUESTIONS OF THE FURTHER ORGANIZATIONAL AND ECONOMIC STRENGTHENING OF THE COLLECTIVE FARMS *

[The Soviet people, under the leadership of the Communist Party, under the wise leadership of our leader, Comrade Stalin, has achieved the greatest victories on all sectors of economic and cultural construction. As a result of the self-sacrifices of workers, peasants, and the intelligentsia of our country there has not only been attained the prewar level, but also a new powerful upsurge of industry, agriculture, and culture. The welfare of workers of the city and countryside is incessantly being increased.] Together with the entire Soviet people, the collective farmers, Machine and Tractor Station workers and state farmers of Moscow Province are working unselfishly for the welfare of their socialist motherland. Relying on the assistance of the state, utilizing the achievements of Soviet agronomy and applying the experience of leading farmers, the collective and state farms in 1949

* This article was published in *Pravda,* April 25, 1950. A footnote said the article was from Khrushchev's speeches at the March 16, 1950, meeting of the Moscow Province Soviet and at a conference of leading farm executives of Moscow Province, March 31, 1950. Translation based on condensed version published and copyrighted by *The Current Digest of the Soviet Press,* II, No. 17, pp. 3–6. Passages [within brackets] omitted from this condensed version were translated by Thomas P. Whitney.

exceeded the prewar level in yield and gross harvest of grain and vegetables. The plan for deliveries of agricultural products [to the state] was fulfilled ahead of schedule. The three-year plan to develop communal animal husbandry is being successfully carried out.

But we must not forget the instructions of our Party and of Comrade Stalin that the Soviet people cannot rest content with what they have achieved. We must bear in mind the fact that there are still serious defects in our work, along with the successes. It must be remembered that many unresolved tasks lie ahead of us. Therefore we must concentrate on eliminating defects; we must not gloss over them, we must bring them out into the open. It is necessary to mobilize the efforts of the collective farmers for the speediest elimination of defects in order that collective farming may grow uninterruptedly, that the collective farms may be strong and prosperous and that every collective farm may obtain high harvests of all crops, steadily improve livestock raising, settle its accounts with the state in good time, increase the communal wealth and raise the income of the farm's communal economy and the payment to farm workers per workday.

I.—The collective farms require constant attention and assistance. The Party and Comrade Stalin teach us that the collective farm system does not lessen but, on the contrary, increases the concern and responsibility of the Party and government for the development of agriculture and that the Party must not reduce but rather increase its contact with the collective farms; it must know everything that is taking place in the collective farms in order to provide timely assistance.

In order that we may achieve a new and mighty upswing in agriculture, Party and Soviet agencies must improve the supervision of collective farms and must occupy themselves continually and more concretely with organizational and economic strengthening of the farms, bearing in mind that this is a major task in collective farming.

Out of all the questions relating to the organizational and economic strengthening of the collective farms, I wish to dwell in particular on the question of enlarging the small collective farms. This is a matter of great importance to the further strengthening of the collective farms and the further development of agriculture.

There are very many small and weak collective farms in Moscow Province. Here are figures grouping collective farms of Moscow Province according to land area:

Less than 100 hectares of plowland	26%
100 to 200 hectares	40%
200 to 300 hectares	18%
More than 300 hectares	16%

Thus, 66 per cent of the total number of collective farms in the province have less than 200 hectares of plowland.

I cite the figures on the number of households in the collective farms:

Less than 15 households	10.3%
16 to 30 households	35.0%
31 to 60 households	37.4%
61 to 100 households	11.7%
More than 100 households	5.6%

Consequently, more than 45 per cent of the collective farms in the province have only up to 30 households each.

Some people say that the existence of a large number of small collective farms is, historically speaking, a special feature of Moscow Province and therefore, they say, this situation cannot be changed. Such arguments are false. The man who holds this view looks backward and not forward, and does not want to achieve further strengthening and speedy economic development of the collective farms. Leaders of the province Soviet executive committee and province agricultural administration, who evidently held this point of view, equipped the small collective farms with outdated machinery; that is, they provided the Machine and Tractor Stations and collective farms in the province with obsolete and hence less productive agricultural machinery.

Whether deliberately or unintentionally, this practice had the effect of retarding and limiting the mechanization of agriculture and was a brake upon the further development of the collective farms.

In the first period of collectivization our collective farms were frequently formed on the basis of existing villages. This was a good principle. At that time the newly organized collectives were still weak. The collective farm managers were only beginning to learn large collective farm administration. There were few agronomists, zootechnicians and other specialists in the villages. In addition, there were very few tractors and other agricultural machines at the time. Obviously, it was inexpedient to form only large collective farms at that time. It was no mere chance that at that time the Party warned against being attracted to building large collective farms with no economic roots in the villages. [Comrade Stalin in 1930 in his essay, "In Answer to Our Comrade Collective Farmers," wrote: "Now the attention of officials must be directed to organizational-economic work of collective farms in villages. When this work shows the necessary success 'giants' will appear by themselves."

During the years of building of collective farms our party has carried out enormous work in strengthening the collective farms. As a result of the victory of the collective farm structure there have taken place great achievements in the countryside. The collective farms have demonstrated their strength and vitality, have shown their enormous superiority over small-scale individual peasant farms and over large-scale capitalist agriculture. The collective farms have incessantly grown and strengthened, are increasing their productivity year by year, are increasing the total harvests of grain and industrial crops.

The collective farms are receiving constant help from the state. The Party and the Soviet government have created in our country powerful factories for manufacture of agricultural machinery which are producing an enormous number of tractors, combines, complex threshing machines, seeders, and other agricultural machines. In collective farms there have been mechanized all basic types of agricultural work for grain culture and also many processes of cultivation and harvest of intertilled crops which have in great measure lightened the labor of collective farms. There has grown up a remarkable corps of collective farm activists—heads of farms, brigadiers, heads of links for intertilled crops, and others. Constant help of agricultural specialists is at the service of collective farms. The collective farm structure has created unlimited possibilities for further vast growth of all branches of socialized agriculture.]

It must be admitted that not all collective farms develop with the same success. While the collective farms in the main are growing from year to year, raising the yield of crops, increasing the productivity of communal livestock and assuring high pay per workday to the collective farmers, there are still no few collective farms which are developing slowly and are not keeping step, as they say, with the over-all growth, not ensuring the necessary increase in the yield of crops and falling behind in the development of communal livestock raising.

An analysis of the state of the collective farms in Moscow Province shows that it is generally the small farms which lag behind, since they cannot make full use of all the advantages offered by large collective economy. Large collective farms develop considerably faster than small.

In the present conditions of highly developed mechanization of agriculture, small collective farms hold back the progress of socialist agriculture. The advantages of large-scale farms over small have been proved by the teachings of Lenin and Stalin. The strength of large-scale farming, Comrade Stalin has pointed out, lies in the fact that a large farm is able to use machinery, to take advantage of scientific data, use fertilizers, raise labor productivity and thus provide the maximum marketed produce.

The advantages of the large farm are fully confirmed by the entire practice of collective farming in our country. This may also be seen from the results of the economic functioning of collective farms in Moscow Province.

One of the important economic indices in agriculture is the cash revenue per hectare of plowland. The annual accounts of collective farms in the province for 1948 show that in the larger collective farms, having up to 400 hectares of plowland, each hectare provides 6.5 times as much cash revenue as in small collective farms having up to 100 hectares of plowland.

Further, take the indivisible funds, which are the foundation of the communal economy of the collective farms. In collective farms having more than 350 hectares of plowland the indivisible funds per hectare of plowland are 6.4 times as great as in the collective farms having up to 100 hectares of plowland.

One could cite other interesting and instructive comparisons. [For example, collective farms which have a tilled area of from 300 to 500 hectares, in comparison with collective farms which have a tilled area of up to 100 hectares, had for every hectare of tilled land: more working horses in almost double the quantity, large horned cattle in more than double the number, pigs in almost quadruple the number.

The monetary income per hectare of tilled area in large collective farms was 6.5 times as much as in small ones.]

Small collective farms expend two to three times as many workdays as large collective farms on maintenance of administrative and service personnel.

Large collective farms are able to expand the construction of communal buildings and buildings for cultural and living needs, barns, granaries and other buildings beyond the powers of small collective farms.

Thus, small collective farms bear no comparison with large. Small farms are in no position to take full advantage of scientific discoveries and have limited possibilities of using agricultural machinery—powerful tractors, combines, complex threshing machines and others. Yet without broad mechanization of agriculture it is impossible to improve agricultural technology, to raise the yield of crops and the productivity of livestock and to attain the required increase in labor productivity.

I have quoted figures for all collective farms in the province on the basis of the annual accounts. When we look at the development of individual collective farms we see a far more striking picture. Many examples from the life of collective farms in the Ukraine are fresh in my memory. Allow me by way of illustration to cite some of them in order to show what results have been obtained by large farms.

The Stalin Collective Farm in Genichesky District, Kherson Province (Chairman, Comrade Litovchenko), has 12,558 hectares of land, including 7,738 hectares of plowland. This collective farm has 720 households, situated in 15 villages. It has approximately 1,000 head of cattle, 400 hogs, 8,092 sheep and 279 horses. All field work is done here with machinery. Thirty-seven tractors from Machine and Tractor Stations work on the collective farm fields. The farm has 15 motors, 13 trucks, 84 cultivators, 22 grain drills and six cotton drills. Two electric power plants of 150 kilowatts have been built on the collective farm. Sheep shearing, water supply and fodder preparation have been mechanized, and the majority of the collective farmers' homes, buildings for cultural and living needs and work premises have been electrified. The collective farm has 140 hectares of gardens, 39 hectares of vineyards and 42 hectares of ponds. Five agricultural specialists work in the collective farm. Two more farms, the Peasant's Labor and the Path to Socialism collectives, have recently been amalgamated with the Stalin Collective Farm, and this farm will now have 14,600 hectares of land, including 9,200 hectares of plowland.

The Lenin Collective Farm, which holds the Order of Lenin, in Chemerovetsky District, Kamenets-Podolsk Province (Chairman, Comrade Boiko), has 2,551 hectares of land, of which 1,924 are plowland. For many years the farm has obtained a grain yield of more than 100 centners per hectare and a beet yield of more than 300 centners per hectare from the entire sown area. The farm has 400 head of cattle, 428 hogs and 301 horses. Five M.T.S. tractors work in this farm. A 50-kilowatt power plant has been built. The chaff cutter, machine shop, mill, grain threshing operations, barns and most of the farmers' homes use electricity. There are auxiliary enterprises—a mill, slaughter house, brick plant, sawmill and smithy. The farm has a club with an auditorium holding 500, a nursery for 150 children, a 15-bed maternity home, a 24-bed hospital, a bath house and a plug-in radio network for the community. The farm employs three agricultural specialists. For their achievements 256 collective farmers of the Lenin farm have been awarded orders and medals of the Soviet Union; 11 hold the title of Hero of Socialist Labor.

There are a considerable number of such large collective farms, developing every branch of their economy, in all the provinces and republics of the Soviet Union.

What is the secret of these collective farms' success? How did they achieve these results? These collective farms achieved remarkable successes because, as large farms, they were able to make the most rational use of machinery, to raise labor productivity, to make wide application of scientific discoveries, to use fertilizers and, as a consequence [of all this], to obtain a large volume of marketable produce.

There are quite a few collective farms in Moscow Province which have achieved great successes. Figures have appeared in the press concerning the Labor Collective Farm in Zagorsk District, which is a merger of 14 small collective farms with a total land area of 2,575 hectares. Whereas many of these collective farms were backward before this amalgamation, the Labor Collective Farm has now become a large and advanced farm of many-sided activity. Before the merger, the majority of the small farms lagged behind and obtained low harvests. In the past two years the yield of the same land has been increased to one and one-half or double, and payment to collective farmers per workday has risen sharply.

I cite comparative data for two collective farms of Konstantinovo District:

	Konstantinovo Village Farm	*Bazykino Village Farm*	*% Difference*
Households	128	15	
Total land	1,772 h	208 h	
1949 Yield per hectare:			
Grain	15.4 c	9 c	170
Potatoes	191.0 c	70 c	270
Cattle per 100 hectares of plowland	38	11.7	320
—Including: cows	13	5	260
Milk per cow	2,123 kg.	1,146 kg.	200
Hogs	45	none	
Indivisible fund per 100 hectares plowland	120,000 r.	4,000 r.	3,000
Capital investments per 100 hectares plowland	10,000 r.	600 r.	1,700

In a small collective farm it is impossible to manage the economy as it should be managed. The fields for crop rotation in small collective farms are not large and it is impossible to use powerful agricultural machines—tractors, combines, complicated threshers, etc.—to proper effect. We have facts indicating that in the larger collective farms, which have 350 to 450 hectares of plowland, the combines have been one and one-half to two times as productive as in collective farms where the plowland area is from 140 to 200 hectares. [And in the large collective farms the productivity of combines was still higher. The productivity of the thresher MK-1100 in large collective farms of Moscow region was 2.4 times as much as in small collective farms. The thresher MK-1100 is the most productive machine and for its servicing in two shifts there are required more than 40 persons. In small farms there are not enough labor-capable people to service it. Therefore in a series of districts where there are many small collective farms threshers are being used unproductively.]

Collective farmers are struggling resolutely to carry out the three-year plan for development of communal animal husbandry. This task is being solved with greater success in large collective farms. These are building modern barns, mechanizing laborious processes, etc. This is beyond the powers of small collective farms. [Collective farm economy must be conducted in a cultured way, with knowledge of the business, with application of the attainments of Soviet agriculture, science, and the experience of the most advanced elements. In order to conduct things with success in a collective farm, in addition to a good chairman, it is necessary to have agricultural specialists, agronomists, an expert in animal husbandry, a veterinarian. But is it possible that a small collective farm can have the trained, educated leader which is required for conduct of collective farm management? For a good leader there is nowhere to develop, to manifest his abilities, in a small collective farm. In addition he has little material incentive since in such a collective farm the pay is small. And how can a small collective farm support agricultural specialists? Of course it cannot, since it does not have the funds for this.]

There has been almost no construction of public and cultural buildings in the small collective farms. Indeed, what kind of construction can there be in a collective farm uniting 15 or 20 households? Can such a collective farm build a club, nursery or maternity home? In such collective farms there has not even been construction of farmers' homes or the most vital farm buildings.

The solution is to enlarge collective farms and build well-arranged villages, to which the collective farmers may move from small and badly laid-out villages. [In these new villages there will be created good living and cultural conditions for the life on collective farms.

The problem of Party, government, and agricultural organizations is to get down to the business of organization of agricultural and collective farm construction with Bolshevik determination. We can and must organize things so as in the near future to re-organize our countryside. There is no doubt that in the near future our collective farms will become still stronger and can build for collective farmers comfortable, high-quality housing, provide cultural, service, and productive buildings and also comfortable field camps in distant fields on farms.]

It is necessary to build enterprises on collective farms for manufacturing building materials—brick and tile yards, woodworking shops and other auxiliary enterprises. It is necessary to train expert builders from among collective farmers and to form them into building brigades. It is also necessary to improve the designing of village and collective farm buildings and to draw up model plans for administrative, public and cultural buildings and collective farmers' homes.

The broad masses of collective farmers understand that the further strengthening of collective farms and the growth of the collective farmers' prosperity and culture will advance considerably more rapidly if small collective farms are amalgamated into larger ones. That this question is now ripe is indicated by speeches of collective farmers at meetings and conferences in their farms, proposing to enlarge the collectives. The members of many farms have decided to merge them to make them economically strong.

During the past two months the number of collective farms in Moscow Province has been reduced by 2,139 as a result of amalgamation. In Kommunistichesky (Communist) District, mergers have reduced the number of collective farms by 98, in Yegoryevsk District by 96, in Zaraisk District by 93 and in Zvenigorod District by 65.

The amalgamation of collective farms affords enormous economic advantages. According to preliminary estimates, the following annual savings will be made by reducing administrative and maintenance personnel through merging collective farms in certain districts: 86,620 workdays in Yegoryevsk District, 92,240 in Mozhaisk District, 92,700 in Zvenigorod District, 88,300 in Taldomsk District, and 79,164 in Kommunistichesky District.

Mergers of collective farms released a considerable number of people to work in brigades and in livestock raising. In Kommunistichesky District, for example, 311 administrative and maintenance workers were released by amalgamation of farms, 336 in Yegoryevsk District, 315 in Mozhaisk, 236 in Zvenigorod, etc. [In Yegoryevsk district alone there can be maintained in collective farms more than 10 agricultural specialists from out of the economy realized as a result of the reduction of administration-management and auxiliary personnel.]

Six collective farms have been merged into the Lenin Collective Farm (in the village of Borisovo, Lenin District). Amalgamation released 14 administrative and maintenance workers. The annual economy through this saving in personnel is 6,750 workdays and 96,000 rubles. Judge for yourself what may be done with such savings, not to mention the fact that it is possible to maintain more than

9 agricultural specialists on these savings. [The enlargement of collective farms is a serious matter. This work must be carried out with intelligence. Special attention must be directed to the advancement of worthy leaders of collective farms. Success of things in every collective farm depends largely on the chairman, the board, the brigadiers. This is the most important thing in a large collective farm. If a collective farm has 50 hectares of land and has an untrained chairman who cannot provide leadership for such a small economic unit, and as a result of enlargement of collective farms one entrusts to him an economy of 500 or 1,000 hectares then only the more will he lack strength and ability for leadership of such a complex economy. Such an approach can only promote the good cause of merger of collective farms. Therefore if collective farmers of one or another collective farm decide to combine with other collective farms, then it is necessary in the first place to think of the selection of a worthy farm chairman. In this work Party and government organizations must help the collective farms. It is necessary more boldly to promote to leadership in collective farms honest, capable, literate people.]

It is impossible to allow administration by official injunction in strengthening collective farms, just as it is impossible to allow it in supervising collective farms generally. It is necessary to make a profound study of the possibilities and to consider the economic and organizational-economic peculiarities of each collective farm. The question of amalgamation must be decided by the collective farmers themselves on a voluntary basis. The business of Party and Soviet organizations is to explain to collective farmers the full advantage of this measure, which accords with the tasks of further strengthening collective farms and raising the material welfare of collective farmers, and not only to explain, but also to supervise this most important work.

II.—The U.S.S.R. Council of Ministers and the Communist Party Central Committee, in their decree on collective farm, Machine and Tractor Station and state farm preparations for spring sowing, set before Party, government and economic agencies the task of devoting increased attention to labor organization on collective farms, strengthening the permanent work brigades and raising productivity of labor of collective farmers. [Why must we strengthen the permanent production brigades? Because this is the basic form of organization of labor in collective farms. The production brigade, given correct organization, gives the possibility of use with maximum productivity of the equipment of the Machinery and Tractor Stations and the means of the collective farms themselves and also fully to make use of the advantages of collective forms of labor.]

Recently *Pravda,* the organ of the Central Committee of our Party, in an article entitled "Against Distortions in Collective Farm Labor Organization," sharply criticized and rightly condemned the corrupt practice of the Kursk Province Party Committee, which, instead of strengthening the work brigade, had adopted a policy of weakening it and substituting independent teams [smaller units] for the brigade. Every farmer is bound to draw the necessary conclusions from this article, because this question is of great importance, concerning, as it does, fundamental questions of collective farming.

Why is the practice of establishing independent teams harmful in grain cultivation? Because this practice is opposed to the mechanization of agricultural production. "Advocates" of the team in grain cultivation pulled the collective farms backward, led them to a weakened state.

It must be observed that there have been defects in the organization of labor on collective farms in Moscow Province, too. The executive committee of the Moscow Province Soviet and the province Agriculture Administration are largely responsible for this. There has been no real struggle to strengthen the work brigade on collective farms in Moscow Province. Some Party and Soviet officials have tried to identify the concept of the brigade and the team. Besides this, teams have been formed outside the brigade. In recent years individual teams have been formed in a number of collective farms for the cultivation of grain crops.

For example, on collective farms in the province in 1948 more than 4,000 teams had their own allotments of land and were engaged in cultivating grain crops. In 1949, also, many such teams were formed for grain cultivation, which proved to be impractical. Teams for grain cultivation led not to strengthening work brigades, but to weakening them and to splitting up the collective economy into small work sectors and, what is most important, held up the mechanization of work in the fields. The officials who praised the team and made it the ideal form of organization of labor in collective farms essentially adopted a policy of returning from mechanization to manual labor and underestimated the importance of mechanization in developing agriculture. . . .

At the same time, it must be emphasized that in cultivating vegetable and other similar crops it is necessary at the present stage to maintain the teams, since the cultivation of these crops is still not sufficiently mechanized.

With the development of mechanization the need to turn over even this type of crop to teams will gradually disappear. This means that in the future the work of collective farmers will be made increasingly lighter.

Of primary importance in strengthening the work brigades is the correct organization of labor. All agricultural officials are bound to devote deep study to the April 19, 1948, decree of the U.S.S.R. Council of Ministers "On Measures for Improving Organization, Raising Productivity and Regulating Payment for Labor on Collective Farms" and to ensure its constant observance in every collective farm. This decree is aimed at eliminating defects in the organization of labor and leveling in payment. Formerly payment was made per workday, regardless of the results of the work. It followed that the brigade that had conducted all field work in time, had done high quality work, and had obtained a higher yield in fewer workdays received less payment in kind and in cash when the collective farm income was divided than a brigade which worked poorly, dragged out the work beyond the deadlines and spent more workdays, while obtaining a considerably smaller harvest. [Now such injustice is removed. If the brigades work well and gather a higher harvest the collective farms of these brigades will receive in addition 1 per cent of workdays for every per cent of over planned harvests for the brigade or of the average harvests for the collective farm. And, on the other hand, if the brigades work badly and receive a low harvest, there will be deducted from the compensations of the collective farms of this brigade 1 per cent of workdays spent on this crop (but not more than 25 per cent in total) for every per cent below planned yield. Such a system of compensation for labor has already been established for collective farms working in animal husbandry. This system of payment of labor excludes leveling, creates in collective farms the incentive for increasing productivity of labor, for receiving large quantities of products of agriculture and animal husbandry.]

Unfortunately, there are still some collective farms in our province which have not yet applied this decree of the government. Party, Soviet and agricultural agencies must explain carefully to all collective farmers the essential nature of the government's decree of April 19, 1948, and see that it is put into effect this year in every collective farm, so that in autumn payment may be made everywhere on the basis of this decree.

High labor discipline is the basis of collective farm development. The struggle to strengthen labor discipline and to organize labor in exemplary manner is of enormous economic and political importance. Where there is no real struggle to strengthen labor discipline against slackers and pilferers of communal property, great damage is done to the communal economy of the collective farms and the interests of honest collective farmers.

It is necessary to give active support to all conscientious officials in their struggle against slackers and parasites, to mobilize all the collective farm public to fight for firm discipline in every collective farm and to create an atmosphere of hatred and public contempt for idle elements and pilferers of communal property.

It is necessary to train collective farm executives and the collective farm *aktiv* in such a way that everyone may understand that allowances of any sort to anyone, be they friends or relatives, are inadmissible in communal collective farm affairs. In any collective farm there are many leading people who are seriously concerned for the communal economy. It is necessary to rally them together and things will improve further.

There are warnings to the effect that in places the communal property of collective farms is not sufficiently well guarded. There are cases of violations of the collective farm statutes—the squandering of land, the theft of collective farm property and violation of the democratic principles of administering collective farms. It is necessary to wage a resolute struggle against those who violate the statutes and those who connive at violation.

It is necessary to explain to all collective farmers that only by strengthening the communal economy of the collective farm and only by increasing communal property can the further growth of the prosperity of collective farmers and the raising of their cultural level be achieved.

In order to bring about the further organizational-economic

strengthening of collective farms, it is necessary to do still more work in educating the masses of the collective farmers and in training thousands and thousands more leading agriculturists. It is necessary to ensure that the broad masses of collective farmers, Machine and Tractor Station workers and state farmers work according to the example and methods of leading collective farmers. It is necessary to organize a universal struggle to obtain good harvests over large areas of entire collective farms and districts.

There is no doubt that farmers in the Moscow Province, by developing socialist competition on a wide scale, will obtain good harvests of all crops this year and the further development of communal livestock breeding, will fulfill all obligations to the state, will raise payment per workday for collective farmers and thereby fulfill the pledges made in their letter to the great leader, Comrade Stalin.

1951:
The Agrogorod Question

The year 1951 in the Soviet Union was characterized by an absence of outstandingly important public events.

In the Far East the Korean conflict continued—but the danger of its erupting into a new World War diminished considerably with the relative stabilization of a front line and the beginning in mid-year of the long and drawn-out armistice negotiations. The Soviet government carefully avoided overt involvement but continued to send large supplies of arms to the North Koreans and the Chinese Communists and also to wage an incessant propaganda campaign against the "imperialists" participating in the U.N. Korean forces.

The international situation continued to be tense and this fact was reflected within the Soviet Union in a never-ending campaign against Western influences, in continual attacks on "sycophancy before foreignism" wherever it could be found in Soviet life. Thus, for one example, the scientific attainments of even such a distinguished and peaceful Westerner as Dr. Albert Einstein were brought under fire in Soviet publications—and his theories labeled as "idealist," a term of opprobrium in the Communist lexicon. This sort of thing was part of a general, continuous probing and delving by ideological experts of the Soviet Communist Party into all departments of Soviet life in search for errors, ideological deviations, and heresies. The keynote for the hairsplitting involved in this "inquisition" had been set by Joseph Stalin himself in 1950 in the course of the curious discussion on linguistics and philology. Stalin had made clear by his own investigations into this obscure area that no fields of intellectual activity were too remote to be neglected in the campaign to build a new society and remold the minds of Soviet people. This was re-emphasized in April when *Pravda* issued a major editorial pronouncement on an opera by a little-known writer by the name of G. Zhukovsky which was entitled *With All One's Heart*. No sooner had *Pravda* revealed the "faults" in this unfortunate work than the entire corps of Soviet critics went hunting for similar errors in other works—in literature, the graphic arts, and elsewhere. When *Pravda* in July discovered editorially errors of nationalist deviation in a poem by an Ukrainian poet, V. Sosyura, entitled "Love the Ukraine," again the wolf pack of Party ideological experts was set on a hunt for other nationalist deviations throughout the country in all areas of culture. Once again in the course of this there was a return to the antisemitic theme struck in early 1949 when *Pravda* at the end of October found that there were still some "antipatriotic critics" lurking in the byways of Soviet literature—and demanded they be ruthlessly exposed.

One of the Russians who became involved in "errors"—though of quite a different kind indeed—during this difficult year was Nikita Khrushchev—and it happened in a curious manner.

Khrushchev, as shown in the previous document in this anthology, had become, shortly after his arrival in Moscow as a new Central Committee secretary, the sponsor for the program of amalgamation or merger of small collective farms into larger units. This farm program had many social-economic implications and by early 1951 when the merger campaign had gone quite far it was time to discuss some of them.

One of the questions brought up by the farm amalgamations was the possibility of creating larger, centrally located farm villages or towns on each of the new enlarged farms—merging into them all the small villages dotting the countryside and bringing all the farm families belonging to one new larger collective farm into the new farm settlement. It should be noted that this would amount to a fundamental rural revolution—since most Russian villages dated from time immemorial and went right back to the days of serfdom in which one village often represented the holdings of one estate-owner. Not only that—it would also have involved large-scale investments in housing and public services to build such new country towns. In the Ukraine Khrushchev had already gotten his name closely associated with development of large rural farm towns which had been christened there "agrogorods" or in other words "agro-cities." The Soviet press had given great publicity to the "agrogorod" idea.

This then was the background for the publication of an article in *Pravda* over Khrushchev's name on March 4, 1951. It was entitled "On Building and Improvements on the Collective Farms."

The Khrushchev article, obviously an important one, being signed by a member of the Politburo and dealing with questions affecting the living conditions and livelihood of all of the Russian peasantry, specifically recommended the amalgamation of small, scattered villages on farms into large, well-built, modern collective farm settlements. It, however, criticized the use of the term "agrogorod" for such new rural towns and indicated preference for the term "collective farm settlements." At the same time the Khrushchev article dealt with one especially tricky matter—that of the individual small orchard and garden plots held by collective farmers throughout the Soviet Union as part of their house lots. Many Soviet collective farmers derived the largest part of the food for their families and also the largest part of their cash income from the intensive cultivation of these individually held garden plots—and this was just about the most sensitive subject in Soviet life. Khrushchev proposed, in building the new "collective farm settlements," to leave the peasants next to their dwellings only little bits of lots—not much more than a few square meters evidently —and to "move" the remainder of their individual plots outside the town, to a special garden area. This was so obviously a step toward eventual confiscation of these removed garden plots that it could easily meet serious resistance on the part of the Russian peasantry—and this could have serious effects on the Soviet food supply.

Thus Nikita Khrushchev was really sticking his neck out in his *Pravda* article. It was one of the most important articles carried in the Soviet press for a long time.

Therefore, it was interesting indeed when on the day after the Khrushchev article *Pravda* came out with the following terse announcement: "Through an oversight of the editorial office, in printing Comrade N. S. Khrushchev's article on 'Building and Improvements in the Collective Farms' in yesterday's *Pravda,* an editorial note was omitted in which it was pointed out that Comrade N. S. Khrushchev's article was published as material for discussion. This statement is to correct the error."

This could only be interpreted as a slap in Khrushchev's face. No one in the Soviet Union believed that the "omission" had been an error. Its publication in this form, on the contrary, indicated that the leadership, in other words Stalin, wished to make clear that this was still an open question, not settled, and that in "discussion" of the article it was therefore permissible to take pot shots at its program and indirectly at its author.

Khrushchev had evidently stepped into a trap. The indications as to who had set the trap for Khrushchev came a little later when statements by Party leaders condemning the Khrushchev proposals appeared in newspapers of Soviet Georgia and Armenia, areas where the influence of Lavrenty Beria was supreme.

Elsewhere the "discussion" did not come out into the open but later it quickly became amply apparent that the Khrushchev program for amalgamation of farm villages had been generally rejected as too costly and as improperly putting the stress on housing questions at a time when the stress should be on increased farm productivity.

Thus Nikita Khrushchev came a cropper over what one might term the "agrogorod deviation." There is every reason to think that the rebuke which Khrushchev suffered in this question still stings—and that the enmities aggravated by it, between Malenkov and Beria on the one hand and Khrushchev on the other, played a role in subsequent Soviet internal politics.

Khrushchev's *Pravda* article of March 4, 1951, is here carried as the third item in this collection of Khrushchev documents:

ON BUILDING AND IMPROVEMENTS ON THE COLLECTIVE FARMS *

I.—The development of socialist agriculture is accompanied by a rise in the living standards of the collective farmers and improvement in their conditions of life. At the same time, there is constant growth in the cultural and everyday demands and requirements of the masses. This is natural. The peasants' work has undergone fundamental change on the collective farms; more and more, it is becoming a kind of industrial labor. Work is performed with the help of modern machinery. The basic processes of agricultural production have been mechanized, which has considerably lightened the work and made it highly productive. A new culture and new ways have come to the

* From a speech at a conference on building and improvements on Moscow Province collective farms, Jan. 18, 1951. *Pravda,* March 4, pp. 2–3. Translation copyrighted by *The Current Digest of the Soviet Press,* III, No. 7, pp. 13–15.

village; the very appearance of the village has changed. The process of eliminating the antitheses between city and countryside is making gradual progress.

"The old village, topped by the church, with the best homes—those of the village policeman, priest and kulak—in the foreground and its lean-to huts of the peasants in the background, has begun to disappear," Comrade Stalin has said. "In its place there is appearing the new village, with its communal farm and business buildings, its clubhouses, radios, motion pictures, schools, libraries and nurseries, its tractors, combines, threshers and automobiles."

The amalgamation of collective farms that has been carried out has created favorable conditions for new and even mightier progress in socialist agriculture. And this will bring in its wake a further growth in people's prosperity and culture.

But in order for the amalgamated collective farms to be able to make full use of all their advantages we must strengthen them in an organizational-economic regard. One of the most important problems is merger of small villages and the erection of new collective farm villages and settlements and municipal improvements.

In past years the advanced collective farms have done much to improve their villages and put them in order. But housing construction and building for cultural and everyday needs have lagged in many artels. One of the reasons for this lag has been the existence of small collective farms, which do not possess sufficient manpower and means to develop the construction of modern public buildings and funds for collective farmers. Collective farmers living in small villages do not have an opportunity to utilize all the advantages that the collective farming system affords for improving culture and everyday life. The small collective farm did not possess the power to establish building crews and expand construction. In a small village one does not erect a school, hospital, maternity home, club, farm studies center and the other public buildings that the collective farmers need.

Housing construction in the artels as a rule was conducted only with the means at the disposal of the collective farmer-homebuilder himself, without the support that should be due from the collective farm. Consequently the entire burden of assembling building materials and performing the building work fell directly on the farmers. The farm members had difficulty in obtaining skilled labor for building their homes—carpenters, joiners, stove setters and chimney masons, roofers, etc. Not always and not everywhere have the collective farms allocated the necessary manpower and draft animals to help the collective farmers build their homes. The farm member was obliged to erect his house only in the days and hours free from work on the collective farm. All this created difficulties for the farm members in building houses and other household structures.

In practice it turned out that the more conscientious and advanced collective farmers, who concerned themselves with developing the collective farm and did not wish to deflect themselves by work on their own personal household, to the detriment of the communal economy, were unable to build new homes for themselves, while the less conscientious collective farmer could build a home for himself sooner than the leading farmer.

In large artels there is an opportunity to organize building crews, to set up enterprises producing building materials—brick, tile, etc.—to hire skilled labor and to develop construction of buildings for cultural and everyday needs and farm structures, and likewise to undertake the building of homes for farm members on a large scale. Large collective farms can and should take the responsibility for erecting housing for collective farmers. This construction should be effected with the facilities of the collective farm, at the expense of the collective farmers for whom the house is built. Naturally, the collective farms will build homes first of all for the collective farmers who work well for the communal economy and, in this way, the outstanding people will be placed in better circumstances than the slipshod farmers. Farmers who work well on the collective farm can repay the farm in a few years for building the home; payment can be made by deductions of workdays or deductions from the cash payments earned by the workdays.

Construction in the collective farms has tremendous political and economic significance. Erecting new settlements and economic centers for artels will make possible further increase in farm production and will bring the everyday life of the collective farmers closer to the conditions of city life. In place of small villages there will arise large, well-ordered collective farm settlements with schools, clubs, public baths, centers for farming study, nurseries, and other institutions to meet cultural and everyday needs. All this meets the wishes of the broad masses of men and women collective farmers. After all, the matter is one of improving the cultural and everyday conditions of their lives.

Quite obviously, construction work on the collective farms demands constant direction and help on the part of Party organizations and Soviet agricultural agencies. As in any matter, but even more so in rural and collective farm construction, it is absolutely impermissible to let things drift of their own accord.

Public production and work buildings should be erected first of all—cattle barns, machine sheds, grain elevators and vegetable storage facilities. Simultaneously, extensive building should be undertaken for cultural and everyday needs and housing construction.

It is necessary to help the collective farms in correctly laying out the new settlements, enlisting the best architects in this work and providing good designs for the collective farm settlements and for both the collective farmers' homes and public buildings. It is necessary to help the collective farms to establish production of building materials and to acquire stocks of them, to organize building crews and to train the required cadres of builders.

II.—Designing and planning agencies are presented with serious demands in connection with the expansion of construction in the countryside.

To draw up a good design for the collective farm village is not an easy matter. One cannot mechanically apply urban structural designs and urban building methods in the villages; nothing good would come of it. Accordingly, to draw up designs for the collective farms one must call upon the most inventive and able architects and construction engineers, capable of bringing a creative approach to the matter and drafting designs fully meeting the requirements of modern collective farm life.

It is imperative that designing and planning work be conducted with the cooperation of agricultural agencies and be geared to the perspectives of development of amalgamated collective farms.

Choice of site for the collective farm settlement is of considerable importance for establishment of the best possible production conditions and the best housing and living conditions for the collective farmers. Therefore correct selection of a site for the collective farm settlement is necessary in setting about the planning of a new collective farm settlement to which farmers of small villages are to be moved. When the populace of small villages is to be moved to existing centers, it is similarly necessary to choose a good spot for building the production and economic center and for erecting housing and community buildings.

In selecting the site for the collective farm settlement it is necessary to see that it is well situated in relation to the artel fields. This does not mean, of course, that the settlement must necessarily be built in the center of the farm's lands, but that is desirable where possible.

The collective farm settlement should not be laid out on both sides of large highways. It is well to put the artel's barn outside the settlement, away from the farmers' homes. Streets in the residential area of the settlement should not be particularly wide.

Standard designs are of great value in building the collective farm settlements. Standard layouts for settlements, providing plans for blocks of streets and squares, should be drawn up; standard designs should be compiled for community buildings, homes and farm buildings, combining economy and simplicity of construction with conveniences in the structures to be erected. The design should indicate the materials from which the structure is to be built, its size and cost.

In planning the settlement, heed should be given to correct placement of village offices and cultural and everyday buildings—the club, farming study center, school, hospital, village Soviet, store, park, stadium, motion picture theater, public baths and other necessary structures. These buildings should have good architectural design and their appearance should be an adornment to the settlement.

The task of building and attractively designing the centers of collective farm settlements should be treated primarily from the viewpoints of expediency, economy and the perspectives of development of the collective farm.

In the new collective farm settlement it will be necessary to make gradual installation of water mains, power lines, street lights and sidewalks. All this should be borne in mind when the building site is selected, the layout of buildings determined and the order and density of construction planned. It is necessary to look ahead and foresee the possible need for future building.

Collective farmers' dwellings will be the most numerous objects of construction in the villages. Particular attention should be devoted to plans for these houses. In drawing up plans, architects and designers should bear in mind one very important circumstance. Villages are not the same now as they were 20 years ago. Numbers of intelligentsia live on the collective farms—teachers, agronomists, doctors and highly qualified M.T.S. mechanics, tractor drivers and brigade leaders. There are many young people in the village who have had a seven- or ten-year schooling. The living standard and cultural level of the collective farmer has grown. His requirements are now different, he wants to improve his everyday life, and one room can no longer satisfy him. It should be arranged so that the collective farmer can have two, three or four rooms. The collective farms can do this, only they need to be given help. The dwellings should be spacious, light, convenient, strongly built, fire-resistant and at the same time inexpensive.

Some architects consider it best to construct settlements of one-family individual dwellings. They base themselves on the view that the collective farmers have allegedly been accustomed to individual homes, and this, they say, is part of the collective farmers' psychology. These comrades are profoundly mistaken. It is not true to think that once people live in individual houses in the countryside they cannot give up this custom. It is we who should give up our old views on the village and on the collective farmers. The present-day collective farmer is capable of understanding all that is best, of appraising rapidly all that is advanced and of appreciating the advantages of an innovation if it is convenient for living.

In the Ukraine, for example, there were architects who said houses with attics were not suitable for the collective farmers. But they were wrong. When houses with attics were built and proved convenient and attractive, the collective farmers very much appreciated them and would not agree to change them for any other single-story house.

In the new collective farm settlements, a single-story house can contain one or two apartments; there can be one-story houses with attics; two-story houses with two to four apartments. The houses need only be skillfully placed, avoiding great disharmony and also monotony. Of course, houses must be built in two or four apartments only with the consent of the collective farmers.

A sufficient variety of types of designs for dwellings must be drawn up, but the final choice should rest with the collective farmers. Our task is to help the collective farmers make the correct decision.

In drawing up plans for dwellings, the arrangement of the collective farmer's [private] farmstead must be carefully thought out, envisaging where and how the house, vegetable cellar, barn and outhouse (if it is in the yard) are to be placed.

A word about private allotments. The larger the build-up area of the settlement, the more expensive will be the construction and improvement work. Advanced collective farmers have understood this. Many of them have expressed the correct opinion that in forming the new settlements and also in reorganizing the old villages a large personal allotment should not be laid out near the house, since in this case the village will occupy a very large area, the length of streets, power lines and water main will be increased, and the cost of all the improvement work inevitably will rise considerably.

Proposals have been made to restrict the personal allotments in the settlement to small proportions, of 10 to 15 one-hundredths of a hectare. This is quite sufficient to build a dwelling and the essential facilities, to plant an orchard of 15 to 20 trees and have a small kitchen garden for growing vegetables. The remainder of the area of personal allotments stipulated by the collective farm statutes will be removed beyond the settlement limits, not in the crop rotation system but in a specially allocated area of collective farmers' personal allotments, immediately adjoining the settlement.

This is a completely correct proposal, which will not harm the collective farmers' interests, but will improve conditions for planning the settlement and greatly reduce manpower and money expenditure on the improvement work.

On the personal allotments which will be beyond the settlement limits, certain work can be mechanized with the agreement of the collective farmers, for example plowing, cultivation and harrowing. All this would lighten the labor of the collective farmer and at the same time help to raise yields.

The importance of field camps will increase in the amalgamated collective farms. Hence a task is to establish field camps at the individual field sectors, simultaneously with construction of the collective farm settlements.

Designing the field camps is not a simple matter. Careful thought must be given to creating better working conditions and conditions for cultured recreation for the collective farmers.

Establishing field camps will make it possible for the collective farms to make large savings in manpower and transportation facilities, and will enable the collective farmers to work more productively on the fields and enjoy good conditions for rest during the field work period.

III.—In designing farm buildings and buildings for cultural and everyday requirements, account must be taken of availability of local building materials and corresponding designs for various structures must be drawn up in accordance with this.

Production of building materials is now one of the most important problems. Proper attention has not been paid to this work. Existing brickyards and tile plants function unsatisfactorily, with interruptions, and erection of new factories and yards is proceeding slowly.

Hitherto many collective farms sought to have their own brickyards, which, however small, would be their own. But small brickyards exclude the possibility of mechanization. Bricks are manufactured by hand methods at such enterprises, and the production cost is very high. It is necessary to build large brickyards and tile works on the collective farms and in some districts, where even after amalgamation there remain not particularly large collective farms, evidently it will be expedient to build large intercollective farm brickyards and tile works. By building such plants, we can mechanize them and thereby ensure high labor productivity. Then production costs will be considerably lower.

It is necessary to establish mass production of cinder blocks and such new materials as mortar blocks, straw insulation matting and other wall and insulation materials, the demand for which will grow. Farm, business and cultural buildings on the collective farms, as well as dwellings should be constructed of fire-resistant materials manufactured from local raw materials.

Along with establishment of a new base for manufacture of building materials, it is necessary to make maximum use of the existing enterprises of the collective farms and local industry, ensuring their uninterrupted operation to produce brick and tile.

We asked engineers to compile comparative data on the cost of various kinds of building materials. Here are the results one gets in the case of wall materials. Silicate brick is 28 per cent cheaper than ordinary red brick; cinder block manufactured with lime is 18 per cent cheaper than the red brick. Blocks made with artificially carbonized lime are 38 per cent cheaper and sand-lime brick, steamed without pressure, 39 per cent cheaper than red brick.

At present, besides ordinary clay brick, cement-sand brick is being manufactured. This has the considerable advantage of not requiring firing. Cement-sand brick is 44 per cent cheaper than clay brick.

Accordingly, mass production should be organized of materials which are cheaper and more advantageous, depending on local conditions.

With extensive development of construction, the collective farms will experience some difficulty in procuring lumber. Therefore it is very important to make maximum use of local resources and so far as possible to reduce the amount of lumber employed, substituting other cheap and lasting materials.

In addition, it is expedient to use the lumber from the collective farm buildings and farmers' dwellings dismantled in moving [the populace of] small villages. Of the dwellings of collective farmers moving to the new collective farm settlement, there will always be found a certain number, the lumber of which will be suitable for making wooden details (window frames, doors, etc.) for the fire-resistant buildings being erected. However, account should be kept of the lumber used on the individual dwelling, so that accounts can be settled afterward among the collective farmers. Upon convincing themselves of the practicality of this proposal, the collective farmers undoubtedly will agree to it.

It is expedient to employ the same procedure in constructing public buildings and farm structures.

The work of making window frames and doors, as well as cabinet trim, is extremely labor-consuming. A great deal of effort and time is required for hand carpentry. This work can be simplified by establishing special intercollective farm or province carpentry shops, well equipped and well supplied with machines and tools.

Mass production of hardware should be organized as enterprises of local industry and industrial cooperatives. In order to do so, standard designs must be adopted for such parts.

IV.—I must dwell in separate detail on certain questions of the organization of construction work on the collective farms. This is very important. Success depends on how the work is organized on the spot as a practical matter, on how it is guided.

I wish to cite the Chapayev Collective Farm, Zolotonosha District [Poltava Province], in the Ukraine Republic, as an example of good organization of building. Here there is a permanent construction brigade of 50 master builders: carpenters, joiners, bricklayers and plasterers. The brigade exists as an independent production unit. It has its own shop and auxiliary buildings. Assigned to it are a small number of draft animals, carts and the necessary small inventory. At the height of the building work, in the period of minimum pressure of field work, the brigade is assigned additional men and draft animals. Collective farm technician Comrade Lyashenko, a graduate of a building trades secondary training school, directs the brigade. The brigade is divided into teams of seven. There are three teams of carpenters, two of joiners, and a team of coopers, wood trimmers and wood workers. One team of three men is engaged in finishing work (fretwork, wood turning, etc.). The teams are headed by the best craftsmen. Each team is given its assignments by the day or week, depending on the size of the task in hand.

Examples of good organization are also to be found in some Moscow Province collective farms. At the Zhdanov Collective Farm, Kimovo District, the construction brigade consists of 17 persons, five bricklayers, eight carpenters and four roofers. Additional help is called upon [as needed]. Work is paid by the piece, according to quotas and a payment scale in farm workdays.

Nevertheless, it must be confessed that many collective farms still do not feel the effect of the proper help by local Party and Soviet agencies and by personnel of village and collective farm building organizations in this important and urgent matter. Construction brigades have not been organized in many artels and when they exist they often work badly.

One of the substantial defects is that on many collective farms plans of construction and improvement work have not been drawn up and neither order of priority nor deadlines have been fixed for the work.

It is imperative to work out and adopt for each artel, with active participation of specialists and at a general meeting of the farm members, a construction program for farm buildings, dwellings and buildings to meet cultural and everyday needs. It should be determined which buildings are to be erected and by what deadlines, and likewise all expenditures and requirements of materials should be calculated and measures outlined for procuring everything needed for construction. Work on improvements in the collective farm settlements should be planned similarly. These projects should be reflected in the collective farms' production plans and their estimates of income and expenditures.

In order to cope with the great volume of construction and to organize the work properly, it is necessary to maintain permanent building brigades in all large artels. Where there are several small collective farms, perhaps it would be expedient, as an exception to the rule, to establish intercollective farm building brigades. Builders who are collective farm members should be enrolled in the construction crews—carpenters, joiners, bricklayers, chimney masons and stove setters, plasterers, roofers and painters. Good, experienced people who know building should be placed at the head of the brigades and their appointment confirmed at meetings of the collective farm administration boards and executive committees of the district Soviets. The construction brigades should be just as complete working units of the collective farm as field brigades or animal husbandry brigades.

There is a shortage of builders now in some artels. Training of building personnel must be organized by training within the brigade. The method of apprenticeship within the brigade is already employed in the 14th Anniversary of October Collective Farm, Krasnokutsk District, Kharkov Province. Young apprentices are assigned to experienced, skilled craftsmen for training.

Collective farms which do not have their own craftsmen to train others in the building trades should call upon craftsmen from other collective farms or building organizations. The districts must systematically conduct seminars for leaders of construction brigades. Large collective farms, having a great volume of building work and extensive production of building materials, should be instructed to add to their staffs on a regular basis engineers, building technicians and technologists who will help improve the technical guidance of construction and of the enterprises producing building materials.

In order to speed the pace of construction and lighten the work of rural builders, it is necessary to see to it that construction brigades are supplied with the necessary tools and machinery. Following the example of leading collective farms, building yards should be set up, with carpentry and metal-working shops for preparing necessary details.

[Industrial] Enterprises and institutions and scientific and educational institutions, as patrons, can provide considerable assistance to the collective farms in organizing building work. It would be well if enterprises or institutions temporarily assigned engineering and technical personnel who might teach building trades to people on the spot and help organize the production of local building materials. It would not be bad if institutes which train professional builders, architects, building-materials technologists, surveyors, plumbers and other specialists were to send students in the senior grades to the collective farms for several months of practice work.

The experience of advanced collective farms demonstrates the wisdom of concentrating building work in one or two places, not spreading it all over the village.

A few words about what the new collective farm villages are to be called. It no longer satisfies the collective farmers to call population centers "villages" or "hamlets." They are therefore looking for names which would define the new type of socialist rural center of population. In the Ukraine, for example, some of the large new villages being built have been termed "agro-cities." It seems to me this cannot be considered apt. The name "city" implies a great deal. If it is to be a city, everything here must meet the high requirements of urban culture.

The question must be approached more modestly; imposing titles should not be sought. In my opinion the name "collective farm settlement" would be very fitting. The name of a new village is an affair of the collective farmers themselves, but it must be ensured that there is no thoughtlessness or haste in its selection.

A noble and majestic task confronts our farmers, architects, engineers and builders! For the first time in history learned scholars are concerning themselves with building villages. In our socialist conditions this is no fantasy, but an actuality. And all our efforts, knowledge and experience should be employed to help reconstruct our collective farm villages.

The architects and building engineers should be imbued with a sense of the full solemnity of the tasks facing them. What a truly noble field of action opens up before them! There is room to show one's ability. It is not an easy matter. It must be remembered that many of the architects do not know the countryside well. We must help them. We will give every support to those who seek advanced, progressive methods in construction, who are thinking about the interests of Soviet people and their own state.

Immense work awaits us on moving [the populace of] small villages and building new collective farm settlements. This work is within the powers of the collective farms. All Party and nonmember Bolsheviks should embark energetically on this work. All workers of agriculture should be imbued with an awareness of the immense responsibility for this sector of work, recalling that building on the collective farms is one of the indispensable conditions for organizational-economic strengthening of the farms. By reorganizing their villages the collective farms will effect tremendous cultural changes and will make a great forward stride on the road to communism.

1952:
The 19th Party Congress

The year 1952 saw a further intensification of some trends in Soviet life which had been developing apace in 1951 and previous years.

There rose, as if by command, a chorus in the Soviet press discovering and condemning "nationalism" in various forms in the Soviet republics. This "nationalism"—"bourgeois nationalism," as it was called—was discovered in ancient folk epics and the works of modern Soviet writers alike. Simultaneously anti-Western and in particular anti-American materials poured forth in all media of Soviet communications. For example, one Soviet reader who wrote to the newspaper *Soviet Art* to ask why there could not be a Soviet "jazz"—"jazz" being a term used in the Soviet Union to describe all modern Western dance and popular music—received his proper come-uppance. He was rebuked and told that "jazz" is inimical to genuine Soviet art, that, in the words of Maxim Gorky (in one of his more anti-American moments), "jazz" is the "music of the fat men"—of the "capitalists." This was typical.

Much more menacing, however, was the drive started by the Soviet propaganda machine in February to convince the Soviet people that Americans were using germ warfare in Korea and China. This campaign culminated in mass meetings throughout the country in early summer at which vitriolic orators hurled bitter epithets at the American "imperialists" and attempted to whip Russians into a fever of hate.

It was in this kind of an atmosphere that Stalin decided to convene the most important meeting of Communists to be held up to then in the postwar period—the 19th Congress of the Soviet Communist

Party. The congress met in October. It heard major reports by Georgi Malenkov, who gave the over-all summary of the world situation and the Party's activities, and by Nikita Khrushchev, who proposed changes in the Party Statutes. The most important pronouncement of the congress period, however, was made by Joseph Stalin in the form of a treatise on the "Economic Problems of Socialism in the U.S.S.R." —published on the eve of the meeting. This document gave portions of an outline for the future directions of development of the Soviet Union—as Stalin envisioned them. It was scheduled to become a new bible for Soviet and other communists. Its issuance overshadowed the congress itself.

The fact that Nikita Khrushchev was assigned the task of proposing the changes in Party Statutes indicated that he had been given a new area of competence in his work as a Central Committee secretary. Evidently he had been put in a position of supervision over Party organizational matters. This was a key spot. It acquired particular significance in connection with the way things were going in Soviet internal affairs.

The 19th Congress ended with the election of new ruling bodies of the Party—a new Central Committee and a new Presidium (to replace the old Politburo) and Secretariat of the Central Committee. Under the new situation all these bodies were greatly enlarged. As Khrushchev later in 1956 described these changes, they evidently represented preparation by Stalin for a purge of many or perhaps all of his immediate colleagues or "comrades-in-arms," as they were styled, in his leadership. Would Khrushchev perhaps himself have eventually fallen victim to this purge? Khrushchev himself has never spoken out on this particular point.

The fourth in this series of Khrushchev documents is his report to the 19th Party Congress on proposed changes in Party Statutes:

CHANGES IN STATUTES OF THE ALL-UNION COMMUNIST PARTY (OF BOLSHEVIKS) *

Comrades! By their heroic struggle in the patriotic war, the Soviet people, guided by the Communist Party, defended the great socialist

* Report delivered at the 19th Congress of the Soviet Communist Party by Khrushchev, *Pravda*, Oct. 13, 1952, pp. 1–3. Translation copyrighted by *The Current Digest of the Soviet Press,* IV, 42, pp. 3–8.

achievements and won victories of world-historic significance. By their self-sacrificing constructive labor since the war, the working people of our country have ensured success in fulfilling the Fourth Five-Year Plan of peaceful economic construction and have made major achievements in all fields of economy, science and culture. Along with the growth of the economy, there has been a steady rise in the material well-being and cultural level of the people.

The victories and achievements are a result of the correct policy of the Communist Party, the wise leadership of the Leninist-Stalinist Central Committee and of our beloved leader and teacher Comrade Stalin. (*Stormy, prolonged applause.*)

The achievements in our country are due to the Party's great and tireless organizing work among the masses for carrying out the brilliant Stalinist plans. The Communist Party's organizing work united all the forces of the Soviet people and directed them toward the common goal of defeating the enemy in the severe years of the war, rapidly restoring and further developing the national economy after the war and successfully fulfilling the plans of communist construction.

The great ideas of Marxism-Leninism light the road to communism for the Soviet people. The strength of our party lies in the fact that it is armed with knowledge of the laws of development of society and is guided in its work by the revolutionary theory of Marxism-Leninism.

Comrade Stalin's speeches collected in the book *On the Great Patriotic War of the Soviet Union,* Comrade Stalin's work *Marxism and Problems of Linguistics* and the resolutions of the Central Committee on ideological problems are of tremendous significance to ideological and educational work in our country.

Comrade Stalin's work *Economic Problems of Socialism in the U.S.S.R.* is a new and invaluable contribution to Marxist-Leninist theory. In creatively developing Marxist-Leninist science, Comrade Stalin arms the Party and the Soviet people with the theory of the nature of the economic laws of present-day capitalism and socialism and the conditions necessary for preparing for the transition from socialism to communism.

Comrade Stalin's work on economic problems, like his other works, is of tremendous importance in solving the problems of building a communist society, in training Party members and all the working people in the spirit of the immortal ideas of Leninism.

Now, when the Soviet people are fighting with new energy to carry out the great program of projects for the building of a communist society, the guiding and organizing role of the Communist Party, as well as the importance of its organizational and ideological-educational work, is further enhanced.

Comrade Stalin teaches that after the correct policy is given, after a problem is correctly solved, success depends on organizational work, on organizing the struggle to carry out the Party's policy.

The tasks facing us make still greater demands on Party organizations, on all Communists, demands which must be taken into consideration in Party work and in building the Party.

Our party is constantly improving its methods of work and changing the forms of Party activity to correspond to the circumstances and new tasks.

Since the time of the 18th Party Congress, the Party has been enriched with new experience of Party activity which should be reflected in the Party Statutes. It is also necessary to take into consideration the fact that certain clauses of the Statutes adopted by the preceding Congress have become obsolete. In this connection it is necessary to make additions and changes in the Party Statutes.

On the Party's New Name and the Definition in the Statutes of the Chief Tasks of the Party.—The Central Committee considers that a need has matured to make the name of our party more precise. It is proposed that the All-Union Communist Party (of Bolsheviks) henceforth be called the Communist Party of the Soviet Union.

It is expedient to make the Party's name more precise for the following considerations:

First, the name "Communist Party of the Soviet Union" is more exact. This title for the Party, which is the ruling party in our country, will correspond more closely to the names of state agencies of the Soviet Union.

Secondly, there is now no need to retain the dual name of the Party, Communist and Bolshevist, since the words Communist and Bolshevik express the same thing.

In the history of our party the addition of the words "of Bolsheviks" to the name of our party had great, fundamental importance. In the prerevolutionary years, when the Party was called the "Russian Social-Democratic Labor Party," the addition of the phrase "of Bolsheviks" indicated membership in the new type of party, the party of

Leninists, which waged an irreconcilable struggle against the Mensheviks and other parties and groups hostile to the proletariat, a struggle for the victory of the socialist revolution and the dictatorship of the proletariat.

After the October revolution, when our party was renamed the Communist Party at the Seventh Congress, the additional words "of Bolsheviks" were retained in its title since they had acquired a recognized status not only in the political life of our country but also beyond its borders.

Thus arose the dual name of the Party—Communist and Bolshevist. But essentially the words Communist and Bolshevik, as I have already said, express the same meaning. And, Comrades, although all of us have grown used to calling Communists Bolsheviks, there is no longer any need to retain the dual designation in the name of the Party and in the Party Statutes.

Further, it is proposed to give the following brief definition, in Section I, of the Communist Party of the Soviet Union and of its chief tasks:

"The Communist Party of the Soviet Union is a voluntary, militant union of Communists holding the same views, formed of people of the working class, the working peasantry and the working intelligentsia.

"Having organized the alliance of the working class and working peasantry, the Communist Party accomplished, through the October revolution of 1917, the overthrow of the rule of the capitalists and landowners, the organization of the dictatorship of the proletariat, the liquidation of capitalism, and abolition of exploitation of man by man, and ensured the construction of a socialist society.

"The chief tasks of the Communist Party of the Soviet Union now are to build a communist society by gradual transition from socialism to communism, to bring about a constant rise in the living standards and cultural level of society, to educate the members of society in the spirit of internationalism, in the spirit of the establishment of fraternal bonds with the working people of all countries, and to strengthen in every respect the active defense of the Soviet country against aggressive actions of enemies."

Although Section I of the Statutes is extremely compact, it profoundly reflects the majestic results of the path traversed by our party and defines its chief tasks for the future.

For more than half a century our party has headed the revolutionary movement, tirelessly cementing its ranks. Joined by clarity of purpose and unity of will and action, the Party now represents as never before a united, militant union of Communists holding the same views, a union such as is set forth in the proposed draft Statutes.

Under the guidance of the Party the great October socialist revolution was accomplished, which overthrew the rule of the capitalists and landowners in our country; the alliance of the working class and peasantry was formed and grew strong. The Communist Party created the world's first socialist state of workers and peasants and achieved the construction of a socialist society. These world-historic achievements are reflected in Section I of the draft Statutes.

All the work of the Communist Party is directed toward a great aim —the building of communism in our country through creating the necessary preliminary conditions for a radical transition from the economy of socialism to another, higher economy, the economy of communism. The building of a communist society has become the practical task of the peoples of the Soviet Union. The tasks set by the Communist Party inspire the Soviet people in the struggle to overfulfill the Fifth Five-Year Plan, to achieve new triumphs in building communism.

Who Can Be a Party Member.—The Communist Party attaches great importance to the question of Party membership, which is a basic question in building the Party. The leaders of the Party, Lenin and Stalin, have always shown great concern for the purity of the Party ranks, for elevating the title of Party member and the significance of Party membership, for organizing and unifying the Party ranks. The Party is strong through the high awareness of every Communist and his responsibility for effecting the ideas and decisions of the Party.

In order to raise still further the title of Communist Party member and the significance of Party membership, it is proposed to reformulate the section in the draft Statutes on who can be a member of the Party:

"Any working person who is a Soviet citizen not exploiting anyone else's labor, accepting the program and Statutes of the Party, taking active part in effecting them, working in one of the Party organizations and carrying out all the decisions of the Party may become a member of the Communist Party of the Soviet Union.

"Members of the Party pay the established membership dues."

As a result of the victory of socialism, exploiting classes have been abolished in our country; exploitation of man by man no longer exists. Soviet society consists of friendly classes. The moral and political unity of the Soviet people has been consolidated.

The statement in the Statutes that any working person who is a Soviet citizen not exploiting anyone else's labor may become a member of the Party consolidates the achievements made by the Party and reflects the proposition that the Communist Party is formed of people of the working class, the working peasantry and the working intelligentsia.

The new tasks facing the Party in the building of a communist society demand of each Communist a greater responsibility for the cause of the Party. Therefore, the proposed section on Party membership points out that a member of the Party can [only] be one who not merely accepts the Party program and Statutes but also takes active part in effecting them and carries out all the decisions of the Party.

On the Duties of Party Members.—In order further to raise the vanguard role of Party members in the building of communism, it is necessary to give a fuller definition in the Statutes of the duties of Party members and to add new clauses to this section.

It is proposed, first of all, to record that it is the duty of a Party member to guard the unity of the Party in every way, as the prime condition of the Party's strength and might.

Concern for guarding the unity of the Party is the cardinal duty of a Communist. Therefore, it will be perfectly correct to begin the exposition of the duties of Party members with this basic requirement.

The inviolable unity and monolithic character of the Party's ranks have always been and will be the source of our Party's might and of its great victories. It is not accidental that the enemies of the Party, the Trotskyite-Bukharinist traitors and betrayers, tried more than once to split the Party's ranks and to shake its unity. Under Stalin's guidance our party has completely routed all attempts of the enemies of Leninism to disrupt the unity of the Party ranks.

The Communist Party came to its 19th Congress monolithically united, firm and mighty as never before, closely rallied around the Central Committee and its brilliant leader and teacher Comrade Stalin. (*Prolonged applause.*)

In the years which have passed since the 18th Congress the Party has grown and become steeled in the struggle against the difficulties of the war and the postwar period. The current period is marked by a further strengthening of Party organizations and by the development of Party democracy.

However, the level of Party political work still lags behind the requirements of life, of tasks advanced by the Party. There are shortcomings and errors in the work of Party organizations.

In his report on the work of the Central Committee, Comrade Malenkov disclosed shortcomings and errors which exist in the work of Party organizations, negative and at times unhealthy manifestations, and pointed out ways to overcome and eliminate them.

It is necessary to center the attention of all Party organizations and all Communists on persistent efforts to carry out Party and state resolutions and directives which embody the policy of our party. It is necessary to increase the effectiveness of every Party organization in every way, to strengthen Party and state discipline, to improve organizational work, and to increase the activeness of Communists in the struggle against shortcomings in the life and work of Party organizations.

The need has arisen to stipulate in the Statutes that it is the duty of a Party member to be an active fighter for the fulfillment of Party decisions.

It should be noted that we have many Party members who have a formal and passive attitude toward fulfilling Party decisions. Unfortunately there are Communists who express their agreement with Party resolutions in words but actually pigeon-hole them, regarding with indifference the matters entrusted them and manifesting little concern or effort for ensuring fulfillment of tasks set. These persons are not disturbed by the fact that the Party and government decisions in the sector entrusted to them are not satisfactorily fulfilled. They take their time, work without energy, and do not manifest initiative or persistence. These officials put off to "tomorrow" what can be done today, and frequently tie up vital matters in red tape.

Some leaders of Party organizations do not wage an adequate struggle against those who have a formal attitude to Party directives; they do poor work in training cadres in the spirit of high responsibility for matters entrusted to them.

A formal, passive attitude to Party decisions is a great evil which the Party must resolutely fight. Such an attitude toward Party decisions on the part of Communists weakens the Party's effectiveness. Therefore it is necessary to record in the Statutes that a passive and formal attitude toward Party decisions is incompatible with membership.

Another evil existing in our Party is that some Communists wrongly suppose that there are two disciplines in our party—one for the rank-and-file and another for leaders.

There are quite a few officials who consider that laws are not written for them. Conceited enough to think they can do what they like, these officials turn the enterprises or institutions under their control into their own domain, where they introduce their own "order" and their own "discipline," casting state discipline aside. They do not take into consideration the decisions of Party organizations or the opinion of the Party masses. There are many scandalous practices of all kinds wherever such bureaucrats with a Party card in their pockets are active.

It is understandable that the Party cannot countenance such a lordly, anti-Party conception of discipline. This evil, too, must be decisively eradicated, since it undermines Party and state discipline and thereby does serious harm to the interests of the Party and the state.

The interests of the Party and state require a heightened sense of responsibility in every Communist for the job entrusted to him, whatever office he may hold, and the strictest observance of Party and state discipline, which must be the same for all members of the Party irrespective of their services and the offices they hold. It is necessary to record in the Statutes that violation of Party and state discipline is a great evil harming the Party and hence incompatible with membership.

Comrades! The Party has always attached great importance to the development of criticism and self-criticism, especially to criticism from below, to the exposure of shortcomings and the fight against ostentatious self-satisfaction and complacency in work. The strength of our party lies in the fact that it is not afraid of criticism and derives energy for further advance from criticism of its shortcomings.

However, it should be recognized that an underestimation of criticism and self-criticism in the life of the Party and state still exists even now in Party organizations. Some officials who are invested with the Party's trust and placed in responsible positions do not draw conclusions for themselves from the repeated Party directives on the necessity of developing criticism and self-criticism; they gloss over mistakes and shortcomings and create an atmosphere of ostentatious self-satisfaction and complacency. Criticism and self-criticism are frequently met with obstinate resistance by some "humbug" Communists.

It has been disclosed that a great deal of harm is done the Party by Communists who shout unceasingly about their devotion to the Party while actually not permitting criticism from below but stifling it.

Suppressors of criticism employ the most diverse forms and methods of persecuting critics. One can find instances of honest people, good workers, being dismissed from their jobs merely because they have spoken out against shortcomings, instances of intolerable conditions created for people who criticize certain officials. There are even cases in which comrades who make correct critical comments are pressured into recanting and promising not to criticize shortcomings again.

It must be noted that sometimes such ugly incidents occur before the eyes of the Party organizations, the duty of which is to combat the slightest suppression of criticism. This is evident from the example of certain Party organizations in Rostov Province where self-criticism was underestimated and the necessary conditions not created for developing criticism from below. This resulted in the fact that bureaucratic officials in some Party organizations dealt highhandedly with Communists who criticized shortcomings; this was the case, for example, in Railroad Borough of the city of Rostov.

Although the Rostov City and Province Party Committees had received reports that various officials of the Railroad Borough Party Committee were connected with thieves and bribetakers and were persecuting Communists who were uncovering abuses, they did not take the necessary measures in good time and the criminals went unpunished for a long while. By a resolution of the Party Central Committee, those to blame for the suppression of criticism and other abuses have been expelled from the Party and prosecuted.

The most decisive struggle must be waged against those who hinder the development of criticism and self-criticism. Only by thorough development of self-criticism and criticism from below can we succeed in overcoming and sweeping aside all obstacles in the path of our advance to communism.

Comrade Stalin teaches that we need self-criticism as we need air or water, that without it, without self-criticism, our Party could not advance; it could not eliminate our shortcomings. Self-criticism is the foundation of our party. The Communist Party is the directing and organizing force of Soviet society; it is the ruling party in our country. Comrade Stalin points out that we ourselves must disclose and correct our errors if we want to advance, that no one else can disclose and correct them. Self-criticism must be one of the most important motive forces in our progress.

Experience shows that mere explanation of the importance of criticism is not enough. It will be perfectly correct to record in the Statutes that it is the duty of a Party member to develop self-criticism and criticism from below, to expose and seek to eliminate shortcomings in work and to remove them, and to fight against ostentatious self-satisfaction and complacency in work. The Statutes must guard Party members who criticize shortcomings in work, and protect them from suppressors of criticism. He who hinders the development of self-criticism, who silences criticism and substitutes ostentation and boastfulness in its place, is unworthy of the lofty title of Party member.

It must be said in this connection that the harmful opinion exists among some Communists that Party members do not have to report shortcomings in work to leading Party bodies. One frequently encounters cases in which responsible officials prevent Communists from disclosing an unfavorable state of affairs to leading Party bodies, on the grounds that this allegedly hinders them in their work. Bosses and bureaucrats still exist who consider that lower officials do not have the right to and should not report shortcomings in work to higher bodies. Some officials even take the path of persecuting persons who report shortcomings in work to leading Party bodies, to the Party Central Committee. It is plain that the Party must wage a merciless struggle against such dignitaries.

The Statutes now record that a Party member has the right to take any statement to any Party body, right up to the Central Committee. As is seen, this is not enough. The Statutes must state that a Party member not only has the right but the duty to report to leading Party bodies, right up to the Central Committee, shortcomings in work, irrespective of the persons involved, and the Statutes must state that those who hinder a Party member from carrying out this duty must be severely punished as violating the will of the Party.

Another great evil which has gained currency among some Communists is concealing the truth from the Party and dishonest and untruthful behavior toward the Party.

Some officials, as is shown by facts uncovered by the Central Committee and the government, try to be cunning with the Party and state, take the path of deceit, of concealing from the state material resources at their disposal. This shows that antistate practices of placing narrow departmental interests above the interests of the state and the interests of the Party have not yet been completely eradicated.

Some officials try to sweeten the state of affairs, engage in window-dressing, in padding reports on plan fulfillment.

One encounters officials who violate or circumvent Soviet laws and produce unfinished products or low-quality goods and pass them off for first-grade, thereby doing great harm to the state and the interests of the consumers.

It is plain that the Party cannot tolerate deceivers in its ranks, because such persons undermine trust in the Party by their criminal actions and morally corrupt the ranks of the Communists. It is not without reason that the saying goes: "He who tells lies cannot be a friend." We must expose deceivers, bring them out into the open, punish them severely and rid ourselves of them. At the same time it is the duty of Party organizations to train Communists in the spirit of truthfulness, honesty and strict observance of the interests of the Party and state.

In view of the above, it is proposed to record in the Statutes that it is the duty of a Party member to be truthful and honest before the Party and never permit concealment or distortion of truth and that untruthfulness of a Communist to the Party and deception of the Party are grave misdeeds incompatible with Party membership.

It must also be stipulated in the Statutes that it is the duty of a Party member to keep Party and state secrets and to display political vigilance, that disclosing Party or state secrets is a crime before the Party and incompatible with Party membership.

The necessity for adding this is dictated by the fact that manifestations of political carelessness and gullibility and instances of disclosing Party and state secrets have become fairly widespread among Communists. Many persons, carried away by economic successes, forget the Party's instruction on the necessity of taking every measure to increase vigilance. We must always remember the capitalist encirclement, remember that the enemies of the socialist state have tried and will try to send their agents into our country for subversive work. In order to achieve their foul purposes, hostile elements try to make their way into offices in the Party, state and economic organizations and to take advantage of careless, talkative individuals who do not know how to keep Party and state secrets.

It is the duty of Party organizations to put a decisive end to political carelessness, to train Communists in the spirit of the strictest guarding of Party and state secrets. Greater political vigilance on the part of Communists, an implacable struggle against any intrigues whatsoever by hostile elements, are important requisites for further strengthening our party and the Soviet state. Every Communist must remember that vigilance is necessary on every sector and under all circumstances.

A decisive condition for successful fulfillment of political and economic tasks is the correct selection, placement and training of cadres on all sectors of Party and state work. As a result of work done by the Party, the composition of executive personnel has improved considerably. But it would be a mistake to assume that there are no shortcomings in this important matter. It must be recognized that a great evil in many Party, state and economic organizations is an incorrect approach to the selection of cadres, selection not on the basis of political or work qualifications but on the basis of friendship, personal loyalties, local allegiance or kinship.

Wherever there is a little family group gathered—friends, relatives or neighbors—there is inevitably created a quiet backwater, a mutual desire to cover up one another's shortcomings; mutual protection is established.

There are instances of directors of some organizations and offices, in deference to family ties and friendship, protecting officials who have failed and shifting them from job to job to the detriment of the interests of the work. Some officials display unprincipled behavior by handing out favorable, eulogistic references to persons who have failed in their work and been removed from office, and thus help them find other responsible work.

Violation of Party principles in the selection of cadres leads to sprinkling the machinery of certain enterprises and institutions with unworthy personnel, crooks and scoundrels, and creates favorable soil for all kinds of abuses.

Some directors of organizations, instead of strictly observing the

Party's demand for correct selection of cadres on the basis of political and work qualifications, try to surround themselves with obsequious persons, flatterers, persons of no ability, while they get rid of honest workers who put heart and soul into their work and combat shortcomings.

It is plain that such selection of workers has nothing in common with the principles established by our party and does harm to the Party.

The task is to place the work of selecting cadres in all sections of the Party, state and economic apparatus on a higher level, to increase the responsibility of directors of enterprises, organizations and institutions in the correct selection of workers.

The Statutes must point out that it is the duty of a Party member to carry out without fail the Party directives on correct selection of cadres with regard to political and work qualifications and must record that violating these directives [that is], the selection of workers on the basis of friendship, personal loyalties, local allegiance, or kinship, is incompatible with Party membership.

The inclusion in the Party Statutes of the new points on the duties of Party members reflects the growth in the political maturity and activeness of Communists and testifies to the broad development of Party democracy which is a distinguishing characteristic of the development of our party. These additions are aimed at further promoting the initiative of the Party masses. They will evoke greater activity on the part of Communists and will be an important means of improving all the organizational and political work of Party organizations, so that the material and spiritual forces and means at the disposal of the Party and state may be used with maximum effectiveness for speeding the pace of our country's advance to communism.

It is further necessary to dwell on additions made concerning the procedure for considering questions of expulsion of Communists from the Party if they are members of elected leading Party bodies. It is proposed to set forth that a primary Party unit cannot adopt a resolution to expel from the Party any Communist who is a member of the Central Committee of the Communist Party of the Soviet Union, the Central Committee of the Communist Party of a Union republic or a territory, province, region, city or district Party committee.

The question of expelling a member of the Central Committee of the Communist Party of a Union republic, a territory, province, region, city or district Party committee from membership in the committee or the Party is decided at a plenary session of the committee concerned by a two-thirds majority.

It is proposed to set forth that the question of expelling a member of the Central Committee of the Communist Party of the Soviet Union from the Central Committee or from membership in the Party is decided by the Party Congress or, in the interval between congresses, by the plenary session of the Central Committee of the Communist Party of the Soviet Union by a two-thirds majority. A person expelled from the Central Committee is automatically replaced by a candidate for membership in the Central Committee in the order established by the Congress in electing candidates to the Central Committee.

These additions testify to the fact that the responsibility of Party members elected to leading Party bodies, responsibility to both the Communists who elected them and to the Party committees concerned is being increased.

As a measure of Party discipline, Party organizations may transfer a member of the Party to the status of candidate, but this measure of discipline is not specified in the Statutes. It is proposed to include in the Statutes that when it is necessary as a measure of Party discipline, a Party organization may transfer a member of the Party to the status of candidate for a period of up to one year.

On the Rights of Party Members.—Our party has always attached and does attach great significance to consistent realization of Party democracy. In its inner life the Communist Party strictly combines the principles of centralism with the principle that [members of] all executive Party bodies are elected, accountable and removable.

The existing Statutes state in the first clause of the section on rights of Party members that a Party member has the right to participate in free and businesslike discussion at Party meetings and in the Party press of political questions of Party policy.

The Party member's right to free and businesslike discussion of questions of Party policy, as set forth in the Statutes, is an inalienable right of each Party member, a right which stems from internal Party democracy. It should be said that in this connection the abovementioned formulation somewhat restricts and imprecisely defines the rights of Party members, limiting them to participation in discussion of practical questions of Party policy. Therefore it is proposed that the section in the Statutes on rights of Party members be put as follows:

"The Party member has the right:

"(a) To take part in free and businesslike discussion, at Party meetings and in the Party press, of matters of Party policy.

"(b) To criticize any Party functionary at Party meetings.

"(c) To elect or be elected to Party bodies.

"(d) To insist on personal participation in all cases when resolutions are adopted concerning his activities or behavior.

"(e) To address any questions or statements to any Party body, at any level, right up to the Central Committee of the Communist Party of the Soviet Union."

On Candidates for Party Membership.—I will dwell on additions to the section of the Statutes on candidates for Party membership. According to the Statutes, all persons wishing to join the Party pass through a candidate stage, which is essential in order that the candidate may acquaint himself with the program, Statutes and tactics of the Party and that the Party organization may verify his personal qualifications.

Many Party organizations do not fulfill these demands satisfactorily; they do not adequately help candidates prepare for entry into the Party and are not concerned with checking on their personal qualifications. Therefore the candidate stage is frequently turned into an empty formality and, for a considerable number of the candidates, is dragged out for a number of years.

Some Party organizations neglect Party candidates, do not draw them into active public and political life, leave the candidates alone and, in fact, decline all responsibility for their training.

There are quite a few comrades who have been candidates a long time, who work well at their jobs in industrial enterprises, on collective farms or in offices, who take part in public life, attend study circles on the history of the Party and raise their ideological level. But because of the Party organizations' lack of attention to these people they continue to remain candidates for a long time.

On the other hand, there are quite a few instances of Party organizations becoming convinced that a candidate cannot join the Party on the basis of his personal qualifications, but nevertheless they do not settle the matter.

The Party cannot countenance these shortcomings. It is necessary to improve Party organizations' work with candidates and to increase the responsibility of the candidates themselves for passing the candidate stage, so that the candidate stage may be a school of Party training and steeling for those entering the ranks of the Party.

In this connection it is necessary to indicate in the section of the Statutes entitled "Candidates for Party Membership" that the Party organization is obliged to help candidates to prepare to become Party members. On the expiration of the candidate term, the Party organization must take up the question of the candidate's Party membership at a Party meeting. If the Party candidate has been unable to prove himself for reasons which the Party organization deems excusable, the primary Party organization may prolong his candidature for a period not exceeding one year. In case it has become clear during the course of the candidature that the candidate's personal qualifications do not justify admission to Party membership, the Party organization adopts a resolution to expel him from Party candidature.

This addition will help improve work with candidates.

On the Supreme Bodies of the Party.—I turn to the question of the supreme bodies of the Party.

On Periods for Convocation of Party Congresses and Plenary Sessions of the Party Central Committee.—It is expedient to establish the following periods for convocation of Party Congresses and plenary sessions of the Party Central Committee: it is proposed to convene regular Congresses not less than once every four years and plenary sessions not less than once every six months.

On All-Union Party Conferences.—Provisions concerning all-Union Party conferences are not included in the proposed draft Statutes.

In present conditions there is no need to convene all-Union Party conferences, since topical questions of Party policy can be discussed at Party Congresses and at plenary sessions of the Central Committee.

On Transformation of the Politburo Into the Presidium of the Party Central Committee.—It is proposed in the draft revised Statutes to transform the Politburo into a Presidium of the Party Central Committee, organized to direct the work of the Central Committee between plenary sessions.

This transformation is expedient because the title "Presidium" better accords with the functions which the Politburo actually performs at the present time.

It is expedient, as experience has shown, to concentrate the current organizational work of the Central Committee in one body, the Secretariat, in which connection the Organizational Bureau of the Central Committee is to be eliminated in the future.

On Reorganization of the Party Control Commission Into the Party Control Committee Under the Party Central Committee.—In the Statutes adopted by the 18th Congress, the Party Control Commission was charged with the tasks of checking on the implementation by Party organizations and Soviet economic agencies, of resolutions of the Party and the Party Central Committee, checking the work of local Party units, calling to account those guilty of violating the Party program and Statutes and Party discipline.

Checkup on the implementation of Party resolutions and the work of local Party organizations is concentrated in the Central Committee, since checkup and verification are an inalienable and most important part of Party guidance. It is necessary to increase the role of Party control bodies in the struggle against violations of Party discipline and against instances of Communists unsatisfactorily fulfilling their duties. Therefore it is expedient to reorganize the Party Control Commission as the Party Control Committee under the Party Central Committee. It is also necessary to establish the office of representative of the Party Control Committee in republics, territories and provinces independent of the local Party bodies.

The Party Control Committee is to be charged with verifying observance of Party discipline by Party members and candidates, and calling to account Communists guilty of violating the Party program and Statutes or of breaches of Party and state discipline, as well as violators of Party ethics (persons guilty of deception of the Party, dishonesty and insincerity in relation to the Party, slander, bureaucracy, moral turpitude, etc.).

It is also proposed to charge the Party Control Committee with examination of appeals against decisions of the local Party bodies on expulsions from the Party and Party penalties.

On More Precise Stipulation in the Statutes of the Tasks of Local Party Organizations.—Comrades! The period which has elapsed since the 18th Congress is characterized by the further strengthening of local Party organizations and by an improvement in all their work.

Success in accomplishing new tasks in the building of a communist society is indissolubly linked with further improvement of all Party-organizational and political work, with intensified ideological training, arming Party members with theory and educating the working people in the spirit of lofty communist consciousness.

Taking into consideration the heightened standards set for local Party organizations and also bearing in mind that their tasks and functions, as experience has shown, are not fully reflected in the existing Statutes, it is necessary to make additions in the appropriate sections of the Statutes.

First of all it is necessary to record that the Central Committees of the Communist Parties of Union republics, the territory committees, province committees, regional committees, city committees and district committees see to undeviating fulfillment of Party directives and guide the activity of local Soviet and public organizations through the Party groups in them.

The fulfillment of Party decisions and directives has been and remains the cardinal duty and obligation of Party organizations, the basis of their work. It is necessary for these tasks to be reflected in the Party Statutes.

Further, it is necessary to reflect in the Statutes the tasks of Party organizations in the matter of developing Party criticism and self-criticism and of educating Communists in an attitude of intolerance of shortcomings in the work of the Party and state.

The Party imposes on every Communist the duty of developing self-criticism and criticism from below, of exposing shortcomings in work and removing them. This places heightened demands on Party organizations. In the development of criticism, as in every cause, things cannot be left to drift: Party organizations must direct the increasing activity of Communists, educate the Communists so that they will wage an uncompromising struggle to remove shortcomings and in this way achieve comprehensive improvement in the work of all Party, state, economic and public organizations.

The stipulation of these tasks in the Statutes stems from the necessity of putting an end to the underestimation of criticism and self-criticism, which is a most important means of developing Party democracy and strengthening the bonds of Party organizations with the masses.

Work on the communist upbringing of working people and the Marxist-Leninist education of Party members occupies a large place in the life of Party organizations.

Party organizations are faced with the task of ensuring a decisive upswing in all ideological work, of systematically improving and perfecting ideological-political training of cadres in all sections of the Party and state apparatus. This is all the more necessary since many Party organizations underestimate ideological work and still do not satisfactorily organize Marxist-Leninist propaganda.

Underestimation of ideological work must be done away with rapidly. The Statutes should record that it is the task of local Party organizations to supervise the study of Marxism-Leninism by Party members and candidates and to see that they acquire the minimum knowledge of Marxism-Leninism, and to organize work on the communist upbringing of the working people.

It is further proposed to provide in the Statutes for the formation of Secretariats in province and territory committees and the Communist Party Central Committees of the Union republics. Experience shows that it is expedient to form Secretariats in the interests of more effective examination of current questions and better organization of checkup on fulfillment. In order to prevent the Secretariats from supplanting the bureaus, the number of secretaries should be reduced to three and the Secretariats should be directed to report the decisions adopted by them to the bureau of the province committee, territory committee or Party Central Committee of the Union republic, as the case may be.

It is also proposed to record in the Statutes that the province committee, territory committee or Union republic Party Central Committee keep the Party Central Committee regularly informed and, at specified times, submit to the Central Committee reports on its activity. This is necessary so that shortcomings in the work of local organizations may be corrected in good time and positive experience in their work may be appraised and studied.

On Periods for Calling Plenary Sessions of Committees of Local Party Organizations.—It is recommended that the Statutes stipulate that plenary sessions of the Union republic Communist Party Central Committees and of the territory committees and province committees be convened not less than once in two months, that plenary sessions of regional Party committees be convened not less than once in one and one-half months and that plenary sessions of city or district Party committees be convened not less than once a month.

The establishment of these periods is due to the necessity of bringing the leadership of the local Party bodies closer to the life of the Party organizations. It will increase the role and activeness of Party committee members in resolving the tasks facing the Party organizations and will promote the further development of Party democracy, development of self-criticism and criticism from below and intensification of checkups on the fulfillment of Party directives and decisions of local Party organizations.

These are the principal changes and additions to the Communist Party Statutes which the Central Committee submits for consideration by this Congress.

The draft revised Statutes have been widely discussed in the primary Party units, at conferences and at Congresses of Communist Parties of the Union republics.

The discussion has taken place everywhere with great participation of the Party masses and full freedom of criticism. The draft revised Statutes have been greeted with deep satisfaction and have been unanimously approved by all Communists and all Party organizations.

The broad discussion of the draft Statutes and the amendments and additions put forward in this connection indicate that all Communists are imbued with great concern for further strengthening the Party and increasing its effectiveness.

The introduction in the Party Statutes of the changes and additions proposed by the Central Committee will contribute to improving the organizational work in all Party organizations and the Party as a whole.

Comrades! Our Communist Party has traveled a glorious path of struggle and victory. Under its guidance the peoples of the Soviet Union have built a socialist society and are demonstrating to the whole world by their world-historic victories the superiority of the socialist economic system over the capitalist; this has tremendous effect in strengthening the camp of peace, democracy and socialism, in rallying all the peace-loving peoples against the instigators of a new war.

By its selfless service to the motherland, our party has won the boundless trust, love and devotion of the Soviet people. The strength of our party is in its indissoluble link with the broad masses of working people. From this life-giving source the Party draws energy for new victories. The ever-growing political and work activity of the workers, peasants and intellectuals of our country is an expression of the Party's deep bonds with the masses and of the boundless trust in the policy and guidance of the Party.

The Soviet people are carrying out with great energy the vast plans of further development of the industry, socialist agriculture, science and culture of Soviet society. Tremendous creative work is going on throughout the whole of our boundless country; new factories and plants and great power stations are being built; new canals and irrigation systems are being constructed. The work of transforming nature is taking on ever broader scope.

Our socialist state, which has withstood all tests with honor, has become even more firm and mighty. The moral and political unity of Soviet society and the friendship of peoples has become still stronger.

The Communist Party is mobilizing its forces and summoning the millions of workers, peasants and intellectuals to carry out the still vaster plans of economic and cultural construction.

The 19th Communist Party Congress, which has heard and discussed the report of Secretary of the Party Central Committee Comrade Malenkov on the work of the Party Central Committee, has unanimously approved the political policy and practical work of the Party Central Committee.

The 19th Congress of our party arms the Party and the Soviet people with a majestic program of work for building a communist society. The tasks set by the Party Congress open up broad perspectives of a mighty and new upswing in economy and culture and a considerable growth in the material well-being of the Soviet people. Accomplishment of these tasks is a great step on the path of our country's gradual transition from socialism to communism.

Success in accomplishing the tasks set forth demands great effort and energy. Comrade Stalin teaches that victory does not come by itself; it must be won in a stubborn fight, overcoming the obstacles and difficulties encountered in our path. The Party is uniting its ranks still more, raising still higher the title of Party member and the significance of Party membership and the role and responsibility of every Communist and every Party organization in the fight for the cause of the Party, the cause of communism.

The Party Statutes being adopted by the Congress are a document of great organizing and mobilizing force. They will be an important means of intensifying the ideological education of Communists, of Party and state cadres, in the spirit of Leninism, and further developing Party democracy and criticism and self-criticism. The Statutes will raise the Party's organizational work to a new and higher level.

Armed with the all-conquering teachings of Marxism-Leninism, the Communist Party rallies the millions of working people of our country still more closely under the great banner of Lenin and Stalin. (*Stormy applause.*)

Long live the mighty Communist Party, truly leading the Soviet people to new victories, to the triumph of communism! (*Prolonged applause.*)

Long live the wise leader of the Party and the people, the inspirer and organizer of all our victories, Comrade Stalin! (*Stormy, unabating applause, turning into an ovation. All rise.*)

1953:
Stalin's Demise, Khrushchev's Rise

The year 1953 was eventful for the Soviet Union and also for Khrushchev.

It began with the announcement in early January of the "discovery" of the so-called "doctors' plot." This was the "case" fabricated by Stalin and some others close to him—the details are still little known—in which leading Soviet physicians, many of them of Jewish origin, were accused of plotting to kill by medical means, on orders from Zionist organizations, and also American and British intelligence services, the political and military leaders of the Soviet Union. This "case" was planned by Stalin in order to set off a purge of the political leadership of the country—and probably the massacre of most of Russia's Jews and much of the rest of the intelligentsia as well. In January and February the Soviet press worked at creating a frenzy of suspicion, a spy-hunting mania, in the country.

But the intended purge did not come off. Stalin died on March 5, 1953—of a stroke if the official announcement can be believed. To his power there succeeded the members of his old Politburo—many or most of them men he had evidently intended to kill off. Among them were: Georgi Malenkov, named immediately as premier; V. M. Molotov, named as foreign minister; Nikolai Bulganin, named as minister of the armed forces; Lavrenty Beria, named as first deputy premier and minister of internal affairs in charge of police and security; and also Nikita Khrushchev.

Khrushchev's role in the post-Stalin regime was not entirely clear at first. The initial announcement following Stalin's death on the assignment of functions in the new regime merely made apparent that he had given up his role as head of the Moscow Party organizations and would "concentrate" on his work in the Central Committee. His continuing prestige was manifested immediately in the fact that he headed the commission charged with organizing Stalin's funeral and that he presided at the funeral itself.

It was more than two weeks after Stalin's death when a brief announcement appeared in the press. The communiqué said that the Central Committee of the Party had met (a week before, as a matter of fact, according to the date given in the announcement) and named a new Secretariat for the Central Committee consisting of five men. Malenkov, it was revealed, had resigned as a secretary. The first name on the list of Party secretaries (out of alphabetical order) was that of Khrushchev. Thus, without so far possessing the formal title, he seemed to have acquired *de facto* the most important position in the Soviet Union—that of first secretary of the Central Committee, the position which had been Stalin's springboard to power.

Yet as things seemed to be for the time being in the new "collective" leadership of the country Khrushchev ranked not first, as one might expect from this position, but about fifth, behind not only Malenkov but also Beria and two others. And for the time being, at least, there was no sign that Khrushchev was in a position to throw his weight around in national affairs.

As soon as Stalin died things began to change rapidly. A number of measures were taken by the new government which had the effect of relaxing in great degree the keen tension prevailing during Stalin's last years and months both internally and in foreign relations. It soon became clear that Russia was entering a new, more promising era.

And it was also clear that there were problems of conflict within the top ranks of the leadership which were unsettled. The first of these involved Lavrenty Beria, police and security chieftain whose power represented a direct threat to all the other Soviet leaders since Beria was not accountable to anyone in the control and operation of his police empire, vast in its dimensions and embracing such varied elements as nuclear energy, counterintelligence, and forced-labor camps. It was in late June that the other heirs of Stalin united against Beria and arrested him.

Within only a few weeks after the announcement of the purge of Beria there were two important happenings. The first was the ending —with Soviet assistance—of the Korean war. This improved greatly the international atmosphere. The second was the explosion by the

Soviet Union of the first H-bomb. This latter event, which caught the world by surprise, was the more ironic in that it had been Beria who had headed Soviet nuclear weapon development right up to this outstanding success.

The Beria purge set the scene for the emergence of Nikita Khrushchev into formal possession of the highest rank in the country. The logic of the situation was very simple. Premier Georgi Malenkov's authority and power had depended on the support of Beria. When Malenkov was induced, for whatever reasons, to go along with the purge of Beria he thereby pulled the rug out from under himself. This did not become immediately apparent, but the fact that Khrushchev had moved into the center of things was made clear in September. At a meeting of the Central Committee early in that month Khrushchev made the keynote address—on the all-important subject of proposed agricultural reforms—and was elected the first secretary of the Central Committee, in other words, the Party's chief executive.

Soon the signs began to accumulate that Khrushchev was the man to watch, that Malenkov's star was declining. And later in the year when Khrushchev went to Leningrad in order to oust from the Party leadership there an appointee and protégé of Malenkov it was apparent that it was he who was calling the shots in appointments to crucial Party posts.

Khrushchev's report to the Central Committee on the agricultural situation delivered on September 3 and published nearly two weeks later is an important document. It revealed in blunt facts and figures that Stalin had left the Soviet Union in the throes of a farm crisis, and that drastic measures were required in order to effect an improvement. It is here presented as the fifth item in this series of Khrushchev documents—fittingly because it is in effect, one might say, his real inaugural address:

ON MEASURES FOR FURTHER DEVELOPMENT OF U.S.S.R. AGRICULTURE *

Comrades! The Soviet people's great successes in developing socialist industry permit the Communist Party and the state to undertake in earnest solution of the task of creating an abundance of consumers' goods in our country.

* Report delivered by Khrushchev to Plenary Session of the Central Committee of the Soviet Communist Party, *Pravda,* Sept. 15, 1953, pp. 1–6. Translation copyrighted by *The Current Digest of the Soviet Press,* V, 39, pp. 11–12, 24–41.

The great Lenin taught that "a large machine industry capable also of reorganizing agriculture can be the only material basis of socialism" (V. I. Lenin, *Works* [in Russian], Vol. XXXII, p. 434). Under the leadership of the Communist Party the Soviet people have developed an integrated heavy industry—the mighty foundation of the socialist economy. With such a foundation available there is now practical possibility for marked advances in all branches of light and food industry and a considerable expansion in consumers' goods output, for the maximum satisfaction of the steadily growing material and cultural needs of the entire society is the basic goal and chief task of socialist production.

In order to organize this marked advance in consumers' goods, however, our agriculture must be rapidly advanced.

A most urgent and important national and economic task at the present stage is to obtain a sharp rise in all branches of agriculture while further developing heavy industry and in two to three years greatly increasing the food supply for our country's entire population as well as guaranteeing the collective farm peasantry a higher level of material well-being.

In this connection the Presidium of the Party Central Committee has considered it necessary to introduce for consideration by the plenary session proposals for realizing a number of urgent measures to ensure the rapid growth and comprehensive development of agriculture.

1. The State of Agriculture and the Task of Creating an Abundance of Farm Produce.—The collective farm system created under the leadership of the Communist Party has a decided advantage over any private-ownership agricultural system, whether small- or large-scale capitalist farming. The world's largest system of socialist agriculture was established and consolidated in place of the old village system with 25,000,000 scattered, parcelled-out private farms. The socialist agricultural system in our country now includes 94,000 collective farms, 8950 Machine and Tractor Stations and more than 4700 state farms.

Our agriculture is the most highly mechanized in the world. It is generally known that modern agricultural equipment in capitalist countries is concentrated in the hands of a few capitalist farmers, and manual labor with primitive equipment predominates on the farms of an overwhelming majority of the working peasants.

The Soviet state has supplied agriculture with the first-class industrial equipment of the M.T.S., thus solving the problem of mechanizing the most important farm work. In 1952 collective farm tasks were mechanized as follows: sowing grain—87 per cent, combine harvesting—70 per cent, plowing fallow land—96 per cent, fall plowing—97 per cent, sowing cotton—98 per cent and planting sugar beets—95 per cent. The mechanization of farm production has greatly eased the collective farm peasantry's work and given our country immense savings in labor. It has permitted our country's agriculture to be based on modern, scientific farming principles.

Armed with modern agricultural equipment, the communal sector on collective farms has developed and strengthened. The collective and state farms have brought about growth in the productivity of socialist agriculture and in its commodity output. From 1926 and 1927 to 1952 and 1953 agricultural output increased as follows: grain—from 10,300,000 to 40,400,000 tons, potatoes—from 3,000,000 to 12,500,000 tons, meat (live weight)—from 2,400,000 to 5,000,000 tons, and milk—from 4,300,000 to 13,200,000 tons. Great successes have been achieved in the output of cotton, sugar beets and several other industrial crops. The growth in agricultural output has permitted the socialist state to increase year after year marketable reserves from agricultural production to cover the raw material needs of industry and satisfy the people's growing demands for foodstuffs.

As the communal sector on the collective farms strengthens and further develops, their wealth grows and the collective farmers' incomes in cash and kind increase. Suffice it to say, the indivisible funds of the collective farms doubled between 1940 and 1952. The collective farmers' actual income is now several times higher than that of the working peasantry before the revolution. A most profound cultural revolution has taken place in the country.

All this testifies to the fact that the collective farm system has radically transformed the bases of production and the daily life of tens of millions of peasants on new, socialist principles. It has opened a broad path to a prosperous and cultured life for all the toilers of the Soviet countryside. The alliance of the working class and the collective farm peasantry has become an invincible force.

However, it must be said frankly that we are making poor use of the immense resources concealed within large-scale socialist agricultural production. We have many backward and even neglected collective farms and entire districts. The crop yield continues low on many collective farms and districts. Agricultural productivity has grown very slowly, particularly in regard to animal husbandry, forage and feed crops, potatoes, and vegetables. An obvious discrepancy exists between the growth rate of our large socialist industry, city population and the material well-being of the working masses on the one hand and the present level of agricultural production on the other.

One may cite several facts by way of illustration. Between 1913 and 1952 the gross output of U.S.S.R. large industry became (in comparable prices) 27 times larger, or, if the output of the means of production is included, 47 times larger. Along with the growth of socialist industry there has occurred an accelerated increase in city population, which more than tripled between 1926 and 1952. As the wealth of socialist society has multiplied the workers' material well-being has continuously grown. Today the actual wages of U.S.S.R. workers and employees are several times greater than before the revolution. This means that our country has grown wealthier every year, that the working people's material prosperity has increased and, in addition, demands on agriculture have become increasingly greater.

Meanwhile, the rate of socialist agricultural development has obviously lagged behind the rate of industrial development and the growth in the population's need for consumers' goods. Suffice it to say that although industrial output increased 2.3 times from 1940 through 1952, gross agricultural output increased (in comparable prices) only 10 per cent.

We are in general satisfying the country's need for grain crops, in the sense that our country is well supplied with bread. We have the necessary state reserves and are exporting wheat on a limited scale. With the growth in the working people's material well-being, the population's demand is moving more and more from bread to meat and dairy products, vegetables, fruits, etc. An obvious discrepancy between the population's growing needs and the production level has been formed during past years, particularly in these branches of agriculture. The lag in a number of important agricultural branches has hindered further development of light and food industry and is an obstacle to increasing the profitability of the collective farms and farmers.

What are the reasons for the inadequate level of agricultural production in general and the lag in a number of important agricultural branches?

The Communist Party has steadily maintained a course of over-all development in heavy industry as essential to the successful development of all branches of the national economy, and it has achieved very great successes on this road. Chief attention was turned to solving this immediate national economic problem, and basic forces and means were directed toward it. Our best cadres were occupied with the work of industrializing the country. We did not have the means for high-speed, simultaneous development of heavy industry, agriculture and light industry. For this it was necessary to provide needed prerequisites. Now these prerequisites exist. We have a mighty industrial base, strengthened collective farms and cadres trained in all branches of economic construction.

There are other reasons, however, for the lag in a number of important agricultural branches, reasons which are rooted in shortcomings in our work, in shortcomings in agricultural leadership—that is to say, reasons which depend on us.

Many such reasons concern mainly the violation of the principle of material self-interest in a number of agricultural branches. The principle of the material self-interest for a factory and for each worker individually in matters of labor expenditure is a basic principle of socialist economy. V. I. Lenin has pointed out that the transition to communism takes many years and that during the transition the economy must build "not on enthusiasm directly but with the aid of enthusiasm born of the great revolution, on personal interest, on personal incentive and on nonsubsidized operations. . . ." Otherwise, Lenin further points out, "you will not achieve communism and you will not lead tens and tens of millions of people to communism" (V. I. Lenin, *Works* [in Russian], Vol. XXX, p. 36).

Meanwhile, facts show that this principle of material self-interest and material incentive for workers is not uniformly applied in a number of important branches of agriculture.

This is above all true in animal husbandry. We have figures which show that receipts from collective farms' deliveries and sales of cotton to the state amounted to from 17 to 36 rubles per workday spent on the crop in the Central Asian republics, for sugar beet 12 rubles in the Ukraine Republic and for technical crops throughout the U.S.S.R.

approximately 18 rubles. In highly mechanized regions such as the North Caucasus collective farms paid eight to 14 rubles per workday unit spent on grain crops. During this time the receipts from deliveries and sales per workday unit earned in animal husbandry averaged only five rubles in the U.S.S.R. as a whole and little more than four rubles in the Ukraine Republic. Thus, animal husbandry, in contrast with other branches of agriculture, is in an unsatisfactory economic state.

The actual preponderance of manual labor in animal husbandry has resulted in great waste in production. Facts also show that present procurement and purchase prices for animal husbandry products are an inadequate incentive to the material self-interest of the collective farms and farmers in developing animal husbandry, and as they now stand do not give the collective farms and farmers due returns. The same can be said for vegetables and potatoes.

Further. The very important Collective Farm Statutes have been violated on many collective farms. Comrade Stalin pointed out that the principle of the proper combination of the collective farmers' communal and private interests, with subordination of private interests to communal, is the cornerstone of the collective system in agriculture. Proceeding from this guiding principle, it was designated in the Collective Farm Statutes that on the collective farm, along with the main, decisive communal sector, each collective farm household be allowed a small holding as private property. This subsidiary holding is necessary as long as the communal sector is still inadequately developed and cannot fully satisfy the communal needs of the collective farm as well as the personal needs of the collective farmers.

This very important principle of collective farming has been violated on many collective farms. This could only lead and actually has led to fewer cattle, sheep and pigs in the personal holdings of the collective farmers.

Violation of the principle of material self-interest of collective farms and farmers is especially great under present conditions. Our industry is growing at a rapid pace. Labor shortages exist. Unemployment has been long forgotten. Every year earnings increase, and the factory workers' lot improves. Under such conditions if work on the communal sector does not give the collective farmer due returns per workday unit and if his personal interests in his private subsidiary holding are also infringed upon, then the collective farmer easily finds another opening for his labor—he goes away to the city and into industry. This is the reason for the reduction in the collective farmers' personal economy and the flow of the rural population from the lagging collective farms.

Unsatisfactory use of the powerful equipment which the state has supplied and is continuing to supply the M.T.S. is obviously a very important cause of the serious lag in certain branches of agriculture. Manual labor still predominates in certain branches and aspects of farm work. With the high level of mechanization in the cultivation of grain crops, sugar beets and cotton, mechanization has lagged in such important branches as animal husbandry and the raising of potatoes, vegetables, flax and a number of other crops. Tractors and other machines are poorly used in many M.T.S.

The unsatisfactory leadership of collective and state farms and M.T.S. by Party, Soviet and agricultural agencies, especially in selecting, placing and training personnel in agriculture and conducting Party-political work in the countryside, is a very important reason for the serious lag in a number of branches of agriculture.

Finally, it is necessary to mention the reasons which depend on the collective farms themselves, on the chairmen and boards of the collective farms and on the collective farmers. Labor discipline is still very low in many collectives, and not all of the collective farmers take full part in farm production. The work of the collective farmers is not well organized everywhere, and there are still numerous instances of carelessness and negligence toward communal property.

Further advances in socialist agriculture aim at raising the people's well-being. It is well known that with the victory of socialism public consumption has steadily grown. Thus the output of consumers' goods has become approximately 12 times greater in the past 28 years, including significant increase in supplying the population with foodstuffs. However, the Soviet people's well-being, their purchasing power and their demands have risen still more rapidly, and the output of foodstuffs far from satisfies the growing needs of the working people. Therefore, the task of improving food supply for the population acquires special importance.

One must take on the task of attaining the level of food consumption established by scientific norms for nourishment necessary to the over-all, harmonious development of a healthy person. In this connection it is highly important to improve the structure of consumption by increasing the production mainly of animal husbandry products and vegetables.

In order to satisfy completely the population's demands for milk and dairy products, 260 centners of milk must be obtained for every 100 hectares of arable land, meadows and pasture in the country. To do this there must be no less than ten cows, each with an average annual milk yield of 2500 to 2600 kilograms, for each 100 hectares of arable land, meadows and pasture.

In order to satisfy the population's need for meat and meat products, 27 centners of meat must be obtained for each 100 hectares of arable land, meadows and pasture. For this it is necessary to develop pig-breeding intensively, obtaining not less than 30 centners of pork for each 100 hectares of arable land.

On every 100 hectares of arable land there must be 340 hens, each with an egg-laying capacity of not less than 110 eggs a year.

Yields of sugar, vegetable and melon crops, fruits, berries and other produce must be considerably increased.

We must reach this level of food production more quickly. The time limits for attaining this level will depend in many ways on us, on our leadership and on the work of the Party organizations. If we exert all our ability, means and efforts in solving this task and do not limit ourselves in our leadership to general directives but are occupied with strengthening each collective and state farm and each M.T.S., then we shall attain this level of consumption in a very short time and for certain produce in two to three years.

We have numerous collective farms already making valuable contributions to the task of setting up a full supply of foodstuffs in our country. Many of these collective farms have advanced from lagging to progressive in two to three years. Let us take, for example, the Molotov Collective Farm in the Ramenskoye District of Molotov Province. Three years ago a number of minor collective farms which lagged considerably behind the Molotov Collective Farm were joined to this farm. Thanks to able management by the collective farm board, headed by such an outstanding organizer of collective farm production as Comrade Puzanchikov, the collective farm as a whole, including the former lagging collectives joined to it, has made great advances and become highly developed and extremely profitable. The average milk yield per cow was raised from 2500 to 4208 kilograms. The yields of all farm crops were raised, including potatoes to 162 centners and vegetables to 294 centners a hectare. The number of livestock increased, and the collective farm began to obtain considerably more animal husbandry products.

The high productivity of animal husbandry and the high yields of all the farm crops permitted the Molotov Collective Farm to increase its monetary income up to 3,000,000 rubles. In 1952 the collective farm spent 612,000 rubles on constructing animal husbandry facilities alone. The collective farmers received up to 25 rubles 80 kopeks in cash per workday unit.

If we compare the norms quoted above as necessary for satisfying the population's demands for animal husbandry products with the showings actually achieved by the Molotov Collective Farm, the following picture is obtained:

The first column in the table below shows the figures necessary per 100 hectares of arable land, meadows and pasture for the country as a whole if it is to meet scientifically based norms of consumption; the second column shows the existing situation on the Molotov Collective Farm in 1952:

Cattle, including cows	20	35
Cows	10	19
Meat (slaughter wt. in centners)	27	31
Milk (centners)	260	710
Milk av. per cow (kilos)	2500 to 2600	4208

In all the results enumerated the Molotov Collective Farm has already exceeded the norms we must achieve for the country as a whole. It should be borne in mind that these figures for the Molotov Collective Farm include only the communal livestock and not the livestock which are the private property of the collective farmers.

If every collective farm in our country attained the level of the Molotov Collective Farm, and this task is possible for any collective farm, then the problem of creating an abundance of farm produce would be solved.

Socialist agriculture has everything necessary to solve in the shortest time the problem of fully supplying the Soviet people with foodstuffs and industry with raw materials. In order to convert these potentialities into reality, however, each collective farm must be strengthened in the organizational and managerial aspect and, above all, intelligent organizers capable of successfully guiding the socialist economy must be put in administrative posts on each collective farm.

Of great importance is raising the material self-interest of collective farms and farmers in increasing crop yields and developing communal animal husbandry. For this purpose the U.S.S.R. Council of Ministers and the Presidium of the Party Central Committee have considered it necessary to increase the present procurement and purchase prices for animal husbandry products, potatoes and vegetables. Thus, the procurement prices for livestock and poultry turned over to the state as obligatory deliveries are more than 5.5 times larger, double for milk and butter, 2.5 times greater for potatoes, and 25 per cent to 40 per cent more on the average for vegetables. As for purchase prices, they have risen an average of 30 per cent for meat and 50 per cent for milk. It is important to note here that retail prices for animal husbandry products, potatoes and vegetables have not risen, but, on the contrary, are dropping every year. The policy of lowering retail prices will be steadily followed.

Under these circumstances it has also been considered expedient to lower the norms for the collective farms' obligatory deliveries to the state of animal husbandry products and the norms for the collective farms' deliveries of potatoes and vegetables. The norms for obligatory deliveries of animal husbandry products from the holdings of workers and employees have been considerably decreased.

With the reduction in the obligatory delivery norms, the collective farms and farmers will have more surplus produce for sale at the higher purchase prices and for sale on the collective farmers' markets. In this connection the present system of purchases by state and cooperative organizations must be reviewed. It is necessary to change from the present purchasing procedure to contracts which permit the state to plan beforehand the amount of produce remaining after obligatory deliveries and guarantee the collective farms and farmers sale of their produce, allowing them to receive cash advances and to obtain manufactured goods in the form of reciprocal sales.

In addition, the Soviet government will spend more than 15,000,000,000 rubles in 1953 and more than 35,000,000,000 rubles in 1954 to implement the urgent measures for further developing agriculture. A large part of these expenditures is earmarked for further additional capital investment in agriculture and for increasing the stake of the collective farms and farmers in developing animal husbandry and raising yields of potatoes and vegetables in order markedly to advance these branches of agriculture in the next few years. As a result of carrying out the above-mentioned measures, the collective farms and farmers will receive more than 13,000,000,000 rubles' extra income in 1953 and more than 20,000,000,000 rubles' extra income in 1954.

Increasing the procurement and purchase prices and reducing the norms for obligatory deliveries are highly important in strengthening the material interest of the collective farms and farmers in further advancing agriculture. However, these measures must be properly evaluated. Their importance and necessity at the present time is obvious, but they do not determine the main path for developing collective farming.

Characteristic of the economy of socialist society is the systematic price reduction which takes place on the basis of improved production, increased labor productivity and greater industrial output. The main way to eliminate the lag in animal husbandry and in the output of potatoes and vegetables and provide a further powerful advance in all branches of agriculture is to raise the level of collective farming, increase its gross and marketed output and reduce expenditures.

There are now hundreds and thousands of advanced collective farms which are making obligatory deliveries to the state of meat, milk, wool, potatoes and vegetables according to the procurement and purchasing prices effective until now and receiving large incomes. These collective farms not only are meeting their obligations to the state successfully but are also ensuring the planned annual growth of the communal funds and high remuneration for the workday. This means that the matter rests not solely on the raising of procurement and purchasing prices but principally on the level of economic development.

This can best be shown on specific collective farms. The 12th of October Collective Farm and the May Day Collective Farm, both in Kostroma District, Kostroma Province, have approximately identical soil and climate conditions, but they get vastly different results. This is disclosed in the following comparative figures for these collective farms in 1952:

	12th of October Collective Farm	May Day Collective Farm
Field, meadow and pasture area (hectares)	998	904
Crop yields (centners per hectare):		
all grains	18.5	7.1
potatoes	195	70
vegetables	164	86
Milk yield per cow (kilos)	5233	1272
Communal livestock (per 100 hectares of fields and meadows):		
cattle, including cows	26	13
cows	10	6
pigs (per 100 hectares of fields)	142	8
poultry (per 100 hectares of fields)	240	15
Animal husbandry products (per 100 hectares of fields, meadows and pasture:		
meat	13	5
milk (centners)	509	85
Monetary income (rubles)	2,109,000	151,000
per hectare of fields, meadows and pasture	2113	167

The reason for the successes on the 12th of October Collective Farm is the correct selection and placement of personnel on this farm. Praskovia Andreyevna Malinina, who understands the work well and knows how to manage farming, heads this collective farm. Comrade Malinina's strength lies in the fact that she and the collective farm board she heads rely on the collective farmers and on the collective farm *aktiv*. The role of the collective farm Party organization in guiding the economy is properly apparent here.

Many such examples can be cited, all showing the collective farms' great opportunities to advance agriculture.

Permit me to undertake a more detailed description of conditions in various branches of agriculture.

2. *Concerning the Situation in Animal Husbandry and Measures for Its Further Development.*—Our most pressing tasks lie in the field of animal husbandry, since lagging there has become chronic and we shall be unable to rapidly improve the situation without decisive measures.

Our animal husbandry was lagging even before the war. Much has been accomplished since the war to restore and further develop animal husbandry. During the period from July, 1945, to July, 1953, cattle in the U.S.S.R. increased 11,300,000 head, sheep and goats 53,900,000 and pigs 25,100,000.

At first glance it seems that these figures for growth, and they are really considerable, present no cause for alarm. This is not actually so.

I cite data on the number of livestock in the U.S.S.R. (in millions, over comparable areas, for the beginning of each year):

	Cattle	Cows	Pigs	Sheep and Goats	Horses
1916	58.4	28.8	23.0	96.3	38.2
1928	66.8	33.2	27.7	114.6	36.1
1941	54.5	27.8	27.5	91.6	21.0
1953	56.6	24.3	28.5	109.9	15.3

These data show that the number of cows at the beginning of 1953 was 3,500,000 less than at the beginning of 1941 and 8,900,000 less than at the beginning of 1928.

While agriculture as a whole, developing according to the principle of expanded reproduction, forged far ahead, animal husbandry developed extremely slowly. The productivity of communal animal husbandry is still low. In certain provinces and republics an especially intolerable situation has arisen in regard to the milk yield. Kirov Province collective farms obtained 727 kilograms of milk per cow in 1952, Novgorod—777, Vologda—819, Kostroma—906, Azerbaidzhan Republic—373, Georgian Republic—457, Kirgiz Republic—537, Armenian Republic—814 and Belorussia—829 kilograms.

The lag in animal husbandry must be overcome as soon as possible and, above all, the communal herd must be rapidly advanced and decisive steps taken to increase the number of livestock and raise their productivity on collective and state farms.

Communal animal husbandry on the collective farms has grown rapidly since the war. By the beginning of 1953 there were 10,200,000 more cattle on collective farms than in 1940, including an increase of 2,800,000 cows, 35,300,000 more sheep and goats, 7,900,000 more pigs and a 58,000,000 increase in poultry.

If we overcome the serious obstacles to the development of communal animal husbandry which have already delayed herd reproduction, collective farm herds can increase even faster. It is a matter of growing feed, constructing buildings and mechanizing labor-consuming processes which in animal husbandry have lagged far behind the communal herd's rate of growth.

Can we surmount these difficulties in a very short time? Yes, without doubt we can and will surmount them if we manage the development of animal husbandry better, select good personnel for work on the farms and train them properly and increase the collective farms' and farmers' personal stake in the development of communal animal husbandry.

In this connection I would like first of all to dwell on animal husbandry procurements. At present the handling of procurements frequently boils down to a mechanical distribution of quotas among the collective farms according to the size of their herds, and the hectare principle in procurements is grossly violated. Advanced collective farms, districts and provinces with highly developed animal husbandry receive increased quotas for animal husbandry products every year, while smaller and, in effect, preferential norms are established for the collective farms not greatly concerned with developing communal animal husbandry. This practice undermines the collective farms' and farmers' personal stake in increasing communal livestock and raising its productivity.

Here is a typical example. Collective farms in Moscow Province supply the state 39.5 liters of milk from each hectare of arable land, meadows and pasture, while collective farms in Ryazan Province supply only 14.8 liters. Lukhovitsy District in Moscow Province and Rybonye District in Ryazan Province have approximately the same conditions for developing animal husbandry. Nevertheless, collective farms in Lukhovitsy District supply the state 57 liters of milk and 5.5 kilograms of meat from every hectare and collective farms of Rybonoye District 31 liters of milk and 4.7 kilograms of meat.

Nothing can explain the fact that on the average the collective farms of the Ukraine are required to supply the state considerably more animal husbandry products than Belorussian collective farms, for example. Thus, for Ukrainian collective farms the norm for meat deliveries has been established at 6.3 kilograms and for milk at 25 liters, while for Belorussian collective farms it is 3.9 kilograms and 12.8 liters respectively. Yet Belorussia has favorable conditions for developing animal husbandry, especially hogs. Belorussian Party and Soviet agencies are not conducting a true struggle to increase the herd and raise its productivity. It is no accident that in 1952 less than one hog was fattened per 100 hectares of arable land on the republic's collective farms and pork made up only 13 per cent of the meat procurements.

What can justify this lack of coordination in establishing delivery norms for collective farms with approximately equivalent possibilities for developing animal husbandry? Procurement officials attempt to justify it by differences in the level of economic development of collective farms, districts and provinces. In their view the more developed economy should yield more: if you have kept more young animals this year and obtained more milk, you receive a larger quota as well. A collective farm has only to exceed its neighbor, and the procurement officials prune it down just as a gardener prunes bushes with clippers in a public garden.

This inadmissible practice must be ended. The per-hectare principle in obligatory deliveries of animal husbandry products established by the Party and the government must be strictly adhered to, so that a single per-hectare norm applies generally within the limits of a single administrative district. Only when the quality of the land varies can there be deviation from the average district norm.

As I have mentioned already, the collective farms' and farmers' personal stake in the development of communal animal husbandry depends to a large extent on procurement prices for animal husbandry products. In connection with the increase in procurement and purchase prices, the collective farms will receive this year additional income from milk and meat deliveries totaling about 3,800,000,000 rubles. Receipts from deliveries and sales of animal husbandry products to the state will become a chief source of collective farm income from animal husbandry.

As a result of the inadequate development of animal husbandry some of the collective farms are behind in their obligatory deliveries of animal husbandry products. Party and government decisions have provided for writing off the collective farms' arrears in deliveries of animal husbandry products, in order to establish additional opportunities for this branch of agriculture to develop rapidly. A similar measure has been proposed in regard to the holdings of collective farmers, workers and employees with arrears in their deliveries of animal husbandry products for the past few years, in order to help them obtain cows more rapidly.

There have been serious errors not only in animal husbandry procurements but also in other areas in the development of animal husbandry. For a number of years the heads of the U.S.S.R. Ministries of Agriculture and Procurements and of State Farms and many directors of local agencies have not displayed proper alarm over conditions in animal husbandry, have accepted the unfavorable situation and failed to present or solve problems of improving animal husbandry which were urgent long ago.

Allow me to give a few examples to illustrate this situation. The situation on collective and state farms is bad in regard to the number of cows. In striving for a general increase in cattle the U.S.S.R. Ministry of Agriculture and Procurements, the U.S.S.R. Ministry of State Farms and many local Soviet agencies have relaxed concern for increasing the number of cows.

In 1952 the collective farms could have increased cows by 1,500,000 head, yet there was an increase of only 500,000 in all. Why? Because, it seems, approximately 1,000,000 cows were delivered to the state instead of hogs and fattened steers, and at the same time 500,000 cows were sold and used for needs within the collective farms. The 1,500,000 cows disposed of in the course of one year equaled 18 per cent of the total number on the collective farms. The number of cows disposed of for the same reason on collective farms in Vologda Province in 1952 equaled 23 per cent of the total herd, in Kazakh Republic—24 per cent and in Kirov, Molotov and Vladimir Provinces—26 per cent.

By the beginning of 1953, 43 per cent of total herd of cattle in the country were cows, as opposed to 51 per cent in 1941. Cows make up 28 per cent of the cattle on collective farms and 31 per cent on state farms.

In order to obtain sufficient milk not less than 50 per cent of the herd should be cows and in suburban districts not less than 60 per cent, while on collective farms in the steppe, semi-steppe and mountain areas of Kazakhstan, Central Asia, the Transcaucasus, North Caucasus, Astrakhan, Chkalov and Chita Provinces, Buryat-Mongol Autonomous Republic and Tuva Autonomous Province not less than 40 per cent should be cows. But how can one talk of an abundance of milk if cows make up only 26 per cent of the herd in Belorussian Republic collective farms, 24 per cent in the Ukrainian Republic and Kursk and Voronezh Provinces, 21 per cent in Rostov Province and 19 per cent in the Moldavian Republic?

There has been considerable decrease in the number of cows in important dairy regions like Vologda, Archangel, Yaroslavl, Tambov, Molotov, Sverdlovsk, Kurgan, Omsk and Novosibirsk Provinces. The slow increase in the head of cows also explains the fact that less butter is now being produced in regions which have long been commercial butter-making centers. In Siberia, for example, 75,000 tons of butter were produced in 1913 and 65,000 tons in 1952.

State farms have also lagged behind in increasing the number of cows. They now possess 1,300,000 cows—500,000 less than in 1935. According to a strange "theory" held by the officials of the U.S.S.R. Ministry of State Farms 200,000 state farm cows are not milked but are used to nurse calves, resulting in an annual loss to the state of not less than 200,000 tons of milk. According to a report by Comrade Soroka, Secretary of the Mountain Altai Province Party Committee, the milking of 2000 Simmental cows was stopped four years ago on Abai Koksin State Farms in Altai Territory. Some of these cows gave up to 3000 kilograms of milk. These state farms provided the state 35,000 centners of milk, but now it is being fed to calves and to a large extent is being wasted and misappropriated.

According to the 1954 plan the number of cows is to be increased to 29,200,000 head, or 4,900,000 head more than at the beginning of 1953, of which 11,500,000 head, or 3,000,000 more, are to be on the collective farms. The plan for cattle is to be considered complete only when the plan for the number of cows is also fulfilled.

As is well known, planning and records on plan fulfillment for all kinds of livestock have for many years been drawn up as of Jan. 1 of each year. Experience has shown that this procedure does only harm. In the effort to meet the plan for increasing the number of livestock, the collective farms have been compelled to keep on the livestock sections prior to Jan. 1 a large number of nonproductive livestock intended for delivery to the state, sale or use as meat, to buy calves from the collective farmers, to fall back on livestock born in autumn and to maintain "rooster" farms.

After the Jan. 1 census collective farms immediately get rid of a considerable number of cattle. Thus, throughout the country as a whole the collective farms provided the state 232,000 head of cattle in December, 1951, and 889,000 head in January, 1952. In December, 1951, Ukraine Republic collective farms provided 16,700 head of cattle and the next month 219,000 head—or 13 times as many. According to estimates of the U.S.S.R. Central Statistical Administration, in the first quarter of 1952 collective farms provided 200,000 more cattle than called for in the meat deliveries plan, because the cattle delivered were exhausted from inadequate and poor feeding during the winter season. This inflicted major losses on the collective farms and on the state.

The economic year in animal husbandry actually ends Oct. 1. By this time feed supplies and preparations for winter shelter are complete and the animals are well fed, thus enabling collective farms to satisfy meat deliveries with summer-fattened livestock of greater weight and in fewer number. Determination of the disposal of livestock (those remaining with the herd, stock selected for slaughter, etc.) is completed on collective farms by the beginning of October. It should be established, therefore, that the economic year in animal husbandry begins Oct. 1.

One of the most serious shortcomings in the development of animal husbandry is the excessively high percentage of barrenness in female livestock and the great incidence of disease, particularly among young livestock. In 1952 collective farms obtained per 100 female breeding stock 11 fewer calves than in 1940, 27 fewer lambs and 163 fewer suckling pigs. On the collective farms of Novgorod, Kostroma and Kurgan Provinces and the Altai Territory in the past three years they have lost every third calf because of disease, in 1952 on collective farms in Vologda and Ivanovo Provinces every second suckling pig, in Voronezh, Tambov and Rostov Provinces every fifth suckling pig and in the Belorussian Republic every fourth suckling pig.

One may cite many other examples of extremely unsatisfactory guidance in development of animal husbandry. But it is not a matter of the number of examples. One thing is clear; in order to rid animal husbandry of its present neglect the guidance of animal husbandry must be resolutely improved along with the carrying out of other measures.

The draft decree lays down measures for bringing about in 1954 considerable increases in all kinds of productive livestock as well as in milk yields, wool shearing and livestock fattening.

In connection with the planned increase in the number of cattle and in their productivity it is intended in 1954 to increase the total volume of meat procurements to 4,100,000 tons (as against 3,000,000 tons in 1952), milk to 14,300,000 tons (as against 10,000,000 tons in 1952), eggs to 4,300,000,000 (as against 2,600,000,000 in 1952) and wool to 230,000 tons (as against 182,000 tons in 1952). I have already stated how animal husbandry procurements are to be carried out at new and higher prices.

The situation in regard to livestock feed on collective and state farms must be resolutely improved. The neglect of feed bases in many areas and on many collective farms has reached utterly intolerable proportions.

The problem of expanding output of a particular feed crop should be handled in relation to soil and climate conditions in a region. But in every region an over-all expansion in yields of succulent feeds, which are essential to a marked increase in milk output, must become the rule. In the central regions, for example, this means potatoes, feed and sugar beets, carrots, eggplants, pumpkins and turnips, and in the southern regions fodder melons, pumpkins, eggplants and beets.

More attention must be paid to raising wheat, sunflowers, kale and certain other silage crops.

Separate mention must be made of such a valuable feed crop as corn. It is no accident that corn growing has become widespread in a number of countries with developed animal husbandry. In the U.S.S.R. corn occupies an extremely small area, even in those regions where it grows best.

Conditions are favorable for corn growing in many provinces of the U.S.S.R. One may cite many examples where increased corn yields have been obtained by Ukrainian collective and state farms. Back in 1948 Comrade Taran, an agronomist on the Comintern State Farm in Poltava Province, obtained an average harvest of 70 centners of corn per hectare over a large area by using the square-cluster method of sowing. On the Chkalov Collective Farm in Dnepropetrovsk Province (Comrade Shcherbina, Chairman) the average corn harvest for five years was 50 centners per hectare. I do not mention the remarkable successes in corn raising of Mark Yevstafyevich Ozerny—the well-known master of this method from the Red Partisan Collective Farm, Likhovka District, Dnepropetrovsk Province—who has obtained high yields year after year and in 1949 got a record harvest of 224 centners of corn per hectare.

In Moscow Province experience has shown that corn provides high yields of silage in the central districts. The square-cluster method of sowing fully ensures harvests of up to 500 and more centners of silage per hectare. Thus the Path of the New Life Collective Farm and the Gorki-II State Farm in Moscow Province have raised no less than 700 to 800 centners of corn for silage on every hectare. If most collective farms were to cultivate not 700 or 800 centners of green feed from every hectare of corn but merely 250 to 300, this would be enough to provide 225 to 260 kilograms of butter per sown hectare.

Certain local officials complain of the feed shortage yet raise the question of reducing corn crops. Our Ukrainian comrades in particular are at fault here. One may ask, what more abundant feed crop can they name?

Vigorous steps must be taken to increase corn yields and considerably expand the area sown to corn for silage. Sowings of corn for silage must be extended in most provinces of the central Black Earth zone and the non-Black Earth belt as well as in areas of Belorussia and the Baltic republics. Increasing the corn sown for silage is important to collective and state farms in the southern regions of the Urals, Siberia, the Far East and the northern regions of Kazakhstan. In increasing yields of corn, sunflowers and other silage crops, silos must be built on every collective and state farm to an extent that ensures ensiling of five to six tons of high-grade fodder per cow.

Party agencies, particularly those in the central Black Earth and non-Black Earth provinces, must determinedly end the failure to realize the value of potatoes as feed.

The utilization and improvement of natural hayfields and pasture has proceeded unsatisfactorily. In 1952 collective farms procured 9.6 centners of hay per head of cattle instead of the 11 centners procured in 1940. It is essential that yields of natural and sown grasses be sharply raised and crops of alfalfa, clover, timothy and esparto be in every way developed. In the southern regions Sudan grass deserves particular attention, since there it yields large quantities of excellent-quality hay. For the northern and southern central regions vetch and oat mixtures are good.

The stall-and-pasture system of sheltering cattle with a green conveyer * should be widely introduced on collective and state farms as an effective measure for increasing the milk yield per cow.

Animal husbandry cannot be advanced if Party, Soviet and agricultural agencies do not actively engage in setting up a stable feed base. Nevertheless, many Party and Soviet officials regard feed output and procurements as a matter of secondary importance. Some comrades have replaced concrete and comprehensive guidance of this work on every collective and state farm with last-minute rushes and high-flown declarations.

For example, here is how Comrade Semin, Secretary of the Vologda Province Party Committee, pictures the solution of problems linked with feed procurements. In a report to a plenary session of the province Party committee, which was later published in the province paper, he stated: "One must be convinced of the fact that the feed base is not primary or fundamental in animal husbandry. First comes leadership, then the feed base." Further, he proposed handling the haying in ten to 15 days by last-minute rush tactics. "Only by a general frontal attack," he said, "can one win this battle." Comrade Semin demands that intercollective farm or district headquarters be set up to organize and direct all operations.

One asks, where are the district Party committees or the district Soviets and what is their role, if some sort of far-fetched intercollective farm headquarters directs the haying? The Vologda Province Party Committee and the province executive committee kept aloof from feed procurements. As a result, 159,000 hectares of natural hay and sown grasses were not yet harvested in the province by Aug. 25 and the plan for laying in silage was only 57 per cent completed.

Unless the feed problem is solved there can be no sharp advance in livestock productivity. We can no longer accept the fact that for more than ten years collective farm milk yields have not exceeded 1000 to 1070 kilograms per cow. This is absolutely inadmissible. After all, advanced holdings like the Karavayevo, Gorki-II, Lesniye Polyany and Kholmogorka State Farms, the 12th of October Collective Farm

* [A method of livestock feeding involving grazing livestock on natural and artificial pasture, as well as planting crops to supply green feed in seasons when grass is scarce.]

in Kostroma Province and the New Life Collective Farm in Archangel Province for a number of years got milk yields of 4500 to 5000 and 6000 or more kilograms per cow by using abundant supplies of succulent feeds.

The problem of increasing productivity in pig raising by an over-all increase in pig fattening deserves serious attention, since pork does not yet have its proper place in the country's meat supply. Over-all yields from pig-raising in 1952 amounted to 1,600,000 tons as against 1,500,000 tons in 1940.

Increasing the wool output is also tremendously important. In many provinces and areas the wool clip per sheep has been high. In 1952 collective farms in Stavropol Territory had on the whole a fine-wool clip of 5.2 kilograms per sheep. Nevertheless, the country is not producing enough wool. Officials in the Kazakh Republic deserve severe criticism. There are now 17,000,000 sheep and goats in the republic, but in 1928 there were more than 19,000,000. Although the number of fine-wooled sheep has more than quadrupled since 1940, the average clip has decreased in this same period from 2.4 to 1.9 kilograms. It is not surprising, therefore, that the plan for wool procurements in Kazakhstan has been only 60 per cent to 70 per cent met.

Further improvement in the mechanization of feed procurements on collective farms is important to solving the feed problem. The amount of work done by M.T.S. in mechanizing haying and ensiling feed has considerably increased in the past three years, but the general level of M.T.S. participation in feed procurement work has remained extremely low and lags sharply behind the level of mechanization already achieved in grain farming.

It is particularly necessary to call attention to mowing and stacking hay in less time. Delays in these operations have resulted in major losses in the quality of the hay. It is common knowledge that hay which has stood too long or has been mown but left unstacked for a long while loses its most valuable nutrient properties. Consequently, when we permit delays in haying we get considerably less feed units per hectare.

In 1954 and 1955 it is planned to raise the level of mechanization in hay-making and raking to 80 per cent, stacking to 65 per cent ensiling to 75 per cent and sowing and cultivating silage and root-feed crops to 95 per cent. It is also planned to extend considerably the work of M.T.S. in fundamentally improving meadows and pasture.

In addition, the level of mechanization in labor-consuming operations on animal husbandry farms must be in every way raised.

It is exceptionally important to provide all livestock with shelter. The sale of building materials to collective farms by the Central Union Consumers' Cooperatives and by local cooperative and state industry must be increased. Where expedient, the collective farms must be required to produce bricks, tiles and lime from their own resources in order to satisfy their needs for the materials mentioned.

We have been concerned thus far with reasons for lags and ways to increase collective animal husbandry. This is our major task. But we cannot forget the livestock on the collective farmers' private holdings. Here too the situation is unsatisfactory. The number of cows which are the personal property of the collective farmers has been reduced by 6,500,000 since the war. The number of collective farmers' holdings without cows has increased to 45 per cent.

The new law on the agricultural tax recently adopted by the U.S.S.R. Supreme Soviet has provided conditions for increasing the collective farmers' interest in acquiring livestock. In addition to developing animal husbandry, local Party, Soviet and agricultural agencies must decisively end the incorrect practice of infringing upon the interests of the collective farmers in regard to personally owned livestock. Only people who do not understand the policy of the Party or the policy of the Soviet state see any danger to the socialist system in the presence of personally owned productive livestock on a collective farmer's private holding within the limits set by the Collective Farm Statutes. We must also eliminate the prejudice that it is disgraceful for a worker or an employee to possess livestock as private property.

The measures proposed for the acquisition of livestock as personal property by collective farmers, workers and employees in no way signify a relaxation in attention to the development of communal animal husbandry on collective and state farms.

The system of increasing communal animal husbandry is the main way and has always been the main way to solve the animal husbandry problem. The time will come when communal animal husbandry will reach such heights that the collective farmer's personal needs for animal husbandry products will be completely satisfied by the communal economy and it will then be disadvantageous to the collective farmer to possess livestock as personal property.

But until we reach this situation, until communal animal husbandry is able to satisfy fully the requirements of the entire population, including the collective farmers, for animal husbandry products, the presence of livestock as the personal property of a collective farm household is not a hindrance but a help to communal animal husbandry and is consequently advantageous both to the collective farmers and to the collective farms and the state.

Thus in the field of further development in animal husbandry, it is necessary:

to improve decisively the guidance of animal husbandry, to select good permanent personnel for work on the livestock sections;

to increase the economic self-interest of the collective farms and collective farmers in the development of animal husbandry;

to take necessary steps to increase the number of communal livestock and raise its productivity in order to gain considerable success in 1954;

to strengthen the feed base in communal animal husbandry and to provide all livestock with an adequate supply of feeds;

to increase the level of mechanization in feed procurements and labor-consuming work on the livestock sections, to build durable shelters for all communal animal husbandry and improve its maintenance and care;

to assist collective farmers in acquiring productive livestock.

Comrades! The rapid advance in animal husbandry is vitally important to the Party and the country and is now a most urgent task of the Party and state in the field of agriculture. We have great and complex work ahead. But however great the difficulties, we must crown this cause with success and in the next two or three years bring about a marked increase in the output of animal husbandry products.

3. On Increasing Production and Procurements of Potatoes and Vegetables.—The next urgent question to be solved is that of increasing production of potatoes and vegetables. Demand for potatoes and vegetables has grown to such an extent that their present production level must be considered completely inadequate. In recent years yields and gross harvests of these crops, far from increasing, have decreased. The area sown to vegetables is 250,000 hectares less than in 1940. The area sown to potatoes has increased in the country as a whole, but in certain provinces it is by no means near prewar level. In Novgorod Province the area sown to potatoes on the collective farms is

38 per cent of the prewar level, in Velikiye Luki 59 per cent and in Smolensk 61 per cent.

The reduced yields permitted in many districts have led to a decrease in the gross harvest of potatoes which is particularly alarming.

The decrease in the gross harvest of potatoes and the inadequate output of vegetables hinders us from markedly improving deliveries of these products to the working people in the cities and industrial centers and the supply of raw material to food industry enterprises. The inadequate potato supply also has, as I have already said, an adverse effect on the development of animal husbandry.

Why is it that, in view of the great possibilities, the production of potatoes and vegetables on collective farms has not increased recently and in many districts has even decreased?

One reason for the lag in potato and vegetable raising is the weak material interest of collective farms and collective farmers in growing these crops. Although we have a whole system of material incentives for other crops—cotton, sugar beets, tea and citrus crops—there is still none for potatoes or vegetables. Inadequate procurement prices, the procurement agencies' incorrect approach in estimating delivery norms and, in particular, the increase in norms for collective farms in suburban districts and food industry areas and the establishment of higher norms for leading collective farms have destroyed the collective farms' stake in increasing production of these crops.

The shortcomings pointed out must be corrected and important material incentives must be established to increase the collective farms' output of potatoes and vegetables. Such incentives are: increasing procurement prices for potatoes and vegetables, lowering the norms for obligatory deliveries, extending purchasing at the higher prices and special consideration in delivering grain to collective farms which have large surpluses of potatoes and vegetables.

But here it must be stated that we have done as much as possible to raise procurement prices. A further rise in procurement prices for potatoes and vegetables is impossible. If we were to extend this policy, trade in potatoes and vegetables would be unprofitable. Then, instead of reducing retail prices for potatoes and vegetables, which the Party and the government are constantly effecting, it would be necessary to raise retail prices, which is not to the people's interest. It goes without saying that the Party and the government cannot and will not do this.

Therefore, our main objective is to use reserves for raising yields, which are still very low despite the fact that the opportunities for increasing them are tremendous. Average-size collective farms get 140 to 150 centners of potatoes per hectare, yet many hundreds of leading collective farms gather 200 to 300 centners. Thousands of leading agricultural workers have achieved still more outstanding results. The Ukrainian collective farmer Marta Khudoly has gathered 800 centners of potatoes per hectare, and Comrades Dianova and Kozhukhantseva, collective farmers of Moscow Province, have gathered more than 500 centners.

If we can raise the potato yield next year on all collective farms only to the level of the average-size collective farms, and this is entirely possible, then potato yields will rise considerably. From this it is clear that the chief source for raising income from potatoes and vegetables lies in expanded yields. A prime necessity for this is thorough mechanization of sowing, planting, cultivating and harvesting potatoes and vegetable crops. Although basic work in sowing and harvesting grain crops has been almost completely mechanized, potato planting on collective farms last year was mechanized only 14 per cent and harvesting less than 6 per cent.

The question of mechanizing the cultivation of potatoes is primarily a question of the planting methods. We shall not solve the question of mechanization if we do not adopt a more progressive method of planting potatoes and vegetables, a method enabling us to mechanize row cultivation fully. Have we such a method? Yes. It is the square-cluster method. Leading collective farms have long used it. The Stalin Collective Farm in Serpukhov District, Moscow Province, began as early as 1943 to plant potatoes by the square-cluster method. In recent years many collective farms, convinced of the advantages of the new method, widely adopted it. For example, last spring this method was used for most of the potatoes planted in Moscow Province. What are the advantages of this method? It permits mechanized cultivation of the plantings in transverse and lengthwise directions and sharply reduces manual labor in tending the plantings. This provides optimum conditions for raising plants and consequently for large harvests.

I shall cite some examples. The Forward to Communism Collective Farm in Ramenskoye District, Moscow Province, has 920 hectares of sown area. Row-planted crops occupy about 460 hectares here, including 277 hectares of potatoes and 120 hectares of vegetables. Of the collective farm's 321 able-bodied collective farmers, 160 are busy in the fields. Thus, there is one collective farmer in the field for about every three hectares of row crops. Could the collective farmers cultivate this area well with horses and manual labor and still get high yields? Of course not. At the start of 1951 the collective farmers began using the square-cluster method of potato planting. At that time there was no machine for square-cluster planting; it was still being tested. They decided to plant with the aid of a cultivator. The collective farmers had reasoned correctly: it was necessary to plant by the square-cluster method even if by hand, without machines. Better to expend more labor and at the same time establish conditions for mechanized work. After the job was mechanized the collective farm got sharply increased yields. In 1952 the harvest of potatoes sown by the square-cluster method amounted to 167 centners per hectare, while only 80 centners per hectare were obtained from row-planted potatoes.

In 1953 almost the entire area sown to potatoes by the collective farm was planted by the square-cluster method. Labor expended by the collective farm in planting of one hectare by the square-cluster method with a four-seed drill amounted to one workday, and for three row workings of the potatoes in two directions by tractor only 0.6 workdays were expended. Thus, with the square-cluster method only 1.6 workdays per hectare were expended on planting and cultivating the potatoes, while with row planting more than 30 workdays were expended on this work. For each workday expended on potatoes planted by the square-cluster method the collective farms received 23 centners of potatoes, while only 1.5 centners were received from the usual method. Labor productivity will be increased still further when a potato-planting machine is put into use. This machine needs qualified workers, and such people are increasing among us. There are already quite a few technically skilled equipment operators who have achieved remarkable results. On the Forward to Communism Collective Farm in Ramenskoye District, Moscow Province, equipment operator Comrade Akimfeyev raised the 8-hectare daily norm of a four-row potato planter to 12.4 hectares. If one estimates that the machine is serviced by eight men, then it appears that in one day one-and-one-half hectares of potatoes were planted per man. On the Voroshilov Collective Farm in Bronnitsy District, Moscow Province, equipment operator Comrade Redkin raised the output of a four-row seed drill to ten to 11 hectares per shift. These are the advantages of the square-cluster method! It must be more widely introduced.

It is necessary to state that officials in the U.S.S.R. Ministry of Agriculture and Procurements have taken an incorrect stand in this matter. They have planned potato planting by the square-cluster method in terms of existing equipment. Inasmuch as we still have few machines, the ministry proposes that we plant only half the area. It is impossible to agree. We must recollect that the square-cluster method grew up on collective farms when we did not have a special machine. Nevertheless, it was applied on advanced collective farms with excellent results.

Next year we must in general plant potatoes by the square-cluster method. Industry is now sharply increasing output of potato planters, but there are still not enough. Potatoes may be planted with a cultivator, with a plow, by the square-cluster method. If we do this as well as mechanize potato cultivation, you may be sure that potato harvests will sharply increase in 1954.

Potatoes planted by the square-cluster method with a cultivator or plow, as is well known, must be planted by hand. This permits introducing manure into the seed holes along with the seed potatoes, which is important in increasing yields. On the same Forward to Communism Collective Farm in Ramenskoye District a half-kilo mixture of manure and mineral fertilizers was introduced into the seed holes during planting with a cultivator in sandy soils. A yield of up to 156 centners per hectare was obtained. Fertilizers are utilized more rationally when introduced into seed holes. Approximately 30 to 40 tons of manure would have to be used on the soil to obtain the abovementioned harvest, but by introducing it into seed holes only ten tons were needed. Every collective and state farm can plant potatoes by the square-cluster method with a cultivator or a plow, at the same time introducing manure and mineral fertilizers into the seed holes. Here everything depends on the leaders, on their understanding of the importance of the new method, on their persistence and skill in organizing the matter—correctly placing people, marking off the fields and other work.

Something must be said about seeds. The people have a wise saying: "Don't expect a good breed from a poor seed." Unfortunately there is among us a negligent and at times criminal attitude toward potato seed. Many collective and state farms sow poor seed and also fail to meet the full sowing norm. Yet the sowing norm for potatoes has particular and even decisive importance in obtaining high yields. For example, progressive collective farms in Moscow Province sow two to three tons of seed per hectare. With good care they obtain a harvest of 20 to 25 tons per hectare. Unfortunately, most collective farms, with the connivance of their leaders, sow one to one-and-one-half tons of potatoes per hectare. It is, of course, impossible to expect high potato yields with such a sowing norm and poor, small seeds and bad cultivation as well.

It is impossible to manage the economy in this fashion. Anyone who permits low sowing norms knowingly condemns the collective farms to low yields. Such workers must be severely brought to book. Each collective farm must have its own potato seeds and must never store them later than September, taking care that the seeds come from the sections with the highest yields, that the potatoes are dry and will store well. The situation resulting from delaying the storage of seed potatoes until the last days of the harvest must be eliminated. Harvesting is often prolonged until the end of October and sometimes even extends into November. The season for sleet arrives, there is frost on the ground and the collective farm has not yet stored its seeds. Thus frozen and damp potatoes are often stored for seed. When the storage bins are opened in the spring half the potatoes are rotten. If every collective and state farm stores its seed potatoes in September, and this must be done, then by spring we will have enough good seed potatoes. The areas sown to early potatoes must be considerably extended, and in the southern regions more attention must be paid to summer potato plantings by the method advocated by T. D. Lysenko.

Comrades! the importance of potatoes to the national economy is great. They are valuable not only as feed but as raw material for alcohol and starch, etc. Potatoes per one unit area give approximately four times more alcohol than do grain crops. Potatoes are excellent feed for animals, particularly for pigs and milk cattle, and for poultry as well.

According to figures cited by Academician D. N. Pryanishnikov, about ten poods of potatoes are used to produce one pood of pork. If 15 tons of potatoes are received per hectare, with a small addition of grain in the ration a pork increase of up to 90 poods will result. If cows are fed potatoes, much milk and butter will be obtained.

The task of further increasing potato output is basic to the further development of agriculture. With enough potatoes we can in the next two years significantly increase output of pork, milk and butter.

Particular attention must be paid to the role of the central non-Black Earth regions in raising potatoes and vegetables. I have in mind Moscow, Leningrad, Ryazan, Tula and certain other provinces and the Belorussian, Latvian, Lithuanian and Estonian Republics, where there are highly favorable conditions for large potato yields. Unfortunately these provinces grow few potatoes or vegetables. The agricultural agencies have until now planned the sowing of vegetable crops incorrectly. If a district is given the task of planting 100 hectares of cabbages, it usually distributes the task among all the collective farms. The same is true with cucumbers, tomatoes and other crops. Economically this principle is completely incorrect. Vegetables need particular conditions and particular soils. Most vegetable crops give considerably higher yields on low-lying damp ground. This is particularly true of cabbages. We give the same tasks to a collective farm with well-watered soils and close to water as to a collective farm without such lands. Collective farms are forced to plant cabbages and other vegetables on unsuitable land and gather low harvests with much labor and material waste.

Where should one plant vegetables? The most correct solution of this task must be sought in concentrating vegetable crops in regions where land is most suited to their cultivation. Party and Soviet organizations in Moscow Province followed such a course and introduced for government consideration a draft decree "Concerning the concentration of sowing and the mechanization of cultivating vegetable crops on the collective farms." The suggestions presented by Moscow Province were approved by the government. Now vegetables and particularly cabbages will be grown on lands most suited to them —on the river floodlands.

While 1373 collective farms in Moscow Province formerly raised vegetables, now commercial truck farming is for the most part concentrated on 252 collective farms, of which 141 are on well-watered lands. Areas sown to vegetables on the river meadows of the Moskva, Oka, Yakhroma, Klyazma and other rivers will be increased from 6000 hectares in 1952 to 12,000 in 1954. As a result of this concentration of vegetable crops and the increase in their yields, Moscow Province will be able to meet almost completely the demands of the population of Moscow and other cities in the province for cabbages, carrots and beets and to a considerable degree for tomatoes and cucumbers.

The question of concentrating vegetable growing in other provinces, territories and republics must be solved along the lines of the Muscovites' example.

The mechanization of row cultivating is particularly important to increasing vegetable yields. It must be considered abnormal that vegetable crops are now largely sown by hand on most collective farms. Why can we not transfer to the square-cluster method? When this question is put to ministry officials they answer that there are no machines for square-cluster planting. But this argument does not stand up! Surely cabbage and tomato seedlings are now usually sown by hand. Consequently, no extra expenditure of workday units is needed to sow them by the square-cluster method. Even if one conceded that planting by this method requires greater labor expenditure, the collective farms would still gain by the work. By planting with the square-cluster method we have the opportunity to mechanize row cultivation by using tractors, and if there are no hitching attachments, we can use horse-drawn cultivators. Prompt cultivation is a sure gain in the harvest. We must, therefore, in the spring of 1954 plant cabbages, tomatoes and eggplants by the square-cluster method. Cucumbers, marrows, pumpkins and watermelons must also be planted by the square-cluster method.

An important way to increase vegetable yields is growing seedlings in peat-humus pots. This valuable proposal was made 20 years ago by Prof. Edelstein, but agricultural agencies unfortunately have done almost nothing for the widespread raising of seedlings in peat-humus pots. Where this method is used, magic results are attained. The Memory of Ilyich Collective Farm in Mytishchi District, Moscow Province, for more than 13 years has obtained harvests of early cabbages of 447 centners per hectare by planting seedlings started in peat-humus pots. Thanks to the use of peat-humus pots the collective farmers have increased the cabbage yield per hectare by 100 centners.

Outside Moscow is the Gorky State Farm, where agronomist Comrade Filatov works. He is a true enthusiast in his work. By growing seedlings in peat-humus pots he gets high and profitable yields of early vegetables. In 1953 the state farm started harvesting and delivering early cabbage to the state by June 25 and cauliflower by June 11. The average yield of early cabbage was 298 centners per hectare and cauliflower 241 centners per hectare. From one hectare of early cabbage 65,000 rubles' profit was obtained and from a hectare of cauliflower 82,000 rubles. In 1952 the state farms by Aug. 1 had delivered to the state early vegetables worth 7,334,000 rubles and in 1953 at this same time 11,154,000 rubles had been realized on early vegetables. Such is the effectiveness of this remarkable new method of increasing vegetable yields. Now the task is to organize the growing of seedlings in peat-humus pots on every state and collective farm which raises vegetables.

Collective and state farms grow extremely small amounts of such valuable vegetables as eggplants, peppers, marrows, tomatoes and green peas. This has limited the food industry's canning output. In the next two to three years these crops must be more widely sown and their yields increased. More watermelons and muskmelons must be grown in regions which are favorable to them.

Finally, hotbeds and hothouses. We will be unable to increase vegetable raising if we do not establish good hotbed and hothouse farming. According to estimates for raising seedlings alone, the collective farms need 14,000,000 hotbed frames, yet the collective farms now have only about 5,000,000. The hotbed frames currently available are sold at a high price. The problems of developing hotbed farming must be decided immediately.

Wherever possible, waste heat from industrial enterprises absolutely must be utilized. Truck-gardening collective farms often do not have enough biological heat for their hotbeds and hotbed grounds and have shortages of coal and wood for heating hothouses as well. Nevertheless, the almost gratuitous amount of heat wasted by industry (steam, hot water) is utilized in only insignificant quantities. Certain collective farms have shown through experience that these heat sources can be successfully used to heat hothouses and hotbeds.

The Third Five-Year Plan Collective Farm in Ukhtomskaya District, Moscow Province, uses waste heat from industry. In 1952 the collective farmers erected a hothouse with an area of 1080 square meters and used waste steam from a factory adjoining the collective farm to heat it. Unfortunately such examples are few. Waste heat from industrial enterprises is not used to heat hotbeds in the Donets Basin or in Leningrad, Gorky, Sverdlovsk and other cities, although the possibilities for this are great.

Collective and state farms must be recommended to use steam as well as electrical heat for hotbeds, which will lighten the collective farmers' work and increase the vegetable yield. For example, the Memory of Ilyich Collective Farm in Moskvoretsky District has used steam heat for hotbeds since 1952. This year it had 1200 hotbed frames under steam heat. By Aug. 1 the collective farm had received an average yield per frame from the hotbeds as follows: 28 kilograms of vegetables grown with steam heat and 19 kilograms grown with biological heat. Twenty-six kilograms of vegetables per workday unit were taken from hotbeds with steam heat and 15 kilograms per workday unit from hotbeds with biological heat.

The workers on this collective farm in 1952 gathered yields of 485 centners per hectare of cabbage and 260 centners per hectare of tomatoes. Monetary income from one hectare of vegetables raised on open ground amounted to 56,000 rubles. In 1952 this collective farm issued per workday unit 22 rubles 76 kopeks in cash alone.

Thus, in order to increase output of potatoes and vegetables it is necessary:

to increase the material interest of the collective farms and the collective farmers in raising these crops;

to mechanize the planting and row cultivation of potatoes and vegetables, extensively introducing the square-cluster method of sowing;

to ensure intense vegetable raising on floodlands and lowlands;

to increase to the maximum accumulations of manure and other local fertilizers and the digging of peat for fertilizer, in order that potatoes and vegetables may be planted on well-fertilized land;

to increase hotbed-heat farming, to raise seedlings in peat-humus pots.

Great are the tasks before us in increasing yields of potatoes and vegetables. We must in the shortest possible time bring yields of these crops to a level which fully satisfies the needs of our country's people. This task is within our power. It must be solved and it will be solved.

4. On Raising the Yields of Grain and Technical Crops.—We must ensure further and more rapid growth in grain yields in order to overcome the lag in the development of animal husbandry and the output of potatoes and vegetables. This is necessary not only to satisfy the population's growing demand for bread but also for rapid advances in all branches of agriculture and, above all, in animal husbandry.

Achievements in the sphere of grain production have been more considerable than in certain other branches of agriculture. We have not only restored within a comparatively short time the grain farming which suffered from the war but have also expanded it. Areas sown to such a valuable food crop as wheat are growing apace. Today areas sown to wheat are 8,100,000 hectares greater than before the war. The Ukraine, areas in the North Caucasus and Crimea have had great successes in growing grain. There areas sown to wheat have been restored and expanded; winter-wheat sowings in particular have increased and the yields raised.

Many collective farms and entire districts have harvested 150 to 200 poods of wheat per hectare. The Stalin Collective Farm in Vurnary District, Chuvash Autonomous Republic, obtained 212 poods of spring wheat per hectare. Winter-wheat yields on collective farms in Bashtanka District, Nikolayev Province, averaged 170 poods per hectare in 1952 throughout the entire sown area.

These are considerable achievements. However, a significant number of the collective and state farms still obtain low yields of grain and of beans in particular. Districts in the non-Black Earth belt, the central Black Earth provinces, the Volga area, western Siberia and Kazakhstan are lagging in this respect.

Collective and state farms have large opportunities for increasing output of wheat, rye, barley, oats and other grain crops year after year.

Particular attention must be paid to wheat. Extensive possibilities exist for increasing output of winter and spring wheat; in addition to the old regions for growing this crop there are many districts in the central Black-Earth provinces, the Volga area, the forest steppes of the Ukraine and a number of the non-Black Earth belt areas. When essential agrotechnical measures are observed, these regions obtain high yields of winter and spring wheat.

Lags must be decisively overcome in the production of feed grain crops, the yields of which continue low.

We do not have enough land sown to groats and crop yields are low. As a result, buckwheat and millet procurements have been sharply curtailed. The importance of buckwheat is common knowledge. But what is the attitude toward raising this crop? As a rule, it is sown at the wrong time and on the worst land, the soil is badly worked, supplementary pollination is not carried out, no bees are brought in, etc. There is no true struggle to increase millet yields, the broad-row sowing method is seldom used, and when it is used the spaces between the rows are not always cultivated. Yet millet or any other crop sown by the broad-row method does not yield high harvests when cultivation is lacking. It must also be noted that we do not adequately encourage raising groats. Forty pounds [metric] of millet is equated to 34 lbs. of wheat or 40 lbs. of rye; this does not help increase the collective farmers' stake in raising millet. Correct equivalents must be established for these crops.

We have opportunities for increasing rice growing in the southern provinces and republics: Transcaucasia, Central Asia, South Kazakhstan and the Far East.

The fact that such a powerful incentive as bonus payments for grain crops is actually not used on many collective farms is a serious shortcoming. Crop-yield indexes for which bonus payment should be made have been raised, but on many collective farms the collective farmers do not receive this payment. There is urgent need to revise the system for distributing bonus payment.

We must not forget Italian millet. Work on this crop must be continued, new high-yield varieties must be discovered and tried out at experimental stations and under collective and state farm conditions.

In the interests of providing the population of the country with every foodstuff, there must be over-all increase in the output of bean crops—peas, string beans, lentils and soybeans.

The area sown to oil-bearing crops on collective farms has been considerably increased since the war and now exceeds the prewar level. There are great possibilities for increasing sunflower yields. Unfortunately sunflower harvests are low. Nevertheless, collective farms and entire districts where sunflower raising has been well organized gather remarkable harvests. For example, collective farms in Maryinka District in Stalino Province have harvested more than 18 centners of sunflower seed per hectare.

If we change to the square-cluster methods in sowing this crop, there will be opportunity to mechanize cultivation efficiently and opportunely and get marked increases in sunflower yields, thus becoming able to satisfy the country's need for vegetable oil.

In addition to sunflowers, we must in every way increase seed crops yields of curly flax, castor oil, peanuts, mustard, chanterelle and other oil-bearing crops.

There have been great achievements in the development of cotton growing. Irrigated land sown to cotton this year exceeds the area sown in 1940 by 317,000 hectares. Cotton yields from irrigated land in 1952 were 6 centners per hectare higher than before the war. Last year 70 per cent more cotton was obtained than in 1940. Hundreds of collective farms got an average cotton yield of 30 to 40 centners per hectare, and many brigades and teams obtained 50 and more centners of cotton per hectare.

Production of this valuable crop must be even further expanded. There are tremendous unutilized reserves for this in the cotton-growing republics. When one recalls that last year a third of the cotton-growing collective farms got harvests of less than 15 centners per hectare, it becomes apparent what could be obtained if these collective farms were to raise yields to only 20 or 25 centners per hectare. This is above all a task for cotton-growing collective farms in Kazakhstan, where cotton yields are still low—11 to 12 centners per hectare on the average. Cotton growing is only slowly increasing in the Kirgiz Republic, Tashauz Province in the Turkmenian Republic and the Kara-Kalpak Autonomous Republic. The great potentialities for increasing cotton growing in Khorezm and Samarkand Provinces of the Uzbek Republic have not been utilized.

The further development of cotton growing has been retarded by poor work to restore and utilize unused irrigated land. Land-amelioration work has been unsatisfactorily conducted.

A considerable expansion in cotton growing must be ensured in as short a time as possible and the demand for this valuable raw material in industry must be fully satisfied.

There have been large achievements in sugar-beet raising. As compared with 1940, the area sown to this crop in 1953 is more than 28 per cent larger, and sugar-beet yields have also increased. Sugar production in the country exceeded the prewar level back in 1950 and has been constantly increasing ever since. The population's need for sugar, however, exceeds its output. Sugar-beet yields must be increased 65 per cent to 70 per cent by the end of the five-year plan, bringing the over-all sugar-beet harvest to approximately 350,000,000 centners annually instead of the 220,000,000 in 1952. This can be achieved by expanding sown areas in the main beet-growing regions and extending the crop to new areas but chiefly by increasing crop yields and gross harvests.

Comparative data for two provinces—Kursk and Kharkov—graphically illustrate the considerable reserves for increasing sugar-beet yields and the amount lost by collective farms and the state because of poor farming methods. These neighboring provinces have identical conditions for developing farming. But these are their different results as shown in the amounts of sugar beets supplied to the state, in centners per hectare:

	Kursk Province	Kharkov Province
1940	92	183
1950	94	190
1951	139	213
1952	96	185

In 1952 Kursk Province collective farms sowed 131,000 hectares to sugar beets but in Kharkov Province the collective farms sowed half as much, or 62,000 hectares. They delivered almost equal quantities of sugar beets to the sugar refineries: 12,600,000 centners from Kursk Province and 11,500,000 centners from Kharkov Province. Different standards in farming methods primarily explain this. Here are figures showing the duration of basic field work in 1952 on sugar beets:

	Kursk Province	Kharkov Province
Sowing	20 days	10 days
Balling	45 "	30 "
Singling	55 "	30 "
Harvesting	70 "	55 "

Considerably better care is taken of the sugar-beet crop in Kharkov Province than in Kursk Province. These data illustrate the unsatisfactory guidance of agriculture in Kursk Province.

Such important technical crops as long-staple flax and hemp demand attention. Many conditions favorable to their development have been established in recent years. A number of collective farms which have fulfilled and overfulfilled plans for delivering flax and hemp have obtained high incomes from these crops—up to 10,000 rubles and more per hectare sown to flax or hemp. Despite the great assistance given by the government since the war to the M.T.S. and collective farms in the flax and hemp regions, the output of these crops remains highly unsatisfactory. A negligent attitude toward raising long-staple flax and hemp can be found in many provinces, territories and republics. Not only have areas sown to these crops not increased, but in the last three years they have declined considerably. The gross harvest and commercial yield of these crops continues low and little concern has been shown for providing collective farms with their own stocks of long-staple flax seed.

Things have gone particularly badly with the restoration and expansion of flax raising in Smolensk, Ivanovo, Kostroma, Kirov, Velikiye-Luki, Bryansk and Tyumen Provinces and in Altai and Krasnoyarsk Territories and with the expansion of hemp raising in the Bashkir Republic, the Mordvinian Autonomous Republic, Orel, Tambov, and Gorky Provinces and in the Belorussian Republic.

One of the chief hindrances to the development of flax and hemp raising is the poor mechanization of cultivating and harvesting work, particularly work on the primary cultivation of these crops.

Every collective farm has to spend much labor on spreading, retting and removing flax from the spreaders. Because of manpower shortages and poor mechanization the collective farms do not handle these operations in good time and lose much of the flax. Agricultural agencies must seriously undertake to mechanize all operations in flax cultivation. The flax-processing experiment conducted in Novosibirsk Province deserves attention. Last year ten collective farms in Maslyanino and Bolotnino Districts of this province by way of experiment delivered flax to the flax mills directly from the fields. Threshing and flax-processing were organized at the mills. As a result, these collective farms' commercial yields of fiber increased three to three and one-half times and seed two to four times.

The U.S.S.R. Ministry of Agriculture and Procurements and the U.S.S.R. Ministry of Consumers' Goods Industry must study this experiment and see to its widespread application. The matter must be set up in such a way that collective farms deliver flax to the flax mills for retting and the mills organize the retting, cleaning and processing of the flax fiber. Hemp mills must be organized to receive the hemp fiber. Work must be done to erect shops in flax and hemp mills for the industrial preparation of the spread flax and hemp and shops for retting flax.

Important tasks confront collective and state farms in further expanding output of tobacco, makhorka [a grain substitute for tobacco], tea, fruits, grapes, citrus and other crops.

Increasing crop yields is a major task in agriculture. A number of important and urgent measures must be implemented for this purpose.

We must set about raising agricultural standards properly. The introduction of crop rotation and its development on many collective and state farms has been badly organized. A chief cause for this is the neglect of raising grass seed.

It is essential that the matter of growing grass seed on collective and state farms be put to rights; yields must be raised and in the next two to three years the fulfillment of plan goals for sown grasses must not only be increased but the necessary reserve stocks must be established. Steps must be taken to enable every collective and state farm to provide its own perennial and annual grass seeds. Thought should also be given to organize commercial seed raising, above all in districts where high harvests of grass seed can be obtained.

More lupine should be cultivated for fertilizer. In many northern regions lupine sowed from seed does not always mature. For the time being, therefore, the collective farms of the northern regions cannot provide themselves with seed for fairly large areas. It is necessary to determine the regions where commercial lupine seed can be cultivated.

Fallow land and arable land turned in good season and well tilled, and sowing at the optimum time are of very great importance in raising crop yields. Low winter-crop yields in many districts can be explained by the fact that these crops are sown on poorly, tardily cultivated and inadequately manured fallow land or on the fresh tillage of an unfallow predecessor. It can hardly be tolerated that many collective farms in the non-Black Earth belt have delayed sowing winter crops until the second half of September and some even until October. It is clear that such a breach of farming methods wastes a considerable part of the winter crops.

One reason for low spring-crop yields in many regions is that they are being sown over large areas on spring tillage, in badly prepared soil and late. The collective farms sowed 38 per cent of the spring crops on spring tillage in 1951, 33 per cent in 1952 and 41 per cent in 1953, and in such provinces as Smolensk, Pskov, Novgorod, Velikiye-Luki, Vologda and Kostroma 80 per cent to 90 per cent of the spring crops were sown on spring tillage in 1953. Clearly, such operations make it difficult to get good yields. This situation is no longer acceptable. The land for all of next year's spring sowing must be plowed this year.

The problem of seed deserves serious attention. Many collective and state farms take poor care of their own seed and borrow in large quantities from the state each year. Much time goes into shipping grain seed and a tremendous amount of labor, funds and transport is nonproductively expended. By spring of 1952 more than 500,000 tons of grain seed, or about 30 per cent of their requirements, were allocated collective farms in the central provinces alone. More than 30,000,000 rubles from state funds, not counting the collective farms' expenditures, went for shipping and cleaning this seed. There is another important point here. Frequently the seed lent is not suited to the soil and climate of the region where it is to be sown. Under such conditions, of course one cannot expect high harvests.

It is time to bring order to seed farming. The transition to graded sowings of all crops must be ensured in 1954 and 1955. This year the government has established a new procedure for laying in seed stocks on the collective and state farms. Seed stocks must be stored at the best times and, above all, selected and graded seed from the yields of the seed-raising sectors planted according to the best farming methods must be used. If there is a lack of selected seed from the seed-raising sectors, then the best seed should be taken from the most fruitful sectors of general sowings prior to meeting the plan for grain deliveries to the state. Everything has been established to enable the collective and state farms to provide themselves fully with the best selected seed of highly fruitful varieties. It is absolutely necessary to end such disgraceful occurrences as the reduction of sowing norms.

The incorrect attitude toward the use of local fertilizers which has arisen in recent years among many agricultural agency officials and leaders on collective farms, M.T.S. and state farms must be condemned as a serious shortcoming. A harmful lack of understanding of the importance of this matter exists. One cannot otherwise explain the situation where plans for manure accumulations and peat procurements are not being fulfilled.

It is well known that manure is a highly valuable fertilizer. By the end of the five-year plan it will be possible to obtain about 400,000,000 tons of manure a year—the equivalent of approximately 20,000,000 tons of mineral fertilizers, or 3.5 times more than industry is now providing. Serious attention must be given to the matter of accumulating, correctly storing and applying manure to the soil. Improper manure storage must be done away with; when badly stored the manure is ventilated and loses its valuable properties. Manure storage bins must be constructed on the livestock sections of every collective and state farm in order to ensure that the manure is completely spread on the fields in good time and turned under. Steps must also be taken to mechanize labor-consuming operations such as loading, unloading and spreading manure on the fields, to organize the manufacture of manure spreaders and loaders and to introduce this equipment on collective and state farms.

In regions with acid turfy-podsol soils liming is of great importance in increasing crop yields, and in regions with saline soil gypsum must be spread. For this purpose the lime output must be sharply increased in enterprises of the building materials industry, local industry and consumers' cooperatives, and gypsum mining must be developed, along with its milling and delivery to the collective farms.

There must be considerable increases in the output of mineral fertilizers for raising crop yields as well as in the utilization of local fertilizers. The government plans to expand mineral fertilizer production, and in 1953 collective and state farms will receive 6,000,000 tons of mineral fertilizers from industry—almost double the amount allocated agriculture in 1940. In following years fertilizer production will be even larger. Proper order must be brought to the storing of mineral fertilizers and they must be used correctly. Bacterial fertilizers must also be used more widely.

Implementation of the matters set forth will raise agricultural standards to a new level and result in major increases in the yields of all agricultural crops.

5. On Improving the Work of Machine and Tractor Stations.— A leading and decisive role in the further advance of agriculture belongs to the Machine and Tractor Stations. There are now 969,000 tractors (in terms of 15 h.p.) on the M.T.S., or 74 per cent more than before the war, 255,000 grain combines, or 66 per cent more than in 1940, and many other machines.

The M.T.S. have received much new equipment since the war. Whereas before the war we had mostly wheel tractors, many diesel and caterpillar tractors have been received in the postwar years and there are now 14 times more than in 1940. New types of cultivator tractors have been built—the Belarus, the KDP-35 and the KhTZ-7, and the manufacture of attachments and equipment has been mastered.

Every year mechanization increases in collective farming, manual labor has been reduced and the collective farmers' work output has risen. This means that further advances in all branches of agriculture depend principally on improving the work of the M.T.S.

Unfortunately it appears that many Party, Soviet and agricultural agency officials have not yet learned that mechanization is that force without which it is impossible to maintain either our rates of development or large-scale production. Many Party, Soviet and agricultural agencies guide the M.T.S. only weakly, neither exercising needed supervision over timely and correct farm work nor busying themselves as they should in selecting and training M.T.S. workers. A main shortcoming in the M.T.S. work is the completely unsatisfactory utilization of equipment. This is a chief reason for the lag in a number of vitally important branches of agriculture.

The attitude toward M.T.S. must be fundamentally changed, serious shortcomings in their work must be resolutely eliminated and the over-all mechanization of farming must be ensured.

The M.T.S.' main task is to raise in every way all collective farm crop yields, ensure the growth of communal animal husbandry while increasing its productivity and expand gross and commercial output in agriculture and animal husbandry on the collective farms being served. The M.T.S. must complete the mechanization of grain and technical crop cultivation, extensively develop the mechanization of labor-consuming processes in animal husbandry and potato and vegetable raising, apply the achievements of science and advanced practice in collective farming, ensure the further organizational and economic strengthening of the collective farms and, on this basis, raise the collective farmers' material well-being.

The M.T.S. must ensure large harvests on all the areas cultivated. This can be done if tractors and other equipment are used productively and the farm work handled rapidly and efficiently. Nevertheless many M.T.S. are not meeting this highly important task. They violate farm practice, prolong the work periods, cultivate the land badly and handle the sowing in a poor fashion, with the result that yields are inadequate. Last year more than half the M.T.S. did not meet the work plan. More than 20 per cent of all the work on spring and winter crops was handled with delays. Important work such as plowing fallow land, plowing to fallow, hay harvesting and ensiling feed is being done poorly. Considerable losses in the harvest have occurred, because a considerable part of the tractors and other equipment stand idle during the time for field work. Shift norms were met by only 34 per cent of the tractor operators. The M.T.S. in Novosibirsk, Kalinin, Smolensk, Yaroslavl, Velikiye-Luki, Pskov and Novorod Provinces and the Belorussian Republic have handled tractor utilization particularly badly.

A main reason for this situation is the failure to provide the M.T.S. with qualified machine equipment operators. The rich and complex machinery of the M.T.S. needs skilled workers, but it is in the hands of seasonal workers assigned from the collective farms for the field work period. The tractor driver is actually not subordinate to the M.T.S. director. If he likes, he goes to work; if he does not go, it is difficult for the director to influence him. Today he drives a tractor, tomorrow he returns to the collective farm or departs for industry. This to a considerable degree explains the low work discipline and the large personnel turnover. Thirty per cent to 35 per cent of the tractor drivers leave the tractor brigades annually, and the staff of tractor-drawn equipment operators is changed several times a year in many tractor brigades.

If we wish decisively to improve the M.T.S. work, we must provide permanent and qualified equipment-operating personnel, who can fully and productively utilize the equipment and ensure the further development of all branches of collective farming. It is therefore necessary to see to it that the tractor drivers, tractor brigade leaders and their assistants, the excavator operators and their assistants and the fuel attendants in the M.T.S. are permanent staff members. During seasons when there is no field work these workers must be employed on related jobs in the repair shops, on mechanization work on the collective farms' animal husbandry sectors and on other duties in the M.T.S. Workers on tractor-drawn farming and digging machinery and combine operators' assistants must be included on the M.T.S. staffs as seasonal workers.

We must also increase the tractor brigade workers' stake in utilizing machinery as productively as possible and gaining large harvests. The present system of paying tractor brigade workers on the basis of workday units and piece rates, whereby workers are paid for norm fulfillments and amount of actual output in relation to crop yields, has been justified in practice and must be adhered to in the future.

An increase is planned in the M.T.S.' cash payments to the tractor brigade workers for workday units. Moreover, they will continue to receive, along with the collective farmers, pay for workday units. Bonuses for overfulfilling harvest plans are maintained. In this connection, the existing system of guaranteed minimum payment in kind with grain has been changed for tractor drivers and other tractor brigade workers. Where before they received the grain from collective farms, the M.T.S. will now issue it. Grain from food crops due to tractor brigade workers for meeting the guaranteed minimum workday units and harvesting with combines and other equipment will be delivered by the collective farms to the state procurement centers along with payment in kind. Food grain for tractor brigade workers will be handed over to the M.T.S. by the procurement organizations.

When our crop yields rise, animal husbandry productivity increases, potato and vegetable growing expands and, thanks to this, collective farm income and pay for workday units rises, the wages of the tractor drivers and other tractor brigade operators will also rise considerably. This will undoubtedly stabilize the personnel situation, thus ensuring optimum utilization of machinery.

Need has arisen to change the system of training tractor and combine operators and workers with other general qualifications. These cadres have been wretchedly trained until now. A fellow takes a course two or three months, is led around a machine a few times and then the steering wheel is put into his hands and there you have a tractor driver. Somehow this tractor driver will ride out to the field in the spring, but if the machine should stop he will sit helplessly by the tractor until a mechanic comes. Thus, output is low, machines frequently break down and the work is poor. The present system of training personnel in brief courses does not guarantee them the necessary technical background. This must be profoundly changed. Tractor drivers and mechanics must be trained for the M.T.S. with broad skills, so that they will be able to work with tractors, combines and other machines and know how to do mechanic's work, repairs and other work. In order to organize training properly the existing schools of mechanization must be reorganized into institutes for mechanization and the periods of training increased. We must shift to the system for training equipment operators which is used in industrial trade schools. Reorganization of the system for training equipment operators must be done quickly. This important work must not be delayed one day.

In recent years many experienced tractor drivers who knew their work well left the M.T.S. for work in industrial combines in the cities. An appeal should be made to the former equipment operators to return to work on the M.T.S. It must be assumed that now, when tractor drivers will be permanent members of the M.T.S. and will receive higher guaranteed wages, many former tractor drivers will willingly return to work on the M.T.S. Directors of enterprises must be warned not to prevent this.

We must consider separately the problem of selecting administrative personnel for the M.T.S. In September, 1951, the government passed a decree "On measures for improving M.T.S. work," which provided for increased pay rates, bonuses for achievements in the harvest and other incentives for M.T.S. administrators.

Nevertheless, many local Party agencies did not take steps to strengthen the M.T.S. with qualified personnel or use the opportunities created by this decree and did little to promote engineering and technical personnel to work on the M.T.S. Meanwhile, the level of the engineering, technical and agronomical training of the overwhelming majority of M.T.S. administrators does not meet the demands of managing large-scale mechanized farming. Here are some figures on the educational backgrounds of M.T.S. officials. Among M.T.S. directors, 22.6 per cent have higher education, 47 per cent secondary or specialized education and 30.4 per cent are practical workers with elementary education. Of the chief engineers 14.8 per cent have higher education, 20.8 per cent secondary or specialized, and 64.4 per cent elementary. Only 1.3 per cent of the shop foremen have higher education, 8.8 per cent have secondary or specialized education and 89.9 per cent are practical workers with elementary education.

Attention must be called to the completely inadmissible situation wherein the posts of directors, chief engineers and shop foremen are filled by people without specialized training. It is understandable that for lack of needed training they frequently cannot cope with the work entrusted them. There is every opportunity for advancing to these posts trained people with specialized education who are capable of successfully guiding the large and highly complex work of the M.T.S.

Here it must be noted that our educational institutions train personnel with higher and secondary skills without consideration of the need for them in agriculture. There are particular lags in training engineers and mechanics for the M.T.S. and state farms. While the number of agricultural specialists increased 53 per cent from 1940 through 1950, the number of those with engineering training rose only 12 per cent.

Further improvement in M.T.S. work depends directly on how we provide the M.T.S. with administrative and engineering and technical personnel. M.T.S. directors should, as a rule, be engineers, mechanics or agronomists with higher education and necessary training in the mechanization of agriculture. Workers with higher, specialized education must be appointed to the posts of chief engineer or chief agronomist on the M.T.S.

It may be asked, what is to be done with the M.T.S. directors who have no specialized training but have proved themselves good organizers? The approach to this work cannot be indiscriminate, of course. We have many M.T.S. directors without specialized training who have nevertheless learned through experience and guide the M.T.S. skillfully. Such workers must be left in their posts and helped to get an education.

In order to strengthen the M.T.S. with administrative, engineering and technical personnel, we must in the immediate future attract engineers and mechanics from industry and other branches of the national economy and send them to the M.T.S. as directors and technical chiefs for repair shops and send the technicians to work as mechanics in the M.T.S.

There is much equipment on the M.T.S. but not enough to handle the tasks ahead of us successfully. Therefore, the U.S.S.R. Council of Ministers and the Party Central Committee have planned a major program for the output of tractors and other equipment. Agriculture is to receive 500,000 general-purpose tractors (in 15-h.p. units), 250,000 cultivator tractors and a large amount of farm machinery and motor vehicles in the period from 1954 through May 1, 1957. Many new-type cultivator tractors, highly productive machinery for cultivating and harvesting technical and feed crops, potatoes and vegetables and equipment for fully mechanizing hay and silage harvesting and labor-consuming work on the animal husbandry sections will be provided.

The industrial ministries must be required to work more actively to design new machines and improve present ones. Inadequate attention on the part of the U.S.S.R. Ministry of Machine Building and the U.S.S.R. Ministry of Agriculture and Procurements has frequently resulted in new and excellent machines greatly needed in farming not being put into production for needlessly long periods or being turned out in very small quantities. Some enterprises have not been meeting plans for manufacturing farm machinery.

Nor is everything well in regard to the quality of the machinery produced. Farm workers have justly complained of this. For a number of years M.T.S. combine operators and workers on M.T.S. and state farms have pointed out serious shortcomings in the C-4 power combine, which is not suited to farm needs, especially in regions with high humidity. Yet the U.S.S.R. Ministries of Machine Building and Agriculture and Procurements have done nothing to eliminate these shortcomings.

The square-cluster method, which permits row tilling with tractor- or horse-drawn cultivators, is extremely important in ensuring large harvests of such cultivated crops as corn, sunflowers, castor-oil plants. However, seeders are necessary to plant by the square-cluster method. True, the Red Star Factory in the city of Kirovograd makes a seeder for square-cluster sowing of corn, sunflowers and other crops, but it has to be adjusted by hand. This method does not work since squares do not result. This procedure must be made automatic and based on a guide wire, as is done on potato planters. Use of this principle on the SSh-6 seeder has given good results.

Seeders must also be made for square-cluster sowings of other cultivated crops, particularly where large sowing densities are required. Institutes and factories must be charged with designing such seeders more rapidly and the U.S.S.R. Ministry of Agriculture and Procurements must test the seeders for production and equip the M.T.S. with them. Only if we shift to mechanized sowing and cultivation can we quickly raise the yields of all cultivated crops. We have no choice. It is the honorable task of industrial enterprise workers, engineers and technicians to meet the goals for producing good-quality machinery in full and on time.

Further attention must be called to organizing repairs and maintenance for tractors and other equipment. One can no longer be resigned to the fact that important M.T.S. equipment has been neglected and put out of commission prematurely. Many M.T.S. do not yet have repair shops, garages, machine sheds or other buildings. This unfavorable situation in the M.T.S. is illustrated by the following: 429 M.T.S. have no repair shops whatsoever and about 5000 have poorly equipped shops which cannot meet repair needs. Many M.T.S. do not have the necessary housing for engineers and mechanics, dormitories for tractor drivers or other buildings. Despite this fact, allotments for constructing housing and production buildings on the M.T.S. were utilized only 80 per cent to 85 per cent in the past three years. Most to blame for this are the local agricultural agency officials who took no steps to make complete use of the allotted funds and the Party agencies which did not give needed supervision to the task.

Such mismanagement must be stopped. In the next three years each M.T.S. must, as a rule, have a standardized repair shop, no less than two or three garages for tractors, enough sheds to house farm machinery, and other production buildings and living quarters. Large funds have been allotted for this. These must be utilized correctly and thriftily and the goals established must be met.

Important here is the organization of material and technical supplying of the M.T.S. with equipment, tools, metals and other material and, in particular, spare parts. Work must be stepped up on the electrification of farming and the collective farmers' daily life on the basis of more complete utilization of electricity from existing rural power plants, the construction of new rural power plants and wind power stations and also by joining the M.T.S. and collective and state farms to the state power systems. It is highly important to provide agriculture with equipment operated by electric cables.

The increased scale of mechanized work on the collective farms has brought the M.T.S. more payment in kind. The present rates for payment in kind are based on the following principle: the bigger the harvest received by the collective farm, the higher the rates of payment in kind. This system has major shortcomings. After all, the harvest yield depends not only on the quality of M.T.S. work but on the quality of the collective farm's work.

It frequently happens that the very same M.T.S. tractor brigade works on two neighboring collective farms, yet one collective farm has a large harvest and the other a low one. The quality of the M.T.S. work on these collective farms was the same. What is wrong here? The truth is, the collective farm with the big harvest sowed higher-grade seeds and used fertilizers, and the second collective farm did not. The first collective farm paid off the M.T.S. in kind at a higher rate than the second, although the M.T.S.' absolute expenditure per hectare was equal on both collective farms. After making payments in kind, each of these collective farms had almost equal amounts of grain and other produce remaining to issue for workday units.

In view of the fact that the present system of making payments in kind for M.T.S. work is not an incentive to the advanced collective farms, fixed rates of payment in kind must be established to encourage the M.T.S. to increase crop yields. The U.S.S.R. Council of Ministers and the Presidium of the Central Party Committee have charged the U.S.S.R. Ministry of Agriculture and Procurements with preparing proposals on this matter.

We must end the incorrect practice of calculating the yields of grain and other farm produce not according to actual harvest but only according to the estimated yields of the unharvested crops. This practice does not help the harvesting of the crop and even retards the struggle against harvest losses, which are still great on collective farms. The present system of determining crop yields does not induce M.T.S. directors to carry work through to the end or be concerned not only for raising the crops but for gathering them without losses. We must base calculations on the harvest actually in the barns and make bonus payments for yields actually gathered, so that M.T.S. workers will be directly interested in the actual harvests of grain and other farm produce.

The production relations of the M.T.S. with the collective farms will continue to be determined by the contracts concluded between them. Changes stemming from the new tasks facing the M.T.S. must be made in the standard contract. It must once more be emphasized that the contract of the M.T.S. with the collective farm has the force of law and its fulfillment is obligatory both for the M.T.S. and for the collective farm. Local Soviet and Party agencies must ensure comprehensive supervision over fulfillment of the contractual obligations of the M.T.S. and collective farms.

Thus, in order to further improve the work of the M.T.S. it is necessary:

to establish permanent staffs of equipment operators with high qualifications and for this purpose to reorganize fundamentally the system of training tractor and combine operators and other equipment operators, replacing short courses with a network of institutes for mechanization;

to strengthen M.T.S. administrative personnel;

to increase the role of the M.T.S. in the struggle further to develop animal husbandry, resolutely to improve the use of equipment and to ensure that farming is done by the best methods and in the best fashion;

to build on each M.T.S. repair shops for tractors and farm machinery and garages and sheds;

to develop work on housing for M.T.S. specialists and workers.

Party organizations must improve guidance of the M.T.S., increasing their role in the organizational and economic strengthening of the collective farms, in the struggle further to develop agriculture. Herein lies the guarantee for success.

6. On the Work of Agricultural Agencies and Increasing Agronomical and Zootechnical Service to the Collective Farms.—Comrades! the tasks of overcoming the lag in particular branches of agriculture and raising all agricultural output to a new, higher level make considerable demands on the U.S.S.R. Ministry of Agriculture and Procurements, the U.S.S.R. Ministry of State Farms, all local agricultural agencies and every agricultural specialist.

Tens of thousands of specialists, devoted to our party and giving all their strength and knowledge to the further development of agriculture, are working in the agricultural agencies. But can we say that the agricultural agencies are on the whole adequate to their task? No, comrades, we cannot. Facts show that the U.S.S.R. Ministry of Agriculture and Procurements and the U.S.S.R. Ministry of State Farms have lagged impermissibly far behind the demands of life and have not taken into account the changes which have occurred in the collective farms, M.T.S. and state farms.

It must be noted that even the apparatus of the U.S.S.R. Ministry of Agriculture and Procurements and its local agencies does not conform to the demands for efficient solution of the problems advanced by the collective farms and M.T.S. The apparatus is very unwieldy; it includes numerous administrations and departments which duplicate one another's work and are frequently idle. It is not surprising that the ministry does not show efficiency and accuracy in guiding local agencies, that it permits bureaucracy and red tape in settling pressing problems. The U.S.S.R. Ministry of Agriculture and Procurements is but feebly linked with practice, is isolated from the collective farms and the M.T.S. With no knowledge of the true state of affairs locally, the ministry nevertheless attempts to regulate from the center all phases of the work of local agricultural agencies, collective farms and M.T.S., issuing instructions which are often locally undesirable.

Ask the comrades from North Caucasus if they have ever asked the ministry how to raise wheat. I am certain the answer will be in the negative. Workers in the Ukraine do not ask the ministry how to raise sugar beets nor do those in Uzbekistan ask how to grow cotton. This is understandable—experienced workers have grown up in the localities. But the ministry officials continue to guide in the old way, proceeding on the false assumption that only they know all and can do all.

V. I. Lenin pointed out: "It would be a mistake to follow one type of decree for everywhere in Russia . . ." (V. I. Lenin, *Works* [in Russian], Vol. XXIX, p. 138). He stated: "To apply one particular stereotype to Central Russia, the Ukraine and Siberia would be the height of stupidity" (*Ibid.,* Vol. XXXII, p. 198). These injunctions are timely today.

The defects in the ministry's work are graphically shown in the work of planning for agriculture. Many unnecessary items which restrict the initiative of the local agencies, M.T.S. and collective farms are included in the plans. Suffice it to say that the planned tasks for the collective farms in agriculture and animal husbandry alone list from 200 to 250 goals. Yet, for example, such measures as removing cross-bred pigs from fattening, sowing "curtains" of tall crops [corn, sunflowers] on fallow land [using the stalks for snow retention, etc.] and many other measures are centrally planned.

An excessively great number of tasks which include many items has brought about an extraordinary inflation in every type of report making. Many agricultural specialists and collective farmers are employed in compiling various summaries, lists and reports. In the course of the year each collective farm presents to district agricultural agencies factual reports covering approximately 10,000 items. Collective farm reports have almost tripled since the war in number of items covered.

Although we criticize the U.S.S.R. Ministry of Agriculture and Procurements, this does not mean that its role has been diminished. On the contrary, the ministry must play an increasingly greater role.

The ministry apparatus must be revised to conform with changed conditions and its staffs considerably decreased.

First of all, the U.S.S.R. Ministry of Agriculture and Procurements must concentrate on planning for agriculture and its various branches, on the material and technical supplying and the financing of agriculture, on farm procurements, on selecting, placing and training personnel, on problems of propaganda and applying advanced experience and scientific achievements and on problems of collective farm organization as well.

In this connection the importance of Union and autonomous republic Ministries of Agriculture and Procurements and territory and province agriculture and procurements administrations must take on increased importance. This means that local agricultural agencies must be strengthened with qualified personnel, their structure must be reviewed, their staffs decreased and the agencies brought closer to production.

It is particularly necessary to say something about agricultural leadership in the Russian Republic. The territory of the Russian Federation contains more than 57 per cent of all the collective farms in the country and more than 62 per cent of the M.T.S. The Russian Federation has more than 62 per cent of all sown area in the U.S.S.R. and more than half of all the cattle in the country.

Notwithstanding, the Russian Federation unlike all other Union republics, until recently has not had a full-fledged Ministry of Agriculture with the necessary rights and powers. Even the republic's M.T.S. were not within the ministry's jurisdiction.

This ministry formerly had the task of concentrating on the output of potatoes and vegetables, but actually it did not have the needed material and technical base even for this. As a result, the ministry had to limit its activity to problems of rabbit breeding, bee keeping and wild life. This sounds fantastic, but unfortunately it is not fantasy but fact.

The Russian Federation with its large and varied agriculture must have a truly full-fledged Ministry of Agriculture and Procurements enjoying the necessary rights and powers. This ministry must be given the leadership of all branches of agriculture, collective farms and M.T.S. in Russian Republic territory.

A no less important question is that of strengthening agronomical and zootechnical aid to the collective farms. We have already done much in this respect and are continuing to do so. Nevertheless, we have far from used our opportunities here.

The state has trained hundreds of thousands of agricultural specialists in higher and secondary schools. In the agricultural agencies alone there are more than 350,000 specialists with higher and secondary education.

How have we used these specialists? Only 18,500 specialists, or merely 5 per cent of the total, are working on the collective farms. There is only one specialist to five collective farms! On the M.T.S. there are 50,000, or 14 per cent, of the specialists working: 75,000, or 21 per cent, are employed in the agricultural agency apparatus and are by no means adequately linked with collective farming.

This problem of utilizing agricultural specialists is not being raised for the first time. In recent years the government has followed the course of increasing the earnings of specialists in the M.T.S. Now the agricultural specialist or engineer in an M.T.S. receives no less and in many cases more than an engineer working in an industrial enterprise. But despite this, most specialists are still warming chairs in various institutions and offices.

How can this abnormal situation be explained? First of all, by the agricultural agencies' antistate approach to the problem of employing specialists. Considering the specialists' chief vocation to be the writing of orders, directives and instructions, the agricultural agency officials try to set them behind office desks. The agricultural agencies have done little to provide each specialist with a sense of professional pride, to awaken in him the spirit of fruitful research, the spirit of an indomitable transformer of agriculture and animal husbandry.

This attitude toward the invaluable fund of agricultural personnel is radically wrong. It is high time to see that specialists work in production—in the collective farms, M.T.S. and state farms—and at their own task, that of increasing harvest yields and developing animal husbandry.

The draft decree provides for sending by the spring of 1954 not less than 100,000 agricultural specialists to work in the M.T.S. so that each collective farm is served by an agricultural specialist and each large collective farm by an agricultural specialist and an animal husbandry specialist. The M.T.S. agricultural specialist, who continuously serves one collective farm, must see to it that the contract between the M.T.S. and the collective farm is met. He is required to see that farming standards are complied with and in no circumstances must permit poor-quality work to be covered up, remembering that the slightest relaxation in his attitude toward the violations of farming standards or any connivance with spoilage producers damages the collective farm and the state. The agricultural specialist must be interested in everything and be an active fighter to introduce into collective farming all that is new and progressive.

It is expedient to make the chief agronomist in an M.T.S. a state inspector for supervising the quality of the work envisaged by the contract between the M.T.S. and the collective farm. Here it would be entirely proper for the chief agronomist for farming methods to be subordinate not to the M.T.S. director but directly to the head of the province agricultural administration. This is necessary if production and farming interests are not to be subordinated to narrow departmental considerations. There are times when an M.T.S. director, in order to obtain greater output per tractor and save on fuel, permits shallow plowing or postpones the start of spring sowing until the soil has dried. The chief agronomist on an M.T.S. must in no circumstances permit violations of farming standards, always basing his work on the fact that high yields can only be obtained by timely and high-quality M.T.S. work. Agricultural specialists must become the true organizers of the struggle for high harvests.

The U.S.S.R. Ministry of Agriculture and Procurements must clearly and accurately define the rights and duties of the chief agronomist on an M.T.S.

As the organizing role of the M.T.S. in collective farming is increased, the present need for district agricultural and procurements agencies obviously will decrease. It is sufficient to include several workers for planning and reporting in the district executive committee makeup, but use must be made of the basic cadres of specialists in the M.T.S. and collective and state farms.

A little time must be spent on such an important question as the propaganda and application in agriculture of scientific achievements and advanced experience. There are many agricultural innovators and advanced collective farms, M.T.S. and state farms in every province, territory and republic. To manage a farm in our time without considering the experience of advanced collective farms, M.T.S. and state farms or innovators' achievements is knowingly to doom it to lagging.

Unfortunately we have poorly propagandized and applied what is new. Each of our collective farms must, if it can be so expressed, make its way in life through its own mind, its own experience, its own practice, and we should be able to arm all collective farms with the great experience which has been accumulated by our advanced farmers.

The ministry and its local agencies have until now adopted an indifferent, passive attitude toward all that is new in agriculture; indeed, they have not noticed it. Many valuable and proven methods for increasing yields have not been applied over the years.

Agricultural leadership implies first and foremost the study, generalization and dissemination of progressive experience and scientific achievements. Agricultural propaganda must at long last become a most important and integral part of all the work of the U.S.S.R. Ministry of Agriculture and Procurements, the U.S.S.R. Ministry of State Farms and their local agencies.

It must be stated that it is not only the ministries and their local agencies who are to blame for the poor situation in regard to the propaganda of advanced experience and scientific achievements. Many Party and Soviet agencies have handed over the important work of agricultural propaganda to a few workers and have themselves held aloof.

Party and Soviet organization officials must not only make speeches on the need to disseminate advanced experience; primarily, they must study this experience and become active organizers in applying it on all collective and state farms. Before urging others, the official must make a thorough, on-the-spot study of advanced methods and ways of managing in order to realize well what he is asking and, when at the collective and state farms, must give needed advice and provide help.

Party and Soviet organization officials should encourage the collective farm chairmen, board members, brigade leaders, team leaders and other workers on lagging collective farms to visit the leading farms and there study in detail all the techniques and methods of their work. It is necessary to find proper ways to influence lagging collective and state farms and see that they base all their work on that of advanced farms.

Our press, particularly the agricultural press, has unsatisfactorily propagandized scientific achievements and advanced experience; there are still few good books published on these problems, and those which are published often have a superficially descriptive nature and do not disclose the essentials of new work techniques and methods.

The output of popular scientific or instructional agricultural films is poor and their quality often leaves much to be desired. Often people with a poor understanding of agriculture are haphazardly recruited to make agricultural films.

A few words about agriculture and animal husbandry classes on collective and state farms. There are now more than 2,500,000 collective farmers and state farm workers attending three-year training courses. This, of course, is considerable. However, instruction in many cases is conducted on a low level and often in isolation from the specific conditions of actual practice. In the present academic year only 60 per cent of the collective farmers taking courses passed their examinations. On 30,000 collective farms, agriculture and animal husbandry classes for the collective farmers were not organized at all.

Agricultural science plays an important role in the further advance of agriculture. It must be noted that Soviet science has made considerable contributions to the progress of agriculture; nevertheless, it still lags behind the production needs and requirements. Some institutes and experimental stations do not do enough work on urgent questions of raising the level of agriculture and animal husbandry. Scientific institutions lack adequate criticism and self-criticism, creative discussion and a free exchange of opinion are absent and often there is cultivated around various scientists an atmosphere of toadying and obsequiousness.

As you know, the government does not stint funds and materials for developing science and scientists have been provided extremely favorable work conditions. Unfortunately, however, we have some scientific workers who defend their dissertations and then actually stop work, for years making no new contribution to science or to collective and state farming. There are also dissertations with neither scientific nor practical importance. The fact that various institutes' experimental bases and stations get lower crop yields and livestock productivity than do advanced collective and state farms discloses the extent to which some research institutes have fallen behind practice.

Every scientific institution must concentrate seriously on solving problems connected with increasing crop yields and developing animal husbandry, as well as on problems of the economics and organization of agriculture and the mechanization and electrification of collective and state farming.

District and province agricultural exhibits must become important in propagandizing scientific achievements and advanced experience and bringing about competition to apply them widely. Before the war such exhibits were held annually in many districts and provinces, but in recent years attention to organizing them has weakened.

This matter must be put right. Agricultural exhibits must be organized annually in district and province centers. Every advanced collective and state farm and every M.T.S. must have an opportunity to display its achievements and its experience at the exhibit. Unlike before, there must be a place at the exhibit for showing the lagging collective and state farms so that they can see their lagging in comparison with better practice. This will encourage them to adopt the techniques and methods of the advanced workers. A proposal has been introduced to adopt a decree opening an all-Soviet agricultural exhibit in 1954.

Thus, in order to improve the work of agricultural agencies and increase agronomical and zootechnical assistance to the collective farms, it is necessary:

to improve the agricultural leadership fundamentally, raising it to the level of the new tasks;

to raise the agricultural agencies' role in developing agriculture, to strengthen their personnel and bring them closer to the M.T.S. and to collective farms;

to improve agrotechnical and zootechnical service to the collective farms, sending no less than 100,000 agronomists and zootechnicians to work on the collective farms, in order that each collective farm is served by one or two specialists;

to increase decisively the propaganda of advanced experience and the achievements of agricultural science.

The above-mentioned shortcomings in the guidance of the collective farms and the M.T.S. apply in full measure to the state farms as well. A major shortcoming in the state farms' work is still the high output cost of grain, meat, milk and other products.

The state has provided everything necessary to handle work well on every state farm, but farming results differ completely, depending on the quality of the leadership.

I will give an example. The Miner State Farm and the Young Communist State Farm, both in October District of Rostov Province, have approximately the same farming conditions, but these are the results of their work in 1952:

	Miner Farm	Young Communist Farm
Sown area (hectares)	3982	3222
Cattle	1190	1117
Cows	352	409
Pigs	813	661
Milk yield per cow (kilos)	3035	1934
Cost per centner of animal husbandry products:		
milk (rubles)	90	114
pork (rubles)	646	1457
Deliveries to the state:		
milk (centners)	9595	6279
meat (centners)	1419	932
Results of work	686,000 rubles' profit	407,000 rubles' loss

What is the reason for such different results? The Miner State Farm is led by the experienced zootechnician Comrade Povarenkin, but the Young Communist State Farm is headed by Comrade Bondarenko, who does not have the necessary training and is a bad organizer. Notwithstanding the fact that he clearly has not met his obligations, the ministry has tolerated him in the post of director for ten years.

Many state farms are headed by poorly trained workers. Of the 2064 directors of state farms under U.S.S.R. jurisdiction in the U.S.S.R. Ministry of State Farms, 644, or 31 per cent, are men who learned on the job and lack even a secondary specialized education. Among those managing sectors, divisions and livestock sectors 93 per cent have no specialized education. Almost three-fourths the workers employed as senior engineering personnel on state farms are such men.

We must see that every state farm is profitable and has a highly marketed output. To achieve this it is necessary to strengthen state farm administrative personnel. Lagging state farms must be put in order, wasteful methods must be eliminated, strict economy must be observed with state funds and the unit cost of products sharply decreased. Some thought must be given to eliminating the existing system of state subsidies, since it breeds a parasitical state of mind among state farm officials and does not encourage them to struggle unflaggingly to improve state farm work.

It is our duty to see that all state farms become models.

7. *Questions of Party Political Work in the Countryside.*—Comrades! Successful solution of the tasks confronting us in agriculture demands great organizational and political work by Party organizations. It would be wrong to assume that the further development of agriculture will come about quietly, smoothly and spontaneously.

At present every material, technical and organizational condition for the further strengthening of the collective farms, M.T.S. and state farms is being provided by the Party and the government. In this connection it is possible that certain of our officials may think that now the work will go on by itself and that they may be entirely complacent. There is nothing more dangerous than such sentiments. They can do immense harm.

Material opportunities and reserves by themselves, without organizational work by province and district Party committees, primary Party units and M.T.S., collective and state farm officials cannot get the results needed. To utilize these reserves and opportunities, all our forces and potentialities must be brought into play, great organizational effort must be applied and the wide masses of collective farmers and workers in M.T.S. trained and guided to solving the task of further advancing agriculture.

Our rural Party forces are not small. There are collective farm Party organizations on 76,000 collective farms. At present there are more than 1,000,000 Communists in the countryside. The army of rural Y.C.L. members numbers more than 2,000,000. If we place and utilize these forces correctly, we shall successfully cope with all our tasks and surmount every difficulty on the way to the goal. For this purpose Party organizations must rely still more on the non-Party *aktiv,* the foremost people in the collective farm countryside.

The measures carried out by the Party in recent years to develop inner Party democracy, criticism and self-criticism have to a considerable extent helped to develop Communists' activity, strengthen Party organizations and consolidate their ties with the masses of working people.

Nevertheless, it must be admitted that there are grave shortcomings in the work of Party organizations in the countryside. In many organizations Party political work is carried on in isolation from economic tasks. There are still officials among us who frequently say that politics is inseparable from economics, that politics must be combined with solving economic tasks, while in practice they separate political activity from the daily work of economic construction. This is to be seen primarily in the state of work with agricultural officials, especially with collective farm chairmen.

To attain success, attention must be concentrated on what is most important, i.e., strengthening the M.T.S. and collective and state farms with qualified, capable personnel, with our best officials. Implementation of the urgent tasks in the sphere of advancing agriculture depends first and foremost on strengthening the M.T.S. and collective and state farms with experienced, tested, honest and devoted leaders, ones capable of organizing the work and selecting and placing people correctly.

No directive, however well and fully it may have been drawn up, will have the required influence on the development of agriculture, if there are not good administrators and capable organizers in the districts. A directive is useless without able officials heading the collective farms.

The collective farms have developed and have become large and diversified economies. While before amalgamation a collective farm had on the average 589 hectares of arable land, at present it has 1693 hectares. Guiding such a holding is a complex and responsible task.

The Party Central Committee and the U.S.S.R. Council of Ministers three years ago adopted a decree on improving collective farm chairmen and other administrators. Considerable work has been done recently to improve the selection of collective farm officials. Many specialists and also practical workers with experience in organizational work have been appointed collective farm chairmen.

However, the matter of strengthening the collective farms with administrative personnel is still unsatisfactory. On only 16,600 collective farms do the chairmen have higher or secondary specialized education. On most collective farms the chairmen are people with elementary education.

Unsatisfactory selection of collective farm chairmen has resulted in frequent changes. Almost one-third the chairmen have held their posts less than one year. Many collective farms have had two or three chairmen in the course of a year. A number of these chairmen were dismissed as incapable or for misdemeanors. There are many cases where district committees have transferred people who showed themselves inefficient or dishonest from one collective farm to another, imposing them on the collective farmers.

We must strengthen the ranks of the collective farm chairmen and improve their training in the immediate future. At the same time very serious attention must be directed to selecting work brigade leaders. With the amalgamation of collective farms, the work brigades have also become larger; experienced people, good organizers and honest collective farmers must be put in charge of them.

The Party has trained excellent cadres in the countryside. In many districts there is a possibility for strengthening the ranks of collective farm chairmen by drawing upon local officials. But there are many districts which will need assistance in this matter. It must be remembered, that in some districts there are particular difficulties in regard to collective farm personnel. These difficulties arose as a result of the large losses in personnel we suffered during the war. Moreover, since the war a large number of the best educated and able collective farmers have transferred to work in industry. The possibilities for promoting good personnel in a number of districts are consequently limited. These districts must get help.

In addition to promoting local personnel and transferring specialists, it is also necessary to select and send Communists from industrial centers to executive work on the collective farms.

At one time the Party sent 25,000 industrial workers into the countryside. They carried out a tremendous amount of work for the socialist reorganization of farming. Moreover, 17,000 Party officials were sent in 1933 to aid the collective farms by work in political departments. Many thousands of industrial officials have been sent at various times to the M.T.S. and collective and state farms. This greatly assisted the collective farm peasantry. An overwhelming majority of the officials sent to rural areas undertook the work with ardor and honorably justified the Party's trust. Although at the outset they did not have the necessary knowledge of agriculture, nevertheless, having extensive political training and experience in organizational work, they rapidly mastered the jobs entrusted them, proved to be capable leaders and did much to strengthen the collective farms. One could give a number of examples of the excellent work of Communists sent by the Party to rural areas. Such people should be given every support by Party organizations, since they are performing a great and noble task for the people and strengthening the ties of the working class with the peasantry.

Today, too, the socialist city can help the collective farm countryside by means of personnel; this is one of the most important ways to strengthen still further the ties between the industrial workers and the peasants—the impregnable basis of the might of Soviet society.

It is completely possible for us to supply all the collective farms with qualified personnel. It is good when a collective farm chairman is an agricultural specialist, preferably one with a higher education. But good, practical organizers must also be valued. We have many examples of remarkable work done by collective farm chairmen who learned on the job.

Above all the lagging collective farms need good organizers. When selecting collective farm chairmen, we must aim at placing in charge of each collective farm an experienced, able organizer, one who knows how to rally the collective farmers and manage a large holding successfully.

Now that a Soviet intelligentsia has grown up among us, why should we not issue a call from the Party and summon the best people from the cities—say, for example, 50,000 Communists—to strengthen rural work? I think that we can do this. It would be well to discuss this matter along with other questions here at the plenary session.

It may be said with entire confidence that if the Party makes such an appeal to the Communists in industrial centers, it will find many who are willing to go voluntarily to rural areas and devote their strength and knowledge to further strengthening the collective farm system. We must send proven Communists, ones who realize the entire importance of this work, who would regard themselves as permanent and not temporary rural officials. They must be surrounded with attention and care.

If we strengthen collective farm personnel, it will end the need for the various kinds of representatives who frequently know nothing about farming and do not always give needed help to the collective farms. Assigning officials to permanent work on the collective farms will be of incomparably greater help than sending representatives.

An urgent task in improving the guidance of agriculture is raising the role of district Party committees and district executive committees in developing collective farms, M.T.S. and state farms. Unless we strengthen the district sector, unless we place Party forces correctly and organize all Party work skillfully, we shall be unable to raise the guidance of the collective and state farms and M.T.S. to the level of the new tasks.

Many rural districts are not well provided with trained Party and Soviet personnel. Officials in many district Party committees and district executive committees do not have the practical qualifications for meeting the increased demands now made of executives. This particularly refers to the secretaries of rural district Party committees. If one judges on the basis of questionnaire data, the situation is more or less satisfactory. More than 90 per cent of the secretaries have Party membership of eight or more years and 80 per cent have secondary or higher education.

What are the weaknesses of executive personnel in rural districts? These are their frequently poor knowledge of agriculture and their lack of necessary experience in organizational work. About half the secretaries of rural district committees have less than five years' experience in Party work. More than one-third the rural district committee secretaries have less than a year's experience in this work. There are personnel heading many district committees and executive committees who have little experience, who find it difficult to guide the district, M.T.S. and collective farms at the required level.

Are there opportunities to strengthen the district sector with needed Party and Soviet personnel? Undoubtedly there are. One has only to place and to utilize people correctly; the apparatus in province, territory and republic centers must be reduced, unnecessary superstructures must be eliminated and many good officials must be transferred to strengthen the district sector, the collective and state farms and M.T.S.

Some provinces do not have the necessary personnel reserves for promotion to Party and Soviet work and must therefore transfer inefficient officials from place to place. Without the help of the Party

Central Committee it would be difficult for such provinces to solve the problem of improving leadership in the districts by means of their own forces. We must aid them. For this purpose several thousands of the best Communists must be selected and sent to work on rural district Party committees and executive committees.

Warning must be given to approach the matter of replacing inexperienced officials thoughtfully and attentively. Weak Party and Soviet workers must be replaced only by stronger, better trained and more experienced workers. If the comrades let go have done well as far as the Party is concerned, it would be expedient to coach them, to send them to refresher courses and to Party schools and make sure that they become good leaders. Clearly, it would be useful to include study of problems of method, economics and the organization of socialist agriculture in the syllabuses of refresher courses for personnel and in Party schools.

Work in the countryside is highly important and honored work. Party organizations should overcome the lordly and bureaucratic attitude toward the village which has arisen among certain Communists, even those occupying responsible posts. There are still workers who consider jobs in rural districts, M.T.S. and collective and state farms to be of secondary importance. Such people do not understand the simple truth that without an advance in agriculture the tasks of communist construction cannot successfully be solved. Communist society cannot be built without an abundance of bread, meat, milk, butter, vegetables and other farm produce.

The attention of Party organizations must be directed to the matter of rapidly developing agriculture. Every sector connected with the guidance of agriculture must be strengthened with personnel. A tremendous army of specialists must be transferred from the apparatus to production; collective farms, M.T.S. and state farms must be strengthened with managerial and mass personnel, and the personnel of district Party committees and district executive committees must be strengthened. This work must be begun immediately and fundamentally completed not later than January or February of next year, so that by spring thousands of capable organizers—Party and non-Party—who have been newly promoted will participate in the active struggle for next year's high harvest and an advance in animal husbandry.

The lack of personal responsibility in the guidance of M.T.S. and collective farms must be eliminated. There is a large apparatus in the districts of Party, Soviet and agricultural agency officials, which amounts to approximately five or six officials for each collective farm. Yet, given all this, no one is actually responsible for conditions on the collective farms and M.T.S. or for political work among the masses.

It may be said that the district committee secretary, the district executive committee chairman, the head of the agricultural department of the rural district executive committee, the M.T.S. director and many others are responsible for the collective farms and M.T.S. But who is actually responsible for a particular collective farm in the district? You will not get a definite reply to this question from anyone, because there is no one responsible for a particular collective farm. Herein lies the fundamental shortcoming in the guidance of collective farms. The guidance of collective farms actually lacks personal responsibility and is formed most frequently in this fashion: a district committee or district executive committee official tours the collective farms in a car, getting around half the district in a day and frequently issuing instructions without leaving the car.

Substantial shortcomings also occur in the guidance of the primary Party units on collective farms. This is above all shown in the fact that district Party committees, with rare exceptions, do not manifest the necessary concern for strengthening Party organizations, rallying around them the *aktiv* from among the non-Party collective farmers. The Marxist-Leninist education of Communists is still badly conducted in many organizations.

Province and district Party committees are not taking necessary steps to raise the role of the collective farm Party organization in performing the tasks confronting the collective farms. Fairly large Party organizations have been formed on many collective farms. The Party organizations on a number of collective farms are headed by secretaries who have been relieved of other duties. At the request of province and district committees, the Party Central Committee set up posts for full-time secretaries in the larger Party organizations on 3747 collective farms. But the Party committees did not everywhere regard the selection of secretaries for collective farm Party organizations seriously. Immature, untrained and sometimes adventitious persons have frequently been recommended for this work.

Mass-political work on many collective farms is carried out at a low level and necessary attention is not being devoted to the working people's political education. There are still officials who, instead of profound, over-all work with collective farmers, employ administrative fiat and violate Soviet law. On many collective farms, M.T.S. and state farms cultural-everyday services for the collective farmers and M.T.S. and state farm workers are badly arranged. In certain districts Party and Soviet agencies pay little attention to providing motion picture installations for the population.

In a number of districts there is a failure to appreciate Y.C.L. organizations, which are a great force in the struggle to advance agriculture. Y.C.L. members and village young people are still only weakly recruited to solve the problem of raising agricultural standards and developing communal animal husbandry.

Women—our glorious collective farm women and the women workers on M.T.S. and state farms—provide outstanding examples of selfless labor in all sectors of collective and state farming and are taking an exceptionally great part in agriculture. It should be stated bluntly that many Party organizations have not kept this in mind and have conducted work among the women unsatisfactorily.

Province and district Party committees are required decisively to remove present serious shortcomings and raise the standard of Party-political work among the broad masses of working people.

To achieve this, the lack of personal responsibility in social-political work in the countryside and in the guidance of M.T.S. and collective farms must be eliminated.

The need to bring Party leaders closer to decisive sectors of production has become urgent. The work of the Party apparatus now must be so rearranged that a given worker conducts work on a given collective farm and is responsible for it, that someone is made to answer for the correct selection and placement of personnel, for political work among the collective farmers and for the performance of tasks confronting a given collective farm.

The following considerations for an exchange of opinions on this question might be stated. It seems to us that for every M.T.S. the rural district committees should have a group of workers, headed by the district Party committee secretary. For example, there are three M.T.S. in a district. In such a district it is possible to form three groups of instructors—one group for each M.T.S.—so that one instructor serves one or a maximum of two collective farms and is responsible to the district Party committee for his work. The role of instructor in the Party apparatus in general and in the district Party communities in particular must be increased. Attention must therefore be paid to selecting and training instructors.

The district committee secretary who heads a group should supervise the instructors under him, serve the collective farms throughout the whole M.T.S. zone, organize Party work among the M.T.S. workers and also on the collective farms and be responsible to the district Party committee for conditions on these collective farms. In order that the guidance of collective farms and primary Party units be concrete, the district committee secretary will have to spend all his working time in the M.T.S. And this is good; there will be less paper work and red tape and more active business. In this connection there no longer is any need for an assistant director for political affairs in the M.T.S. The bureau of the district Party committee, headed by the first secretary, must guide the work of the groups serving the M.T.S. and collective farms and also manage the entire economic and cultural life of the district.

Carrying out these measures will, in our opinion, facilitate an advance in all organizational Party work and end the lack of personal responsibility in guiding the collective farms, M.T.S. and primary Party units.

The shortcomings in the manner and methods of province Party committees' guidance of agriculture should also be mentioned. The Party Central Committee has every reason for demanding an improvement in this guidance. We have facts at our disposal which indicate that many Party and Soviet officials have not penetrated deeply into collective farm affairs. Such workers have not studied collective farming and advanced experience properly, are superficial and supplant businesslike assistance to the collective farms with administrative fiats and last-minute rushes.

There are even certain secretaries of province Party committees who are not well informed about agriculture and do not care to study it, who get away with general formulas, and superficial instructions of little benefit. Can one consider normal a situation where the leader of a province Party organization cannot even name a single collective farm with high yields, a good collective farm chairman or an advanced brigade leader. Or can it be tolerated that a province committee secretary or a Union republic Party Central Committee has no definite or clear idea of the advantages of advanced work methods in agriculture and is ignorant of how the collective farms of the province are conducting the work of providing livestock with feed or which crops, for example, are best raised for silage, what of these crops are gathered by the collective and state farms, and so on? Unfortunately we still have several such leaders.

It is necessary to end decisively the superficial approach to the guidance of agriculture. In order to guide correctly the on-the-spot situation must be studied, conditions on the collective farms, M.T.S. and state farms must be looked into, work must be done with the personnel in general and with the chairmen of collective farms in particular, and advanced experience must be learned and applied. Party and Soviet officials do not have to be agricultural specialists, but they must be well versed in farming problems. And this is within every worker's grasp if he wants to be a truly useful worker. I think such a demand is absolutely just.

Comrades! In every district of the country there are now many economically strong collective farms with large harvests and high animal husbandry productivity which are successfully meeting obligations to the state, obtaining big incomes and annually ensuring a high distribution of produce and money to the collective farmers for workday units. Implementation of the measures laid down for the further advance of agriculture will ensure large and new growth in the incomes of collective farms and farmers. The collective farmers' cultural-everyday requirements are greatly increasing and will continue to do so. In this connection it is necessary to mention certain problems of building cultural and service structures and the planning of the collective farm villages. Many officials ask how to proceed with this work. There can be only one answer—this task must be in conformity with specific conditions. Where the collective farms have been strengthened and have the appropriate material potentialities, and there are many such collective farms, work must be done first and foremost on the construction of farm buildings and the improvement of the collective farm villages as well.

As the communal economy grows, the collective farms have the opportunity to use part of their income to construct communal buildings—kindergartens, nurseries and lying-in homes—and to provide women better conditions for work in collective farming and for more active participation in public life. The economically strengthened farms can allocate funds to build clubs and thereby establish more favorable conditions for social-political and cultural-enlightenment work among the collective farmers. The collective farms should be advised to assist collective farmers in making repairs and constructing housing and outbuildings, in acquiring planting stock for fruit trees for their private holdings, in getting supplies of fuel and in satisfying other needs of the collective farmers.

In this the chief thing to be remembered is raising the crop yield, advancing animal husbandry and developing all branches of agriculture. Only on the basis of a mighty new advance in agriculture can one solve the problems in sphere of planning and organizing cultural-everyday services for the collective farm village, of further improving the collective farmers' culture and living conditions. Constant concern for raising the working people's material and cultural standards of living is a most important duty for all Party and Soviet organizations.

I want to touch on yet another question. It is the matter of the holdings of private peasants [i.e., ones not belonging to the collective farms]. It is well known that in the Baltic republics—Lithuania, Latvia and Estonia—there are many such holdings. Now, when collectivization in these republics has been basically accomplished, certain local officials have raised the question of what is to become of private peasants' holdings and what should be our attitude toward them? To our way of seeing it, there can be no two opinions here. In the other republics and provinces the removal of the population from private farmholds was almost completed before the war, in conformity with the government's decision. We are in favor of gradually eliminating the system of private peasant holdings and setting up amalgamated collective farm settlements. This will ensure more favorable conditions for an advance in collective farming and will permit the collective farmers' cultural and everyday living conditions to be improved and good schools, hospitals, lying-in homes and children's institutions to be built.

But it would be incorrect to show haste in the practical solution of this question. Party and Soviet agencies must weigh the local conditions in every way with the collective farmers and rely on them to decide the question of where, when and how to carry out this matter. We are confident that a correct solution will be found. The collective farmers themselves will not want to live on private farmholds and will raise the question of the need for improving cultural and everyday conditions.

The implementation of large-scale measures for the further advance of agriculture will depend a great deal on the Party organizations' work among the masses. The creative powers of farm workers are inestimable and they must be more actively applied. Party workers and all Communists should explain extensively the tasks of developing agricultural and socialist competition to increase crop yields and animal husbandry productivity. For this it is necessary to be always in the midst of the masses and work with them in every way, to know people and their needs and requirements well, to be able to note useful innovations in good time and support them and to anticipate possible breakdowns and failures. In all their work Party organizations should rely on the advanced people on collective farms, M.T.S. and state farms, the masters of farming and animal husbandry whose ranks will grow and multiply day by day.

Party organizations must be required:

to ensure an advance in all organizational-Party and mass-political work and link Party-political work more closely with the performance of economic tasks;

to take urgent steps to strengthen district Party committees, M.T.S., collective and state farms with personnel and raise work with personnel in all branches of agriculture to a higher level;

to end the incorrect view of some officials that work in the countryside is work of secondary importance;

to eliminate the lack of personal responsibility in the management of collective farms, rearrange the work of the apparatus of district Party committees and bring the Party agencies closer to the collective state farming;

to improve province and district Party committees' guidance in agriculture, decisively halt the use of administrative fiat by certain officials and end the superficial, bureaucratic approach to the management of collective farms, M.T.S. and state farms.

Party organizations must rouse all men and women collective farmers, M.T.S. workers and agricultural specialists to fight to increase the yield of all farm crops and develop communal animal husbandry, to reach the point where each collective farm successfully meets its obligations to the state in delivering farm produce, has seed and other stocks and assures a further strengthening of the collective economy and higher payments for the collective farmers' workday.

Comrades! The land of the Soviets is at the height of its powers and is confidently advancing along the path to communism. The practical solution of the problem of the establishing in our country, on the basis of the powerful advance in socialist industry as the leading force in the national economy, an abundance of agricultural produce is a most important and integral part of the program for communist construction. This problem now confronts us as a vital, nationwide problem. Its successful solution will also facilitate the further strengthening of the alliance between the working class and collective farm peasantry.

We may voice firm our confidence that under the Communist Party's leadership, the working class, the collective farm peasantry, our intelligentsia and all the Soviet people will perform this task in the shortest time. Our country will make a great step forward along the path to communism!

1954: *The Thaw*

The Khrushchev touch in public affairs—drastic, bold, imaginative, sweeping, and also risk-taking—is vividly illustrated by the first major measure in the post-Stalin era to become associated closely with his name and Party leadership—the virgin lands drive. This was launched in early 1954, to become a semipermanent feature, evidently, of Soviet life. Russia had a bad agricultural problem, as Khrushchev himself had announced and explained the previous September. Important measures had been taken at that time to increase the incentives of the Russian peasantry to produce more food—but they were not enough. It was clear that much more must be done—and quickly. But what?

This was a subject considered by the new collective leadership. One approach to it might have been the broad liberalization of the collective farm system so as to permit on a much wider scale individual private farming. But this approach was beyond the grasp of the Soviet leadership whose members considered that the collective farm system was a permanent, unchangeable aspect of the Soviet Communist system whose preservation was more important than expeditious solution of the food problem. Another approach could have been the pouring of large capital investments into existing cultivated areas so as to provide greatly increased quantities of fertilizer, more and better farm machinery, and much else as well. This approach, in order to be completely effective, would probably also have required that capital and materials be diverted to the production of greatly increased quantities of consumer goods for farmers so as to give them heightened incentives to produce and sell more. Some members of the leadership, including probably Georgi Malenkov, evidently favored this kind of a plan.

But Nikita Khrushchev acted as the sponsor for a very different approach. In the eastern areas of the Soviet Union, in particular in southern Siberia and northern Central Asia, there were enormous plains of uncultivated, relatively arid virgin lands. They were being used—not very efficiently—only as grazing lands by seminomadic Kazakhs. The Khrushchev plan was to plow up these plains, millions of hectares of them, making use of big gang plows, to sow them to grain, and then to harvest with big fleets of combines. Who would do it? Khrushchev proposed to mobilize Soviet youth by the hundred thousand and ship them out east to new state farms on the virgin lands in order to carry out his project. There, it was hoped, they would raise gigantic crops which would solve the shortage of Soviet feed grains—at least in part. There were many other aspects of the Khrushchev farm program, but this was the most dramatic feature. Would the big crops actually materialize or would there be, as so often there was on these Central Asian plains, destructive drought? Khrushchev was seemingly staking his political future in large part on the weather in the virgin land areas during the coming several years.

Khrushchev got the approval of the Party's Central Committee for his plan and the drive was launched with great fanfare. His report on this to the Central Committee in late February was one of the most important policy statements of the postwar period.

That the new first secretary's prestige and authority were steadily increasing became obvious to all Soviet citizens when on his sixtieth birthday on April 17 the leading newspapers splashed his photograph on their front pages, publishing a decree of the government granting him a special decoration—and also listing congratulatory messages received from abroad for the occasion.

On May Day of 1954 the official photographs for the occasion singled out not just Georgi Malenkov, but both Khrushchev and Malenkov, each in an identical pose, setting the two of them apart from the rest of the leaders—and establishing them as equals of each other. This began a period in which Malenkov and Khrushchev appeared everywhere together looking like identical twins, forming what appeared to be a kind of duumvirate or two-man rule. Yet all the time Khrushchev seemed to be gaining in the public attention given his own role.

Much was happening during this year of 1954. Russians, at first hesitant to believe there would be a new deal, and cautious about venturing onto new ground, began at last to feel they were really out from under the Stalin tyranny and terror. Its name was given to the era by a famous writer, Ilya Ehrenburg, who wrote a short novel called *The Thaw*. In it Ehrenburg depicted in statements which he put into the mouths of his fictional characters the new hopefulness in the air after the death of Stalin, and also the revulsion of people against what had gone before. The novel aroused a storm of controversy and was severely criticized by reviewers. Other writers also took a relatively fresh outlook on things in plays, novels, and critical essays. One literary monument of the period was an article in a literary magazine by a writer and critic by the name of V. Pomerantzev calling for "sincerity" in literature—in other words, realistic frankness about some of the more negative aspects of life on which there had previously been enforced silence. These writers were all criticized in the press—but nothing worse happened to them.

One of the most potent factors in the feeling of more comfortable, freer life coming over the country was the fact that police terror had in considerable part been relaxed following the Beria affair. As cases of persons exiled and imprisoned for political "crimes" under Stalin were reviewed some survivors of his purges had begun to trickle in from concentration camps, a few at first and then more. Other persons, some of them once famous revolutionaries, were permitted to emerge from enforced obscurity or exile.

There was a new deal in science where the grip of such ideological dictators as Trofim Lysenko was loosened. There was much more freedom of thought and research.

It was in this year that the Soviet leaders began to see much more of people, their country, and the world—and to be seen much more themselves. In Moscow the collective leadership began to attend en masse diplomatic receptions and other functions and to meet foreign officials, diplomats, and also Russians. There were trips abroad. Khrushchev went in 1954 to Warsaw and Prague, and then to China, for instance. On the way back from China he toured the Soviet Far East and Siberia, seeing and learning much as he went along. (Under Stalin, who did not like to get out and travel, the other leaders were also expected to spend their time mostly in their Moscow offices—and hardly ever went traveling inside Russia or abroad.)

All this and much else as well added up to big change. This was reflected in many ways in Nikita Khrushchev's own utterances. As the year went on he spoke out on other subjects than just agriculture and farm problems. He talked about foreign affairs and toward the year's end in a speech which became famous, in part because of his references to the bad state of plumbing in a hotel which he visited in Sverdlovsk and his mention of his own days as a plumber in this connection, he was even able to lay down the line to Soviet construction experts on architecture and building.

This speech on building and architecture is the sixth of the Khrushchev documents selected for this collection:

ON WIDE-SCALE INTRODUCTION OF INDUSTRIAL METHODS, IMPROVING THE QUALITY AND REDUCING THE COST OF CONSTRUCTION *

Comrades! It is a long time since we have had an all-Union conference of builders, and a great need has arisen to hold such a gathering. I think that this present conference will greatly benefit not only construction work but all our work both in industry and in the other branches of the national economy.

Under the leadership of the Communist Party, the Soviet people have achieved tremendous successes in the industrialization of our country. [These successes are the pride of the working class, the collective farm peasantry, and the intelligentsia of the Soviet Union. These successes gladden our friends abroad.]

The industrialization of the Soviet land has been carried out, thanks to the fact that our party has undeviatingly put into practice the precepts of Lenin and Stalin. [This was our chief task and it remains the chief task for the future also. We must also in the future by all means develop heavy industry. Heavy industry is the basis of the economy, the source of economic might of the socialist state, of its defense capabilities, the source of prosperous and cultural life of the

* Speech by Khrushchev, Dec. 7, 1954, delivered at the All-Union Conference of Builders, Architects and Workers in the Building Materials Industry, in Construction Machinery and Road Machinery Industries and in Design and Research Organizations, *Pravda,* Dec. 28, 2–4. Translation based on condensed translation published and copyrighted by *The Current Digest of the Soviet Press,* VI, No. 52, pp. 7–14 and 33. Passages omitted from this condensation translated [within brackets] by Thomas P. Whitney.

workers.] Only on the basis of a further development of heavy industry will we be able successfully to promote all branches of the national economy, steadily raise the well-being of the people and ensure the inviolability of the frontiers of the Soviet Union. (*Prolonged applause.*)

That is the main thing. The further development of heavy industry —an increase in the output of metal, coal, oil, electric power, chemical products, the development of heavy machine building, machine tool construction and the production of forge-press equipment—is the powerful basis for successful development of all branches of industry and agriculture.

Relying on the progress in developing heavy industry, the Party and government are devoting great attention to expanding the production of consumers' goods.

Much work has been conducted this year in carrying out the decisions of the Party Central Committee plenary sessions on further development of agriculture. As is well known, the Communist Party has made it one of the most important tasks to increase grain output by raising the yield in all parts of the country and developing virgin and idle lands.

The year 1954 was the first year of the struggle to translate into reality the program for markedly advancing agriculture. You know that in 1954 in a number of the provinces of the Ukraine, the Volga region and other southern areas of the country there has been exceptionally unfavorable weather. Because of the drought in these areas we had a serious grain shortage. But the country has been well supplied this year by Siberia, especially the Altai Territory and Kazakhstan. The collective farmers, workers at Machine and Tractor Stations and state farms and the Party organizations of the Altai Territory and a number of provinces in Siberia and Kazakhstan have worked well and done much for the country. Despite the grain shortage in the southern areas, 271,000,000 poods more grain had been procured by Dec. 5, 1954, throughout the country than by the same date in 1953.

The report by the Party Central Committee and the U.S.S.R. Council of Ministers published in the press Nov. 8 acquaints us with the results of the agricultural year. You have read this report and know that in 1954 we have procured considerably more grain, meat, milk and vegetables than last year. Indeed, the increase is very great. Certain people will ask: Why, despite the increase in the volume of procurements and purchases of agricultural produce this year, are needed products nevertheless not always to be found in the shops? How has this come about? It is because the demand for consumers' goods has increased to a tremendous extent and because the people now have more money. Prices have been reduced by billions of rubles, the real wages of workers and employees and collective farmers' incomes have risen considerably. (*Applause.*)

And for this reason, no matter how we increase the output of goods, the demand of the population is still not being fully satisfied. In meetings and talks with collective farmers in various parts of the country I have several times had occasion to hear the wish that there were more sugar on sale, more footwear, woolen fabrics—all, of course, of good quality. The demand for high-quality goods has increased. This stems from the fact that the measures carried out by the Party and the government have created conditions for a considerable rise in the purchasing power of the working people. Our task is to satisfy more fully the population's growing demands. For this reason the struggle to increase output of grain, potatoes, vegetables, meat, textiles and other goods must continue and be continued in the future consistently and persistently. . . .

One may say with confidence that in 1955 not less than 20,000,000 additional hectares of land will be sown as a result of the development of virgin and idle lands. (*Applause.*) [By increasing the production of grain we are creating conditions for the further powerful upsurge of all branches of agriculture. This is especially necessary for the development of animal husbandry.]

We mainly need grain for fodder, since we have enough grain for bread. With an increase in the amount of feed grain, collective and state farms will produce more meat, milk, butter, eggs and wool. We also need more grain in order to set up major grain reserves in the country and also to expand grain trade with other nations.

The measures being carried out by the Party and government to develop industry and agriculture have the goal of further strengthening the might of the Soviet state and systematically improving the well-being of our people. An important part in this work belongs to the workers of the constantly growing building industry—our builders, workers of the building materials industry, machine builders supplying equipment to the construction projects, architects and designers and our entire large army of builders. That is why the Communist

Party Central Committee and the U.S.S.R. Council of Ministers decided to call this conference, in order to discuss with you pressing problems of construction, to bring to light existing shortcomings and to outline concrete measures for fundamental improvement in construction work.

Urgent Problems in the Industrialization of Construction.—Comrades! Construction is going on in our country on a tremendous scale. For an idea of the volume of construction, it should be recalled that the Soviet state has spent more than 900,000,000,000 rubles on capital construction since the war. During this time more than 8000 major state industrial enterprises have been restored or constructed and put into operation. Every year the building of homes, schools and hospitals expands; during postwar years a total of more than 200,000,000 square meters of housing space have been built for workers and employees in cities and settlements and in rural areas about 4,500,000 dwellings for collective farmers and the rural intelligentsia.

In 1954 the volume of construction work throughout the country has increased to more than 2.5 times that in 1946. In 1954 alone expenditures on capital construction equal the total expenditures for this purpose during the entire Second Five-Year Plan.

A major step forward has been taken in the construction of enterprises for heavy industry, the very foundation of our economy. In 1954 and in the future we must concentrate on the construction of new enterprises for the coal, oil, metallurgical and machine building industries, of new power stations and other industrial enterprises. At the same time, large-scale housing construction is being developed throughout the country. Suffice it to say that in 1954 alone there will be built in the cities and workers' settlements in the country a total of more than 30,000,000 square meters of living space and in rural localities about 400,000 dwellings. [In order successfully to deal with the tasks which stand before us in the field of construction it is necessary by all means to develop and perfect our construction industry. It is necessary decisively to put an end to amateurish work in the organization of the construction business.]

Essential to a marked improvement in construction is the further industrialization of construction work. [At present we have the necessary conditions for the broad industrialization of construction. What are these conditions? In the first place we have trained large cadres of skilled workers and specialists. In construction organizations of the country and in the construction materials industry there work many thousands of remarkable masters of their work, innovators in the field of production. We have factories which can provide builders with modern equipment which lightens labor and increases its productivity. There has been created and expanded a productive basis which permits the provision of construction with prefabricated reinforced concrete designs and parts, and with construction materials.

As the present meeting has shown, there are still many faults in the construction business, alongside definite successes. It is necessary decisively to bring out into the open faults and to mobilize all our forces for their elimination. We must reveal faults boldly and sharply and point out those who are specifically to blame because these faults do not exist by themselves alone but are created by some or other officials. Criticism must not be indefinite. It is necessary to criticize those officials who permit mistakes and are to blame for specific faults, and also to criticize those who see these faults but who reconcile themselves to them and do not struggle for their elimination.]

The Party Central Committee and the U.S.S.R. Council of Ministers in the decree "On Developing Production of Reinforced-Concrete Structural Parts" outlined an extensive program for increasing the output of reinforced concrete. This program will ensure the transition to industrial methods in construction.

Extensive development of the production of precast reinforced-concrete sections and parts will have a tremendous economic effect. Builders know that until recently there were disputes as to how we should proceed in construction—by the use of precast sections or of poured concrete. We shall not name any names or reproach those workers who tried to get builders to use poured concrete. I think that these comrades themselves now feel that they had the wrong attitude. Now it seems clear to everyone that we must proceed along a more progressive path, along the path of using precast reinforced-concrete sections and parts. (*Applause.*) [What consequences will the use of poured concrete have in construction? It inevitably leads to filth on the construction area, the use of all kinds and designs of timbering, to the overexpenditure of iron, to the loss of cement, the loss of inert materials and concrete.

And what does the use of prefabricated parts give? The use of prefabricated reinforced concrete gives the possibility of factory manufacture of parts just as in machinery industries, permits transition to factory methods of construction.]

Precast construction opens before us great possibilities for savings in money and materials and for raising output, consequently increasing the wages of builders. Thus, for example, by replacing steel sections with reinforced-concrete ones the expenditure of metal in single-story industrial buildings is cut by not less than half. As compared with that expended in using poured concrete, the labor involved is 20 per cent to 25 per cent less. Moreover, reinforced-concrete sections are considerably more resistant to corrosion; they are durable and fire-resistant.

The decree of the Party Central Committee and the U.S.S.R. Council of Ministers envisages building in the next three years 402 plants and 200 work areas for the production of reinforced-concrete structural parts. During these three years the output of precast reinforced-concrete will increase five times, in connection with which the output of cement will increase more than one and one-half times and inert materials more than one and one-half times.

Discussing the nature of construction employing precast reinforced-concrete structural parts, some comrades ask what form of construction should be given preference: girder-and-panel or large blocks without a girder frame. It seems to me that the time has not come to make a definite decision in favor of either. We must provide opportunity for development of both kinds. Perhaps both methods will justify themselves, since we build structures for all kinds of functions and in conditions which vary.

Experience will show [which of the two—girder-and-panel construction or construction employing large blocks without a girder frame—will be more vital. There are advantages to each of these two methods. At this meeting there have spoken proponents of both types of construction, but neither has proven the inacceptability of the one or the other method.

It is completely unquestionable that simultaneously with the construction of buildings with the use of reinforced wall panels we must broadly develop the construction of buildings from large and small wall blocks.] The cost of large-block construction is 12 per cent lower than the cost of building with brick, and the extent of assembly work increases from 38 per cent to 85 per cent. Labor productivity increases sharply when the large-block method is employed. In eight hours two bricklayers complete 3.5 cubic meters of wall. In the same period two assembly workers can assemble a 25-cubic meter wall of large blocks.

The use of reinforced-concrete units, parts and large blocks should be introduced without waiting for completion of plants producing reinforced-concrete items, particularly since special plants are not required for making wall blocks. The blocks can be produced at the construction site, using electricity or steam to heat the concrete. No complex equipment is needed. [The arrangement of floors and ceilings is one of the basic aspects of work in the construction of buildings. The question of selection of design for prefabricated floor and ceiling panels gets much attention from designers and builders.

Certain comrades proposed to use only the "multi-hollow" panels of the design of Engineer Makarov. The production of these panels is not complicated and should be organized on the broadest possible scale. But, in my view, multiribbed panels for floors and ceilings have great advantages. The future belongs to them: on the preparation of these panels there is spent less material and especially, most importantly, less metal. The design of the panels provides better sound insulation and the cost of the multiribbed panels is significantly lower than that of panels of other designs. However, where it is not possible to prepare multiribbed panels in factory conditions, it is useful to organize the production of "multi-hollow" panels. By the broad use of panels for floors and ceilings we shall evict from construction projects the "handicrafters" who use poured concrete.

It is necessary to speak also of faults in the arrangement of stairways. At the present time stairways and landings are being delivered to many construction projects from reinforced concrete factories with poorly finished surfaces. Therefore at the construction projects they are forced, in installing the stairway assemblies and landings, to finish them on the spot. The same thing happens in numerous cases with wall, floor, and ceiling panels. This is incorrect. All work in the finishing of reinforced concrete parts must be carried out fully at factories. Stairways must be delivered with finished under and upper surfaces. Stairway landings also must have finished under-surfaces and a face covered with tiles or mosaics. In order to preserve the surfaces during the period of construction work they must be covered with paper held in place by boards.

At the factory it is necessary also to carry out the finishing of wall, ceiling, and floor panels. Pieces must arrive at the construction project in completed form, completely ready for installation. Otherwise what advantage shall we receive from prefabrication if we prepared a prefabricated part at the factory, install it on the eighth floor, and then have to consider how to get to it in order to clean or polish its surface? Concrete designs must be light, without excessive weight.

We must direct special attention to the use of thin-walled streamlined prefabricated parts. Such parts in comparison with heavyweight concrete parts have great advantages.

Weight is reduced by approximately 33 per cent, expenditure of cement by 20 per cent, cost by 15 per cent.

The presence in factories of vibrators, vibrotables, mechanical punches, and other machines permits in the preparation of parts and designs the use of hard concrete instead of plastic concrete. Hard concrete gives the possibility of immediate removal from forms and the production of parts of great strength. The effectiveness of the application of hard cement consists also in the increased speed of production because of the reduction in the number of forms, the improvement in the quality of parts, economy of metal in forms, and lowered expenditure for assembly and disassembly of forms. We must approach these questions from the point of view of economy. Only in those places where there are no factories, where there has not been organized factory production of reinforced concrete parts, should we use for the time being plastic concrete.]

Extensive use of reinforced-concrete parts in building will make it possible to reduce considerably the use of lumber and metal. It should be recognized, comrades, that we have not yet learned properly to conserve and use economically such very valuable materials as lumber and metal. Such extravagance cannot be tolerated any longer.

Many people complain that there is no lumber. And that is true, there is a shortage of it. However, much lumber is used extravagantly. Take, for example, the Ministry of Transportation. Railroad ties are made only from wood, and only kilometer-posts made out of steel are erected. Signal towers and conduits are all made from metal. Surely it is possible to make all these things out of reinforced concrete. Why, for example, do we not learn from the Czechs, who make remarkable reinforced-concrete ties and save lumber in so doing. Take a trip there and have a look. They are our friends, and they will willingly share their experience.

Comrades Bulganin, Mikoyan and I and other members of the delegation during our trip through China saw many signal towers and poles made out of reinforced concrete and made well. We should take over this useful experience.

During our trip through the Far East we visited a number of factories and saw that many of them were built mainly from metal, that reinforced concrete was seldom used at all. Why? Because certain directors make the framework of workshops entirely from metal, trying to prove that this enables them to complete the construction more quickly. But this is incorrect.

Comrades, we must resolutely put a stop to the extravagant expenditure of metal. Only what is essential should be built of metal. Everything in building which can be replaced by concrete or reinforced concrete should be replaced. (*Applause.*)

In discussing the problems of industrializing construction, we cannot ignore the question of developing the production of building materials which will be needed in great quantities. It seems to me that both the State Planning Committee and many of us present here are at fault in one serious respect. In developing the building materials industry, we have until recently been wrong in stressing the building of brickyards at a time when we needed to develop the cement industry in every way. (*Applause.*) [Brick, as a basic construction material, has been used and is being used in places where construction is being carried out in main by hand. In this case there is great significance to the weight of the wall material, the weight of the brick. In our times, given concrete, electric motors, lifting cranes, and other machinery, it is impossible to continue to work in ancient ways. Everyone knows how much time and labor is necessary for the manufacture of brick. In quarries they get clay, process it, form the raw material into shapes, then dry it, carry it to the brick ovens, bake the bricks, transport the bricks to warehouses, transport them to construction projects, raise them to the scaffolding, put them in place in the wall—and all this is done many times, moving every brick like a piece of a mosaic.]

Is it not better, instead of bricks, to make concrete wall blocks two, three, five tons in weight for use with existing hoists? Building with blocks produces high labor productivity and a high output. It is no accident that in many other countries concrete and not bricks is widely used in building. [At the present time when there are before us the tasks of broad industrialization of construction, it is necessary by all means to develop the cement industry in order to assure a significant increase in the production of concrete.]

However, one should by no means conclude from this that we should forget about expanding brick production through utilization of existing opportunities at the existing brickyards. . . .

Comrades! Successful introduction of industrial methods and the improvement of the work of building organizations largely depend on the level of organizational and technical guidance in building.

The capacities of small building organizations do not permit the industrialization of construction work, increased rates of output and lower costs. Therefore, it is necessary to consolidate building organizations. There are at present in the Soviet Union more than 7500 contracting construction organizations, a third of which have annual volumes of work of not more than 5,000,000 rubles. Leningrad, for example, has 133 construction organizations building to order, Kiev has 107, Rostov 56, etc. And how many dwarf-sized construction organizations are there at factories, as part of the factory organization itself? They are too numerous to count. The number of construction organizations does not decrease but grows year by year.

We cannot seriously raise the question of industrializing construction work if we continue to increase the number of building organizations. Anyone can see that small and consequently weak building organizations are not able to use industrial work methods. We must resolutely begin to consolidate building organizations. Without this there can be no talk of industrializing construction.

The experience in consolidating construction organizations in Moscow has been quite instructive. A single organization, the Chief Moscow Building Administration, has been formed from 56 building trusts of the Moscow Soviet plus those of ministries and departments. When the question of establishing this central administration was discussed there was much talk to the effect that the Moscow Soviet would be unable to cope with so large an organization, and fears were expressed that the residential building program would fall through if the ministries divorced themselves from this work. One might have expected some organizational defects leading to failure to fulfill the plan in the first year of the Chief Moscow Building Administration. But all these fears proved groundless. [The chief of Glavmosstroi, Comrade Kucherenko, has reported here on the results of the enlargement of construction organizations and reported that the obligation of Muscovites to put into operation in the current year 900,000 square meters of living space will be fulfilled and that simultaneously there will be realized an increase in the backlog for construction in 1955 over last year.

These results show that the new organization has made a significant step forward, inasmuch as the backlog for construction is the chief thing, I would say, even the main thing from among main things. (*Applause.*) Everyone can understand that it is impossible rhythmically to carry out construction work without having a normal backlog. If there is no backlog, then skilled workers are used not in their skills—but on earth work and on auxiliary work. As a result the productivity of labor of workers is lowered, the expenses of construction increase, and the periods of completion of work are interrupted. With a backlog it is possible to carry out work rhythmically, without interruption, using workers according to their skills. The creation of a normal backlog of work can be managed only by large-scale organizations.]

Construction organizations should be consolidated in Leningrad, Kiev and other cities in imitation of the Moscow example. [But this work must be executed in a well-thought-out, reasonable way. The creation of powerful construction organizations is necessary because this will give the possibility of realizing on a wide scale the use in construction of prefabricated reinforced concrete designs and parts, the introduction of complex mechanization of construction works, the raising of the productivity of labor, the speeding up of tempos, the improved quality and lowered costs of construction.]

The experience of Moscow and other cities proves the need to set up specialized building organizations—truly specialized and not complex ones, since only such organizations are capable of introducing building methods. (*Applause.*)

Specialized construction organizations make it possible to organize the workers' labor better, to make it better-skilled labor and to utilize equipment more efficiently. For example, the Foundation Digging Trust has been set up in Moscow to plan foundations, dig them, build foundations and cellar walls (of concrete or ferroconcrete parts and blocks). There are trusts which do general construction work—assembling walls of large blocks or reinforced-concrete panels, installing staircases, ceilings, and other work. A specialized organization builds partitions and does interior finishing. Plumbing is installed by another specialized organization. Others do electrical work, install elevators, etc.

Only with strict specialization is it possible to achieve high productivity and good-quality work. The wages of the workers, too, will rise under such conditions. Where there is no specialization and all types of work are carried out by the same trust or office, the workers' wages are not high. Today a man works as a mason or a painter and tomorrow he is a hod carrier. Understandably, under such conditions wages are not high.

The specialization of building organizations will make them more mobile, more flexible and efficient. Before starting construction of a factory or apartment house, it is essential that an organization specialized in excavation and planning work should plan the site, lay the foundations and install all the underground pipes and cables. At the same time, another specialized organization should prepare for the assembly and erection of the building from precast sections. Such organization of construction will make it possible to carry out work in accordance with a coordinated schedule, assembling the sections of the building and also installing technological equipment if it is a factory that is being built. We have had many examples of such construction organization both during the war and since. [It is clear that a specialized organization cannot be all the time in one place: having completed its job it is obliged to move to another job. The most correct solution one must consider is the creation of specialized territorial construction organizations, but not everywhere have conditions become right for such a solution. Therefore for the time being we must create specialized organizations in the ministries.

Our country carries out on a large scale the construction of industrial enterprises, apartment buildings, schools, hospitals, and other projects. This construction has vitally important significance. We are obliged sharply to increase tempos, improve quality, and lower the cost of construction. For the solution of the given problem there is only one path—that is the path of the broadest industrialization of construction.]

Remove Shortcomings in Design, Improve Work of Architects.—Comrades! Successful industrialization, improvement in the quality and reduction in the cost of building depend to a considerable extent on design organizations, on the work of architects and designers.

The interests of industrializing construction dictate the need to reorganize the work of design organizations and to make standardized designing and application of existing standardized designs the chief thing in their work.

Widespread use of reinforced-concrete parts, sections, large blocks and new and effective materials is a new element in building techniques which imperatively requires us to give up obsolete design methods. (*Applause.*)

Nevertheless, many workers in design organizations underestimate the importance of standardized designs.

This is shown by the following. Of the 1100 construction and design organizations in the country only 152 even partially engage in standardized designing. From 1951 to 1953 inclusive, not more than 1 per cent of the allocations for design work was used on standardized designing. In 1953 only 12 per cent of the total volume of industrial building was carried out according to standardized designs. And matters have not improved very much in 1954.

I have had occasion to talk to many engineers and architects about design. They are all agreed that standardized designs considerably simplify and improve construction work. In practice, however, many architects, designers in industrial building and sometimes even technicians follow only their own plans.

Why does this happen? One apparent cause is that we have tolerated shortcomings in training architects. Many young architects who have scarcely crossed the threshold of the institute and have not yet got properly on their feet follow the example of masters of architecture and wish to design only buildings of an individual character, are in a hurry to build monuments to themselves. While Pushkin created for himself a monument unwrought by human hands, many architects want to create for themselves monuments "wrought by human hands" in the form of buildings built according to individualized designs. (*Laughter, applause.*)

It must be realized that if we were to build all industrial constructions, housing and other buildings according to separate designs the rates of building would be considerably slower and its cost would increase tremendously.

Many planners, architects and designers do work creatively and produce much that is new and useful, but there are also major shortcomings in this matter. Certain planners do not take into account the new sections, parts and materials being manufactured by plants of the building industry but continue to base their work on backward building methods.

Take housing construction. Why not choose the best designs for housing and repeat them many times in construction work? Let architects submit their designs for such buildings in competition!

It is now essential to select the best designs for large-block residential buildings. Design organizations of the Moscow Soviet drafted design solutions for residential buildings with walls of large panels or blocks. The solution proposed by I. V. Zholtovsky, Member of the U.S.S.R. Academy of Architecture, was recognized at that time as one of the best. Since then blueprints could have been drawn from this plan, adopted as standard and used for building large-block residential construction for several years. Yet this has not been done.

Why are there 38 standardized designs for schools in use at the present time? Is this expedient? Apparently it has come about because many officials have a spendthrift attitude toward building. We must select a limited number of standardized designs for apartment houses, schools, hospitals, buildings for kindergartens and nurseries, stores and other buildings and installations and carry out mass building only according to these designs for, let us say, five years. At that time let us have a discussion and if there are no better designs, let us extend the use of these for another five years. What is wrong with that, comrades?

What are the advantages of building according to standardized designs? They are very great once one decides to build, there is already a plan in existence and it is known how large the site must be, what parts and materials will be needed and how many workers will be required. Everything is clear. Such conditions will help us to accelerate construction work and to reduce its cost considerably.

Or take questions of designing industrial buildings and installations. Designs for industrial buildings, like standardized designs for apartment houses, call for many identical sections and identical spans. Columns and girders and other elements in each span remain unchanged. Standardized designs for industrial building should be drawn up with a view to the possibility of placing production and auxiliary shops of different branches of industry in these buildings. Buildings for different purposes can be built from the same units. To achieve this it is essential to draw up standardized designs for industrial buildings, making use of uniform arrangements of columns, uniform heights and loads, uniform stairwells, uniform apertures for windows and doors, and the like.

The use of such standardized designs will make it possible to organize the factory manufacture of structural parts and sections and abandon conventional construction for the assembling of buildings, carrying out this work in short periods of time. We must achieve this, comrades.

To introduce standardized designs we must be determined and persistent, for we may meet resistance in this matter. Evidently there are some people who need a good explanation of the necessity for standardized designs.

The use of standardized designs in building will have a tremendous effect on economizing, speeding up and improving construction work. Of this there is no doubt. (*Stormy applause.*)

Comrades, I want to give you my impressions and make certain observations on the work of architects. First of all, I wish to address President of the Academy of Architecture Comrade Mordvinov. You and I, Comrade Mordvinov, have often met on work in Moscow. I know you as a good organizer; you showed this in the high-speed belt-line construction during the development of Bolshaya Kaluzhskaya Street. High-speed belt-line construction was then being carried out for the first time, and with the participation of Comrade Mordvinov. But Comrade Mordvinov has changed since the war. Mordvinov is not the same. As they sing in the opera "The Tsar's Bride," "I do not recognize Grigory Gryaznov!" (*Laughter, applause.*)

Extravagance can frequently be observed in our construction work, and it is mainly the fault of many architects, who commit excesses in the architecture of buildings built according to individual designs.

Such architects are stumbling blocks on the road to the industrialization of building. In order to build successfully and rapidly, it is necessary to build according to standardized designs, but this, apparently, does not suit certain architects.

Comrade Mordvinov's report and the speeches of some architects at this conference showed that they avoid the questions of economy in construction and are not interested in the cost per square meter of residential space.

Architects, like all builders, must make a sharp turn toward problems of construction economy, must study them thoroughly. It must always be remembered that one of the most important is the cost of erecting the building, the cost per square meter of space.

An architect, if he wishes to keep abreast of life, must know and be able to use not only architectural forms, ornaments and various decorative elements; he must know the new progressive materials, reinforced-concrete sections and parts and, most of all, must have an excellent understanding of construction economy. Because in designing buildings they forgot the main thing, the cost per square meter of site, and were carried away by needless adorning of facades and many other redundant features, Comrade Mordvinov and many of his colleagues were criticized at the conference.

Many unnecessary decorations of various kinds which bespeak a lack of taste in certain architects are sometimes added to apartment-house facades. Even the builders have found it difficult to execute these adornments.

The construction of multistoried buildings has had a major influence on this matter. In designing multistoried buildings architects have been chiefly interested in creating a silhouette, without regard for what the construction and maintenance of these buildings would cost.

The complicated relief of walls, which is designed exclusively for decorative purposes, causes excessive maintenance expenditure and major heat losses. This is why, for example, in the building of the Smolensk Square annual overexpenditures on fuel amount to 250,000 rubles. This is for one building alone.

Here are some figures on the distribution of area in multistoried buildings.

In the building at Krasniye Vorota, 28.1 per cent of the total space is devoted to working area, 23.1 per cent to auxiliary premises, 14.9 per cent is occupied by technical equipment and service premises and 33.9 per cent is structural area. In the building on Smolensk Square 30 per cent of the total space is devoted to working area, 24 per cent to auxiliary premises, 11 per cent to technical equipment and service premises and 35 per cent to structural area.

It can be seen from these figures how little area in these multistoried buildings is devoted to the main purpose and how much to structural area. And what is structural area? It is the area occupied by walls and sections. This area has been greatly exaggerated in multistoried buildings in order to provide a silhouette. One cannot live and work in this area—one can only look at it. (*Stir in the hall; laughter, applause.*)

It may be said that multistoried buildings are nonetheless beautiful, that one should not criticize them because they have been praised. In our opinion, it is better to criticize shortcomings, for unless we do so now imitations of the multistoried buildings will spread and the so-called "structural areas" will expand inordinately. (*Laughter, applause.*)

During Comrade Mordvinov's speech I asked him about the cost of the multistoried Ukraina Hotel, which is being built according to his design. The cost of one square meter of the main functional area of the Ukraina Hotel is 175 per cent of the cost of this area in the Moskva Hotel.

Surely it is not permissible that in one and the same city, Moscow, the difference in the construction cost of two buildings designed by different architects is 600 to 800 rubles for every square meter of living space?

Nor can one be resigned to the fact that the cost of exterior decoration for many apartment-house blocks in Moscow comprises, in relation to the total building cost, 15 per cent to 20 per cent and even 30 per cent instead of the normal 8 per cent to 9 per cent.

Comrades! We have no disagreement with the architects on basic matters—on the need to build comfortable homes and dwelling units. And these are important matters, a question of people's living comforts. The number of large and small apartments, their floor space, ceiling heights—on such questions, as a rule, there is no divergence of opinion. But differences always arise as soon as we come to the problem of the architectural design of building facades. The question of the artistic-architectural treatment of a building has proved most complex.

Certain architects have been carried away with putting spires on buildings, with the result that such buildings resemble churches. Do you like the silhouette of a church? I do not wish to argue about tastes, but in apartment houses, such an appearance is not necessary. The modern apartment house must not be transformed by architectural design into a replica of a church or a museum. This affords the residents no comfort, and only complicates the utilization of the building and raises its cost. Yet certain architects do not take this into consideration.

Architect Zakharov, for example, submitted plans for construction on Bolshaya Tula Street in Moscow of apartment houses which differ little in their outlines from churches. He was asked to explain this and answered: "We have brought our plans into harmony with the tall buildings; the silhouette of the buildings must be clear." These, it would seem, are the sort of problems which occupy Comrade Zakharov most of all. He needs beautiful silhouettes, but the people need apartments. They do not want to admire silhouettes but a place to live! (*Applause.*) In the blueprints for the apartment-house project on Lyusinov Street, the architect had decided to place pieces of sculpture at the building corners, from the eighth floor up. On the highest floor, it was planned to cut off the corners; in these sliced-off corners windows were to be built and it was proposed to place pieces of sculpture on the window sills along the outer wall. A pentagonal room with a window in the corner is awkward, not to mention the fact that the people in this room would have to look at the back of the piece of sculpture for their entire life. It is understandable that life in such a room would not be especially pleasant. It is well that these houses were not built, and that Comrade Zakharov was restrained from such artistry.

And all this is called architectural-artistic decoration of the building! No, comrades, these are distortions in architecture, these spoil materials and cause unnecessary expenditure. Moscow organizations took a correct stand when they dismissed Comrade Zakharov from management of the architectural studio. But it should have been done sooner for the good of the work.

Two large factories making reinforced-concrete parts opened at the beginning of this year in Moscow and are producing, but we have as yet only one approved design for a girder-and-panel structure. Who is guilty of holding back the designing? Many architects are to blame and particularly Comrade Vlasov, Chief Architect of the city of Moscow. He is a good architect, but sometimes he lacks the necessary persistence.

It is necessary in every way to support and encourage good work in designing, and especially in standardized designing. It is necessary to consider and perhaps revise the accepted system of payment for the work of the designers. We should establish a system of payment which will better stimulate their work. (*Applause.*)

The serious shortcomings in the work of design organizations and of individual architects can in many ways be explained by improperly based principles emanating from the Academy of Architecture and a number of chief architects. . . .

Leading architects constantly stress the artistic aspect, and say little about the cost and comfort of housing and other buildings. It is understandable that we must struggle against any such divorce of architecture from the vital tasks of construction.

Some architects try to justify their incorrect stand on waste in designs by referring to the need to combat constructivism. But they waste state funds under the guise of fighting constructivism.

What is constructivism? Here is how the Large Soviet Encyclopedia, for instance, defines this tendency: "Constructivism . . . substitutes barren technical aspects 'born of the construction design' (hence the name constructivism) for artistic design. Demanding functional 'logic,' 'rationalism,' in construction the constructivists actually reached esthetic admiration of form unrelated to content . . . The consequence of this is the antiartistic, dull 'box style' characteristic of modern bourgeois architecture . . . Constructivism was sharply criticized in many Party directives and decrees . . ." (Large Soviet Encyclopedia, 1953, Vol. XXII, p. 437.)

This definition of constructivism is, of course, not exhaustive. But the description of constructivism I have cited showed the groundlessness of some architects disguising themselves in phrases about fighting constructivism while actually sacrificing convenience of internal design and use of the building for the sake of facades, that is, for form's sake, and thereby showing a disregard for the essential needs of people.

Some architects, declaiming about the need to combat constructivism, go to the opposite extreme—they decorate building facades excessively and often unnecessarily, thus wasting state funds.

Buildings which lack towers, superstructures and porticos with columns or have facades which are not adorned with sham detail are called boxes and condemned as relapses into constructivism. Such architects should probably be called constructivists in reverse, since they themselves are lapsing into "esthetic admiration of form divorced from content."

It is impossible to resign oneself any longer to the fact that many architects hide behind phrases about the struggle against constructivism and about socialist realism in architecture while spending the people's funds extravagantly.

Constructivism must be combated by sensible means. One must not be carried away with architectural decorations and esthetic adornment; one must not build absolutely unjustified towers or place pieces of sculpture on them. We are not against beauty but against superfluities. Building facades should be beautiful and attractive because of the good proportions of the entire building, the good proportions of the window and door openings, the skillful arrangement of balconies, the correct utilization of the texture and color in the facing materials and honest delineation of the parts and sections of the walls in large-block and large-panel construction. [Every project must be worked out taking into account economic expenditure of funds for construction. Buildings must be durable and economic in operation. Architects must learn to count the money of the people. This is a very serious question. By my address I am touching on an open wound of the architects. But for this I gave my word not to content myself with half a word. To be friendly, to smile at one another, and then to squander funds of the people—that is a bad, unprincipled friendship. It's necessary to be friendly with those people who multiply the forces of the socialist state, to support people who work in the interests of the people.]

Comrades! It must be said that among architects, including those in the Academy of Architecture, there are many who have come out actively against the incorrect ideas of individual architects, but their objections have not been taken into consideration. You, Comrade Mordvinov, and your assistants have stifled the voices raised against embellishments and sham details in architecture. (*Applause.*)

The cogent remarks of architect Comrade Gradov were heard with great interest at this conference. Speaking of the tasks of Soviet architecture, Comrade Gradov and certain other comrades quite correctly pointed out the need to overcome formalistic distortions and stagnation in architecture. They spoke of the necessity for critically utilizing the classical heritage, of the fact that architecture should be subordinated to the vital needs of our society and that for this it was necessary to link architecture more closely to modern technology and construction work in all its ramifications, to develop widespread creative initiative and innovation in architecture and to eliminate every manifestation of monopolism and suppression of criticism. It is impossible not to agree with these conclusions and proposals.

During the period of preparation for the present conference, Comrade Gradov sent a letter to the Party Central Committee, in which he set forth his critical observations on architectural problems. How did Comrade Mordvinov react to this criticism? He took every possible step to prevent Comrade Gradov from speaking at this conference. This fact testifies that an atmosphere has not been created in the Academy of Architecture for free exchange of opinions on creative questions, for the development of criticism.

It is also necessary to say that the State Committee for Construction Affairs has feebly guided the work of the Academy of Architecture and pays almost no attention to the state of affairs in regard to standardized designing and urban planning and building.

An incorrect approach on the part of certain architects toward planning and superfluities in the architectural decoration of buildings has unfortunately become quite widespread. . . .

In this connection I want to relate the impressions we gathered from visiting Sverdlovsk. Sverdlovsk is a large and fine city; you see in it the might of the Soviet Union. It has large factories which produce fine machinery. But there are great defects in the municipal construction and improvement of this large center. For instance, a tower with a spire was erected on the front of the city executive committee building when it was rebuilt. Construction of the spire alone cost almost 2,000,000 rubles, while reconstruction of the entire building cost 9,000,000. Probably a large part of this expenditure was due to work connected with adapting the facade to the tower and erecting the tower. Two schools for 400 pupils each could have been built with the funds expended on the spire alone.

There is a large five-story building on one of the Sverdlovsk streets.

"This is a mill," Comrade Kutyev, secretary of the province Party committee, told us, and added: "but we want to build a new mill and make this one into a hotel."

"What do you mean; rebuild it?" we asked him.

"Yes," he affirmed, "we plan to change the mill into a hotel."

"Why change a mill into a hotel?" we said. "Wouldn't it be better to build a new hotel instead?"

Judge for yourself. Does it make sense to turn a structure used as a mill into a hotel and build a new mill? (*Laughter, applause.*) You could build a new hotel for that money, and it would be better and cheaper. Where is common sense, where is the economic logic?

We traveled on. The province committee secretary told us:

"Here is a bridge which we are also planning to change."

"What do you want to do to it?"

"Cover it with asphalt."

The bridge is made of granite blocks. It will outlive our grandsons, while asphalt would not last more than ten years. Why, then, spoil a granite bridge?

When we reached the building of the province Party committee, the province secretary said:

"Here is our province committee building. We are planning to rebuild it."

"How and why?"

"We don't like the facade; it should all be changed."

What does that mean? What would it cost to rebuild a six-story building? Surely it is cheaper to build a new structure than to rebuild the old.

Listening to such ideas, one recalls the immortal Shchedrin ridiculing the governor who tore down everything his predecessor had built. It seems that some of the ways which the great Russian satirist Shchedrin ridiculed are still among us! (*Applause.*)

This harmful itch to rebuild costs the state dear. Only officials who have lost a sense of responsibility for the work entrusted to them could act thus. Comrades Bulganin, Mikoyan and I warned the Sverdlovsk officials that they would be punished if they continued to act in this manner and to engage in unnecessary rebuilding.

There is much waste in building medical and cultural structures. In 1953 construction was completed of a Sochi sanatorium of the Ministry of the Shipbuilding Industry. Officials of this ministry and the chairman of the Sochi City Soviet Executive Committee considered the facade too plain. It was proposed to redo the completed facade. Eight hundred thousand rubles were allocated for the reconstruction. For this sum one could build a residential structure with 20 two-room apartments.

There are reasons for believing that the waste and other excessively expensive rebuilding done locally are due in many cases to the advice of the architects. If one looks into the matter, it appears that this was the policy in the work of the Russian Republic Council of Ministers' Architectural Affairs Administration. This administration conducted a competition in 1953 for the best building erected in cities and settlements of the Russian Federation. Which buildings won prizes?

A nursery was built in the settlement of Vatutenka, Moscow Province. Because its proportions are exaggerated, there are 91.9 cubic meters of space per child, compared to the 24 allowed by the norm. The building is loaded down with stucco decoration. The exterior architecture is of "palace" style. With the funds spent on this building one could build three nurseries. Yet the designers won first prize. What for? For wasting funds? (*Laughter.*)

You may ask, who was chairman of the jury in this contest? Comrade Chernyshev—Executive Secretary of the Union of Soviet Architects, formerly Chief Architect of Moscow. Too bad that so experienced an architect permitted himself to stray from the correct path. I think it would be useful to annul the jury's decision in this contest as mistaken. (*Applause.*) [In the city of Ufa there has been built according to a standard project a cinema theatre. The facade of the building was redesigned with the application of a multitude of costly decorations. The cost of the decorative work was more than 30 per cent of the general cost of the building. The author of the project was granted a first prize.

In the surgical section of Sanatorium No. 66 in Yalta there was permitted a rise in the planned solution in the event of more than 1.5 times. The author of this project also was granted a money prize.

All of these facts indicate that the Administration for Architectural Affairs Attached to the Council of Ministers of the Russian Republic incorrectly orients architects in their work, and takes no interest in the economics of construction.]

After this conference we should hold conferences in the cities and ministries of architects, designers and builders so that they may talk "heart to heart" and find a common language. I am convinced that the majority of the architects will correctly understand our demands. (*Applause.*) And those who do not understand should be corrected. [Comrade Vishnevsky who spoke here made the proposal that sales prices be confirmed and the cost of construction of buildings by districts and cities established on the basis of the cost of a square meter of living space. It is possible that this will help eliminate lavishness in projects. I think that such a proposal is correct.

It is necessary to put an end to serious faults in the projecting and planning of cities. Our party organizations and government organs must occupy themselves on a daily basis with this important matter.]

One reason for the defects in the work of the architects which I have mentioned here is that in many cases they have not had supervision and help from local Party and Soviet organizations. The responsibility of local agencies for construction and municipal improvement must be heightened.

Until recently designs for city plans of the Soviet Union were submitted for approval by the Union government. Under that state of affairs confirmation of designs was held up for long years. . . . It seems to me that the need has arisen to revise the system of approving designs for municipal construction, granting greater authority to local agencies. (*Applause.*) On the other hand, evidently it would be logical to require the State Committee for Construction Affairs to intensify supervision over the performance of this work locally, so that there may be no disorders of the kind we saw in Sverdlovsk. [If we organize in a serious way the matter of standard projects, and decisively improve the work of architects and designers, if we direct attention to questions of economy, heighten the responsibility of our local organs, if we give them more initiative, we shall in all probability have new big successes in the construction business, in reduction of its cost and increase in quality.]

Raising Standards Is the Most Important Task of Builders.—Comrades! The question of raising the standard of construction deserves particular attention. We must build not only rapidly but also well and lastingly, valuing the honor of our building trade-mark. Buildings should be suitable for habitation and use. Poor construction work soon requires repairs, and this necessitates additional expense. This is true of all types of construction.

Above all, I would like to say something about the quality of apartment-house construction. [Are we making walls, ceilings, and floors of good quality in buildings? I consider that they are of very good quality. In buildings for apartment houses, schools, hotels, and others the walls, floors, and ceilings are being built in such a way that they will stand for hundreds of years. This is indubitable inasmuch as reinforced concrete is being widely used in construction. But one has to say directly that the finishing of buildings is often being done poorly. Even more than this, many officials are reconciling themselves to obviously dishonest bad work in finishing buildings. Many comrades have with full justice spoken of this at this meeting.]

Recently Comrades Bulganin, Mikoyan and I had occasion to visit many cities in the Far East, Siberia and the Urals. We were well received. This is understandable; after all, we were exacting guests and might criticize or might even do more than criticize. So they tried to put us up comfortably. (*Laughter, applause.*) In Sverdlovsk we stayed at a hotel. The hotel had been built well and firmly. One may suppose that we were not given the worst rooms. (*Laughter.*) But we noticed that the plumbing units had been very badly built and the quality of the finishing work was not high. We sent for the hotel manager and the city officials and pointed out to them how bad the work was!

Obviously, requisite exactingness during construction had been lacking. The quality of the tiles was bad, and they had been carelessly laid. The pipes in the sanitation units were covered with rust and obviously someone had hastily painted them and the pipes along the walls just before our arrival with some kind of gray paint. The pipe joints had been very badly made and I, as a former metalworker, was extremely indignant. Even before the revolution the pipe joints in mines were cleaner and better finished than those in this hotel at Sverdlovsk.

While in Sakhalin we stayed at a hotel built for servicemen. The hotel was well built, but the bathrooms and sanitation units had been badly finished. The quality of the facing tiles was poor, and they had been laid very carelessly.

These cases, and there are many of them, should be mentioned to builders and a resolute improvement in standards should be demanded. Comrade Yudin, Minister of the Building Materials Industry, and other officials of the building materials industry have no need to give themselves airs; they ought to learn something from our friends in Czechoslovakia, who make very good building materials and parts. (*Applause.*) One can also learn something in this matter from the German Democratic Republic, where good facing tiles are produced. It should be said outright that certain comrades learn little from others and, more important, do not want to learn. (*Applause.*)

Apartment houses are often turned over for occupancy with much work left unfinished, causing inconveniences to the tenants.

It is essential to pay particular attention to improving the standard of wood fittings. In many houses window transoms and doors are badly made. And you know that when a person enters a house, he pays attention first and foremost to the door—how it closes, whether there are any cracks in it, and how it is painted; he also looks to see how the windows have been made and what the metal parts are like. We must struggle resolutely and constantly to raise the standard of finishing work. It is necessary also to finish the staircases in apartment houses well.

Much remains to be done in improving soundproofing in housing. It is particularly necessary to show concern for inter-apartment soundproofing; it should be faultless. In this respect the demands of soundproofing should be met in the partitions between apartments and between floors.

There are many defects in the work of laying floors. Parquet floors are laid over a foundation, but the quality of the foundation used is frequently unsatisfactory and it emerges between the parquet blocks. It is necessary to improve the laying of parquet floors.

Linoleum production should be increased. Floors covered with linoleum are not inferior to parquet, and they are more hygienic and decorative. Caring for these floors is simpler than caring for parquet ones. Everyone knows that parquet floors need polishing. This is a complicated task and requires additional expense. One should value the labor of women and lighten their work as far as possible.

Kitchen furnishings are often of poor quality. This is not because we do not know how to do better, but because we are not demanding of quality; we use unseasoned lumber and bad paint. We must put an end to these shortcomings. We must also develop more extensively the production of good furniture for schools, hospitals and apartments.

Ceramics are the best material for finishing outer walls. Ceramic facing is durable, attractive and its colors do not fade. At the conference here, Comrade Melia, the designer of a machine for semidry pressing, reported on this press, which turns out cheap ceramic products in various sizes and colors. Architects should get to know this material and work with Comrade Melia on creating new types of tile facing materials.

The tasks of raising building standards make it essential to be more exacting toward the Ministry of the Building Materials Industry and toward the heads of enterprises producing building materials. Good-quality materials will permit reducing the cost and raising the standard of construction. [Low quality of construction work is abetted in many cases by the fact that in cities there is no active control over construction. In this connection it is necessary to raise the question of improvement of work of the State Architectural-Construction Inspection. On this matter various considerations have been brought out. Comrades propose to give the right to officials of the State Architectural-Construction Inspection to stop construction, to strictly punish those to blame for poor construction, to heighten responsibility for the quality of work, etc. It is advisable, evidently, to study these proposals and to provide various measures of coercion to bad builders. It is necessary to strengthen inspection and increase demands on builders so that in the future they should build well and with good quality. I think that we shall do this.

The improvement in quality of all construction work—whether the matter concerns industrial, housing, or any other type of construction—that is a matter of great state significance. Concern for the high quality of work must be manifested both by the builders themselves—beginning with the heads of the ministries and ending with every worker—and also by all local Party, government, trade union, and Komsomol organizations. In such constant and mass-scale control the quality of construction will be raised to the level of the high demands of our people.]

On Certain Problems of Planning and Economy in Building.—Many who spoke at the conference mentioned serious defects in planning construction and allocations among numerous building projects, the protracted schedules for construction work and the unsatisfactory supply of building materials, all of which lead to increased construction costs.

Great harm is caused by distributing funds over many buildings. [I want to name several "bearded" construction projects supplementary to those already named at the meeting. The Ministry of Ways of Communication has been building ever since 1940 the railroad line from Askiz to Abaza. The cost of this construction is 74 million rubles. Over a period of 13 years there have been spent 64 per cent of all the funds. For 1955 there is planned an expenditure of 5 million rubles. With such planning the construction of this railway is going to continue for 19 years.]

The Ministry of Inland Shipping has been building a wharf in Yaroslavl Province since 1949. The construction cost is approximately 50,000,000 rubles. In five years 10,000,000 rubles have been expended, and 3,000,000 have been allocated for 1955. At this pace the construction job will go on for almost 20 years. Can one possibly build so slowly and expend funds so uneconomically? We must end this practice, comrades!

If these structures are needed, let us build them faster and not drag out the construction for tens of years.

Permit me to read a letter received by the Communist Party Central Committee from Comrades Skripkin and Nesterov, directors of an electric bulb factory under construction, and Comrade Blyum, head of the planning department of Construction Trust No. 13. Here is what they write:

"Construction Trust No. 13 has been working for many years on ten large construction projects. The cost of each construction project comes to tens of millions of rubles. Each year, including 1954, from 11 to 40 structures are planned for each of the projects. Work is going on simultaneously on more than 100 of these structures. The trust has only 900 workers in all. Each structure gets 10 to 15 workers on the average. Some structures are large factory shops, boiler rooms and apartment houses.

"The reason for this fragmentation is that all the ministries for which we build include in their annual plans as many structures and as much expenditure as possible, without regard for the capacity of the building organizations.

"Plants which have an approved list of construction jobs and are well financed insist on construction work on all the structures in their plan. These demands are backed up by telegrams and orders from the ministries. Consequently the building organization is obliged to maneuver, to work on all the structures simultaneously, forcing the pace on them in turn, first at one, then at another factory project. As a result, most of the structures included in the plan are not completed, retarding the opening of the plants.

"Simultaneous work of the same kinds on a large number of structures creates difficulties. For this reason, most factories begun back in 1951 could have been finished in two years but are taking five to seven years to build. The funds spent on this construction work are frozen capital. Moreover, considerable freezing of funds occurs because of the stocks of equipment lying in the contractors' storehouses, equipment which is not being used year after year because the factories are not being completed on time. A difficult supply situation has an adverse effect on the utilization of workers and machinery, and quality of the work deteriorates.

"It is necessary to cease the practice of planning to work on construction and assembly tasks at a number of large plants simultaneously. The U.S.S.R. State Planning Committee should assign the program of construction work in a planned manner among ministries contracting for the work to be done and ministries contracting to accept the orders for work, being guided by the principle of concentrating allocations of funds and supplies and not the principle of dividing them in fragments among the various construction projects."

The critical observations in this letter and the conclusions of the letter's writers are quite correct. The defects mentioned in the letter occur in many cities and many ministries. It is necessary to cease dividing construction funds and supplies into small driblets.

How should one fight these defects? The struggle against dispersal of funds should be waged first and foremost by Ministers and all department heads. The U.S.S.R. State Planning Committee is also bound to give particular attention to this matter. Perhaps supervision by inspectors should be organized, without increasing staffs but entrusting the task to officials who would not only collect information but would check up on how the funds allocated for construction were being used, on whether or not the interests of the state were being violated.

Most important, it is necessary to observe strictly the rule that construction is not to begin without a design, a budget and blueprints. (*Applause.*) But what happens in practice? Hardly has the decision to build been adopted when the report comes flying in: Construction has begun. Yet actually there is not even a design in existence. We know that before beginning construction the site must be well prepared, roads built, water supplies provided, power lines put in, and a complete design readied. Who is supposed to see to the observation of this rule? The State Planning Committee. But it is difficult for this body to do it alone. The ministries ordering construction work and those performing it must also see to it. [In planning construction it is necessary to take into consideration productive capacity, possibilities, and needs of construction organizations and the construction industry. Funds for capital construction must be allotted given only the presence of projects. The ministries and organizations and also the State Planning Commission must improve the planning of construction. Sometimes our comrades who work in planning and supply organizations forget that even the least inexactitude in their calculations can cost the state many millions of rubles.]

We lose a great deal because construction projects do not always receive metals and other supplies in the requisite variety. [I cite two examples and builders themselves can cite innumerable others. Builders need reinforced concrete wire of a diameter of 5.5 mm. There isn't any. They are told to take wire 1 mm. thicker—6.5 mm. in diameter. It would seem that this is not a big difference. Is it worth having a fight for the sake of 1 mm.? However, for part of the projects of the Ministry of Construction in 1953 this one millimeter caused an over-expenditure of 4,800 tons of metal: This is already a figure which the State Planning Commission is fighting. And correctly. There, comrades, is what this millimeter costs.

At the construction projects of the Chief Administration for Construction of Oil Pipelines projects provide for the use of thin-walled pipeline pipes. In reality industry supplied pipes with thick walls. Therefore in 1953 the over-expenditure of metal for the given administration alone constituted 3,400 tons which resulted in a higher cost of work by 3,260,000 rubles.

It is clear that such squandering of metal and other construction materials should not take place.

It is necessary to note that questions of economy of construction are not being adequately considered by ministries and administration, by the State Committee on Construction, by the State Planning Commission, and by the Ministry of Finances.]

Comrade Ionas and others who have spoken at this conference have mentioned that at the present time there has arisen in building a situation where estimates have lost their significance. And it works out in practice, therefore, that the higher the estimated cost of the work completed, the better the indexes for plan fulfillment and the greater the fund for wages and overhead. It is no accident that builders primarily strive to take on expensive jobs. [In recent years the technics of construction, the mechanization of construction work, the organization of labor, materials, and design for construction have changed in significant degree. At the same time the system of financing, the norms for construction, various rules and instructions connected with the subcontracting activity of construction organizations have remained just as they were in 1936 and 1938. All of this has had a negative effect on the development of the construction business. It is necessary, evidently, as this was done after the All-Union Meeting of Builders in 1935, to work out and adopt measures to put in order the system for financing of construction.]

Problems of the planning and economics of construction should be studied constantly and thoroughly. It is necessary for the builders to concern themselves constantly with economic analysis of construction, to introduce concrete proposals for improving planning practice. Along with this, it is necessary to authorize a group of officials, perhaps from the State Bank (*stir in the hall*), a group which would not be dependent on the ministries and departments, to concern itself systematically with problems of the economics of construction. Is the bank for some reason not to the liking of some of you, comrades? Evidently the bank is not to the liking of some people because it is the kind of institution that counts money, and some would like to receive money without counting. But this won't happen. (*Applause.*)

Increase Labor Productivity and Provide Cadres of Skilled Builders.—Of exceptionally great importance is the question of further increasing labor productivity in construction. In order to ensure steady increase in labor productivity, it is necessary first and foremost to organize work at the building sites correctly, to make better use of manpower and machinery, to save raw materials and other supplies and to establish stable and skilled cadres of builders. Increased labor productivity is prerequisite to an increase in builders' wages and the improvement of their material welfare.

Certain comrades who spoke at the conference raised the question of increasing builders' wages. A note received by me mentions the same thing. In this connection it is essential to give some clarification. It is well known that we have always linked wage increases with increased labor productivity. The increase in labor productivity must keep ahead of the rise in wages. Under this condition alone can our society constantly have socialist accumulations necessary to expanding production and on this basis increase the people's material wellbeing. This is the only correct path, for we can only bring about an increase in the working people's welfare while developing the whole of our national economy. Everyone should realize that a correct correlation must be observed in this country between the presence of goods and presence of money in circulation and money possessed by the population. Only then will there be a stable currency, will the ruble be strong and valid. Only then will real earnings grow consistently. Otherwise, not.

Consequently, in order to increase the real wages of the working people it is essential to ensure steady increase in labor productivity and in the amount of work done by each worker.

How do matters stand in regard to increasing the productivity of labor?

In the 19th Party Congress directives on the Fifth Five-Year Plan the increase in labor productivity is envisaged as approximately 50 per cent for industry and 55 per cent for construction, with an increase in real wages of not less than 35 per cent.

In four years the productivity of labor has increased 33 per cent in industry and 32 per cent in construction. Real wages have increased 37 per cent during this period, or in other words, the level envisaged for the entire five-year plan has already been passed. Consequently, we are greatly overexpending the wage fund. These figures show that there are in industry and construction serious defects in the utilization of machinery and in the organization of labor. Failing to meet plans for increasing the productivity of labor, many heads of departments, enterprises and building organizations are taking the path of increasing the number of workers and employees, with resultant overexpenditures of the wage fund. [It is well known that in construction there are enormous reserves for upping the productivity of labor and consequently also for increasing the wages of workers. These include the mechanization of construction work, the correct use of the powerful equipment with which our projects are equipped, the transition to industrial methods of construction, the increasing of the skills of workers, the better use of advanced experience of innovators, and the strengthening of production discipline.

There are many examples to show what big possibilities exist for increasing the productivity of labor and the growth of wages. Here is one of them. Let us take for comparison two schools from among the many school buildings built in Moscow in 1954. One of them is that on Tokmakovo Street built with brick walls and the other in Kutuzov settlement made from large concrete blocks. See what a difference there is in the expenditure of labor on construction. To lay the brick walls, to make the cornices, floors and ceilings, stairways, and partitions there were spent 7,360 worker days—in the brick building. For the same work in the large concrete block building—1,780, in other words, 24 per cent of the labor expenditure on the brick building. The average output of a worker in the brick school was 268 rubles per worker day and in the large concrete block construction 1,432, i.e., 5.4 times as much. Taking into consideration all work in the school with brick walls the output per worker day constituted 142 rubles, and in the second school 261 rubles, 1.8 times as much. The use of tower cranes: on the construction of the brick school there were spent 314 machine-shifts, and on the second 164 machine-shifts, i.e., 52 per cent. That, comrades, is where lie our reserves for growth in the productivity of labor and increase in wages.]

A most important requisite for increasing labor productivity is specialized training for workers and improvement of their skills. This matter is inextricably connected with the task of setting up stable cadres of workers. In construction the turnover of manpower is inadmissibly great. This occurs because training for new workers is not properly organized at many projects. A collective farmer arrives at the construction site without any skills, qualifications, and he is put down, as is well known, as an unskilled worker. And so he works as an odd-job man; his output is low, he has no special trade and his earnings are not great. He begins to look around, and then a comrade comes up to him and says: "Look here, give up this work and go into a factory. There you will have a trade in six months, you will receive a rating and perhaps even a place to live." He looks around and is off; after six months at the factory he has learned a trade and is earning twice or three times as much as at the construction site. Is that not true? (*Shouts of: "Yes, quite right!"*) Skilled laborers—excavator operators, truck drivers, concrete workers, assembly workers and stone masons—do not leave construction. They have a trade and they work at their specialties, fulfilling their work norms and earning quite well.

If every builder were helped to master some trade well and helped to become a skilled worker who could use machinery proficiently, he would then love his work and say with pride: "I am a builder!" Unfortunately, there is still little concern for new workers being shown at construction sites. In the Soviet Union there is no unemployment, and no worker has any difficulty in finding a job. In order to keep workers in construction, it is necessary to train them and help them to master some kind of trade.

Besides this, we need, comrades, without doubt, to devote more attention to systematizing wages. Is it really normal for a number of different wage scales to operate in almost every department? This has been justly pointed out by the speakers here. The proposals on systematizing payments to builders working in various departments deserve support. [It is necessary to eliminate the abnormal situation in which in one and the same city the builders of one and the same specialty and skill receive different wages only because they are working at construction projects of different institutions which have different pay schedules. This, evidently, is taking place also because many economic executives have begun to retreat from the previously established system of payment for labor, taking into account the special aspects of individual zones, the so-called belt system. It is necessary to say also that the trade unions are not manifesting in this matter the necessary activity.

The economic and trade union organizations are obliged to use more correctly the material possibilities which they have for stimulating the growth of productivity of labor at construction projects and increasing production for each worker. This will assure a still more powerful upsurge of our construction, the growth of real wages, the incessant increase of the living standards of the builders, their material and cultural welfare.]

The problem of creating stable skilled cadres of builders cannot be solved without training specialists in the intermediate and higher levels. We have infinitely better conditions than formerly for training specialists. The general educational level of the mass of building workers has risen. From the ranks of the workers cadres of fine organizers are coming, the number of specialists who can handle industrial methods of building is increasing. Many construction projects equipped with advanced technology can and should become good schools for training building specialists.

We must seriously improve on-the-job training for specialists. More attention must be paid to expanding and improving correspondence and evening study institutions, not only the specialized secondary schools but also the higher ones. This will be of great advantage to the entire national economy. If the Ministry of Higher Education were to analyze at present the number of students accepted for the first-year courses at higher educational establishments and the number graduating from them, it would see that there is a considerable dropping out from the higher school. Moreover, by no means all graduates from higher educational establishments are working at their specialties. The efficiency, if one may express it thus, of certain higher educational establishments is not great.

On the other hand, the higher and secondary educational establishments or their branches at the larger factories do turn out highly skilled cadres of specialists, ones who are trained without leaving their jobs but continue to work at the same enterprise.

The Stalin Automobile Plant, for example, has its own institute. Many workers are studying in it without leaving their jobs. A good job is being done there in selecting students from among the workers' collective. A worker comes to the plant, learns to love his enterprise and his trade. Having secondary education, he willingly studies in an evening course, attends school or the evening institute, graduates, obtains the grade of technician or engineer while working at the plant. The only difference is that, having begun his courses an ordinary worker or skilled worker, once graduated, he becomes a skilled worker, technician or engineer and sometimes even a shop head. [It seems to us that along with the improvement in the preparation of specialists in existing secondary and higher educational institutions it is necessary more broadly to develop the preparation of specialists from among the practicing workers, occupied at construction projects, who are fulfilling the obligations of engineering-technical officials and heads of sectors and projects. The preparation of this type of official should be organized both without separation from production and also with separation. The preparation of specialists without separation from production can be longer, but this path has its advantages. For the person completing higher education without separation from production knows his business more deeply, has more practical experience. Many engineers enriched by knowledge of science and production, made wise by experience, on completing their last examination, can boldly direct an enterprise. (*Applause.*) Those who attend higher educational institutions in person have as a rule good knowledge, but they need a definite time in order to study production and accumulate the necessary practical experience.

The tasks of further improvement of the construction business in the country, of its industrialization, put before Party, economics, trade union, and Komsomol organizations the demand for basic improvements of all work with cadres of builders. Builders are carrying out a big business, vitally important for the country. It is our duty to surround them with concern and attention. This means that we must make a deeper acquaintance of the growing needs of builders and satisfy them more completely, improve their housing and living condition, organize more effectively mass-political and cultural-indoctrination work, more broadly expand socialist competition among builders for fulfillment and overfulfillment of plans for increasing labor productivity.]

Some Observations on Road and Rural Construction.—Comrades! Allow me to make a few remarks about road and rural construction. There is no need to say here how important good roads are to our country with its enormous expanses.

We need to develop the construction of cement roads. These are the very best roads. (*Applause.*) An asphalt road is a ten-year road, a cement road lasts 100 years. We must turn toward the development of the cement industry with a view to building cement roads. As they say, we are not so rich that we can afford to build cheaply. If you build expensively, that is to say, with good basic materials, you will forget how long ago you built! (*Applause.*)

Much work needs to be done in constructing production buildings and housing on collective and state farms and M.T.S. as well as in constructing grain storehouses. And here we must make extensive use of precast reinforced concrete and possibly of block construction. For example, at an M.T.S. it is possible to carry out block as well as frame construction. In doing so, widespread use should be made of local building materials. Blocks can be made of coquina, limestone or brick. All local reserves and materials should be put to the service of construction.

Unfortunately, little initiative is as yet being shown in the use of local building materials. Reeds are very good material for rural construction. In a number of regions of the Ukraine and other republics houses have been built of reeds for centuries. It is a wonderful material; it does not rot, and it provides good insulation. But it is still being poorly utilized. "Stromite" panels for walls in frame construction and for partitions and roofing must be made from wood shavings, straw and reed. Composite reed and straw materials should be produced. [Last spring the secretary of the Astrakhan Regional Committee of the Party, Comrade Ganenko, came to me with the request that the supply of lumber for the region be increased. It is well known that timber is needed for the most important construction projects.

I said at the time to Comrade Ganenko: "You have in your region remarkable growths of reeds! That's pure gold, and is it not a construction material?" He replied: "Yes, we have reeds here." I continued: "And isn't it possible to build out of reeds at least sheepfolds? You can't find a better material than reeds for these purposes." Comrade Ganenko agreed with this. But though much time has passed since this conversation the matter has not particularly moved forward.]

There is a great amount of reed in Kazakhstan—nearly 70 per cent of all the reed growing in the country. During our visit to the regions developing virgin lands in Kazakhstan we discussed with the republic leaders the question of utilizing the reed. Comrades Ponomarenko, Brezhnev, Taibekov and other Kazakhstan officials found specialists experienced in the production of reed panels and they have set about using reed in farm construction.

There is a lot of reed in Uzbekistan, Turkmenia and in the Ukraine —on the flats of the Dniester, on the Bug and on the Danube. It is possible to build various farm buildings and even houses from reeds and to make remarkable things, but it is still not being used in the right way. It is essential to draw attention to this!

Much attention should be given to constructing collective farm homes and to planning of villages, hamlets, kishlaks and auls well. When people were poor, they had no chance for good accommodations and improving their lot. Nowadays things are different. As a result of the advance of their economy, the advanced collective farms have large incomes and pay high wages to the collective farmers for workday units. However, the homes of many collective farmers are unsightly.

Houses should be built which correspond to the growing cultural requirements of the collective farmers. At present many collective farms and farmers have the funds for building new houses, but they are unable to purchase the necessary building materials since the latter are not being produced in sufficient quantities.

Comrades, let us think about altering this situation. Let the collective farms and farmers who have the chance build as many production premises, cultural and service buildings and homes as possible and build them as well as possible. People should be encouraged to build and should be helped to do it. (*Applause.*) And in order that construction on the land should move along successfully, the output of building materials for rural construction must be organized.

For this purpose it is essential for republic and province organizations to develop their local building materials industry. This local industry should be based not only on the production of brick but chiefly on the production of cement. It is necessary for cement plants to be built by both Union and republic organizations. Then the country will have more cement to use for the needs of rural construction.

In our country major work is being done to expand the production of consumers' goods. Many people think of consumers' goods only as items such as shoes, suits, fur coats and many other articles of everyday use. But are not materials for building houses also consumers' goods? Building materials for housing are also essential consumers' goods.

The production of cement, slate, tile and other building materials for sale in rural areas should be developed in every way. There is need to organize extensively the production of precast sections and parts for farm buildings of various kinds and for small homes on collective farms, in settlements and suburban areas, with a view to selling them to the working people. This is advantageous both to the state and the population.

By increasing the output of building materials and sending them to the villages we shall considerably hasten the transformation of our villages and settlements, making them beautiful and pleasing to the eye, villages which adorn the life of man. (*Applause.*)

Finally, a word should be said about building motion picture theaters. We still lack sufficient movie theaters in cities and particularly in villages. We must build more, turn out more films and better. This is a great and necessary matter for further progress in the people's culture, for spiritual growth in Soviet people.

Comrades! [From year to year the power of the Soviet state is growing. The economy of our country is developing at rapid tempos. And the welfare and culture of the people are incessantly improving. This is the result of the correct, Leninist policy of the Communist

Party. All our successes are clear evidence of the monolithic unity of the Soviet people, of its loyalty to the great cause of communism.

For the 37 years which have passed since the victory of the great October Socialist Revolution our country has been transformed from the backward country which it was under Tsarism into an advanced powerful socialist power. The historical victories of our peoples have literally shaken the world. This is the result of the enormous advantages of the socialist structure.

The great Lenin created our Communist Party, tempered it in revolutionary battles, and guided it in the great cause of communist construction and the entire people followed the Party.

Now the entire world recognizes the might of the Soviet Union as a great world power and the imperialists must take this into consideration. This the Soviet people attained under the experienced leadership of the Communist Party. This is the result of the realization of the ideas of Marx, Engels, Lenin, Stalin. (*Stormy, long-continued applause.*)] With our achievements as a base and continuing to develop heavy industry in every way, we shall steadily strengthen the might of our homeland, will struggle for a further advance in the national economy and for improving the people's welfare. In this great creative work of communist construction a tremendous part belongs to the great army of builders.

Comrades! At our conference, which has been successfully held, many proper proposals have been advanced. These are all of great interest and great value. Thousands of builders in all parts of the Soviet Union will hear about these proposals and about the positive experience which we have had. The conference has shown that our builders are fully aware of the tasks facing them and that they ardently wish to improve the work of building industrial enterprises in order to strengthen untiringly the industrial might of the Soviet state and to provide the country with more housing and other buildings of good quality.

[If we communicate all of the positive experience of which we have spoken at this meeting, and work as needed for the realization of the proposals which have been made, for the introduction of advanced methods and ways, if we will decisively struggle for the elimination of faults, then we will receive an enormous economy of funds and materials, we shall obtain a more rapid turnover in funds, accelerate the tempos, and improve the quality of construction.]

It is necessary to instruct Comrade Sokolov, Chairman of the State Committee for Construction Affairs, the Ministers of all ministries and particularly the building ministries to study the record of the conference and all the speeches. We must also ask the comrades who were unable to speak here to submit the theses of their remarks, which should also be considered. After generalizing all the conference record, concrete proposals should be drawn up. These should be divided into three groups: Group I—proposals which should apply to the country as a whole; Group II—those which can and should be applied by Union ministries; and Group III—those concerning Union republics and provinces. The necessary checkup on application of these proposals should be established.

[Particular attention must be directed to the communication of advanced ways and methods of construction. (*Applause.*)]

It would also be well to hold similar conferences locally and in individual ministries. At these conferences advanced experience should be generalized, particularly experience in introducing industrial methods, and all our shortcomings should be criticized, should be, as they say, "ground with emery," without fear of stepping on friends' corns. This will help to bring to light tremendous opportunities and potentialities and put them to use in our common cause.

I will end my speech, comrades, by expressing confidence that builders, architects, designers, workers in the building materials industry, construction and highway machine building, design and research organizations will carry out honorably the tasks laid upon them by the Party and government, will raise still higher the level, rate and quality of our construction work, and will open up factories, mines, power stations and plants more rapidly, will build cheaper, better and more beautiful housing, schools and hospitals. . . . I wish you new successes, comrades! (*Stormy, prolonged applause. All rise.*)

1955:
Malenkov Out

It was more or less clear that the duumvirate arrangement between Khrushchev and Malenkov was both instable and impermanent. And in late 1954 and early 1955 there appeared signs that a denouement was near. Still, when it did actually come it was a surprise inside and outside the Soviet Union.

Two particular public signals of an internal crisis turned up before the results of the actual showdown became apparent. One of them consisted in oblique indications in the press of an intraparty discussion of the Stalinist thesis of priority for heavy industry in Soviet economic development. This is a permanent issue in the Soviet Union—and a basic one. Priority for heavy industry means that heavy industry, producing basic metals and fuels and also in particular machinery, including both capital goods and armaments, is supposed, according to this thesis, to develop at a more rapid rate than light industry producing largely consumer goods. The slogan of "priority for heavy industry," in other words, is a slightly different Communist version of the famous slogan of "guns instead of butter"—except that it would have to read "guns and capital goods instead of butter." The point of the discussion of this subject at the end of 1954 and the beginning of 1955 was evidently that Premier Georgi Malenkov had made a key point of his program for the country a big immediate increase in consumer goods production. The opposition to Malenkov, led by Khrushchev, then could contend that Malenkov was subverting the basic program of "priority for heavy industry." On such a platform Khrushchev could be certain of having the support of the Stalinists in the leadership such as Molotov and Lazar Kaganovich—and also, no doubt, of the Soviet army.

It was all a question of relative emphasis—and of political maneuvering.

The other particular signal of an internal political crisis which turned up at about the end of 1954 was the curt announcement in December of the trial and execution of the former minister of State Security, V. S. Abakumov, and several of his colleagues for alleged complicity in organizing the "Leningrad case" in 1949–50 which had resulted in the death of Politburo member, Nikolai Voznesensky, and other friends of the late Andrei Zhdanov. The question at stake here seemed to be not the "Leningrad case" itself, but of its relationship to members of the Soviet leadership. Obviously Georgi Malenkov—like the dead Lavrenty Beria—had profited politically from the "Leningrad case." Obviously the raising of this issue at this time could be directed against Malenkov—and was.

Malenkov resigned as Soviet premier in early February 1955 at a Supreme Soviet Session. He did not even read his own resignation statement. He was replaced as premier by Nikolai Bulganin, a relative nonentity.

Thus Nikita Khrushchev vanquished his principal opponent on his path to power. Thus he became the dominant personality in the leadership of the country.

It seems clear that one of the key elements—perhaps the crucial element—in the political support which Khrushchev was able to muster in his showdown with Malenkov was the Soviet military, headed by career officer and war hero, Marshal Georgi Zhukov. For whatever reasons, Zhukov backed Khrushchev in all of the internal political crises in the Soviet Union internally and abroad. In both areas his moves were characterized by boldness, imagination, and also opportunism.

In agriculture Khrushchev launched a gigantic campaign to convince Soviet farmers to go over to the culture of corn—maize—as a principal fodder crop. It was the Khrushchev thesis that corn, grown under the climatic conditions of the Soviet Union mainly for use as green silage, was the most efficient fodder crop and would help in large part solve the problem of increasing the country's supply of meat and other animal products. It was in connection with the Khrushchev corn program that he sent to the United States the first important Soviet nondiplomatic delegation to visit America for many years. This was the farm delegation which toured Iowa and other farm states in

July and August. The group got much attention in the American press and served a political purpose of emphasizing the possibility and practicability of cultural exchanges between the United States and the Soviet Union even under circumstances in which there remained no little hostility in political relations between the two countries.

The findings of the Soviet farm delegation acted to strengthen Khrushchev's determination to push ahead with his plans for far-reaching farming reforms.

In foreign policy Khrushchev during 1955 developed a free-wheeling, double-pronged strategy which at one and the same time saw the Soviet Union seeking visible relaxations of tensions with the West on one front and cementing and strengthening relations within the Communist bloc and increasing the influence of Communist nations on the newly independent countries of Asia and Africa on the other hand.

In May the military alliance between the Communist bloc and East European nations was formalized with the signing of the Warsaw Pact, an arrangement which gave the Soviet Union a considerable measure of control over the armed forces of Eastern European nations and furnished a legal basis for a continued stay of Soviet troops in certain East European countries, in particular Hungary and Roumania. Simultaneously with the conclusion of the Warsaw Pact the Soviet government finally signed that same month the Austria State Treaty which put an end to the Soviet occupation of parts of Austria.

In May and June the world was treated to the extraordinary sight of Khrushchev flying to Belgrade in order to make a public confession to President Tito of Soviet error in the 1948 break with Communist Yugoslavia. Khrushchev, evidently, was hoping that he could bring President Tito back into the Kremlin fold. The visit resulted in greatly improved Soviet-Yugoslav relations, in continued maintenance by Tito's Yugoslavia of an independent course in international affairs, and in substantial Soviet expenditures for economic aid to Yugoslavia which was having the best of both worlds by receiving American aid at the same time.

It was in July that Khrushchev had his first experience with a summit meeting at Geneva where he and Premier Bulganin met with President Eisenhower and other Western leaders in order to inaugurate a period of what Soviet propagandists optimistically christened "the spirit of Geneva." No substantial agreement of substance came out of the conference—but there was an air of greater cordiality in international affairs as a result of it.

While going to Geneva Khrushchev at the same time had his representatives working out a large-scale deal for the sale to Egypt of Communist arms. This was the beginning of the Soviet policy of fishing in the troubled waters of the Middle East, by giving material support to Arab nationalism in its anti-Israeli and anti-Western trends.

As Khrushchev himself took a more direct hand in foreign affairs he also took the opportunity to kick in the teeth his erstwhile foreign minister, V. M. Molotov, who represented the more conservative, dogmatic "Stalinist" line of Soviet political leadership. Use was made of an inexact ideological formulation by Molotov in a speech delivered before the Supreme Soviet early in 1955 to force him to make a public confession of error in the press which amounted to a personal and political humiliation.

Throughout 1955 the campaign to develop the virgin lands of the Soviet East continued apace. Khrushchev made much of this drive, and as the seventh item in this collection of Khrushchev documents there has been selected an address which he delivered in January 1955 to a group of Soviet young people headed for the East. In it he says in effect: "Go East, young man!"

MOSCOW MEETING OF YOUNG COMMUNISTS AND YOUNG PEOPLE WHO HAVE EXPRESSED A DESIRE TO SET OFF TO DEVELOP VIRGIN AND IDLE LANDS: SPEECH BY COMRADE N. S. KHRUSHCHEV *

Allow me to greet you, Comrades, in the name of the Communist Party Central Committee and to wish you the greatest success in your labors for the welfare of our great Soviet motherland. (*Applause.*)

Comrades! It is a fine thing that you have decided to set off to develop the virgin lands and by your efforts reinforce the volunteers already working there and represented by speakers at this meeting. When we talked about these virgin lands last year, they seemed farther from Moscow than today. At that time few Muscovites had visited the distant regions of Kazakhstan and the Altai and, consequently, few had a specific, clear idea of those lands.

* *Pravda,* Jan. 8, 1955, p. 2. Translation copyrighted by *The Current Digest of the Soviet Press,* VII, No. 1, pp. 12–13, 22.

It is different now that thousands of people have gone to the virgin lands, have been there, have set to work there in fitting fashion and have written letters. True, the letters have been of all kinds; some were tearful, that must be said. But most of the letters have been confident. People have expressed firm faith in succeeding in the work entrusted to them. These letters are splendid documents of our times, testifying to the optimistic spirit of our glorious young people who set out to master the idle lands. As a result it is easier for the Young Communist League to appeal to young people to follow the example of those who left last year to master the new steppe expanses of Siberia and Kazakhstan. That is good.

I think that this year we will complete, in the main, the assembling of cadres for the new state farms and Machine and Tractor Stations of the idle-land districts. Is that right, Comrades, or will this task hang over to next year?

(*Voices from the audience:* We'll finish it!)

Yes, evidently we will have to finish it. It is very important to the country. You know that the Party and government have planned to put 28,000,000 to 30,000,000 hectares of new land under cultivation by 1956. I call attention to the figure of 30,000,000; it is better than 28,000,000 because it is larger and, consequently, we shall have more grain. (*Applause.*)

It seems to me that there are none among us who doubt that these lands will be put under the plow. We shall plow and sow 20,000,000 hectares this year, but 10,000,000 remain. Therefore next year we shall have 30,000,000 additional hectares sown. And 30,000,000, Comrades, is a great deal, it is a great addition to what already exists.

Along with development of the new lands we will find something in the old districts, we will plow up pasturage where it is low in grass yield and plant it to grain and other crops yielding high harvests. And then a very large figure will be added to the present harvests of grain, potatoes, vegetables and technical crops.

I would like to share my impressions with you, Comrades. As you know, last year I had occasion to visit the virgin lands in Kazakhstan, the Altai and Novosibirsk and Omsk Provinces. I have lived a long time, and I spent my childhood in the Ukraine. I know its riches. And it seems to me that it would be hard to find richer soil in the Soviet Union than exists in the Ukraine! But, Comrades, the soil of Kazakhstan and the Altai is much richer! Of course, I am not speaking of all the soil of Kazakhstan and the Altai, there is poor soil there too, but on the whole there are considerably better lands here than in the Ukraine.

But these blessed lands were left to the rabbits until recently and wild goats roamed here. It is high time that we set about developing the virgin lands. It is said that there is little rainfall there. But there is not a drop more rainfall in the southern Ukraine. Consequently this argument does not stand up. The only thing one can say is that there are underpopulated and in some instances entirely unpopulated districts here. But, with your active support, with the support of all our young people, this difficulty will be overcome.

It must be said that the virgin lands have been eyed since ancient times. Efforts to solve the problem were made under Tsarism. But nothing came of them; under the capitalist system in Russia people could not be roused to master the virgin lands. It is different in our Soviet conditions. The Soviet people have created a mighty industry which is equipping agriculture with a wealth of machinery. Soviet people fully realize that development of the virgin lands is in the interests of strengthening the might of our state, in the interests of increasing the people's living standard. Hence the tremendous enthusiasm of the young people. They can work fruitfully, making use of the wealth of machinery which the state is sending into the new-land districts. The state has provided the virgin lands with tens of thousands of tractors, combines and other machines. The Young Communist League and our glorious young people are responding eagerly to the Party's call.

It is a fine thing that it is young people who are going to the virgin lands. All those who come are working directly in production. You know that many have to come to wilderness where housing has not yet been built and necessary articles of everyday life are lacking. It is easier for a young man or girl to bear these temporary difficulties than a large family. Comrades Lomteva and Kasatkin, two Young Communists who have already been working in the virgin lands, have spoken here. The winter cold gave their spirits a pick-up there! Evidently things were not so gay for them as they described them to us today. But people are working there, unfrightened by the difficulties. They realize that we have done things that were harder. Do you remember where the soldiers rested during the war? They rested where they fought. If the country needs it, our people do not spare any efforts. It is pleasant to see and realize that people have spoken from this platform who are plowing virgin fields and mastering the soil. And we will not abandon this land after a year or two. We must settle on it firmly, once and for all. For this it is desirable that you marry there. (*Applause.*)

What is a married person? It means that the person wants to build a family, to settle firmly in a new place. And he who founds a family is a good citizen. The more people we have, the stronger will our country be. Bourgeois ideologists have invented many cannibalist theories, including the theory of overpopulation. They think about how to reduce the birth rate and the growth of population. Matters are different among us, Comrades. If we were to add 100,000,000 to our 200,000,000, it would be too few!

I wish to take this opportunity and, speaking here, to dwell on one question. Some comrades hold against us the allegation that the tax on unmarried persons and persons without children, a law adopted at one time, is a bad one. Comrades, if anyone is to be scolded for this law, it is myself most of all. I proposed this law. Comrade Malenkov is present here, he can confirm this. I presented a proposal to Comrade Stalin to draft and adopt such a law, and the law was drafted and ratified. I consider it a good law. Only it should be viewed not from the bystander's position but in state fashion. What does the law say? If you have no children or have only one or two, pay a tax. Why? Because, if each family were to have only one or two children, the country's population would not grow, it would decline. And we have to think of the development of society. Therefore each family should have at least three children and should give them a good upbringing! (*Prolonged applause.*)

Some people ask: Why should persons who have two children and particularly those who have none pay a tax? Here is why. We have people who either do not marry or do not have children after marriage, for reasons which we shall not discuss here. But such people live in society and enjoy all its benefits. Then they grow old. Who, one asks, will look after them when they lose the capacity to work? The same young people who will have been raised by our fine mothers of large families. So Comrade Stalin proposed aiding large families. At whose expense? At the expense of those who live and do not think of the morrow. We must think of the morrow, for we must think of our socialist society, we must look to its development. Then we shall be strong and rooted in our socialist society and no power will be able to tear up these roots.

It appears, Comrades, that the law of the tax on single and childless persons is a correct law, a good law, it benefits our state.

I wish to return to the question of developing the virgin lands. The lands in the East of our country are rich. We must go eastward beyond the Altai. What lands there are in Krasnoyarsk Territory! We often live under the impression of all kinds of literature, good and bad, describing Siberia. More often than not, it describes it as a place where people served their terms of exile under Tsarism. Under the impression of these descriptions people sometimes obtain an utterly wrong idea of these regions. Take that same Krasnoyarsk. It is a territory which does not know drought, and there is splendid soil here!

Comrades, I was in the Far East recently and visited Khabarovsk Territory. It is one of the richest territories, yet it still has a small population, and it must be developed. We now ship potatoes from Omsk to Sakhalin, while in neighboring Khabarovsk Territory marvelous soil, from which one could obtain large crops, lies idle. This land could yield potatoes and rice and soy and corn and melons. Whatever you sow on this soil grows, and grows well. Yet this soil is still very little used.

And Vladivostok? On our return from our recent trip to China Comrades Bulganin, Mikoyan and I visited Vladivostok. A fabulous place! A very beautiful city, laid out on hills, with picturesque bays and islands, all covered with greenery, amid nature's bounty! What sunlight! When we were in Vladivostok you here were shivering in the first winter freeze, but we were going about in light coats and enjoying fine, sunny weather.

And, as Lenin said, Vladivostok, far as it is, is a city of ours! Maritime Territory has inexhaustible possibilities for development of agriculture and particularly animal husbandry. Grasses grow in this territory as in the jungle, yet we still send meat, butter and other dairy products there. This must be corrected.

And Sakhalin? It too is a very picturesque and fruitful land, with good, moist climate, perhaps too moist. But Soviet people live there too and not only live there but feel fine and do good and useful work.

In a word, we must develop the empty lands in the East and settle down firmly on those lands.

When we were in Komsomolsk, that young city, and in other new

Far Eastern cities, when we talked with workers and employees there, we were particularly struck by the [local] patriotism of the inhabitants of the new cities. The enthusiasm with which they spoke of how they were building up their cities! They pleaded with us to help them improve their cities. Among them were many Muscovites who had gone there in the past to build these cities.

That is a good trait—the birth of love for one's city! Some of us can say that there's no need to agitate among us, we know it ourselves. But sometimes weak things float to the surface on a strong patriotic wave, along with everything healthy. (*Laughter, animation in the hall.*) When the difficulties come, then spirits drop and some may find themselves back in Moscow. Well, we are sending you off with honor, but we will take you back without pleasure. (*Laughter.*) Yes, and without honor!

You are leaving to master the new lands; that is good. You have to build a great deal there. In fact, in many districts where new lands are being put to the plow there is no lumber; but take the Ukraine, take our Donets districts. You will find Ukrainians living in cottages of *saman.** I myself once lived in a *saman* cottage—it was warm in winter and always cool in summer. That is its advantage.

There are many lakes in Kazakhstan, where many of you are going. The republic has the greatest reed thickets. This is a golden material for building both housing and farm structures. It need only be skillfully used. You will have to make homes in the new lands of Kazakhstan and you will have to build your cottages well there. You can do it. True, at first, perhaps, you will have an earthen floor. Too bad. But in time you will build a wooden floor. Even Moscow wasn't built in a day, as they say. You must set yourself up well, to set examples not only in matters of work—that, of course, is most important—but also in everyday living. You must bring your city culture to the steppes so that even the stranger may see immediately that here live people resettled from Moscow, they live well and neatly. This is a very important matter.

Build schools, children's centers, nurseries and kindergartens. One of the new settlers spoke here and said that they will have a ten-year school and that he will be studying next year. It is very important that

* [*Saman*—Brick made of clay mixed with dried manure, straw and horsehair or other fibrous material.—Ushakov's *Explanatory Dictionary of the Russian Language*.]

many of you, if you lack a secondary education, obtain it. You must seek to accomplish this; there is every opportunity to do so. You must obtain secondary education, you must be masters of machinery, then labor productivity will be different and the accumulation of socialist wealth will be different and life will be considerably better.

Comrades! To raise the people's living standards it is necessary to develop agriculture, to obtain more food products and more raw materials for industry.

But you must know that for all the successes of our country we are indebted to the victory of the general line of the Party, the line which was outlined by Lenin, which was undeviatingly carried out by the Party under Stalin's leadership and which has been carried out by our entire party. This is the triumph of the line of industrializing the country. Without developing heavy industry, without developing coal mining and the metallurgical and chemical industries, without developing machine building, we could not have developed our national economy, we could not have ensured victory in the hard war years. We live in a capitalist encirclement. Our successes bring joy to our friends and infuriate our enemies. We must constantly strengthen the might of our motherland, and fight for a firm and lasting peace throughout the world.

The Soviet people, engaged in peaceful labor, will devote all their efforts to the great cause of communist construction. We are convinced that the victory will be ours because we are guided by the teaching of Marx-Engels-Lenin-Stalin!

Our successes are great. But we cannot rest content, we must work better! And another thing we need is more self-criticism. We must be more demanding of ourselves and indulge less in boasting. We cannot rest content with what we have accomplished; today it suffices, tomorrow it is already insufficient. Criticism and self-criticism must sweep the dust and mold from our administrative agencies and then the strong young shoots of all that is progressive in our economy will grow more rapidly.

Comrade Kasatkin, who went to the virgin lands from the Manometer Plant, spoke here. It was very pleasing to hear that in his first year of work on the virgin lands he and his group won the right to show at the All-Union Agricultural Exhibition. I think that each of us will fight for the right to be exhibitors at the All-Union Agricultural Exhibition. Going to the virgin lands, you must not disgrace the capital, you must not discredit the group from which you went. I think it would even be somehow disappointing if you did not become participants in the exhibition. As I see, you don't agree—are you frightened? (*Animation in the hall. Applause.*)

We have machinery, the soil is good, we have the knowledge, and there will be more of all these things. What is needed? Persistence. If you don't succeed the first year, don't give up, fight for another year, in the third year victory is sure. There are no difficulties which man cannot overcome if he knows what he is fighting for and if he is armed with knowledge and works persistently.

What is the All-Union Agricultural Exhibition? It is nationwide evidence that in a short time we can obtain a sufficiency of all the food products necessary for the country. What is happening now? Each year there is more food, and still there are not enough goods. Why is this? Because each year the working class increases, wages rise, prices drop, the number of consumers grows. Is this bad? No, it is very good. But it is necessary that production not lag behind the growth in the public's demands. Good work, correctly organized labor, the ability to utilize our means—all this will enable us to accomplish our tasks in the quickest possible time.

In 1955 we must substantially increase the output of agricultural products. We must develop grain farming and animal husbandry; there must be more vegetables, potatoes, cotton, flax, hemp and other crops.

I wish you great achievements, Comrades! We expect truthful letters from you reporting your successes in developing the virgin lands, in work for the good of the motherland, in work to strengthen its might. (*Stormy, prolonged applause. All rise.*)

1956:
De-Stalinization

The entire year of 1956 was colored by the important events at the 20th Congress of the Soviet Communist Party held in Moscow in February.

Overshadowing everything else at this Congress in its tremendous impact on the Soviet Union and the entire international Communist movement was the speech delivered on February 25 to a closed session of the Congress by Nikita Khrushchev in which he made public a lengthy, trenchant, and outspoken condemnation of Joseph Stalin for serious errors and for using methods of police terror to rule the country. Using the term of the "personality cult of Joseph V. Stalin" or, as it might alternately be translated, the "cult of the individual," Khrushchev recounted how Stalin had liquidated on false charges, using evidence extracted by physical torture, thousands of loyal Communists. It was a shocking revelation.

Although the speech has never so far been published in the Soviet Union, versions of it were read to Communist Party members and other Soviet citizens throughout the country at meetings called for this particular purpose. The soul-searching, ferment, and unrest which this caused was intense and nationwide and extended outside the Soviet Union where it ultimately led to Poland's bloodless October "revolution" and to the ill-fated revolution in Hungary in that same month.

The impact of the Khrushchev speech on Stalin was greatly heightened when in June the United States government made public a version of the address which it had obtained from Communist sources. With this it was made clear to everybody that even the worst things which had been said about Stalin's methods of rule by his enemies were less horrible than the actual truth.

The 20th Congress set the stage for Khrushchev to carry out a whole series of political measures in the direction of further liberalization of the Soviet system. For example, in April a new law abolished the Stalinist practice of use of special criminal procedures for political prisoners. Another decree about the same time repealed the onerous law of 1940 which made absenteeism and leaving a job without official permission a criminal offense on the part of Soviet workers. In the field of international affairs the Communist Information Bureau—the Cominform—was abolished in April. In the spring of this year Khrushchev made his first visit to one of the important Western powers—Great Britain. He was generally well received and his prestige increased greatly both at home and abroad as a result of the journey despite his violent outburst when he was questioned by British Socialists on the whereabouts of many Social-Democrats of Russia and Eastern European countries persecuted or liquidated by the Soviet Communists.

One of the most important and far-reaching consequences of the de-Stalinization program of 1956 was the release from Soviet concentration camps and other forms of imprisonment of most of the thousands of political prisoners still held in them even after Stalin's death. These people, representing those relatively few who had survived, returned home each with his own story of the mistreatment to which he had been subjected. As a result, since there were many of them, the entire country got to know a great deal more about the nature of the police terror applied under Stalin.

It was not surprising, considering the far-reaching implications of de-Stalinization, that it would soon go so far as to endanger in one and another way the continuing absolute rule of the Soviet Communist Party over the Soviet Union and Eastern Europe.

Inside the Soviet Union writers were in the forefront of vocal protests which went further than criticism merely of Stalin and extended to criticism of the system itself. In a collection of essays and stories called "Literary Moscow" several short story writers depicted in vivid colors some of the despair, dishonesties, and barrenness characteristic of some areas of contemporary Soviet life, particularly in the countryside. One novelist, V. Dudintsev, published a novel entitled *Not By Bread Alone* which served as a rallying point for critical feelings on the part of Soviet young people. In essence the Dudintsev work, though wholly Communistic in outlook and spirit, was a ringing condemnation of Soviet bureaucracy and the insincerity, dishonesty, and falseness of officialdom. Its hero, a young inventor, was hounded by his persecutors into forced labor in Siberia until his important invention eventually realized its justification. So bitter was the Dudintsev diatribe against the scheme of things that it brought down on his head official condemnation. So widespread was the unrest among Soviet students toward the end of the year that drastic measures were taken by the government to suppress it. Though this repression did not in any sense compare with Stalinist terror, it did represent a political repression and showed that broad freedom of speech was still incompatible with the authoritarian nature of the regime.

The consequences abroad of de-Stalinization were even more serious. Communist Poland succeeded in establishing its independence of direct rule from Moscow in October in a Soviet-Polish crisis which came close to erupting into hostilities. Khrushchev himself flew to Warsaw in order to attempt to deal with the situation but was met by a display of unity and determination of the Polish Communist leadership, headed now by Wladislaw Gomulka, which forced him to retreat abruptly to Moscow. Fortunately he listened to the wiser persons among his advisers and did not attempt to deal with the Polish situation by military force. As a result, in the end, the outlines of a Soviet-Polish modus vivendi, satisfactory to both sides, were worked out without bloodshed.

This was not so in Hungary where acute discontent and unrest led to revolution suppressed with great bloodshed by Soviet armed forces. The Hungarian revolt was a blow to Soviet prestige at home and abroad and it brought about an immediate reassertion all along the line of the absolute authority of the Soviet Communist Party.

It was during the immediate period of the Hungarian revolution that the eruption of the Suez crisis gave Khrushchev a chance to divert Soviet attention toward foreign happenings by his threat to send Soviet volunteers and other aid to Egypt for the struggle against the British, French, and Israeli forces. The effect of the Soviet position in the Suez crisis was to enable Khrushchev to recoup some of the prestige which he had lost as a result of the events in Hungary.

As the eighth in this collection of Khrushchev documents there is selected here his speech of February 25, 1956, on "the personality cult of Joseph V. Stalin." This represents the single most important—and most interesting—public statement in Khrushchev's long career:

SPEECH BY N. S. KHRUSHCHEV ON THE STALIN CULT DELIVERED FEB. 25, 1956, AT A CLOSED SESSION OF THE 20TH CONGRESS OF THE SOVIET COMMUNIST PARTY *

Comrades! In the Party Central Committee report to the 20th Congress, in a number of speeches by delegates to the Congress, and earlier at plenary sessions of the Party Central Committee, quite a lot has been said about the cult of the individual leader and its harmful consequences.

After Stalin's death the Party Central Committee began to implement a policy of explaining concisely and consistently that it is impermissible and foreign to the spirit of Marxism-Leninism to elevate one person, to transform him into a superman possessing supernatural characteristics akin to those of a god. Such a man supposedly knows everything, sees everything, thinks for everyone, can do anything, is infallible in his behavior.

Such a belief about a man—specifically about Stalin—was cultivated among us for many years.

The objective of the present report is not a thorough evaluation of Stalin's life and work. Concerning Stalin's merits, an entirely sufficient number of books, pamphlets and studies had already been written in his lifetime. Stalin's role in the preparation and execution of the socialist revolution, in the Civil War, and in the fight for the construction of socialism in our country is universally known. Everyone knows this well. At present we are concerned with a question which has immense importance for the Party now and in the future—[we are concerned] with how the Stalin cult gradually grew, the cult which became at a certain specific stage the source of a whole series of exceedingly serious and grave perversions of Party principles, of Party democracy, of revolutionary legality.

Because not all as yet realize fully the practical consequences re-

* The Soviet official stenographic account of the proceedings of the 20th Congress of the Soviet Communist Party reported that Khrushchev delivered a speech to a closed session of the congress on the Stalin cult on Feb. 25, 1956. The Soviet press to date has never published the text of this report. However, this version of it in English translation (with a few minor stylistic changes) was released on June 4, 1956, by the U. S. State Department with the comment that it is a text prepared for the guidance of the leadership of a Communist Party outside the U.S.S.R.

sulting from the cult of the individual leader, the great harm caused by the violation of the principle of collective direction of the Party, and because immense and limitless power was gathered in the hands of one person, the Party Central Committee considers it absolutely necessary to make the material pertaining to this matter available to the 20th Congress of the Communist Party of the Soviet Union.

Allow me first of all to remind you how severely the founders of Marxism-Leninism denounced every manifestation of the cult of the individual leader. In a letter to the German political worker Wilhelm Bloss, Marx stated: "Because of my antipathy to any cult of the individual, I never made public during the existence of the International the numerous addresses from various countries which recognized my merits, and which annoyed me. I did not even reply to them, except sometimes to rebuke their authors. Engels and I first joined the secret society of Communists on the condition that everything making for superstitious worship of authority would be deleted from its statutes. [Ferdinand] Lassalle subsequently did quite the opposite."

Some time later Engels wrote: "Both Marx and I have always been against any public manifestation with regard to individuals, with the exception of cases when it had an important purpose; and we most strongly opposed such manifestations as during our lifetime concerned us personally."

The great modesty of the genius of the revolution, Vladimir Ilyich Lenin, is known. Lenin had always stressed the role of the people as the creator of history, the directing and organizing role of the Party as a living and creative organism, and also the role of the Central Committee.

Marxism does not negate the role of the leaders of the working class in directing the revolutionary liberation movement.

While ascribing great importance to the role of the leaders and organizers of the masses, Lenin at the same time mercilessly stigmatized every manifestation of the cult of the individual leader, inexorably combated "hero-and-the-crowd" views—views alien to Marxism—and countered all efforts to oppose a "hero" to the masses and to the people.

Lenin taught that the Party's strength depends on its indissoluble unity with the masses, on the fact that the people—the workers, peasants and intelligentsia—follow the Party. "Only he will win and retain power," said Lenin, "who believes in the people, who submerges himself in the fountain of the people's living creativeness."

Lenin spoke with pride of the Bolshevist Communist Party as the leader and teacher of the people; he called for submitting all major questions to the opinion of knowledgeable workers, to the opinion of their party; he said: "We believe in it, we see in it the wisdom, the honor, and the conscience of our epoch."

Lenin resolutely stood against every attempt aimed at minimizing or weakening the directing role of the Party in the structure of the Soviet state. He worked out Bolshevist principles of Party direction and norms of Party life, stressing that the guiding principle of Party leadership is its collegiality. As early as in the prerevolutionary years Lenin called the Party Central Committee a collective of leaders and the guardian and interpreter of Party principles. "During the period between Congresses," pointed out Lenin, "the Central Committee guards and interprets the principles of the Party."

Emphasizing the role of the Party Central Committee and its authority, Vladimir Ilyich pointed out: "Our Central Committee constituted itself as a closely centralized and highly authoritative group . . ."

During Lenin's life the Party Central Committee was a real expression of collective leadership of the Party and the country. Being a militant Marxist revolutionist, always unyielding in matters of principle, Lenin never imposed by force his views upon his co-workers. He tried to persuade; he patiently explained his opinions to others. Lenin always diligently saw to it that the norms of Party life were realized, that the Party Statutes were enforced, that the Party Congresses and Central Committee plenary sessions took place at the proper intervals.

In addition to V. I. Lenin's great accomplishments for the victory of the working class and working peasants, for the victory of our party and for the application of the ideas of scientific communism to life, his keen mind expressed itself also in that he detected in Stalin in time those negative characteristics which resulted later in grave consequences. Fearing the future destiny of the Party and of the Soviet country, V. I. Lenin gave a quite correct characterization of Stalin, pointing out that it was necessary to consider the question of transferring Stalin from the position of Secretary-General because Stalin was excessively rude, did not have a proper attitude toward his comrades, was capricious and abused his power.

In December 1922, in a letter to the Party Congress Vladimir Ilyich wrote: "Having become Secretary-General, Comrade Stalin has acquired immeasurable power in his hands, and I am not sure that he will always know how to use this power with sufficient caution."

This letter, a political document of tremendous importance, known in Party history as Lenin's "testament," has been distributed among the delegates to the 20th Party Congress. You have read it, and will undoubtedly read it again more than once. You might reflect on Lenin's plain words, in which expression is given to Vladimir Ilyich's anxiety concerning the Party, the people, the state and the future direction of Party policy.

Vladimir Ilyich said: "Stalin is too rude, and this failing, which is quite tolerable in our midst and in relations among us Communists, becomes intolerable in the office of Secretary-General. Therefore, I propose to the Comrades that they think of a way of removing Stalin from this post and appointing to it another person who in all other respects differs from Comrade Stalin in one advantage alone, namely, that he be more tolerant, more loyal, more courteous and more considerate to comrades, less capricious, etc."

This document of Lenin's was made known to the delegates to the 13th Party Congress, who discussed the question of transferring Stalin from the position of Secretary-General. The delegates declared themselves in favor of retaining Stalin in this post, hoping that he would heed Vladimir Ilyich's critical remarks and would be able to overcome the defects which caused Lenin serious anxiety.

Comrades! The Party Congress should become acquainted with two new documents, which confirm Stalin's character as already outlined by Vladimir Ilyich Lenin in his "testament." These documents are a letter from Nadezhda Konstantinovna Krupskaya [Lenin's wife] to [Lev Borisovich] Kamenev, who was at that time head of the Political Bureau, and a personal letter from Vladimir Ilyich Lenin to Stalin.

I will now read these documents:

"Lev Borisovich! Because of a short letter which I had written in words dictated to me by Vladimir Ilyich by permission of the doctors, Stalin allowed himself yesterday an unusually rude outburst directed at me. This is not my first day in the Party. During all these 30 years I have never heard from any Comrade one word of rudeness. The cause of the Party and of Ilyich is not less dear to me than to Stalin. At present I need maximum self-control. I know better than any doctor what one can and what one cannot discuss with Ilyich, because I know what disturbs him and what does not; in any case, I know better than Stalin. I am turning to you and to Grigori [Zinoviev], as much closer comrades of V.I., and I beg you to protect me from rude interference with my private life and from vile invective and threats. I have no doubt as to what will be the unanimous decision of the Control Commission, with which Stalin sees fit to threaten me; however, I have neither the strength nor the time to waste on this foolish quarrel. And I am a living person and my nerves are strained to the utmost.—N. KRUPSKAYA."

Nadezhda Konstantinovna wrote this letter on Dec. 23, 1922. Two and a half months later, in March, 1923, Vladimir Ilyich Lenin sent Stalin the following letter:

"To Comrade Stalin.

"Copies to: Kamenev and Zinoviev.

"Dear Comrade Stalin! You permitted yourself a rude summons of my wife to the telephone and a rude reprimand of her. Despite the fact that she told you that she agreed to forget what was said, nevertheless Zinoviev and Kamenev heard about it from her. I have no intention to forget so easily what is being done against me, and I need not stress here that I consider as directed against me what is being done against my wife. I ask you, therefore, to weigh carefully whether you are agreeable to retracting your words and apologizing or whether you prefer the severance of relations between us." (*Stir in the hall.*) "Sincerely, LENIN—March 5, 1923."

Comrades! I shall not comment on these documents. They speak eloquently for themselves. Since Stalin could behave in this manner during Lenin's life, could thus behave toward Nadezhda Konstantinovna Krupskaya, whom the Party knows well and values highly as a loyal friend of Lenin and as an active fighter for the cause of the Party since its creation, we can easily imagine how Stalin treated other people. These negative characteristics of his developed steadily and during the last years acquired an absolutely insufferable character.

As later events proved, Lenin's anxiety was justified: In the first period after Lenin's death Stalin still paid attention to his [Lenin's] advice, but later he began to disregard the serious admonitions of Vladimir Ilyich.

When we analyze Stalin's practice in directing the Party and the country, when we pause to consider everything Stalin perpetrated, we must be convinced that Lenin's fears were justified. Stalin's negative characteristics, which in Lenin's time were only incipient, turned during the last years into grave abuse of power by Stalin, which caused untold harm to our party.

We have to consider this matter seriously and analyze it correctly in order that we may preclude any possibility of a repetition, in any form whatever, of what took place during the life of Stalin, who absolutely did not tolerate collegiality in leadership and in work and who practiced brutal violence not only toward everything which opposed him, but also toward what seemed, to his capricious and despotic character, contrary to his concepts.

Stalin acted not through persuasion, explanation and patient cooperation with people, but by imposing his concepts and demanding absolute submission to his opinion. Whoever opposed this concept or tried to prove his viewpoint and the correctness of his position was doomed to removal from the leading collective and to subsequent moral and physical annihilation. This was especially true during the period following the 17th Party Congress, when many prominent Party leaders and rank-and-file Party workers, honest and dedicated to the cause of communism, fell victim to Stalin's despotism.

We must affirm that the Party fought a serious fight against the Trotskyites, rightists and bourgeois nationalists, and that it disarmed ideologically all the enemies of Leninism. This ideological fight was carried on successfully, and as a result the Party was strengthened and tempered. Here Stalin played a positive role.

The Party led a great political ideological struggle against those in its own ranks who proposed anti-Leninist theses, who represented a political line hostile to the Party and to the cause of socialism. This was a stubborn and a difficult fight but a necessary one, because the political line of both the Trotskyite-Zinovievite bloc and of the Bukharinites led actually toward the restoration of capitalism and capitulation to the world bourgeoisie. Let us consider for a moment what would have happened if in 1928–1929 the political line of right deviation had prevailed among us, or orientation toward "cotton-dress industrialization," or toward the kulak, etc. We would not now have a powerful heavy industry, we would not have the collective farms, we would find ourselves disarmed and weak in a capitalist encirclement.

It was for this reason that the Party led an inexorable ideological fight and explained to all Party members and to the non-Party masses the harm and the danger of the anti-Leninist proposals of the Trotskyite opposition and the rightist opportunists. And this great work of explaining the Party line bore fruit; both the Trotskyites and the rightist opportunists were politically isolated; the overwhelming Party majority supported the Leninist line and the Party was able to awaken and organize the working masses to apply the Leninist Party line and to build socialism.

Worth noting is the fact that even during the progress of the furious ideological fight against the Trotskyites, the Zinovievites, the Bukharinites and others, extreme repressive measures were not used against them. The fight was on ideological grounds. But some years later, when socialism in our country had been fundamentally established, when the exploiting classes had been generally liquidated, when the Soviet social structure had radically changed, when the social base for political movements and groups hostile to the Party had shrunk sharply, when the ideological opponents of the Party had long since been defeated politically, then the repression directed against them began.

It was precisely during this period (1935–1937–1938) that the practice of mass repression through the state apparatus was born, first against the enemies of Leninism—Trotskyites, Zinovievites, Bukharinites, long since politically defeated by the Party—and subsequently also against many honest Communists, against those Party cadres which had borne the heavy burden of the Civil War and the first and most difficult years of industrialization and collectivization, which had fought actively against the Trotskyites and the rightists for the Leninist party line.

Stalin originated the concept "enemy of the people." This term automatically rendered it unnecessary that the ideological errors of a man or men engaged in a controversy be proved; this term made possible the use of the most cruel repression, violating all norms of revolutionary legality, against anyone who in any way disagreed with Stalin, against those who were only suspected of hostile intent, against those who had bad reputations. This concept, "enemy of the people," actually eliminated the possibility of any kind of ideological fight or the making of one's views known on this or that issue, even issues of a practical nature. In the main, and in actuality, the only proof of guilt used, contrary to all norms of current law, was the "confession" of the accused himself; and, as subsequent investigation has proved, "confessions" were obtained through physical pressures against the accused.

This led to glaring violations of revolutionary legality, and to the fact that many entirely innocent persons, who in the past had defended the Party line, became victims.

We must assert that, in regard to those persons who in their time had opposed the Party line, there were often no sufficiently serious reasons for their physical annihilation. The formula "enemy of the people" was specifically introduced for the purpose of physically annihilating such individuals.

It is a fact that many persons who were later annihilated as enemies of the Party and people had worked with Lenin during his life. Some of these persons had made mistakes during Lenin's life, but, despite this, Lenin benefited by their work, he corrected them and he did everything possible to retain them in the ranks of the Party; he induced them to follow him.

In this connection the delegates to the Party Congress should familiarize themselves with an unpublished note by V. I. Lenin directed to the Central Committee's Political Bureau in October 1920. Outlining the duties of the Control Commission, Lenin wrote that the commission should be transformed into a real "organ of Party and proletarian conscience."

"As a special duty of the Control Commission there is recommended a deep, individualized relationship with and sometimes even a type of therapy for the representatives of the so-called opposition—those who have experienced a psychological crisis because of failure in their Soviet or Party career. An effort should be made to quiet them, to explain the matter to them in a way used among Comrades, to find for them (avoiding the method of issuing orders) a task for which they are psychologically fitted. Advice and rules relating to this matter are to be formulated by the Central Committee's Organizational Bureau, etc."

Everyone knows how irreconcilable Lenin was with the ideological enemies of Marxism, with those who deviated from the correct Party line. At the same time, however, Lenin, as is evident from the given document, in his practice of directing the Party demanded the most intimate Party contact with people who had shown indecision or temporary nonconformity with the Party line, but whom it was possible to return to the Party path. Lenin advised that such people should be patiently educated without the application of extreme methods.

Lenin's wisdom in dealing with people was evident in his work with cadres.

An entirely different relationship with people characterized Stalin. Lenin's traits—patient work with people; stubborn and painstaking education of them; the ability to induce people to follow him without using compulsion, but rather through the ideological influence on them of the whole collective—were entirely foreign to Stalin. He [Stalin] discarded the Leninist method of persuading and educating; he abandoned the method of ideological struggle for that of administrative violence, mass repressions and terror. He acted on an increasingly larger scale and more stubbornly through punitive organs, at the same time often violating all existing standards of morality and of Soviet law.

Arbitrary behavior by one person encouraged and permitted arbitrariness in others. Mass arrests and deportations of many thousands of people, execution without trial and without normal investigation created conditions of insecurity, fear and even desperation.

This, of course, did not contribute toward unity of the Party ranks and of all strata of the working people, but, on the contrary, brought about annihilation and the expulsion from the Party of workers who were loyal but inconvenient to Stalin.

Our party fought for the implementation of Lenin's plans for the construction of socialism. This was an ideological fight. Had Leninist principles been observed during the course of this fight, had the Party's devotion to principles been skillfully combined with a keen and solicitous concern for people, had they not been repelled and wasted, but rather drawn to our side, we certainly would not have had such a brutal violation of revolutionary legality and many thousands of people would not have fallen victim of the method of terror. Extraordinary methods would then have been resorted to only against those people who had in fact committed criminal acts against the Soviet system.

Let us recall some historical facts.

In the days before the October revolution two members of the

Central Committee of the Bolshevist party, Kamenev and Zinoviev, declared themselves against Lenin's plan for an armed uprising. In addition, on Oct. 18 they published in the Menshevist newspaper *Novaya zhizn* a statement declaring that the Bolsheviks were making preparations for an uprising and that they considered it adventuristic. Kamenev and Zinoviev thus disclosed to the enemy the Central Committee's decision to stage the uprising and that the uprising had been organized to take place within the very near future.

This was treason against the Party and against the revolution. In this connection V. I. Lenin wrote: "Kamenev and Zinoviev disclosed the decision of their party's Central Committee on the armed uprising to Rodzyanko and Kerensky. . . ." He put before the Central Committee the question of Zinoviev's and Kamenev's expulsion from the Party.

However, after the great socialist October revolution, as is known, Zinoviev and Kamenev were given leading positions. Lenin put them in positions in which they carried out most responsible Party tasks and participated actively in the work of leading Party and Soviet bodies. It is known that Zinoviev and Kamenev committed a number of other serious errors during Lenin's life. In his "testament" Lenin warned that "the October episode of Zinoviev and Kamenev was not, of course, fortuitous." But Lenin did not pose the question of their arrest and certainly not their shooting.

Or let us take the example of the Trotskyites. At present, after a sufficiently long historical period, we can speak about the fight with the Trotskyites with complete calm and can analyze this matter with sufficient objectivity. After all, around Trotsky were people whose origin cannot by any means be traced to bourgeois society. Part of them belonged to the Party intelligentsia and a certain part were recruited from among the workers. We can name many individuals who in their time joined the Trotskyites; however, these same individuals took an active part in the workers' movement before the revolution, during the socialist October revolution itself, and also in the consolidation of the victory of this greatest of revolutions. Many of them broke with Trotskyism and returned to Leninist positions Was it necessary to annihilate such people? We are deeply convinced that had Lenin lived such an extreme method would not have been used against many of them.

Such are only a few historical facts. But can it be said that Lenin did not decide to use even the most severe means against enemies of the revolution when this was actually necessary? No, no one can say this. Vladimir Ilyich demanded uncompromising dealings with the enemies of the revolution and of the working class, and when necessary resorted ruthlessly to such methods. You will recall only V. I. Lenin's fight with the Socialist Revolutionary organizers of the anti-Soviet uprising, with the counterrevolutionary kulaks in 1918 and with others, when Lenin without hesitation used the most extreme methods against the enemies. Lenin used such methods, however, only against actual class enemies and not against those who blundered, who erred, and whom it was possible to lead through ideological influence and even retain in the leadership.

Lenin used severe methods only in the most necessary cases, when the exploiting classes were still in existence and were vigorously opposing the revolution, when the struggle for survival was decidedly assuming the sharpest forms, even including a civil war.

Stalin, on the other hand, used extreme methods and mass repressions at a time when the revolution was already victorious, when the Soviet state was strengthened, when the exploiting classes were already liquidated and socialist relations were rooted solidly in all phases of national economy, when our party was politically consolidated and had strengthened itself both numerically and ideologically. It is clear that here Stalin showed in a whole series of cases his intolerance, his brutality and his abuse of power. Instead of proving his political correctness and mobilizing the masses, he often chose the path of repression and physical annihilation, not only against actual enemies, but also against individuals who had not committed any crimes against the Party and the Soviet government. Here we see no wisdom but only a demonstration of the brutal force which had once so alarmed V. I. Lenin.

Lately, especially after the unmasking of the Beria gang, the Central Committee has looked into a series of cases fabricated by this gang. This disclosed a very ugly picture of brutal willfulness connected with the incorrect behavior of Stalin. As facts prove, Stalin, using his unlimited power, allowed himself many abuses. He acted in the name of the Central Committee, not asking for the opinion of the Committee members or even of the members of the Central Committee's Political Bureau; often he did not inform them about his personal decisions concerning very important Party and government matters.

In considering the question of the cult of the individual leader, we must first of all show everyone what harm this caused to the interests of our party.

Vladimir Ilyich Lenin had always stressed the Party's role and importance in directing the socialist government of workers and peasants; he saw in this the chief precondition for successfully building socialism in our country. Pointing to the great responsibility of the Bolshevist party, as the ruling party in the Soviet state, Lenin called for the most meticulous observance of all norms of Party life; he called for the realization of the principles of collegiality in the direction of the Party and the state.

Collegiality of leadership flows from the very nature of our party, a party built on the principles of democratic centralism. "This means," said Lenin, "that all Party business is accomplished by all the Party members—directly or through representatives—who, without any exceptions, are subject to the same rules; in addition, all administrative members, all directing collegiums, all holders of Party positions are elected, are accountable for their activities and are subject to recall."

It is known that Lenin himself offered an example of the most careful observance of these principles. There was no matter so important that Lenin himself decided it without asking for advice and approval of the majority of the Central Committee members or of the members of the Central Committee's Political Bureau.

In the most difficult period for our party and our country, Lenin considered it necessary regularly to convoke Congresses, Party conferences and Central Committee plenary sessions, at which all the major questions were discussed and at which resolutions, carefully worked out by the collective of leaders, were adopted.

We can recall, for example, the year 1918, when the country was threatened by the attack of the imperialist interventionists. In this situation the Seventh Party Congress was convened in order to discuss a vitally important matter which could not be postponed—the matter of peace. In 1919, while the Civil War was raging, the Eighth Party Congress met, adopted a new Party program and decided such important matters as the relationship with the peasant masses, the organization of the Red Army, the leading role of the Party in the work of the Soviets, correction of the social composition of the Party, and other matters. In 1920 the Ninth Party Congress was convened and laid down the guiding principles pertaining to the Party's work in the sphere of economic construction. In 1921 the Tenth Party Congress accepted Lenin's New Economic Policy and the historic resolution entitled "On Party Unity."

During Lenin's lifetime, Party Congresses were convened regularly; always, when a radical turn in the development of the Party and the country took place, Lenin considered it absolutely necessary that the Party discuss at length all the basic questions of domestic and foreign policy and questions bearing on the development of the Party and the state.

It is very characteristic that Lenin addressed to the Party Congress, as the highest Party body, his last articles, letters and remarks. During the period between Congresses, the Party Central Committee, acting as the most authoritative directing collective, meticulously observed the principles of the Party and carried out its policy.

So it was during Lenin's lifetime.

Were our party's sacred Leninist principles observed after the death of Vladimir Ilyich?

During the first few years after Lenin's death Party Congresses and Central Committee plenary sessions took place more or less regularly, but later, when Stalin began increasingly to abuse his power, these principles were brutally violated. This was especially evident during the last 15 years of his life. Was it a normal situation when 13 years elapsed between the 18th and 19th Party Congresses, years during which our party and our country experienced so many important events? These events demanded categorically that the Party should have adopted decisions pertaining to the country's defense during the patriotic war [World War II] and to peacetime construction after the war. Even after the end of the war a Congress was not convened for more than seven years.

Central Committee plenary sessions were hardly ever called. Suffice it to mention that during all the years of the patriotic war not a single Central Committee plenary session took place. It is true that there was an attempt to call a Central Committee plenary session in October 1941, when Central Committee members from the whole country were called to Moscow. They waited two days for the opening of the plenary session, but in vain. Stalin did not even want to meet and to talk to the Central Committee members. This fact shows how demoralized Stalin was in the first months of the war and how haughtily and disdainfully he treated the Central Committee members.

In practice Stalin ignored the norms of Party life and trampled on the Leninist principle of collective Party leadership.

Stalin's willfulness vis-à-vis the Party and its Central Committee became fully evident after the 17th Party Congress, which took place in 1934.

Having numerous data showing brutal willfulness toward Party cadres, the Central Committee created a Party commission under the control of the Central Committee Presidium; it was charged with investigating what had made possible the mass repressions against the majority of the Central Committee's members and candidates elected at the 17th Congress of the All-Union Communist Party (Bolsheviks).

The commission has familiarized itself with a large amount of materials in the N.K.V.D. archives and with other documents and has established many facts pertaining to the fabrication of cases against Communists, to false accusations, to glaring abuses of socialist legality which resulted in the death of innocent people. It became apparent that many Party, Soviet and economic activists who were branded in 1937–1938 as "enemies" were actually never enemies, spies, wreckers, etc., but were always honest Communists; they were only so stigmatized, and often, no longer able to bear barbaric tortures, they charged themselves (at the order of the investigating judges—falsifiers) with all kinds of grave and unlikely crimes. The commission has presented to the Central Committee Presidium lengthy and documented materials pertaining to mass repressions against delegates to the 17th Party Congress and against members of the Central Committee elected at that Congress. These materials have been studied by the Central Committee Presidium.

It was determined that of the 139 members and candidates of the Party Central Committee who were elected at the 17th Congress, 98 persons, i.e., 70 per cent, were arrested and shot (mostly in 1937–1938). (*Indignation in the hall.*)

What was the composition of the delegates to the 17th Congress? It is known that 80 per cent of the voting participants in the 17th Congress joined the Party during the years of the [Bolshevist] underground before the revolution or during the Civil War; this means before 1921. By social origin the basic mass of the delegates to the Congress were workers (60 per cent of the voting members).

For this reason it was inconceivable that a Congress so composed would have elected a Central Committee, a majority of which would prove to be enemies of the Party. The only reason why 70 per cent of the Central Committee members and candidates elected at the 17th Congress were branded enemies of the Party and of the people was that honest Communists were slandered, accusations against them were fabricated, and revolutionary legality was gravely undermined.

The same fate befell not only the Central Committee members but also the majority of the delegates to the 17th Party Congress. Of 1966 delegates with either voting or advisory powers, 1108 persons were arrested on charges of counterrevolutionary crimes, i.e., decidedly more than a majority. This very fact shows how absurd, wild and contrary to common sense were the charges of counterrevolutionary crimes made, as we now see, against a majority of the participants in the 17th Party Congress. (*Indignation in the hall.*)

We should recall that the 17th Party Congress is historically known as the Congress of Victors. Delegates to the Congress were active participants in the building of our socialist state; many of them had suffered and fought for Party interests during the prerevolutionary years in the underground and at the Civil War fronts; they fought their enemies valiantly and often nervelessly looked into the face of death. How then can we believe that such people could prove to be "two-faced" and had joined the camp of the enemies of socialism during the era after the political liquidation of the Zinovievites, Trotskyites and rightists and after the great accomplishments of socialist construction?

This was the result of the abuse of power by Stalin, who began to use mass terror against the Party cadres.

What is the reason that mass repressions against activists increased more and more after the 17th Party Congress? It was because at that time Stalin had so elevated himself above the Party and above the nation that he ceased to consider either the Central Committee or the Party. While he still reckoned with the opinion of the collective before the 17th Congress, Stalin in even greater measure ceased to reckon with the views of the members of the Party's Central Committee and even the members of the Political Bureau after the complete political liquidation of the Trotskyites, Zinovievites and Bukharinites, when the Party had achieved unity as a result of that fight and socialist victories. Stalin thought that now he could decide all things alone and all he needed were statisticians; he treated all others in such a way that they could only listen to and praise him.

After the criminal murder of S. M. Kirov, mass repressions and brutal acts of violation of socialist legality began. On the evening of Dec. 1, 1934, on Stalin's initiative (without the approval of the Political Bureau—which was passed two days later, casually) the secretary of the Presidium of the Central Executive Committee, Yenukidze, signed the following directive:

1. Investigative agencies are directed to speed up the cases of those accused of the preparation or execution of acts of terror.

2. Judicial organs are directed not to hold up the execution of death sentences for crimes of this category in order to consider the possibility of pardon, because the Presidium of the U.S.S.R. Central Executive Committee does not consider it possible to accept petitions of this sort.

3. Agencies of the N.K.V.D. [Commissariat of Internal Affairs] are directed to carry out the death sentences against criminals of the above-mentioned category immediately after the passage of sentence.

This directive became the basis for mass abuses of socialist law observance. During many of the fabricated court cases the accused were charged with the "preparation" of terroristic acts; this deprived them of any possibility that their cases might be re-examined, even when they stated before the court that their "confessions" were secured by force, and when, in a convincing manner, they disproved the accusations against them.

It must be asserted that to this day the circumstances surrounding Kirov's murder hide many things which are inexplicable and mysterious and demand a most careful examination. There are reasons for the suspicion that the killer of Kirov [Leonid V.] Nikolayev, was assisted by someone from among the people whose duty it was to guard Kirov's person. A month and a half before the killing, Nikolayev was arrested on the ground of suspicious behavior, but he was released and not even searched. It is an unusually suspicious circumstance that when the Chekist assigned to protect Kirov was being brought in for interrogation, on Dec. 2, 1934, he was killed in an automobile "accident" in which no other occupants of the car were harmed. After the murder of Kirov, top functionaries of the Leningrad

N.K.V.D. were given very light sentences, but in 1937 they were shot. We can assume that they were shot in order to cover the traces of the organizers of Kirov's killing. (*Stir in the hall.*)

Mass repressions grew tremendously from the end of 1936 after a telegram from Stalin and Zhdanov, dated from Sochi Sept. 25, 1936, was addressed to Kaganovich, Molotov and other members of the Political Bureau. The content of the telegram was as follows:

"We deem it absolutely necessary and urgent that Comrade Yezhov be nominated to the post of People's Commissar for Internal Affairs. Yagoda has definitely proved himself to be incapable of unmasking the Trotskyite-Zinovievite bloc. The O.G.P.U. is four years behind in this matter. This is noted by all Party workers and by the majority of the representatives of the N.K.V.D." Strictly speaking we should stress that Stalin did not meet with and therefore could not know the opinion of Party workers.

This Stalinist formulation that the "N.K.V.D. is four years behind" in applying mass repression and that there is a necessity for "catching up" with the neglected work directly pushed the N.K.V.D. workers onto the path of mass arrests and executions.

We should state that this formulation was also forced on the February–March plenary session of the Party Central Committee in 1937. The session resolution approved it on the basis of Yezhov's report, "Lessons Ensuing From the Harmful Activity, Diversion and Espionage of the Japanese-German-Trotskyite Agents," stating:

"The Plenum of the Party Central Committee considers that all facts revealed during the investigation into the matter of an anti-Soviet Trotskyite center and of its followers in the provinces show that the People's Commissariat of Internal Affairs had fallen behind at least four years in the attempt to unmask these most inexorable enemies of the people."

The mass repressions at this time were made under the slogan of a fight against the Trotskyites. Did the Trotskyites at this time actually constitute such a danger to our party and to the Soviet state? We should recall that on the eve of the 15th Party Congress in 1927 only about 4000 votes were cast for the Trotskyite-Zinovievite opposition, while there were 724,000 for the Party line. During the ten years that passed between the 15th Party Congress and the February–March Central Committee plenary session Trotskyism was completely disarmed; many former Trotskyites had changed their former views and worked in the various sectors building socialism. It is clear that there was no basis for mass terror in the country in this situation of socialist victory.

Stalin's report at the February–March Central Committee plenary session in 1937, "Deficiencies of Party Work and Methods for the Liquidation of the Trotskyites and Other Double-Dealers," contained an attempt at theoretical justification of the mass terror policy under the pretext that class war must allegedly sharpen as we march forward toward socialism. Stalin asserted that both history and Lenin taught him this.

Actually, Lenin taught that the application of revolutionary violence is necessitated by the resistance of the exploiting classes, and this referred to the era when the exploiting classes existed and were powerful. As soon as the nation's political situation had improved, when, in January 1920, the Red Army took Rostov and thus won a most important victory over Denikin, Lenin instructed Dzherzhinsky to stop mass terror and to abolish the death penalty. Lenin justified this important political move of the Soviet state in the following manner in his report at the session of the All-Union Central Executive Committee Feb. 2, 1920:

"We were forced to use terror because of the terror practiced by the Entente, when strong world powers threw their hordes against us, without scruples over any type of conduct. We would not have lasted two days had we not been ruthless in meeting these actions of the officers and White Guards; this meant the use of terror, but this was forced upon us by the terrorist methods of the Entente.

"But as soon as we attained a decisive victory, even before the end of the war, immediately after taking Rostov, we gave up the use of the death penalty and thus proved that we intend to carry out our program in the manner that we promised. We say that the application of violence stems from the decision to crush the exploiters, the big landowners and the capitalists; as soon as this was accomplished we gave up the use of all extraordinary methods. We have proved this in practice."

Stalin deviated from these clear and plain precepts of Lenin. Stalin put the Party and the N.K.V.D. to using mass terror when the exploiting classes had been liquidated in our country and when there were no serious reasons for the use of extraordinary mass terror.

This terror was actually directed not at the remnants of the defeated exploiting classes but against honest workers of the Party and of the Soviet state; lying, slanderous and absurd accusations were made against them—accusations of "double-dealing," "espionage," "sabotage," preparation of fictitious "plots," etc.

At the February-March Central Committee plenary session in 1937 many members actually questioned the rightness of the established course regarding mass repressions under the pretext of combating "double-dealing."

Comrade Postyshev most ably expressed these doubts. He said:

"I have philosophized that the severe years of the struggle have passed; Party members who lost their backbone broke down or joined the camp of the enemy, healthy elements fought for the Party. Those were the years of industrialization and collectivization. I never thought it possible that after this severe era had passed Karpov and people like him would find themselves in the camp of the enemy." (Karpov was a worker in the Ukrainian Central Committee whom Postyshev knew well.) "And now, according to the testimony, it appears that Karpov was recruited in 1934 by the Trotskyites. I personally do not believe that in 1934 an honest Party member who had trod the long road of unrelenting fight against enemies, for the Party and for socialism, would now be in the camp of the enemies. I do not believe it. . . . I cannot imagine how it would be possible to travel with the Party during the difficult years and then, in 1934, join the Trotskyites. It is an odd thing. . . ." (*Stir in the hall.*)

Using Stalin's formulation, namely, that the closer we are to socialism, the more enemies we will have, and using the resolution of the February-March Central Committee plenary session, adopted on the basis of Yezhov's report, the provocateurs who had infiltrated the state security agencies, together with unconscionable careerists, began to protect with the Party name the mass terror against Party cadres, cadres of the Soviet state and ordinary Soviet citizens. Suffice it to say that the number of arrests based on charges of counterrevolutionary crimes grew tenfold between 1936 and 1937.

It is known that brutal willfulness was practiced against leading Party workers. The Party Statutes approved at the 17th Party Congress were based on Leninist principles expressed at the 10th Party Congress. They stated that to apply an extreme measure such as expulsion from the Party against a Central Committee member, against a Central Committee candidate, or against a member of the Party

Control Commission, "it is necessary to call a Central Committee plenary session and to invite to the plenary session all Central Committee candidate members and all members of the Party Control Committee"; only if two-thirds of the members of such a general assembly of responsible Party leaders found it necessary, only then could a Central Committee member or candidate be expelled.

The majority of the Central Committee members and candidates elected at the 17th Congress and arrested in 1937–1938 were expelled from the Party illegally through gross violation of the Party Statutes, since the question of their expulsion was never studied at a Central Committee plenary session.

Now when the cases of some of these so-called "spies" and "saboteurs" were examined it was found that all their cases were fabricated. Confessions of guilt of many arrested and charged with enemy activity were gained with the help of cruel and inhuman tortures.

At the same time Stalin, as we have been informed by members of the Political Bureau of that time, did not show them the statements of many accused political activists who retracted their confessions before the military tribunal and asked for an objective examination of their cases. There were many such declarations, and Stalin doubtless knew of them.

The Central Committee considers it absolutely necessary to inform the Congress of many such fabricated "cases" against the members of the Party Central Committee elected at the 17th Party Congress.

An example of vile provocation, of odious falsification and of criminal violation of revolutionary legality is the case of the former candidate member of the Central Committee Political Bureau, one of the most eminent workers of the Party and of the Soviet government, Comrade Robert I. Eikhe, who had been a Party member since 1905. (*Commotion in the hall.*)

Comrade Eikhe was arrested April 29, 1938, on the basis of slanderous materials, without the sanction of the Prosecutor of the U.S.S.R., which was finally received 15 months after the arrest.

Investigation of Eikhe's case was made in a manner which most brutally violated Soviet legality and was accompanied by willfulness and falsification.

Eikhe was forced under torture to sign ahead of time a protocol of his confession prepared by the investigative judges, in which he and several other eminent Party workers were accused of anti-Soviet activity.

On Oct. 1, 1939, Eikhe sent his declaration to Stalin in which he categorically denied his guilt and asked for an examination of his case. In the declaration he wrote: "There is no more bitter misery than to sit in the jail of a government for which I have always fought."

A second declaration of Eikhe has been preserved which he sent to Stalin Oct. 27, 1939; in it he cited facts very convincingly and countered the slanderous accusations made against him, arguing that this provocatory accusation was on the one hand the work of real Trotskyites whose arrests he had sanctioned as First Secretary of the West Siberian Territory Party Committee and who had conspired to take revenge on him, and, on the other hand, the result of base falsification of materials by the investigative judges. Eikhe wrote in his declaration:

". . . On Oct. 25 of this year I was informed that the investigation of my case has been concluded and I was given access to the materials of this investigation. Had I been guilty of only one-hundredth of the crimes with which I am charged, I would not have dared to send you this pre-execution declaration; however, I have not been guilty of even one of the things with which I am charged and my heart is clean of even the shadow of baseness. I have never in my life told you a word of falsehood and now, when I stand with both feet in the grave, I am also not lying. My whole case is a typical example of provocation, slander and violation of the elementary basis of revolutionary legality. . . .

"The confessions which were made part of my file are not only absurd but contain some slander of the Communist Party Central Committee and the Council of People's Commissars because correct resolutions of the Party Central Committee and of the Council of People's Commissars which were not made on my initiative or with my participation are presented as hostile acts of counterrevolutionary organizations performed at my suggestion. . . .

"I am now alluding to the most disgraceful part of my life and to my really grave guilt before the Party and you: that is, my confession of counterrevolutionary activity. . . . The case is as follows: not being able to suffer the tortures to which I was put by Ushakov and Nikolayev—and especially by the former—who utilized the knowledge that my broken ribs have not properly mended and have caused me great pain—I have been forced to accuse myself and others.

"The majority of my confession has been suggested or dictated by Ushakov, and the remainder is my reconstruction of N.K.V.D. materials from Western Siberia for which I assumed all responsibility. If some part of the story which Ushakov fabricated and which I signed did not properly hang together, I was forced to sign another variant. The same thing was done to Rukhimovich, who was at first designated as a member of the reserve network and whose name later was removed without telling me anything about it; the same was also done with the leader of the reserve network supposedly created by Bukharin in 1935. At first I wrote my name in, and then I was instructed to insert Mezhlauk. There were other similar incidents.

". . . I ask and beg you that you again examine my case and this not for the purpose of sparing me but in order to unmask the vile provocation which wound itself like a snake around many persons, in large measure through my meanness and criminal slander. I have never betrayed you or the Party. I know that I perish because of vile and mean work of the enemies of the Party and of the people, who fabricated the provocation against me."

It would appear that such an important declaration was worth an examination by the Central Committee. This, however, was not done, and the declaration was transmitted to Beria, while the terrible maltreatment of the Political Bureau Candidate, Comrade Eikhe, continued.

On Feb. 2, 1940, Eikhe was brought before the court. Here he did not confess any guilt and said as follows:

"In all the so-called confessions of mine there is not one letter written by me with the exception of my signatures under the protocols, which were forced from me. I have made my confession under pressure from the investigative judge, who from the time of my arrest tormented me. After that I began to write all this nonsense. . . . The most important thing for me is to tell the court, the Party and Stalin that I am not guilty. I have never been guilty of any conspiracy. I shall die believing in the truth of Party policy, as I have believed in it during my whole life."

Eikhe was shot Feb. 4. (*Indignation in the hall.*) It has been definitely established now that Eikhe's case was fabricated; he has been posthumously rehabilitated.

Comrade Rudzutak, candidate member of the Political Bureau, member of the Party since 1905, who spent ten years in a Tsarist hard labor camp, completely retracted in court the confession which was forced from him. The protocol of the session of the Collegium of the Supreme Military Tribunal contains the following statement by Rudzutak:

". . . The only plea which he places before the court is that the Party Central Committee be informed that there is in the N.K.V.D. an as yet not liquidated center which is craftily manufacturing cases, which forces innocent persons to confess; there is no opportunity to prove one's nonparticipation in crimes to which the confessions of various persons testify. The investigative methods are such that they force people to lie and to slander entirely innocent persons in addition to those who already stand accused. He asks the court that he be allowed to inform the Party Central Committee of all this in writing. He assures the court that he personally never had any evil designs in regard to the policy of our party because he had always agreed with the Party policy pertaining to all spheres of economic and cultural activity."

This declaration of Rudzutak was ignored, despite the fact that Rudzutak was in his time the chief of the Central Control Commission, which was called into being in accordance with Lenin's concept for the purpose of fighting for Party unity. In this manner fell the chief of this highly authoritative Party agency, a victim of brutal willfulness: he was not even called before the Central Committee's Political Bureau because Stalin did not want to talk to him. Sentence was pronounced on him in 20 minutes and he was shot. (*Indignation in the hall.*)

After careful examination of the case in 1955 it was established that the accusation against Rudzutak was false and that it was based on slanderous materials. Rudzutak has been rehabilitated posthumously.

The way in which the former N.K.V.D. workers manufactured various fictitious "anti-Soviet centers" and "blocs" with the help of provocatory methods is seen from the confession of Comrade Rozenblum, Party member since 1906, who was arrested in 1937 by the Leningrad N.K.V.D.

During the examination in 1955 of the Komarov case Rozenblum revealed the following fact: When Rozenblum was arrested in 1937 he was subjected to terrible torture, during which he was ordered to confess false information concerning himself and other persons. He was then brought to the office of Zakovsky, who offered him freedom on condition that he make before the court a false confession fabricated in 1937 by the N.K.V.D. concerning "sabotage, espionage and diversion in a terroristic center in Leningrad." (*Stir in the hall.*) With unbelievable cynicism Zakovsky told about the vile "mechanism" for the crafty creation of fabricated "anti-Soviet plots."

"In order to illustrate it to me," stated Rozenblum, "Zakovsky gave me several possible variants of the organization of this center and of its branches. After he detailed the organization to me, Zakovsky told me that the N.K.V.D. would prepare the case of this center, remarking that the trial would be public.

"Before the court were to be brought four or five members of this center: Chudov, Ugarov, Smorodin, Pozern, Shaposhnikova (Chudov's wife) and others, together with two or three members from the branches of this center. . . .

" 'The case of the Leningrad center has to be built solidly and for this reason witnesses are needed. Social origin (or course, in the past) and the Party standing of the witness will play more than a small role.

" 'You yourself,' " said Zakovsky, " 'will not need to invent anything. The N.K.V.D. will prepare for you a ready outline for every branch of the center; you will have to study it carefully and to remember well all questions and answers which the court might ask. This case will be ready in four or five months or perhaps a half year. During all this time you will be preparing yourself so that you will not compromise the investigation and yourself. Your future will depend on how the trial goes and on its results. If you begin to lie and to testify falsely, blame yourself. If you manage to endure it, you will save your head and we will feed and clothe you at the government's cost until your death.' "

This is the kind of vile thing which was then practiced. (*Stir in the hall.*)

Even more widely was falsification of cases practiced in the provinces. The N.K.V.D. headquarters of Sverdlovsk Province "discovered" the so-called "Ural uprising staff"—an organ of the bloc of rightists, Trotskyites, Socialist Revolutionaries, church leaders—whose chief supposedly was the Secretary of the Sverdlovsk Province Party Committee and member of the All-Union Communist Party

Central Committee, Kabakov, who had been a Party member since 1914. The investigative materials of that time show that in almost all territories, provinces and republics there supposedly existed "rightist Trotskyite, espionage-terror and diversionary-sabotage organizations and centers" and that the heads of such organizations as a rule—for no known reason—were first secretaries of province Party committees or republic Central Committees. (*Stir in the hall.*)

Many thousands of honest and innocent Communists have died as a result of this monstrous falsification of such "cases," as a result of the practice of forcing accusations against oneself and others. In the same manner were fabricated the "cases" against eminent Party and State workers—Kossior, Chubar, Postyshev, Kosarev, and others.

In those years repressions on a mass scale were applied which were based on nothing tangible and which resulted in heavy cadre losses to the Party.

The vicious practice was condoned of having the N.K.V.D. prepare lists of persons whose cases were under the jurisdiction of the Military Collegium and whose sentences were prepared in advance. Yezhov would send these lists to Stalin personally for his approval of the proposed punishment. In 1937–1938, 383 such lists, containing the names of many thousands of Party, Soviet, Young Communist League, army and economic workers were sent to Stalin. He approved these lists.

A large part of these cases are being reviewed now and a great part of them are being voided because they were baseless and falsified. Suffice it to say that from 1954 to the present time the Military Collegium of the Supreme Court has rehabilitated 7679 persons, many of whom were rehabilitated posthumously.

Mass arrests of Party, Soviet, economic and military workers caused tremendous harm to our country and to the cause of socialist advancement.

Mass repressions had a negative influence on the moral-political condition of the Party, created a situation of uncertainty, contributed to the spreading of unhealthy suspicion, and sowed distrust among Communists. All sorts of slanderers and careerists were active.

Resolutions of the January plenary session of the Party Central Committee in 1938 brought some measure of improvement to the Party organizations. However, widespread repression also existed in 1938.

Only because our party possesses such great moral-political strength was it possible for it to survive the difficult events in 1937–1938 and to train new cadres. There is, however, no doubt that our march forward toward socialism and toward the preparation of the country's defense would have been much more successful were it not for the tremendous loss in cadres suffered as a result of the baseless and false mass repressions in 1937–1938.

We justly accuse Yezhov of the degenerate practices of 1937. But we have to answer these questions: Could Yezhov have arrested Kossior, for instance, without the knowledge of Stalin? Was there an exchange of opinions or a Political Bureau decision concerning this? No, there was not, as there was none regarding other cases of this type. Could Yezhov have decided such important matters as the fate of such eminent Party figures? No, it would be a display of naïveté to consider this the work of Yezhov alone. It is clear that these matters were decided by Stalin, and that without his orders and his sanction Yezhov could not have done this.

We have examined the cases and have rehabilitated Kossior, Rudzutak, Postyshev, Kosarev and others. For what causes were they arrested and sentenced? The review of evidence shows that there was no reason for this. They, like many others, were arrested without the prosecutor's knowledge. In such a situation there is no need for any sanction, for what sort of sanction could there be when Stalin decided everything? He was the chief prosecutor in these cases. Stalin not only agreed to, but on his own initiative issued arrest orders. We must say this so that the delegates to the Congress can clearly understand and themselves assess this and draw the proper conclusions.

Facts prove that many abuses were committed on Stalin's orders without reckoning with any norms of Party and Soviet legality. Stalin was a very distrustful man, sickly suspicious; we knew this from our work with him. He could look at a man and say: "Why are your eyes so shifty today?" or "Why are you turning so much today and avoiding looking me directly in the eyes?" The sickly suspicion created in him a general distrust even toward eminent Party workers whom he had known for years. Everywhere and in everything he saw "enemies," "double-dealers" and "spies."

Possessing unlimited power, he indulged in great willfulness and strangled a person morally and physically. A situation was created in which one could not express one's own will.

When Stalin said that one or another should be arrested, it was necessary to accept on faith that he was an "enemy of the people." Meanwhile, Beria's gang, which ran the organs of state security, outdid itself in proving the guilt of the arrested and the truth of materials which it had falsified. And what proofs were offered? The confessions of the arrested, and the investigative judges accepted these "confessions." And how is it possible that a person confesses to crimes which he has not committed? Only in one way—because of application of physical methods of pressuring him, tortures, bringing him to a state of unconsciousness, depriving him of his judgment, taking away his human dignity. In this manner were "confessions" acquired.

When the wave of mass arrests began to recede in 1939, and the leaders of territorial Party organizations began to accuse the N.K.V.D. workers of using methods of physical pressure on the arrested, Stalin dispatched a coded telegram on Jan. 20, 1939, to the secretaries of province and territory committees and republic Central Committees of the Party, to the Peoples' Commissars of Internal Affairs and to the heads of N.K.V.D. organizations. This telegram stated:

"The Party Central Committee explains that application of methods of physical pressure in N.K.V.D. practice is permissible from 1937 on, in accordance with permission of the Party Central Committee. . . . It is known that all bourgeois intelligence services use methods of physical influence against the representatives of the socialist proletariat and that they use them in their most scandalous forms. The question arises as to why the socialist intelligence service should be more humanitarian against the mad agents of the bourgeoisie, against the deadly enemies of the working class and of the collective farm workers. The Party Central Committee considers that physical pressure should still be used obligatorily, as an exception applicable to known and obstinate enemies of the people, as a method both justifiable and appropriate."

Thus, Stalin had sanctioned in the name of the Party Central Committee the most brutal violation of socialist legality, torture and oppression, which led, as we have seen, to the slandering and self-accusation of innocent people.

Not long ago, only several days before the present Congress, we summoned to the Central Committee Presidium session and interrogated the investigative judge Rodos, who in his time investigated and interrogated Kossior, Chubar and Kosarev. He is a vile person with a bird brain, and morally completely degenerate. And it was this man who decided the fate of prominent Party workers; he made judgments also concerning the politics in these matters, because, having established their "crime," he provided therewith materials from which important political implications could be drawn.

The question arises whether a man with such an intellect could alone conduct the investigation in a manner to prove the guilt of people such as Kossior and others. No, he could not have done it without proper directives. At the Central Committee Presidium session he told us: "I was told that Kossior and Chubar were enemies of the people and for this reason I, as an investigative judge, had to make them confess that they were enemies." (*Indignation in the hall.*)

He could do this only through long tortures, which he did, receiving detailed instructions from Beria. We must say that at the Central Committee Presidium session he cynically declared: "I thought that I was executing the orders of the Party." In this manner Stalin's orders concerning the use of methods of physical pressure against the arrested were in practice executed.

These and many other facts show that all norms of correct Party solution of problems were invalidated and everything was dependent upon the willfulness of one man.

The power accumulated in the hands of one person, Stalin, led to serious consequences during the great patriotic war.

When we look at many of our novels, films and historical "scholarly studies," the role of Stalin in the patriotic war appears entirely improbable. Stalin had foreseen everything. The Soviet Army, on the basis of a strategic plan prepared by Stalin long before, used the tactics of so-called "active defense," i.e., tactics which, as we know, allowed the Germans to come up to Moscow and Stalingrad. Using such tactics, the Soviet Army, supposedly thanks only to Stalin's genius, turned to the offensive and subdued the enemy. This type of novel, film and "scholarly study" entirely ascribes to Stalin's strategic genius the epic victory gained by the armed might of the land of the Soviets, by our heroic people.

We have to analyze this matter carefully because it has a tremendous significance not only from the historical, but especially from the political, educational and practical point of view.

What are the facts of this matter?

Before the war our press and all our political-educational work was characterized by its bragging tone: when an enemy violates the sacred Soviet soil, then for each blow of the enemy we will answer with three blows and we will battle the enemy on his own soil and we will win without much harm to ourselves. But these positive statements were not based in all areas on concrete facts, which would actually have guaranteed the immunity of our borders.

During the war and after the war Stalin put forward the thesis that the tragedy which our nation experienced in the first part of the war was the result of the "unexpected" attack of the Germans against the Soviet Union. But, comrades, this is completely untrue. As soon as Hitler came to power in Germany he undertook the task of liquidating communism. The fascists said this openly; they did not hide their plans. To attain this aggressive end all sorts of pacts and blocs were created, such as the famous Berlin-Rome-Tokyo Axis. Many facts from the prewar period clearly showed that Hitler was going all out to begin a war against the Soviet state and that he had concentrated large armed units, together with armored units, near the Soviet borders.

Documents which have now been published show that by April 3, 1941, Churchill, through his Ambassador to the U.S.S.R., Cripps, personally warned Stalin that the Germans had begun regrouping their armed units with the intent of attacking the Soviet Union. It is self-evident that Churchill did not do this at all because of his friendly feeling toward the Soviet nation. He had in this his own imperialist goals—to bring Germany and the U.S.S.R. into a bloody war and thereby to strengthen the position of the British Empire. Just the same, Churchill affirmed in his writings that he sought to "warn Stalin and call his attention to the danger which threatened him." Churchill stressed this repeatedly in his dispatches of April 18 and in the following days. However, Stalin took no heed of these warnings. What is more, Stalin ordered that no credence be given to information of this sort, in order not to provoke the initiation of military operations.

We must state that information of this sort concerning the threat of German armed invasion of Soviet territory came in also from our own military and diplomatic sources; however, because the leadership was conditioned against such information, such data were dispatched with fear and assessed with reservation.

Thus, for instance, information sent from Berlin May 6, 1941, by the Soviet military attaché, Capt. Vorontsov, stated: "Soviet citizen Bozer . . . communicated to the assistant naval attaché that according to a statement of a certain German officer from Hitler's headquarters, Germany is preparing to invade the U.S.S.R. May 14 through Finland, the Baltic countries and Latvia. At the same time Moscow and Leningrad will be heavily raided and paratroopers landed in border cities. . . ."

In his report of May 22, 1941, the assistant military attaché in Berlin, Khlopov, communicated that ". . . the attack of the German Army is reportedly scheduled for June 15, but it is possible that it may begin in the first days of June. . . ."

A cable from our London Embassy dated June 18, 1941, stated: "As of now Cripps is deeply convinced of the inevitability of armed conflict between Germany and the U.S.S.R. which will begin not later than the middle of June. According to Cripps, the Germans have presently concentrated 147 divisions (including air force and service units) along the Soviet borders. . . ."

Despite these particularly grave warnings, the necessary steps were not taken to prepare the country properly for defense and to prevent it from being caught unawares.

Did we have time and the capabilities for such preparations? Yes, we had the time and capabilities. Our industry was already so developed that it was capable of fully supplying the Soviet Army with everything it needed. This is proved by the fact that although during the war we lost almost half of our industry and important industrial and food production areas as the result of enemy occupation of the Ukraine, North Caucasus and other western parts of the country, the Soviet people were still able to organize the production of military equipment in the eastern parts of the country, install there equipment taken from the western industrial areas, and supply our armed forces with everything necessary to destroy the enemy.

Had our industry been mobilized properly and in time to supply the army with the necessary materiel, our wartime losses would have been decidedly smaller. Such mobilization had not been, however, started in time. And already in the first days of the war it became evident that our army was badly armed, that we did not have enough artillery, tanks and planes to throw the enemy back.

Soviet science and technology produced excellent models of tanks and artillery pieces before the war. But mass production of all this was not organized and as a matter of fact we started to modernize our military equipment only on the eve of the war. As a result, at the time of the enemy's invasion of the Soviet land we did not have sufficient quantities either of old machinery which was no longer used for armament production or of new machinery which we had planned to introduce into armament production. The situation with antiaircraft artillery was especially bad; we did not organize the production of antitank ammunition. Many fortified regions had proved to be indefensible as soon as they were attacked because the old arms had been withdrawn and new ones were not yet available there.

This pertained, alas, not only to tanks, artillery and planes. At the outbreak of the war we did not even have sufficient rifles to arm the mobilized manpower. I recall that in those days I telephoned to Comrade Malenkov from Kiev and told him, "People have volunteered for the new army and demand arms. You must send us arms."

Malenkov answered me, "We cannot send you arms. We are sending all our rifles to Leningrad, and you will have to arm yourselves." (*Stir in the hall.*)

Such was the armament situation.

In this connection we cannot forget, for instance, the following fact. Shortly before the invasion of the Soviet Union by the Hitlerite army, Kirponos, who was Chief of the Kiev Special Military District (he was later killed at the front), wrote to Stalin that the German armies were at the Bug River, were preparing for an attack and in the very near future would probably start their offensive. In this connection Kirponos proposed that a strong defense be organized, that 300,000 persons be evacuated from the border areas, and that several strong points be organized there: antitank ditches, trenches for the soldiers, etc.

Moscow answered this proposition with the assertion that this would be a provocation, that no preparatory defensive work should be undertaken at the borders, that the Germans were not to be given any pretext for the initiation of military action against us. Thus, our borders were insufficiently prepared to repel the enemy.

When the fascist armies had actually invaded Soviet territory and military operations began, Moscow issued the order that the German fire was not to be returned. Why? Because Stalin, despite evident facts, thought that the war had not yet started, that this was only a provocative action on the part of several undisciplined sections of the German Army, and that our reaction might serve as a reason for the Germans to begin the war.

The following fact is also known. On the eve of the invasion of the territory of the Soviet Union by the Hitlerite army, a certain German citizen crossed our border and stated that the German armies had received orders to start the offensive against the Soviet Union on the night of June 22, at 3 o'clock. Stalin was informed about this immediately, but even this warning was ignored.

As you see, everything was ignored; warnings of certain army commanders, declarations of deserters from the enemy army, and even the open hostility of the enemy. Is this an example of alertness of the head of the Party and chief of state at this particularly significant historical moment?

And what were the results of this carefree attitude, this disregard of clear facts? The result was that already in the first hours and days the enemy destroyed in our border regions a large part of our air force, artillery and other military equipment; he annihilated large numbers of our military cadres and disorganized our military leadership; consequently, we could not prevent the enemy from marching deep into the country.

Very grievous consequences, especially in reference to the beginning of the war, ensued from Stalin's annihilation of many military commanders and political workers in 1937–1941 because of his suspiciousness and through slanderous accusations. During these years repressions were instituted against certain parts of the military cadres, beginning literally at the company and battalion commander level and extending to the higher military centers; during this time the cadre of leaders who had gained military experience in Spain and in the Far East was almost completely liquidated.

The policy of large-scale repressions against the military cadres led also to undermined military discipline, because for several years officers of all ranks and even soldiers in the Party and Young Communist League cells were taught to "unmask" their superiors as hidden enemies. (*Stir in the hall.*) It is natural that this caused a negative influence on the state of military discipline in the first war period.

And, as you know, we had before the war excellent military cadres which were unquestionably loyal to the Party and to the fatherland. Suffice it to say that those of them who managed to survive despite the severe tortures to which they were subjected in the prisons showed themselves real patriots from the first war days and fought heroically for the glory of the fatherland. I have here in mind such comrades as Rokossovsky (who as you know, had been jailed), Gorbatov, Meretskov (who is a delegate to the present Congress), Podlas (he was an excellent commander who perished at the front) and many, many others. However, many such commanders perished in camps and jails, and the army saw them no more.

All this brought about the situation that existed at the beginning of the war and which was a great threat to our fatherland.

It would be incorrect to forget that after the first severe disaster and defeats at the front Stalin thought that this was the end. In one of his speeches in those days he said: "All that Lenin created we have lost forever."

After this, Stalin for a long time actually did not direct the military operations and ceased to do anything whatever. He returned to active leadership only when some members of the Political Bureau visited him and told him that it was necessary to take certain steps immediately in order to improve the situation at the front.

Therefore, the threatening danger which hung over our fatherland in the first period of the war was largely due to the faulty methods of directing the nation and the Party by Stalin himself.

However, we speak not only about the moment when the war began, which led to serious disorganization of our army and brought us severe losses. Even after the war began, the nervousness and hysteria which Stalin demonstrated, interfering with actual military operations, caused our army serious damage.

Stalin was very far from an understanding of the real situation that was developing at the front. That was natural because during the whole patriotic war he never visited any section of the front or any liberated city except for one short ride on the Mozhaisk Highway during a stabilized situation at the front. To this incident were dedicated many literary works full of fantasies of all sorts, and many paintings. Simultaneously, Stalin was interfering with operations and issuing orders that did not take into consideration the real situation at a given section of the front and which could not help but result in huge personnel losses.

I will allow myself in this connection to bring out one characteristic fact that illustrates how Stalin directed operations at the fronts. There is present at this Congress Marshal Bagramyan, who was once the Chief of Operations in the Headquarters of the Southwestern Front and who can corroborate what I will tell you.

When there developed an exceptionally serious situation for our army in the Kharkov region in 1942, we correctly decided to drop an operation whose objective was to encircle Kharkov, because the actual situation at that time would have threatened our army with fatal consequences if this operation were continued.

We communicated this to Stalin, stating that the situation demanded changes in operational plans so that the enemy would be prevented from liquidating a sizable concentration of our army.

Contrary to common sense, Stalin rejected our suggestion and issued the order to continue the operation aimed at the encirclement of Kharkov, despite the fact that at this time many army concentrations were themselves actually threatened with encirclement and liquidation.

I telephoned to Vasilevsky and begged him, "Alexander Mikhailovich, take a map" (Vasilevsky is present here) "and show Comrade Stalin the situation which has developed." We should note that Stalin planned operations on a globe. (*Animation in the hall.*) Yes, comrades, he used to take the globe and trace the front line on it. I said to Comrade Vasilevsky: "Show him the situation on a map; in the present situation we cannot continue the operation which was planned. The old decision must be changed for the good of the cause."

Vasilevsky replied that Stalin had already studied this problem and that he, Vasilevsky, would not see Stalin further concerning this matter because the latter did not want to hear any arguments on the subject of this operation.

After my talk with Vasilevsky I telephoned to Stalin at his villa. But Stalin did not answer the telephone and Malenkov was at the receiver. I told Comrade Malenkov that I was calling from the front and that I wanted to speak personally to Stalin. Stalin informed me through Malenkov that I should speak with Malenkov. I stated for the second time that I wished to inform Stalin personally about the grave situation which had arisen for us at the front. But Stalin did not consider it convenient to raise the phone and again stated that I should speak to him through Malenkov, although he was only a few steps from the telephone.

After "listening" in this manner to our plea, Stalin said, "Let everything remain as it is!"

And what was the result of this? The worst that we had expected. The Germans surrounded our army concentrations, and consequently we lost hundreds of thousands of our soldiers. This is Stalin's military "genius"; this is what it cost us. (*Stir in the hall.*)

On one occasion after the war, during a meeting of Stalin with members of the Political Bureau, Anastas Ivanovich Mikoyan mentioned that Khrushchev must have been right when he telephoned concerning the Kharkov operation and that it was unfortunate that his suggestion had not been accepted.

You should have seen Stalin's fury! How could it be admitted that he, Stalin, had not been right! He is, after all, a "genius," and a genius cannot help but be right! Everyone can err, but Stalin considered that he never erred, that he was always right. He never acknowledged to anyone that he made any mistake, large or small, despite the fact that he made not a few mistakes both in the matter of theory and in his practical activity. After the Party Congress we shall probably have to re-evaluate many wartime military operations and to present them in their true light.

The tactics on which Stalin insisted without knowing the essence of the conduct of battle operations cost us much blood until we succeeded in stopping the opponent and going over to the offensive.

The military know that as early as the end of 1941, instead of great operational maneuvers flanking the opponent and penetrating behind his back, Stalin demanded incessant frontal attacks and the capture of one village after another. Because of this we paid with great losses until our generals, on whose shoulders rested the whole weight of conducting the war, succeeded in changing the situation and shifting to flexible maneuver operations, which immediately brought substantial changes in our favor at the front.

All the more shameful was the fact that after our great victory over the enemy, which cost us so much, Stalin began to downgrade many of the commanders who had contributed so much to the victory over the enemy, because Stalin excluded every possibility that services rendered at the front should be credited to anyone but himself.

Stalin was very much interested in the assessment of Comrade Zhukov as a military leader. He asked me often for my opinion of Zhukov. I told him then, "I have known Zhukov for a long time; he is a good general and a good military leader."

After the war Stalin began to relate all kinds of nonsense about Zhukov, among other things the following: "You praised Zhukov, but he does not deserve it. It is said that before each operation at the front Zhukov used to behave as follows: He used to take a handful of earth, smell it and say, 'We can begin the attack,' or the opposite, 'The planned operation cannot be carried out.' " I stated at that time, "Comrade Stalin, I do not know who invented this, but it is not true."

It is possible that Stalin himself invented these things for the purpose of minimizing the role and military talents of Marshal Zhukov.

In this connection Stalin very energetically popularized himself as a great leader; in various ways he tried to implant among the people the fiction that all victories gained by the Soviet people during the great patriotic war were due to the courage, daring and genius of Stalin and of no one else. Exactly like Kuzma Kryuchkov [a famous Cossack who performed heroic feats against the Germans], he put one dress on seven persons at the same time. (*Animation in the hall.*)

A propos of this, let us take, for instance, our historical and military films and some literary works; they make us feel sick. Their true objective is propagation of praise for Stalin as a military genius. Let us recall the film "The Fall of Berlin." Here Stalin alone acts; he issues orders in a hall in which there are many empty chairs, and only one man approaches him and reports something to him—that is Poskrebyshev, his loyal shield-bearer. (*Laughter in the hall.*)

But where is the military command? Where is the Political Bureau? Where is the government? What are they doing, with what are they occupied? There is nothing about them in the film. Stalin acts for everybody; he does not reckon with anyone; he asks no one for advice. Everything is shown to the people in this false light. Why? In order to surround Stalin with glory, contrary to the facts and contrary to historical truth.

The question arises: And where are the military on whose shoulders rested the burden of the war? They are not in the film; with Stalin in, no room was left for them.

Not Stalin, but the Party as a whole, the Soviet government, our heroic army, its talented leaders and brave soldiers, the whole Soviet people—these are the ones who assured the victory in the great patriotic war. (*Stormy and prolonged applause.*)

The Central Committee members, Ministers, our economic leaders, leaders of Soviet culture, directors of territorial Party and Soviet organizations, engineers and technicians—every one of them in his own post gave generously of his strength and knowledge toward ensuring victory over the enemy.

Our hard core showed exceptional heroism; surrounded by glory are our whole working class, our collective farm peasantry and the Soviet intelligentsia, who under the leadership of Party organizations overcame untold difficulties and, bearing the hardships of war, devoted all their efforts to the cause of defending the fatherland.

Great and brave deeds were accomplished during the war by our Soviet women, who bore on their backs the heavy load of production work in the factories, on the collective farms and on various economic and cultural sectors; many women participated directly in the great patriotic war at the fronts; our brave youth contributed immeasurably at the front and at home to the defense of the Soviet fatherland and the annihilation of the enemy.

Immortal are the services of the Soviet soldiers, of our commanders and political workers of all ranks; after the loss of a considerable part of the army in the first war months, they did not lose their heads and were able to reorganize in the course of combat; in the course of the war they created and toughened a strong and heroic army, and not only withstood the strong and cunning enemy, but crushed him.

The magnificent and heroic deeds of hundreds of millions of people of the East and of the West during the fight against the menace of fascist subjugation which loomed before us will live centuries and millennia in the memory of thankful humanity. (*Stormy applause.*)

The main role and the main credit for the victorious conclusion of the war belongs to our Communist Party, to the armed forces of the Soviet Union, and to the tens of millions of Soviet people raised by the Party. (*Stormy, prolonged applause.*)

Comrades, let us reach for some other facts. The Soviet Union is justly considered a model multinational state because we have in practice assured the equality and friendship of all the peoples who inhabit our great fatherland.

All the more monstrous are the acts, initiated by Stalin, which are gross violations of the basic Leninist principles of the nationalities policy of the Soviet state. We refer to the mass deportations from their native territory of whole nations, including all [their] Communists and Young Communists, without any exception; this deportation action was not dictated by any military considerations.

Thus, already at the end of 1943, when there occurred a permanent breakthrough on the fronts of the great patriotic war benefiting the Soviet Union, a decision was taken and carried out concerning deportation of all the Karachai from the lands on which they lived. In the same period, at the end of December 1943, the same lot befell the whole population of the Kalmyk Autonomous Republic. In March 1944, all the Chechen and Ingush people were deported and the Chechen-Ingush Autonomous Republic was liquidated. In April 1944, all Balkars were deported to faraway places from the territory of the Kabardino-Balkar Autonomous Republic and the republic itself was renamed the Kabardian Autonomous Republic. The Ukrainians avoided this fate only because there were too many of them and there was no place to which to deport them. Otherwise, he would have deported them too. (*Laughter and animation in the hall.*)

Not only no Marxist-Leninist, but also no man of common sense can grasp how it is possible to make whole nations responsible for inimical activity, including women, children, old people, Communists and Young Communists, to use mass repression against them and to expose them to misery and suffering for the hostile acts of individual persons or groups of persons.

After the conclusion of the patriotic war the Soviet people stressed with pride the magnificent victories gained through great sacrifices and tremendous efforts. The country experienced a period of political enthusiasm. The Party came out of the war even more united; Party cadres had been tempered and hardened in the fire of the war. In such conditions nobody could have even thought of the possibility of some plot in the Party.

But it was precisely at this time that the so-called "Leningrad case" was born. As we have now proved, this case was fabricated. Those who innocently lost their lives included Comrades Voznesensky, Kuznetsov, Rodionov, Popkov and others.

As is known, Voznesensky and Kuznetsov were talented and

eminent leaders. Once they stood very close to Stalin. Suffice it to mention that Stalin made Voznesensky first assistant to the Chairman of the Council of Ministers and Kuznetsov was elected Secretary of the Central Committee. The very fact that Stalin entrusted Kuznetsov with the supervision of the state security agencies shows the trust Kuznetsov enjoyed.

How did it happen that these persons were branded enemies of the people and liquidated?

Facts prove that the "Leningrad case" is also the result of willfulness which Stalin exercised against Party cadres.

Had a normal situation existed in the Party Central Committee and in the Central Committee Political Bureau, cases of this nature would have been examined there in accordance with Party practice, and all pertinent facts assessed; as a result, such a case, as well as others, would not have happened.

We must state that after the war the situation became even more complicated. Stalin became even more capricious, irritable and brutal; in particular, his suspicion grew. His persecution mania reached unbelievable dimensions. Many workers were becoming enemies before his very eyes. After the war Stalin separated himself from the collective even more. He decided everything alone, without any consideration for anyone or anything.

The arrant provocateur and vile enemy, Beria, who had murdered thousands of Communists and loyal Soviet people, cleverly took advantage of this incredible suspicion. The elevation of Voznesensky and Kuznetsov alarmed Beria. As we have now proved, it was Beria who "suggested" to Stalin the fabrication by him and by his confidants of materials in the form of declarations and anonymous letters, and in the form of various rumors and talk.

The Party Central Committee has examined this so-called "Leningrad case"; persons who suffered innocently are now rehabilitated and the glorious Leningrad Party organization has been restored to honor. Abakumov and others who fabricated this affair were brought before a court; their trial took place in Leningrad and they received their just deserts.

The question arises: Why is it that we see the truth of this case only now, and why did we not do something earlier, during Stalin's lifetime, to prevent the loss of innocent lives? It was because Stalin personally supervised the "Leningrad case," and the majority of the Political Bureau members at that time did not know all of the circumstances in these matters, and could not therefore intervene.

When Stalin received certain materials from Beria and Abakumov, without examining these slanderous materials he ordered an investigation of the "case" of Voznesensky and Kuznetsov. With this their fate was sealed.

Instructive in the same way is the case of the Mingrelian nationalist organization which supposedly existed in Georgia. As is known, decisions were adopted on this case by the Party Central Committee in November 1951 and March 1952. These decisions were made without prior discussion with the Political Bureau. Stalin had personally dictated them. They made serious accusations against many loyal Communists. On the basis of falsified documents it was shown that there existed in Georgia a supposedly nationalist organization, the objective of which was liquidation of Soviet rule in that republic with the help of imperialist powers.

In this connection, a number of responsible Party and Soviet workers were arrested in Georgia. As was later proved, this was a slander directed against the Georgian Party organization.

We know that at times there have been manifestations of local bourgeois nationalism in Georgia, as in several other republics. The question arises: Could it be possible that in the period during which the above-mentioned resolutions were adopted nationalist tendencies had grown so much that there was danger of Georgia's leaving the Soviet Union and joining Turkey? (*Stir in the hall, laughter.*)

This is, of course, nonsense. It is impossible to imagine how such assumptions could enter anyone's mind. Everyone knows how Georgia has developed economically and culturally under Soviet rule.

Industrial production in the Georgian Republic is 27 times as great as before the revolution. Many new industries have arisen in Georgia that did not exist there before the revolution: iron smelting, an oil industry, machine building, etc. Illiteracy, which in prerevolutionary Georgia embraced 78 per cent of the population, has long since been eliminated. Could the Georgians, comparing the situation in their republic with the hard situation of the working masses in Turkey, have aspired to join Turkey? In 1955 Georgia produced 18 times as much steel per capita as Turkey. Georgia produces nine times as much electric power per capita as Turkey. According to data of the 1950 census, 65 per cent of Turkey's total population is illiterate, and 80 per cent of the women. Georgia has 19 institutions of higher learning, which have about 39,000 students; this is eight times as many as in Turkey (per 1000 inhabitants). The prosperity of the working people has grown tremendously in Georgia under Soviet rule.

It is clear that as the economy and culture develop, and as the socialist consciousness of the working masses in Georgia grows, the source from which bourgeois nationalism draws its strength evaporates.

As it turned out, there was no nationalist organization in Georgia. Thousands of innocent persons fell victim to willfulness and lawlessness. All of this happened under the "inspired" leadership of Stalin, "the great son of the Georgian people," as Georgians liked to refer to Stalin. (*Stir in the hall.*)

Stalin's willfulness showed itself not only in decisions concerning the domestic life of the country but also in the international relations of the Soviet Union.

The July plenary session of the Central Committee studied in detail the reasons for the development of conflict with Yugoslavia. It was a shameful role that Stalin played there. The "Yugoslav affair" contained no problems that could not have been solved through Party discussions among comrades. There was no substantial basis for the development of this "affair," it was entirely possible to have prevented the rupture of relations with that country. This does not mean, however, that the Yugoslav leaders did not make mistakes or did not have shortcomings. But these mistakes and shortcomings were monstrously magnified by Stalin, which resulted in the breaking of relations with a friendly country.

I recall the first days when the conflict between the Soviet Union and Yugoslavia began artificially to be blown up. Once, when I came from Kiev to Moscow, I was invited to visit Stalin, who, pointing to the copy of a letter lately sent to Tito, asked me, "Have you read this?" Not waiting for my reply, he answered: "I will shake my little finger—and there will be no more Tito. He will fall."

We have paid dearly for this "shake of the little finger." This statement reflected Stalin's mania for greatness, but he acted just that way: "I will shake my little finger—and there will be no Kossior"; "I will shake my little finger once more, and Postyshev and Chubar will be no more"; "I will shake my little finger again—and Voznesensky, Kuznetsov and many others will disappear."

But this did not happen to Tito. No matter how much or how little Stalin shook not only his little finger, but everything else that he could shake, Tito did not fall. Why? The reason was that, in this case of disagreement with the Yugoslav comrades, Tito had behind him a state and a people who had gone through a severe school of fighting for liberty and independence, a people who gave support to their leaders.

You see to what Stalin's mania for greatness led. He had completely lost a sense of reality; he demonstrated his suspicion and haughtiness not only in relation to individuals in the U.S.S.R., but in relation to whole parties and nations.

We have carefully examined the case of Yugoslavia and have found a proper solution which is approved by the peoples of the Soviet Union and of Yugoslavia, as well as by the working masses of all the people's democracies and by all progressive humanity. The liquidation of the abnormal relationship with Yugoslavia was done in the interest of the whole camp of socialism, in the interest of strengthening peace in the whole world.

Let us also recall the "case of the doctor-plotters." (*Stir in the hall.*) Actually there was no "case" outside of the declaration of the woman doctor Timashuk, who was probably influenced or ordered by someone (after all, she was an unofficial collaborator of the agencies of state security) to write Stalin a letter in which she declared that the doctors were applying allegedly improper methods of medical treatment.

Such a letter was sufficient for Stalin to reach an immediate conclusion that there were doctor-plotters in the Soviet Union. He issued orders to arrest a group of eminent Soviet medical specialists. He personally issued advice on the conduct of the investigation and the method of interrogation of the arrested persons. He said Academician Vinogradov should be put in chains, another one should be beaten. Present at this Congress as a delegate is the former Minister of State Security, Comrade Ignatyev. Stalin told him curtly, "If you do not obtain confessions from the doctors we will shorten you by a head." (*Tumult in the hall.*)

Stalin personally summoned the investigative judge, gave him instructions, advised him on the investigative methods to be used; these methods were simple—beat, beat and, once again, beat.

Shortly after the doctors were arrested, we members of the Political

Bureau received transcripts of the doctors' confessions of guilt. After distributing these, Stalin told us, "You are blind as young kittens; what would happen without me? The country would perish because you do not know how to recognize enemies."

The case was so presented that no one could verify the facts on which the investigation was based. There was no possibility of trying to verify the facts by contacting those who had made the confessions of guilt.

We felt, however, that the case of the arrested doctors was questionable. We knew some of these people personally, for they had once treated us. When we examined this "case" after Stalin's death, we found it to be fabricated from beginning to end.

This ignominious "case" was set up by Stalin; he did not, however, have the time in which to bring it to a conclusion (as he conceived that conclusion), and for this reason the doctors are still alive. Now all have been rehabilitated. They are working in the same places they were working before; they treat top individuals, not excluding members of the government; they have our full confidence; and they execute their duties honestly, as they did before.

In organizing the various dirty and shameful cases, a very base role was played by the rabid enemy of our party, the agent of foreign intelligence, Beria, who had stolen into Stalin's confidence. In what way could this provocateur gain such a position in the Party and in the state as to become the First Vice-Chairman of the Council of Ministers of the Soviet Union and a member of the Central Committee's Political Bureau? It has now been established that this villain climbed up the government ladder over an untold number of corpses.

Were there any signs that Beria was an enemy of the Party? Yes, there were. As far back as in 1937, at a Central Committee plenary session, the former People's Commissar of Public Health, Kaminsky, said that Beria had worked for the Mussavat intelligence service. But the Central Committee plenary session had barely concluded before Kaminsky was arrested and then shot. Did Stalin examine Kaminsky's statement? No, because Stalin believed in Beria, and that was enough for him. And when Stalin believed in anyone or anything, then no one could say anything that was contrary to his opinion; anyone who would have dared to express opposition would have met the same fate as Kaminsky.

There were other signs also. The declaration which Comrade

Snegov made to the Party Central Committee is interesting. (Incidentally, he was also rehabilitated not long ago, after 17 years in prison camps.) In this declaration Snegov writes:

"In connection with the proposed rehabilitation of the former Central Committee member, Lavrenti Kartvelishvili, I have entrusted to the hands of the representative of the Committee on State Security a detailed deposition concerning Beria's role in the disposition of the Kartvelishvili case and concerning the criminal motives by which Beria was guided.

"In my opinion it is indispensable to recall an important fact pertaining to this case and to communicate it to the Central Committee, because I did not consider it suitable to include in the investigation documents.

"On Oct. 30, 1931, at the session of the Organizational Bureau of the All-Union Communist Party Central Committee, Kartvelishvili, Secretary of the Transcaucasus Territory Committee, delivered a report. All members of the Executive of the territory committee were present; of them I alone am alive.

"During this session J. V. Stalin made a motion at the end of his speech concerning the organization of the Secretariat of the Transcaucasus Territory Committee composed of the following: First Secretary, Kartvelishvili; Second Secretary, Beria. (This was the first time in the Party's history that Beria's name was mentioned as a candidate for a Party position.)

"Kartvelishvili answered that he knew Beria well and for that reason refused categorically to work with him. Stalin proposed then that this matter be left open and that it be settled in the process of the work itself. Two days later a decision was arrived at that Beria would receive the Party post and that Kartvelishvili would be deported from the Transcaucasus."

This fact can be confirmed by Comrades Mikoyan and Kaganovich, who were present at that session.

The long unfriendly relations between Kartvelishvili and Beria were widely known. They date back to the time when Comrade Sergo [Ordzhonikidze] was active in the Transcaucasus; Kartvelishvili was Sergo's closest assistant. The unfriendly relationship impelled Beria to fabricate a "case" against Kartvelishvili.

It is characteristic that in this "case" Kartvelishvili was charged with a terroristic act against Beria.

The indictment in the Beria case contains a discussion of his crimes. Some things should, however, be recalled, especially since it is possible that not all the delegates to the Congress have read this document. I wish to recall Beria's bestial disposition of the cases of Kedrov, Golubev, and Golubev's mother by adoption, Baturina, persons who wished to inform the Central Committee concerning Beria's treacherous activity. They were shot without any trial and the sentence was passed ex post facto, after the execution.

Here is what the old Communist, Comrade Kedrov, wrote to the Central Committee through Comrade Andreyev (Comrade Andreyev was then a Central Committee secretary):

"I am appealing to you for help from a gloomy cell of Lefortovo prison. Let my cry of horror reach your ears; do not remain deaf; take me under your protection; please help remove the nightmare of interrogations and show that this is all a mistake.

"I suffer innocently. Please believe me. Time will testify to the truth. I am not an agent-provocateur of the Tsarist Okhrana; I am not a spy; I am not a member of an anti-Soviet organization, of which I am accused on the basis of denunciations. I am also not guilty of any other crimes against the Party and the government. I am an old Bolshevik, free of any taint; I have honestly fought for almost 40 years in the ranks of the Party for the good and the prosperity of the people. . . .

"Today I, a 62-year-old man, am threatened by the investigative judges with more severe, cruel and degrading methods of physical pressure. They [the judges] are no longer capable of becoming aware of their error and of recognizing that their handling of my case is illegal and impermissible. They try to justify their actions by picturing me as a hardened and raving enemy and are demanding increased repressions. But let the Party know that I am innocent and that there is nothing which can turn a loyal son of the Party into an enemy, even right up to his last dying breath.

"But I have no way out. I cannot divert from myself the swiftly approaching new and powerful blows.

"Everything, however, has its limits. My torture has reached the extreme. My health is broken, my strength and my energy are waning, the end is drawing near. To die in a Soviet prison, branded a vile traitor to the fatherland—what can be more monstrous for an honest man? And how monstrous this is! Unsurpassed bitterness and pain grips my heart. 'No! No! This will not happen; this cannot be,' I cry. Neither the Party nor the Soviet government nor People's Commissar L. P. Beria will permit this cruel, irreparable injustice. I am firmly certain that given a calm, objective examination, without foul rantings, without anger and without the fearful tortures, it would be easy to prove the baselessness of the charges. I believe deeply that truth and justice will triumph. I believe. I believe."

The old Bolshevik, Comrade Kedrov, was found innocent by the Military Collegium. Despite this, he was shot at Beria's order. (*Indignation in the hall.*)

Beria also cruelly treated the family of Comrade Ordzhonikidze. Why? Because Ordzhonikidze had tried to prevent Beria from realizing his shameful plans. Beria had cleared from his way all persons who could possibly interfere with him. Ordzhonikidze was always an opponent of Beria, which he told Stalin. Instead of examining this matter and taking appropriate steps, Stalin permitted the liquidation of Ordzhonikidze's brother and brought Ordzhonikidze himself to such a state he was forced to shoot himself. (*Indignation in the hall.*) Such was Beria.

Beria was unmasked by the Party Central Committee shortly after Stalin's death. The particularly detailed legal proceedings established that Beria had committed monstrous crimes, and Beria was shot.

The question arises why Beria, who had liquidated tens of thousands of Party and Soviet workers, was not unmasked during Stalin's lifetime. He was not unmasked earlier because he had very skillfully utilized Stalin's weaknesses; feeding him with suspicions, he assisted Stalin in everything and acted with his support.

Comrades, the cult of the individual acquired such monstrous proportions chiefly because Stalin himself, using all conceivable methods, supported the glorification of his own person. This is confirmed by numerous facts. One of the most characteristic examples of Stalin's self-glorification and of his lack of even elementary modesty is the edition of his "Short Biography," which was published in 1948.

This book is an expression of the most dissolute flattery, an example of making a man into a godhead, of transforming him into an infallible sage, "the greatest leader," "sublime strategist of all times and nations." Finally, no other words could be found with which to exalt Stalin to the heavens.

We need not give here examples of the loathsome adulation filling this book. All we need to add is that they all were approved and edited by Stalin personally and some of them were added in his own handwriting to the draft text of the book.

What did Stalin consider essential to write into this book? Did he want to cool the ardor of his flatterers who were composing his "Short Biography"? No! He marked the very places where he thought that the praise of his services was insufficient.

Here are some examples characterizing Stalin's activity, added in Stalin's own hand:

"In this fight against the skeptics and capitulators, the Trotskyites, Zinovievites, Bukharinites and Kamenevites, there was definitely welded together, after Lenin's death, that leading core of the Party . . . that upheld the great banner of Lenin, rallied the Party behind Lenin's behests, and brought the Soviet people onto the broad road of industrializing the country and collectivizing the rural economy. The leader of this core and the guiding force of the Party and the state was Comrade Stalin."

Thus writes Stalin himself! Then he adds:

"Although he performed his task of leader of the Party and the people with consummate skill and enjoyed the unreserved support of the entire Soviet people, Stalin never allowed his work to be marred by the slightest hint of vanity, conceit or self-adulation."

Where and when could a leader so praise himself? Is this worthy of a leader of the Marxist-Leninist type? No. It was precisely against this that Marx and Engels took such a strong position. This was always sharply condemned by Vladimir Ilyich Lenin, too.

In the draft text of his book appeared the following sentence: "Stalin is the Lenin of today." This sentence appeared to Stalin to be too weak, so in his own handwriting he changed it to read: "Stalin is the worthy continuer of Lenin's work, or, as they say in our party, Stalin is the Lenin of today." You see how well it is said, not by the people, but by Stalin himself.

It is possible to give many such self-praising appraisals written into the draft text of that book in Stalin's hand. Especially generously does he endow himself with praises pertaining to his military genius, to his talent for strategy.

I will cite one more insertion made by Stalin concerning the Stalinist military genius. He writes: "The advanced Soviet science of warfare received further development at Comrade Stalin's hands. Comrade

Stalin elaborated the theory of the permanently operating factors that decide the outcome of wars, [the theory] of active defense and the laws of counteroffensive and offensive, of the cooperation of all services and arms in modern warfare, of the role of big tank masses and air forces in modern war, and of the artillery as the most formidable of the armed services. At the various stages of the war Stalin's genius found the correct solutions that took account of all the circumstances of the situation." (*Stir in the hall.*) And further, writes Stalin: "Stalin's military mastery was displayed in both defense and offense. Comrade Stalin's genius enabled him to divine the enemy's plans and defeat him. The battles in which Comrade Stalin directed the Soviet armies are brilliant examples of operational military skill."

This is how Stalin was praised as a strategist. Who did this? Stalin himself, not in his role as a strategist, but in the role of author-editor, one of the main creators of his self-adulatory biography.

Such, comrades, are the facts—the shameful facts, we should say.

And one additional fact from the same "Short Biography" of Stalin. As is known, the "History of the Communist Party of the Soviet Union (Short Course)" was written by a commission of the Party Central Committee.

This book, incidentally, was also permeated with the cult of the individual leader and was written by a designated group of authors. This fact was reflected in the following formulation in the proof copy of the "Short Biography" of Stalin:

"A commission of the Party Central Committee, under the direction of Comrade Stalin and with his most active personal participation, has prepared a 'History of the Communist Party of the Soviet Union (Short Course).'"

But even this phrase did not satisfy Stalin. The following sentence replaced it in the final version of the "Short Biography":

"In 1938 appeared the book, 'History of the Communist Party of the Soviet Union (Short Course),' written by Comrade Stalin and approved by a commission of the Party Central Committee." Can one add anything more? (*Stir in the hall.*)

As you see, a surprising metamorphosis turned a work produced by a group into a book written by Stalin. It is not necessary to state how and why this metamorphosis took place.

A pertinent question comes to mind: If Stalin is the author of this book, why did he need to praise the person of Stalin so much and to transform the whole post-October historical period of our glorious Communist Party into solely the product of "the Stalin genius"?

Did this book properly reflect the efforts of the Party in the socialist transformation of the country, in the construction of socialist society, in the industrialization and collectivization of the country, and also other steps taken by the Party in undeviatingly traveling the path outlined by Lenin? This book speaks principally about Stalin, about his speeches, about his reports. Everything without the smallest exception is tied to his name.

And when Stalin himself asserts that he himself wrote the "History of the Communist Party of the Soviet Union (Short Course)," this calls at the least for amazement. Can a Marxist-Leninist write about himself thus, praising his own person to the heavens?

Or let us take the matter of the Stalin Prizes. (*Stir in the hall.*) Not even the Tsars created prizes which they named after themselves.

Stalin recognized as the best a text of the national anthem of the Soviet Union which contains not a word about the Communist Party; it contains, however, the following unprecedented praise of Stalin: "Stalin brought us up in loyalty to the people/He inspired us to great labors and feats."

In these lines of the anthem the whole educational, directing and inspirational activity of the great Leninist party is ascribed to Stalin. This is, of course, a clear deviation from Marxism-Leninism, a clear debasing and belittling of the role of the Party. We should add for your information that the Presidium of the Central Committee has already adopted a decision concerning the composition of a new text of the anthem which will reflect the role of the people and the role of the Party. (*Loud, prolonged applause.*)

And was it without Stalin's knowledge that many of the largest enterprises and cities were named for him? Was it without his knowledge that Stalin monuments were erected throughout the country—these "memorials to the living"? It is a fact that Stalin himself, on July 2, 1951, signed a decision of the U.S.S.R. Council of Ministers concerning the erection of an impressive monument to Stalin on the Volga-Don Canal. On Sept. 4 of the same year he issued an order making 33 tons of copper available for the construction of this impressive monument. Anyone who has visited the Stalingrad area must have seen the huge statue which is being built there, and that on a site which hardly any people frequent. Huge sums were spent to build it at a time when people of this area had been living in huts since the war. Consider yourself, was Stalin right when he wrote in his biography that ". . . he never allowed . . . the slightest hint of vanity, conceit or self-adulation?"

At the same time Stalin gave proofs of his lack of respect for Lenin's memory. It is not a coincidence that, despite the decision taken more than 30 years ago to build a Palace of Soviets as a monument to Vladimir Ilyich, this Palace was not built, its construction was always postponed, and the project allowed to lapse.

We cannot fail to recall the Soviet government resolution of Aug. 14, 1925, concerning "the establishment of Lenin Prizes for educational work." This resolution was published in the press, but to this day there are no Lenin Prizes. This, too, should be corrected. (*Stormy, prolonged applause.*)

During Stalin's lifetime, thanks to known methods which I have mentioned, and quoting facts, for instance, from the "Short Biography" of Stalin, all events were explained as if Lenin played only a secondary role, even during the October socialist revolution. Many films and many literary works incorrectly presented and inadmissibly belittled Lenin.

Stalin loved to see the film, "Unforgettable 1919," in which he was shown on the steps of an armored train and where he practically vanquished the foe with his own saber. Let Kliment Yefremovich [Voroshilov], our dear friend, find the necessary courage and write the truth about Stalin; after all, he knows how Stalin fought. It will be difficult for Comrade Voroshilov to undertake this, but it would be good if he did. Everyone will approve of it, both the people and the Party. Even his grandsons will thank him. (*Prolonged applause.*)

In speaking about the events of the October revolution and the Civil War, the impression was created that Stalin always played the main role, as if everywhere and always Stalin had suggested to Lenin what to do and how to do it. But this is slander of Lenin. (*Prolonged applause.*)

I shall probably not be sinning against the truth when I say that 99 per cent of the persons here heard and knew very little about Stalin before 1924, while Lenin was known to all; he was known to the whole Party, to the whole nation, from children to graybeards. (*Stormy, prolonged applause.*)

All this has to be thoroughly revised, so that history, literature, and the fine arts properly reflect V. I. Lenin's role and the great deeds of our Communist Party and Soviet people, the creator-people. (*Applause.*)

Comrades! The cult of the individual leader caused the employment of faulty principles in Party work and in economic activity; it brought about gross violation of inner-Party and Soviet democracy, sterile administration by fiat, deviations of all sorts, covering up of shortcomings and varnishing of reality. Our country gave birth to many flatterers and specialists in false optimism and deceit.

We should also not forget that due to numerous arrests of Party, Soviet and economic leaders, many workers began to work uncertainly, showed overcautiousness, feared everything that was new, feared their own shadows and began to show less initiative in their work.

Take, for instance, Party and Soviet resolutions. They were prepared in a routine manner, often without considering the concrete situation. This went so far that Party workers read their speeches even at the smallest sessions. All this produced the danger of formalizing Party and Soviet work and of bureaucratizing the whole apparatus.

Stalin's reluctance to consider life's realities and the fact that he was not aware of the real state of affairs in the provinces can be illustrated by his direction of agriculture.

All those who interested themselves even a little in the national situation saw the difficult situation in agriculture, but Stalin never even noted it. Did we tell Stalin about this? Yes; we told him; but he did not support us. Why? Because Stalin never traveled anywhere, did not meet city and collective farm workers; he did not know the actual situation in the provinces.

He knew the countryside and agriculture only from films. And these films had dressed up and beautified the existing situation in agriculture.

Many films pictured collective farm life as if the tables bent under the weight of turkeys and geese. Evidently Stalin thought that it was actually so.

Vladimir Ilyich Lenin looked at life differently. He was always close to the people; he used to receive peasant delegates, and often spoke at factory gatherings; he used to visit villages and talk with the peasants.

Stalin cut himself off from the people and never went anywhere. This lasted tens of years. The last time he visited a village was in January 1928, when he visited Siberia in connection with grain deliveries. How then could he have known the situation in the provinces?

And when he was once told during a discussion that our situation on the land was a difficult one and that the livestock situation was especially bad, a commission was formed and charged with drafting a resolution entitled "Means Toward Further Development of Livestock Raising on Collective and State Farms." We worked out this draft.

Of course, our proposals of that time did not contain all possibilities, but we did chart ways in which livestock raising on the collective and state farms could be improved. We proposed then to raise the prices of animal products to create material incentives for the collective farmers and M.T.S. and state farm workers in the development of livestock. But our draft was not accepted and in February 1953 was laid aside entirely.

What is more, while reviewing this draft Stalin proposed that the taxes paid by the collective farms and by the collective farmers should be raised by 40,000,000,000 rubles. According to him, the peasants were well-off and the collective farmer would need to sell only one more chicken to pay his tax in full.

Imagine what this would have meant. Certainly 40,000,000,000 rubles is a sum which the collective farmers did not realize for all the products which they sold to the government. In 1952, for instance, the collective farms and the collective farmers received 26,280,000,000 rubles for all their products delivered and sold to the government.

Did Stalin's position rest, then, on data of any sort whatever? Of course not.

In such cases facts and figures did not interest him. If Stalin said anything, that meant it was so—after all, he was a "genius," and a genius does not need to count, he only needs to look and can immediately tell how it should be. When he expresses his opinion, everyone has to echo it and to admire his wisdom.

But how much wisdom was contained in the proposal to raise the agricultural tax by 40,000,000,000 rubles? None, absolutely none, because the proposal was not based on an actual assessment of the situation but on the fantastic ideas of a person divorced from reality. We are currently beginning slowly to work our way out of a difficult agricultural situation. The speeches of the delegates to the 20th Congress please us all. We are glad that many delegates speak, that there are conditions for the fulfillment of the Sixth Five-Year Plan for animal husbandry, not during the period of five years, but within two to three years. We are certain that the commitments of the new Five-Year Plan will be met successfully. (*Prolonged applause.*)

Comrades! If today we sharply criticize the cult of the individual leader which was so widespread during Stalin's lifetime and if we speak about the many negative phenomena generated by this cult which is so alien to the spirit of Marxism-Leninism, various persons may ask: How could it be? Stalin headed the Party and the country for 30 years, and many victories were gained during his lifetime. Can we deny this? In my opinion, the question can be asked in this manner only by those who are blinded and hopelessly hypnotized by the cult of the individual leader, only by those who do not understand the essence of the revolution and of the Soviet state, only by those who do not understand in a Leninist manner the role of the Party and of the people in the development of Soviet society.

The socialist revolution was accomplished by the working class and the poor peasantry, with the partial support of the middle peasants. It was accomplished by the people under the leadership of the Bolshevist party. Lenin's great service consisted in that he created a militant party of the working class; he was armed with Marxist understanding of the laws of social development and with the science of proletarian victory in the struggle with capitalism, and he steeled this party in the crucible of the revolutionary struggle of the masses of the people. During this struggle the Party consistently defended the interests of the people, became their experienced leader, and led the working masses to power, to the creation of the first socialist state.

You remember well Lenin's wise words that the Soviet state is strong because of the awareness of the masses, because history is created by the millions and tens of millions of people.

Our historic victories were attained thanks to the organizational work of the Party, to the many local organizations, and to the self-sacrificing work of our great people. These victories are the result of the great drive and activity of the people and Party as a whole; they are not at all the fruit of Stalin's leadership, as was pictured during the period of the cult of the individual leader.

If we are to consider this matter as Marxists and as Leninists, then we must state unequivocally that the leadership practice which came into being during the last years of Stalin's life became a serious obstacle in the path of the development of Soviet society.

Stalin often failed for months to take up exceedingly important problems—the solution of which could not be postponed-—concerning the life of the Party and state. During Stalin's leadership our peaceful relations with other nations were often threatened because one-man decisions could and often did cause great complications.

In the recent years when we managed to free ourselves of the harmful practice of the cult of the individual leader and took several appropriate steps in the sphere of domestic and foreign policies, everyone saw how activity grew before their very eyes, how the creative activity of the broad working masses developed, how favorably all this influenced the development of the economy and of culture. (*Applause.*)

Some comrades may ask us: Where were the members of the Political Bureau of the Central Committee? Why did they not assert themselves against the cult of the individual leader in time? Why is this being done only now?

First of all we have to consider the fact that the members of the Political Bureau viewed these matters in a different way at different times. Initially, many of them backed Stalin actively because Stalin was one of the strongest Marxists and his logic, his strength and his will greatly influenced the cadres and Party work.

It is known that Stalin, after Lenin's death, especially during the first years, fought actively for Leninism against the foes of Leninist theory and against those who deviated. Basing itself on Leninist theory, the Party, headed by its Central Committee, started on a great scale the work of socialist industrialization of the country, agricultural collectivization and the cultural revolution.

At that time Stalin gained great popularity, sympathy and support. The Party had to fight those who attempted to lead the country away from the correct Leninist path; it had to fight Trotskyites, Zinovievites and rightists, and the bourgeois nationalists. This fight was indispensable. Later, however, Stalin, abusing his power more and more, began to fight eminent Party and government leaders and to use terroristic methods against honest Soviet people. As we have already shown, Stalin thus treated such eminent Party and government leaders as Kossior, Rudzutak, Eikhe, Postyshev and many others.

Attempts to oppose groundless suspicions and charges resulted in the opponent falling victim of the repression. This characterized the fall of Comrade Postyshev.

In one of his speeches Stalin expressed his dissatisfaction with Postyshev and asked him, "What are you actually?"

Postyshev answered clearly, "I am a Bolshevik, Comrade Stalin, a Bolshevik."

This assertion was at first considered to show a lack of respect for Stalin; later it was considered a harmful act, and consequently resulted in Postyshev's annihilation and in his being branded without reason as an "enemy of the people."

In the situation which then prevailed I talked with Nikolai Alexandrovich Bulganin. Once when we two were traveling in a car, he said: "It has happened sometimes that a man goes to Stalin by invitation, as a friend. And when he sits with Stalin, he does not know where he will be sent next, home or to jail."

It is clear that such conditions put every member of the Political Bureau in a very difficult situation. And when we also consider the fact that in the last years Central Committee plenary sessions were not convened and that the sessions of the Political Bureau occurred only occasionally, from time to time, then we shall understand how difficult it was for any member of the Political Bureau to take a stand against one or another unjust or improper procedure, against serious errors and shortcomings in the practice of leadership.

As we have already shown, many decisions were taken either by one person or in a roundabout way, without collective discussions. The sad fate of Political Bureau member Comrade Voznesensky, who fell victim to Stalin's repressions, is known to all. It is characteristic that the decision to remove him from the Political Bureau was never discussed, but was reached in a devious fashion. The same is true of the decision to remove Kuznetsov and Rodionov from their posts.

The importance of the Central Committee Political Bureau was reduced and its work was disorganized by the creation within the Political Bureau of various committees—the so-called "quintets," "sextets," "septets" and "novenaries." Here is, for instance, a resolution of the Political Bureau of Oct. 3, 1946:

"Stalin's Proposal:

"1. The Political Bureau Committee for Foreign Affairs ('sextet') is to concern itself in the future, in addition to foreign affairs, with matters of internal construction and domestic policy.

"2. The sextet is to add to its roster the Chairman of the U.S.S.R.

State Economic Planning Commission, Comrade Voznesensky, and is to be known as a septet.

"Signed: Secretary of the Central Committee, J. Stalin."

What a card player's terminology! (*Laughter in the hall.*) It is clear that the creation within the Political Bureau of such committees—"quintets," "sextets," "septets" and "novenaries"—was against the principle of collective leadership. The result of this was that some members of the Political Bureau were thus kept from participation in the most important state matters.

One of the oldest members of our party, Kliment Yefremovich Voroshilov, found himself in an almost impossible situation. For several years he was actually deprived of the right of participation in Political Bureau sessions. Stalin forbade him to attend the Political Bureau sessions and to receive documents. When the Political Bureau was in session and Comrade Voroshilov heard about it, he telephoned each time and asked whether he would be allowed to attend. Sometimes Stalin permitted it, but always showed his dissatisfaction. Because of his extreme suspicion, Stalin toyed also with the absurd and ridiculous suspicion that Voroshilov was a British agent. (*Laughter in the hall.*) It's true, a British agent. A special tapping device was installed in his home to listen to what was said there. (*Indignation in the hall.*)

By unilateral decision Stalin had also cut off another man from the work of the Political Bureau—Andrei Andreyevich Andreyev. This was one of the most unbridled acts of willfulness.

Let us consider the first Central Committee plenary session after the 19th Party Congress when Stalin, in his talk at the plenary session, characterized Vyacheslav Mikhailovich Molotov and Anastas Ivanovich Mikoyan and suggested that these old workers of our party were guilty of some baseless charges. It is not excluded that, had Stalin remained at the helm for another several months, Comrades Molotov and Mikoyan would probably not have delivered any speeches at this Congress.

Stalin evidently had plans to finish off the old members of the Political Bureau. He often stated that Political Bureau members should be replaced by new ones.

His proposal after the 19th Congress concerning the selection of 25 persons to the Central Committee Presidium was aimed at removing the old Political Bureau members and bringing in less experienced persons, so that these would extol him in all sorts of ways.

We can assume that this was also a design for future annihilation of the old Political Bureau members and in this way a cover for all the shameful acts of Stalin which we are now considering.

Comrades! In order not to repeat errors of the past, the Central Committee has declared itself resolutely against the cult of the individual leader. We consider that Stalin was excessively extolled. However, in the past Stalin undoubtedly performed great services to the Party, to the working class and to the international workers' movement.

This question is complicated by the fact that all that we have just discussed was done during Stalin's life, under his leadership and with his concurrence; here Stalin was convinced that it was necessary for the defense of the interests of the working classes against the plotting of the enemies and against the attack of the imperialist camp. He saw this from the position of the interests of the working class, the interests of the working people, the interests of the victory of socialism and communism. We cannot say that these were the deeds of a giddy despot. He considered that this should be done in the interests of the Party, of the working masses, in the name of defense of the revolution's gains. In this lies the whole tragedy!

Comrades! Lenin often stressed that modesty is an absolutely integral part of a real Bolshevik. Lenin himself was the living personification of the greatest modesty. We cannot say that we have been following this Leninist example in all respects. Suffice it to point out that we have called many cities, factories and industrial enterprises, collective and state farms, Soviet institutions and cultural institutions after the private names—as if they were the private property, if I may express it so—of various government or Party leaders who were still active and in good health. Many of us participated in the act of assigning our names to various cities, districts, factories and collective farms. We must correct this. (*Applause.*)

But this should be done calmly and slowly. The Central Committee will discuss this matter and consider it carefully to prevent errors and excesses. I can remember how the Ukraine learned about Kossior's arrest. The Kiev radio used to start its programs thus: "This is the Radio Station [named for] Kossior." When one day the programs began without naming Kossior, everyone was quite certain that something had happened to Kossior, that he probably had been arrested.

Thus, if today we begin to remove the signs everywhere and to change names, people will think that the comrades in whose honor the given enterprises, collective farms or cities are named also met some bad fate and that they have also been arrested. (*Stir in the hall.*)

How is the prestige and importance of this or that leader judged? By the number of cities, industrial enterprises, factories, collective and state farms that bear his name. Is it not time we ended this "private property" and "nationalized" the factories, the industrial enterprises, the collective and state farms? (*Laughter, applause, voices: "Right."*) This will benefit our cause. After all, the cult of the individual leader is manifested also in this way.

We should consider the question of the cult of the individual leader quite seriously. We cannot let this matter get out of the Party, especially not to the press. It is for this reason that we are considering it here at a closed Congress session. We should know the limits; we should not give ammunition to the enemy; we should not wash our dirty linen before their eyes. I think that the delegates to the Congress will understand and assess all these proposals properly.

Comrades! We must resolutely abolish the cult of the individual leader once and for all; we must draw the proper conclusions concerning both ideological-theoretical and practical work.

It is necessary for this purpose:

First, in a Bolshevist manner to condemn and to eradicate the cult of the individual leader as alien to Marxism-Leninism and not consonant with the principles of Party leadership and the norms of Party life, and to fight inexorably all attempts at bringing back this practice in one form or another.

To return to and actually practice in all our ideological work the very important Marxist-Leninist theses about the people as the maker of history and the creator of all mankind's material and spiritual benefits, about the decisive role of the Marxist party in the revolutionary struggle to change society, about the victory of communism.

In this connection we shall be obliged to do much to examine critically from the Marxist-Leninist viewpoint and to correct the widespread, erroneous views connected with the cult of the individual leader in the spheres of history, philosophy, economics and other sciences, as well as in literature and the fine arts. It is especially necessary that in the immediate future we compile a serious textbook of the history of our party, edited in accordance with scientific Marxist objectivism, a textbook of the history of Soviet society, a book pertaining to the events of the Civil War and the great patriotic war.

Secondly, to continue systematically and consistently the work done by the Party Central Committee during the past years, work characterized by scrupulous observance—in all Party organizations, from bottom to top—of the Leninist principles of Party leadership; characterized above all by the main principle, collective leadership; characterized by observance of the norms of Party life described in the Statutes of our party; and, finally, characterized by wide practice of criticism and self-criticism.

Thirdly, to restore completely the Leninist principles of Soviet, socialist democracy expressed in the Constitution of the Soviet Union; to fight willfulness of individuals abusing their power. The evil caused by acts violating revolutionary socialist legality which accumulated over a long period as a result of the negative influence of the cult of the individual leader must be completely corrected.

Comrades! The 20th Congress of the Communist Party of the Soviet Union has manifested with new strength the unshakable unity of our party, its cohesiveness around the Central Committee, its resolute will to accomplish the great task of building communism. (*Stormy applause.*) And the fact that we present in all their ramifications the basic problems of overcoming the cult of the individual leader, a cult alien to Marxism-Leninism, as well as the problem of liquidating its burdensome consequences, is evidence of the great moral and political strength of our party. (*Prolonged applause.*)

We are absolutely certain that our party, armed with the historic resolutions of the 20th Congress, will lead the Soviet people along the Leninist path to new successes, to new victories. (*Stormy, prolonged applause.*)

Long live the victorious banner of our party—Leninism! (*Stormy, prolonged applause, culminating in an ovation. All rise.*)

1957:
Party Purge and the Sputniks

The year 1957 was a busy year for the Soviet Union and for Khrushchev personally. It was the year in which he carried out his program for reorganization of the Soviet economy along regional lines. It was the year in which he succeeded in ousting from the Soviet leadership all of his rivals left over from Stalin's Politburo. It was the year in which he fired Marshal Zhukov as head of the Soviet armed forces. It was the year in which the Soviet Union fired the first intercontinental ballistic missile and penetrated into space with the launching of the first two Sputniks. It was the year of the fortieth anniversary of the Bolshevik Revolution.

Plans for a far-reaching reorganization of the Soviet economy arose from a real need to decentralize the administrative machinery of rapidly growing and increasingly complex Soviet industry. From the very start of the Bolshevik regime control over Soviet industrial enterprises, no matter how far away they were from Moscow, had been kept firmly in the national capital where ministries and chief administrations of ministries overseeing activities in various branches of the economy reserved to themselves the right to decide questions, sometimes even the most minute questions, concerning their enterprises. It was one thing to operate the economy on this basis when it was poorly developed and not too large and complicated—and quite another situation when the Soviet Union had emerged by the mid-1950's as the second-ranking industrial power of the world. As industry grew there bureaucracy, red-tape, and inefficiency also grew apace. Efforts to resolve this problem by creation of ever more numerous and more highly specialized ministries, still centered in

Moscow, were not effective and only made things increasingly cumbersome. By late 1956 the Soviet government decided to consider the basic reorganization of economic administration so as to put it, for the most part, on a territorial basis in which individual regions would have a considerable measure of economic autonomy under the general over-all supervisory and planning authority of the central government in Moscow.

The plan for reorganization of the economy also, as it happened, became closely involved in the inner politics of the Soviet leadership. Such a reorganization meant the shifting and moving of thousands of important officials. Whoever controlled appointments and changes in personnel to be made during such a reorganization might well end up controlling the country. It was just at this time that Khrushchev's various rivals within the Presidium of the Central Committee of the Party who had formerly themselves been in sharp rivalry with each other began to think about the possibilities of combining their forces.

Despite the emergence of the danger of a united opposition to himself within the Party Presidium, Khrushchev was nevertheless able through his control over the Party Secretariat and the apparatus of government to maintain his control over the economic reorganization program. It was Khrushchev who presented his plan to the Supreme Soviet in early May. It was enacted—to be put into effect over the course of subsequent months of that year.

Khrushchev manifested much political activity—in connection with the reorganization plan and also with continuing agricultural problems —in the first half of 1957. In one of his speeches of that year—in the city of Gorky on April 8—he made a proposal which amounted to a plan for virtual cancellation of the Soviet national debt. It was a project for refunding of Soviet bond issues which had been sold to Soviet workers on the basis of salary deductions in previous years. As Khrushchev worked it out the government would be paying back to its citizens but very little, if any, of the amounts they had invested in these bonds. On the other hand, the annual bond drives which were naturally highly unpopular would cease. On the balance it could be guessed that the ending of the annual bond drive would be more popular than the plan for refunding the bonds was unpopular—and that there was a net gain in popularity from the Khrushchev proposal.

It was likewise in the first half year of 1957 that Khrushchev advanced his much-publicized campaign to "overtake the United States in the per capita production of meat, butter and milk in the near future." This project was unveiled by Khrushchev in a speech in Leningrad on May 24. It was bold and calculated to appeal to Russian national pride. It was also, of course, specious. As Khrushchev had had much opportunity to learn, progress in increasing food production under Soviet conditions can come only slowly. It was in connection with this dramatic plan that Khrushchev made a proposal calculated to have much appeal to the Soviet peasantry—for abolition of compulsory deliveries to the state at low prices of produce from the private plots of collective farm families.

It was in May and June of 1957—in part while Khrushchev was out of the country on a state visit to Finland—that the opposition to him within the Party Presidium managed to reach agreement on a plan to evict him from the leadership and to secure the support of an overwhelming majority within the Presidium. As a result when Khrushchev returned from Finland he was faced with a demand by most of his colleagues in the Presidium that he resign.

In this dangerous crisis Khrushchev set about mobilizing support for himself within the Central Committee of the Party through his crucial control of the Secretariat. Instead of resigning he demanded a meeting of the full membership of the Central Committee. In addition he sought, again through Marshal Zhukov, to assure himself of the support of the Soviet military. In this he was apparently successful. As a result of his political maneuvering he was able when the Central Committee met in late June to secure a resounding victory and to expel his chief rivals, including in particular Georgi Malenkov, Lazar Kaganovich, and V. M. Molotov from the Party leadership and to force all of them, except only Molotov, abjectly to admit to the Central Committee their errors and to seek its forgiveness. For the time being he allowed certain of the individuals who had opposed him, in particular Klimenty Voroshilov and Premier Nikolai Bulganin, to remain in the leadership, but without either prestige or significant power.

The great Moscow Youth Festival of the summer of 1957 which saw the capital turn itself inside out in order to entertain thousands of young people from all over the world was thus a kind of a colorful celebration of Khrushchev's narrow escape from political oblivion and his seemingly final triumph.

The late summer and fall of 1957 was the period in which the world was startled by Soviet accomplishments in rocketry. On August

26 the Soviet government announced that it had successfully fired an intercontinental ballistic missile. The announcement was met with much skepticism abroad. It was followed, however, by Soviet accomplishments which were beyond any question and which proved Soviet leadership in this crucial area of science and weaponry. On October 4 the first artificial space satellite—promptly christened "Sputnik," which is the Russian word for satellite—was launched. It was followed on November 3 by the launching of Sputnik II which contained the dog passenger, Laika.

Khrushchev's victory over his rivals in June had increased his strength and authority in leadership of the country—but had once more highlighted the importance of the Soviet military in politics. In the upshot Marshal Zhukov, spokesman of the Soviet officer corps, had been named a full member of the Party Presidium, the first career military man to be given such a post. And Zhukov, in a speech he made in Leningrad after the purge of the "anti-party opposition"—as the Khrushchev opposition was immediately labeled—had spoken out bluntly on the dissension in the political leadership. It was clear that Zhukov, so long as he occupied his position as head of Soviet armed forces, could under certain circumstances, challenge, possibly successfully, Khrushchev. This strong position of the military was something Khrushchev and the Communist Party leadership was unlikely long to tolerate. It was not entirely a surprise, therefore, when Khrushchev acted in late October, at a time when Zhukov was out of the country, to replace him, to oust him from the leadership, and to secure a condemnation by the Central Committee of the Party of positions he had taken demanding noninterference of the Party in army affairs. Thus Khrushchev dealt quickly and curtly with the man who till then had been his most powerful and important political ally in the post-Stalin era. But Khrushchev no longer needed Zhukov and looked on him as a threat.

The Zhukov ouster and the second Sputnik were timed for the fortieth anniversary of the Bolshevik Revolution on November 7. For this occasion Communist delegations came from all over the world and joined, after a discussion of problems and issues in the international Communism movement, in a joint statement predicting, of course, the triumph of Communism on a world-wide scale and the downfall of capitalism and imperialism.

In 1957, still under the shadow of the Hungarian Revolution, still concerned with widespread unrest and discontent among intellectuals and young people, the Soviet leadership was much concerned with the problem of keeping Soviet writers and other creative artists in line. One of the most important Soviet documents of the year was a two-page pronouncement on literature and art published in *Pravda* in late August over the signature of Khrushchev. In this statement Khrushchev reasserted the right claimed by the Party to control the activity of writers and other creative artists. It is this statement which has been selected as the ninth in this series of Khrushchev documents:

FOR CLOSE TIE BETWEEN LITERATURE AND ART AND THE LIFE OF THE PEOPLE *

The Communist Party, guided by V. I. Lenin's precepts that literature and art are an integral part of the nationwide struggle for communism, has always attached and continues to attach prime importance to the activities of writers, artists, sculptors, composers and all workers of Soviet culture, to the flourishing of our multinational Soviet socialist culture.

Soviet literature and art have strong ties with the life of the people and with their struggle for the cause of communism. It was noted at the 20th Party Congress that our men of letters and artists are true helpers of the Communist Party in carrying out the great tasks of building a new society and bringing up the working people in the spirit of communism.

Questions pertaining to the development of literature and art cannot be considered apart from the urgent tasks now being solved by the Communist Party and the Soviet people for a further advance of our country's economy and culture, in the struggle to build a communist society.

I.—The 20th Party Congress, as is known, set great tasks in the sphere of developing industry, agriculture and cultural work and raising the people's living standards. Not much time has passed since the Congress, but the successes achieved in this period in carrying out the

* *Pravda,* Aug. 28, pp. 3–4. The article is described as an abridged version of Khrushchev's speeches made at a writers' conference in the Central Committee of the Soviet Communist Party on May 13, 1957, at a reception for writers, artists, sculptors, and composers on May 19, 1957, and at a Party meeting in July, 1957. English translation copyrighted by *The Current Digest of the Soviet Press,* IX, No. 35, pp. 4–10.

policy outlined by the Congress are truly enormous. The industry of our country is successfully fulfilling the goals of the Sixth Five-Year Plan. Many bourgeois politicians are openly saying that they are frightened by the rate of growth of Soviet industry, frightened by the influence of the Soviet example on the working people of the whole world. And you and I know very well how convincing our example is to the minds of the working people in all countries.

At the recent session of the U.S.S.R. Supreme Soviet, which discussed the reorganization of the management of industry and construction, it was noted that in the years of Soviet rule the volume of industrial output in our country has increased more than 30 times, while the output of the machine-building and metalworking industries has increased 180 times and the output of electric power almost 100 times.

These facts are eloquent testimony that our country, following the course indicated by Lenin, has become a mighty socialist power. The present reorganization of the management of industry and construction is of enormous importance to the further development of the Soviet Union's economy.

Shifting the center of gravity of industrial management to the areas in which industry is located will make it possible to manage the economy in a more concrete and practical manner, to give even greater scope to the initiative of the masses and to increase the role and responsibility of the local agencies. Questions pertaining to the work of industry and construction will no longer be decided by the ministries and chief administrations but directly on the spot, in the economic regions.

Presumably not everyone agrees with me on this question. Some will say so openly and some will not. That is their business. I must remind you that when the question of developing the virgin lands was being decided by the Communist Party and our government there were many then too who did not understand the importance of this matter. The same thing happened in the reorganization of industrial management. Some were against it. An attachment for what was old was felt here. The old was convenient; one had grown used to it. But what is old and obsolete must be scrapped. We can no longer live as we used to. We must move on.

If the Soviet people have achieved great successes by developing the virgin and idle lands, the measures carried out by the Communist

Party to improve the work of our industry will yield even greater results. The reorganization of economic management now under way will bring the Soviet people not only material benefits but also a new flourishing of culture, because the cultural forces will be more evenly distributed and the centers of the economic regions will grow more rapidly as cultural centers as well.

After publication of the theses of the report of the reorganization of industry and construction, some writers showed that they did not understand the new processes at work in our lives and proved to be insufficiently prepared to evaluate correctly the state of the national economy at the present stage, when the question of improving the forms of industrial management is being raised persistently. This, by the way, showed that such writers were divorced from life. We are certain, however, that life will soon show these comrades how wrong they are.

The Party has given much attention in recent years to the further advance of agriculture. You know in what a difficult position it was a few years ago. You probably remember what hue and cry our enemies raised in the capitalist countries when, at the September plenary session of the Central Committee in 1953, we spoke openly about the shortcomings in the management of agriculture. Our enemies shouted that this spelled the collapse of the collective farms, the collapse of our whole cause.

In these years the Party and all the Soviet people have done extensive work to advance agriculture, and today every Soviet person is enjoying its benefits. Why, then, did our agriculture lag far behind for a long time? This happened because no one in the center really wanted to learn the true state of affairs on the spot. Stalin, as is known, never went anywhere, did not consult with workers in agriculture and did not heed local workers, while the people whom he delegated in the center to supervise agriculture concealed great shortcomings from him and engaged in misrepresentation. The principle of material incentives for workers in increasing the output of farm products was grossly violated.

Let me cite at least the following examples. Soon after the war I paid a visit to the village where I was born and called on my cousin. She had an orchard.

"You have fine apple trees," I told her.

"I'm going to cut them down in the autumn," she replied.

"Why?" I asked.

"I have to pay high taxes," she said. "It's not profitable to have an orchard."

I told J. V. Stalin about this talk and reported that the collective farmers were cutting down their orchards. He replied that I was a Populist [Narodnik], that I had a Populist attitude and that I was losing the proletarian class feeling.

Here is another example. Did we not used to send thousands of people from the cities to harvest potatoes on the collective farms, while the collective farmers themselves took no part in the harvesting? Yes, this used to happen. And why didn't the collective farmers want to help with the harvesting of the potatoes? Because we paid extremely low prices for potatoes. It cost the collective farm more just to bring the potatoes to the procurement center than it received for them.

We had to change this situation, to find suitable price levels and to offer the collective farmers a material stake in agricultural production. One cannot get very far in this matter without material incentives to the collective farmers. This must not be forgotten when speaking about the output of produce so vital to the people as grain, meat, butter and potatoes. But unfortunately one still finds "hard-heads" among us who are incapable of understanding this truth. Those who have lost contact with life and with the interests of the people are incapable of understanding that by clinging stubbornly to the old ways they can ruin matters and cause irreparable damage to the interests of the people. Such people are also to be found among workers on the ideological front. They live under the spell of outworn concepts, bookish schemes, dogmas and formulas.

It must be admitted that scholastic, bookish concepts are rather tenacious and not infrequently make themselves felt in our work. Those who harbor these views are afraid of everything new, raise an uproar, shy away in terror and lose the faculty of soberly analyzing the situation and of understanding the need to carry out urgent measures dictated by the course of social development. When the Central Committee proposed the introduction of a new system of agricultural planning, the conservative people opposed this measure. They tried to frighten the Central Committee, saying that if we abandoned centralized crop planning, the collective farmers would stop sowing wheat and we would have nowhere to go for bread. Life has made a laughingstock of these conservatives. Millions of collective farmers ardently supported the new system of planning and lent their active support to this matter, and as a result we have benefited greatly.

The 20th Party Congress showed that our country now has all the necessary conditions for accomplishing the U.S.S.R.'s principal economic task in an historically short time—to catch up with and surpass the most highly developed capitalist countries in per capita output. Accomplishment of this task, which Lenin on the eve of the October Revolution called a major task of a socialist state, will further strengthen the U.S.S.R.'s economic might and considerably increase the people's standard of living.

The workers and peasants of our country followed the Bolshevist party and Lenin in October 1917 in the fight to overthrow the landowner-capitalist system in order to win freedom and build a new and better life. How was this better life to be expressed? In the fact that a person would be a free citizen and master of his own fate, that he would work not for exploiters but for himself and have an abundance of all that he needed for a cultural and secure life. The Communist Party believes that its primary duty is constant concern about a steady rise in the working people's well-being. Our present task is to see that in the next few years our country has a sufficiency of such necessities as bread, meat, butter, milk and other consumer goods. You know what efforts are now being exerted by the Party to expand housing construction in every way both in the cities and in the countryside in order to provide the working people of our country with good housing.

As a result of the measures carried out in recent years, our agriculture now stands at such a level of development that it can successfully cope with the task of catching up with the United States in the next few years in the per capita production of meat, milk and butter. What is the situation at present in the production of meat, butter and milk in our country and in the United States? In 1956 the Soviet Union produced 32.3 kg. of meat per capita and the United States produced 102.3 kg. We produced 2.8 kg. of butter per person, while the U.S.A. produced 3.8 kg. We produced 245 kg. of milk per capita, while the U.S.A. produced 343 kg. As you see, we are as yet far behind the U.S.A. in the per capita output of butter, milk and particularly meat. The figures I have cited show what a tremendous task we have set ourselves. Are we equal to it? The skeptics try to frighten us by saying that we have taken on an impossible burden. They do not believe in the potentialities of the socialist economy, do not know the country, do not understand the soul of our people, do not believe in their inexhaustible forces.

We would not be Communists, pupils and followers of Lenin, if we were disheartened by the difficulties that arise in the struggle to improve the people's well-being. We are fully aware that the task before us is great and complex, but the Communist Party and the Soviet people will accomplish it. Our firm confidence is based on accurate calculations of the actual possibilities of socialist agriculture and on consideration of the experience of leading collective farms.

The task set by the Party has received the approval and support of all the people. A mighty upsurge of initiative among the working people is growing throughout the country. The collective farmers are pledging to increase the output of meat, butter and milk by three, five, ten and more times. This is their reply to the faint in heart and the skeptics.

Collective-farm animal husbandry is now on the rise. In these conditions, the Party Central Committee is discussing the question of ending, as early as 1958, obligatory deliveries of farm products by the collective farmers from their private plots. We now have every possibility of doing this. Implementation of this measure is of most vital importance to millions of the working people.

I would also like to speak about other measures being carried out by the Party to ensure continued improvement in the living conditions of the peoples of the Soviet Union. The rapid growth of our industry, the systematic rise in labor productivity and extensive application of the latest achievements of science and technology for mechanizing production will enable us in the near future to change over to the seven-hour working day and, in underground work in the coal and mining industries, to the six-hour working day. In capitalist countries mechanization and automation of production bring with them a deterioration in the working people's living conditions and mass unemployment of the working class. In our socialist country things are quite different. The more perfect the technology of production becomes, the more rapid the growth in the productivity of social labor and the higher the working people's living standards. The time is not far away when, following the introduction of the seven-hour working day, we will change over to the six-hour working day. This will create even more favorable conditions for the comprehensive development of spiritual culture, for the comprehensive development of the personalities of the citizens in the socialist society. The growth of material culture is the basis for the growth of spiritual culture. With a low level of material culture the spiritual culture of the entire society cannot flourish. These two factors are interdependent.

The Soviet Union is a multinational socialist state uniting on a voluntary basis 15 fraternal Union republics with equal rights. On their paths of socialist development the formerly oppressed nations, after receiving state independence, acquired unlimited possibilities for a growth of their economies and cultures, and they have made great strides forward in a short time. It must be said frankly that we have not yet vividly shown as we should those great historic changes that have taken place in the lives of the peoples of our republics in the years of Soviet rule. Our literary men and artists are still in great debt to the people in this respect. I would like to advise writers and artists to observe more closely and delve more deeply into the life of all the nationalities of our country. A thousand living examples will then show them how the lives of the people have changed and with what wonderful successes they are approaching the 40th anniversary of the Great October Socialist Revolution.

During the past few years I have made several trips to Kazakhstan, Uzbekistan and Tadzhikistan and have also visited Kirgizia and the Baltic republics—Lithuania, Latvia and Estonia. I was also in Georgia, but that was long ago. In each of our Union republics enormous successes have been scored in economic and cultural work, and numerous qualified cadres have appeared.

What an amazing flourishing of the economy and culture we have in our Soviet republics! What wonderful people have grown up and developed there under the conditions of a Soviet society, under the leadership of the Communist Party, in the course of the historic struggle for communism! Meeting and talking to these people, one experiences a feeling of bitterness and regret that in their works our writers and artists so seldom succeed in portraying our people properly, in showing that they are new people, born and raised in the epoch of socialism. These new people are fighters for the freedom and happiness of mankind; they embody the high spiritual qualities and traits of communist morality. Stronger ties with the daily life of the people and their labor will help writers and artists to overcome their obsolete notions about our people, to know their soul, their character, their thoughts and hopes, and to create truthful and vivid images of our contemporaries in stories, novels, poems and plays and in films, painting and music.

The 20th Party Congress pointed out in its decisions that for the further rise and flourishing of the economy and culture it was necessary in every possible way to extend the rights and increase the role of the Union republics and consistently to carry out the Leninist nationality policy. The Party and the government have done a great deal in this direction since the Congress, and the results are having a favorable effect on the life of all the republics.

In connection with this, I would like to speak in particular about the major measures carried out by the Party Central Committee and the Soviet government to expand the rights of the Russian Republic. The Russian Federation deservedly enjoys the respect of all the fraternal peoples of the Soviet Union. Together with the Russian people, all the socialist nations of the U.S.S.R. speak affectionately of Mother Russia. It is known that even in prerevolutionary times prominent representatives of the democratic Russian intelligentsia maintained close relations with the leading intellectual representatives of all the peoples of Russia, actively opposed national oppression and had a favorable influence on the development of the culture of various nations and nationalities.

Under the leadership of the Bolshevist Party, the heroic Russian working class led the struggle of the working people of all nationalities against hated Tsarism, against the bourgeois-landowner system, and assured the victory of the socialist revolution. In the course of the great socialist transformation in our country, the Russian people have done much, very much indeed, to help the formerly oppressed peoples of the country to overcome their age-old economic and cultural backwardness and to raise them to their own level. The great and lofty deeds of the Russian people both in the years of peaceful construction and in the period of war trials earned them the warm gratitude and respect of all the peoples of our country. This in no way belittles the outstanding importance of all the peoples in the fraternal family of socialist nations of the U.S.S.R. All the peoples of our Soviet Union are making their great contribution to the building of communism.

The invincible strength of the Soviet system lies in the indestructible fraternal friendship of all the peoples of our multinational land of Soviets.

It must be admitted, comrades, that until quite recently the Russian Federation did not have the full rights relative to its importance and place in the state. This abnormal situation has been corrected since the 20th Party Congress. The Russian Republic Bureau of the Party Central Committee has been established. This operative agency of the Central Committee, which deals with all the affairs of the Russian Federation, directs all spheres of Party, economic and cultural life of the Russian Republic on behalf of the Party Central Committee. The Russian Republic Council of Ministers has been vested with all the rights necessary to guide industry, agriculture and cultural work. The recent reorganization of the management of industry and construction and the establishment of 70 economic councils for the economic administrative regions of the Russian Republic will permit more practical management of the development of the republic's economy.

The measures to expand the rights of the Union republics are of great importance and offer even broader opportunities for their comprehensive development.

Comrades! Our strength lies in the unity of our Party ranks, in the indestructible unity of all Soviet peoples, rallied around the Party Central Committee. With this monolithic and indivisible unity of our ranks we need fear no intrigues by the forces of world reaction.

II.—Some adherents of "pure theory" try to present the activities of our party and the measures it carries out as something in the nature of narrow expediency. Individual supporters of such views may also be found among writers. Such errors cannot be left unanswered. Let us see just how one should understand the relationship of theory and practice from the Marxist point of view. No Marxist-Leninist would ever think of belittling the importance of revolutionary theory. As Lenin said, there can be no revolutionary practice without revolutionary theory.

The theory of Marxism-Leninism is the expression of the fundamental interests of the working class, the fundamental interests of the working people. It is not a dogma, but a guide to practical revolutionary action. At every new stage of historical development life poses its tasks, which stem from the requirements of society. A creative approach to theory, the ability to develop and advance the science of

Marxism-Leninism consists of correctly understanding the new urgent tasks of social development on the basis of scientific generalization of the experience of life and of outlining ways for practical accomplishment of these tasks.

The decisions of the 20th Party Congress are an example of the creative development of Marxist-Leninist theory. The political course of our party charted by the Congress expresses the fundamental interests of the Soviet people at the present stage of the struggle for communism. These fundamental interests of the people are to assure the continued powerful development of socialist industry, primarily of heavy industry, and a sharp rise in agriculture and on this basis to improve the working people's material well-being in every way.

The measures carried out by the Communist Party in recent years both in the sphere of Party and state work and in the sphere of advancing the economy and raising the people's living standards show that the work of our party is based on the indivisible unity of theory and practice. In the last years of Stalin's life this unity of theory and practice was disrupted. This is what is not understood by those who have isolated themselves from life, who think of themselves as high priests and interpreters of Marxist-Leninist science but who have in fact broken with Leninism in practice and slid onto the path of factional, schismatic activities directed against the fundamental interests of the Party and the fundamental interests of the people. The June plenary session of the Central Committee exposed and ideologically routed the anti-Party group of Malenkov, Kaganovich and Molotov, and of Shepilov, who joined them. These people had opposed the Leninist course outlined by the 20th Party Congress. Our whole party and all the Soviet people unanimously approved the decision of the June plenary session of the Party Central Committee, aimed at further strengthening the Leninist unity of the Party.

I know people who pose as theoreticians but whose theoretical "wisdom" essentially boils down to the juggling of quotations from the classics of Marxism-Leninism—with or without reason. Pretending to be theoreticians, these sorry scholars cannot understand the important Marxist truth that people must first of all eat, drink, have homes and clothe themselves before they are in a position to engage in politics, science and art. These Talmudists and pedants forget that the people took power into their own hands precisely in order to develop the forces of production, to multiply society's wealth, to improve their well-being and to create better living conditions as rapidly as possible.

If Marx, Engels and Lenin could rise again, they would ridicule those pedantic quotation lovers who, instead of studying the life of modern society and developing theory creatively, try to find the proper classical quotation on what to do with a Machine and Tractor Station in such and such a district. It would be absurd to comb Marx and Engels for instructions on what to do about deliveries of farm products by the collective farmers from their own holdings, for example.

It must be admitted that some of our economists and philosophers have shut themselves off from life, from the practice of building communism. It is even possible to find economists who, when speaking about wages under present-day conditions, cite examples quoted by Marx almost a hundred years ago in his famous *Capital.* There are not many such people, of course, but unfortunately one does come across them now and then. Such economists cannot cite concrete examples from life because they do not really know life. They are not theoreticians, but parrots who have learned a few phrases by rote and keep repeating them. Such "theoretical" work is not worth a thing!

We Communists are men of vigorous revolutionary action. Our task, as we see it, is to transform the world, to build a communist society. The strength of our theory lies in the fact that it is closely linked to life, that it generalizes the creative experience of millions, that it defends the basic interests of the working people, who comprise the majority of the world's population. The strength of Marxist-Leninist theory lies in the fact that it is revolutionary in essence, that it cannot tolerate stagnation, routine and inertia, that it lights the way to a communist future, that it leads the people forward, helping them to conquer every difficulty and obstacle on the road toward this goal.

Marxist-Leninists stand forth as the creators of a new life, as men of great revolutionary thought, bold imagination and soaring dreams. At the same time they are close to the earth and stand with both feet on the ground of reality. They are sober politicians who weigh real conditions and potentialities in their actions, and they are unafraid of difficulties, never conceal contradictions and are able openly and honestly to tell their people the truth, bitter as it may sometimes be. The disciples and followers of Lenin—the Communists

—set themselves the boldest tasks for the welfare and happiness of the people and spare no efforts to realize them.

Let us recall, comrades, what great importance Lenin attached to the practical activity of our party in the sphere of economic development. He said that if we could provide 100,000 tractors the peasants would say that they were for the communia, that is, for communism. And when a plan was worked out for the electrification of Russia, Lenin called it the second program of our party.

The great plans for building communism worked out by the 20th Party Congress are a militant program of our activities at the present stage of the country's development. These plans provide for a gigantic growth of production forces on the basis of continuous technical progress in order considerably to increase the output of food products and consumer goods and take a big new step forward along the road to communism.

Realization of the plans outlined by the 20th Congress is of great international importance. It will be a new blow of crushing force to the ideologists of the capitalist world, who in their hostile attacks on socialism make wide use of such a passing, temporary factor as the per capita output of goods in the most developed capitalist countries.

All honest, unprejudiced people can see how with every year of rapid development of our national economy the difference between the levels of per capita production in our country and in the most developed capitalist countries sharply narrows. We already hold second place in the world in volume of industrial output. Even the fiercest enemies cannot deny the economic might of the Soviet Union and the rapid rate of its economic development.

The outstanding successes of the Soviet Union, the Chinese People's Republic and all socialist countries are having a devastating effect on the opponents of socialism and throwing them into confusion. It is these successes of the socialist countries that are responsible for the growing attraction of the ideas of socialism in all countries, successes to which the enemies of socialism ascribe an almost supernatural character. It is for this reason that we are sometimes blamed for events in places where we have never set foot. To understand, assimilate and properly elucidate the essence of the great socialist transformation is the major task of our ideological workers.

In speaking of the tasks of ideological workers, it is impossible to ignore the question of the cult of the individual and the elimination of its consequences. Our party's condemnation of the J. V. Stalin cult, which is alien to the spirit of Marxism-Leninism, evoked widespread response both within our country and abroad. The Soviet people, the Communist and Workers' Parties and all of our friends abroad warmly approved and unanimously supported the decisions of the 20th Congress and the well-known resolution of the Party Central Committee on eliminating the consequences of the cult of the individual. The enemies of socialism sought to use criticism of the cult of the individual for their own sordid ends and organized a shrill slander campaign against our country and the socialist camp as a whole. They would very much like to sow confusion in the ranks of the fighters for peace, democracy and socialism, weaken the influence of the ideas of Marxism-Leninism, shake the unity of the countries in the socialist camp and slander and compromise the Communist Parties in the eyes of the peoples. Everyone can now see that these base calculations of the enemies of socialism have suffered disgraceful failure.

The Communist and Workers' Parties quickly saw through and exposed the schemes of the imperialists and dealt a crushing blow to the instigators and organizers of ideological sabotage, as well as to all opportunist elements who sought to revise the principles of Marxism-Leninism.

In the intense ideological struggle our Soviet intelligentsia has proven itself politically mature, steadfast and loyal to the ideas of Marxism-Leninism. Together with all the Soviet people it has demonstrated its unity and solidarity in the great struggle for the cause of communism. It must be admitted, however, that among the intelligentsia there were individuals who began to feel the ground slipping out from under them and displayed a certain shakiness and vacillation in evaluating a number of complex ideological questions connected with eliminating the consequences of the cult of the individual.

How are the shakiness and vacillations of certain representatives of literature and the arts to be explained? I think that this happened because some comrades had a one-sided and incorrect understanding of the essence of the Party's criticism of the Stalin cult. They tried to interpret this criticism as a sweeping denial of the positive role of J. V. Stalin in the life of our party and country and embarked on the false path of prejudiced searching for only the darker sides and mistakes in the history of our people's struggle for the triumph of socialism, ignoring the world-historic successes of the Soviet state in building socialism.

In answer to the question "What place will Stalin take in history?" put to me by the editor of the American newspaper *The New York Times,* I said that Stalin would take his due place in the history of the Soviet Union. Although he had great faults, Stalin was a devoted Marxist-Leninist, a devoted and stanch revolutionary. Stalin made many mistakes in the latter period of his activity, but he also did much that was beneficial to our country, to our party and to the entire international workers' movement. Our party and the Soviet people will remember Stalin and give him his due.

In order correctly to understand the essence of Party criticism of the cult of the individual, it is necessary to realize profoundly that we see two sides to Comrade Stalin's activity—the positive side, which we support and highly value, and the negative side, which we criticize, condemn and reject.

For a long time J. V. Stalin held the leading position in the Central Committee of our party. All his work was linked with the accomplishment of great socialist transformations in our country. The face of our country changed radically in those years as a result of the implementation of Lenin's plans for building socialism. Let us recall what Russia was before the victory of the Great October Revolution. It was an economically and culturally backward country, reduced by Tsarism to the position of a semicolonial state. Look what the land of Soviets is today! The Soviet Union is a great and mighty socialist power exerting a decisive influence on the course of world history and enjoying the profound respect of the working people of the entire world.

The great successes in the development of our country were achieved under the leadership of the Communist Party and its Central Committee, in which J. V. Stalin played a leading role. Socialism was built in the U.S.S.R. under conditions of bitter struggle against class enemies and their agents in the Party—Trotskyites, Zinovievites, Bukharinists and bourgeois nationalists. This was a political struggle. The Party was right to expose them as enemies of Leninism, as opponents of socialist construction in our country. They were condemned politically and condemned justly.

Stalin did useful work in this struggle. This cannot be stricken from the history of the struggle of the working class, peasantry and intelligentsia of our country for socialism, from the history of the Soviet state. It is for this that we value and respect Stalin. We were sincere in our respect for J. V. Stalin when we wept at his bier. We are sincere now in evaluating his positive role in the history of our party and the Soviet state. Each of us believed in Stalin, and this belief was based on the conviction that the work that we did with him was in the interests of the revolution, in the interest of the working class and of all the working people.

Our party and all of us resolutely condemn Stalin for the gross mistakes and distortions that inflicted serious harm on the cause of the Party and the cause of the people. We lost many honest and devoted people, workers of our party and the Soviet state, who were slandered and who suffered innocently. Many of them have already been rehabilitated. The Party has condemned those incorrect methods of leadership which developed in the period of the cult of the individual and is consistently and persistently working to restore the Leninist norms of Party life and principles of leadership and to broaden Soviet socialist democracy in every way.

How can it have happened that Stalin, who maintained a correct stand in the struggle against the enemies of Leninism, committed such gross and serious mistakes? This is a complicated question, comrades. This was Stalin's tragedy, caused to a large extent by major faults in his personality and character, to which V. I. Lenin referred in December 1922 in his letter to the Party Congress. These faults of Stalin developed above all in the final period of his life, when he began to be responsible for gross violations of the Leninist norms of Party life, neglected the principles of collective leadership and decided many major Party and state questions by himself, when his ties with the cadres and masses of the working people weakened. The situation was also worsened by the fact that Stalin's personal failings were exploited by the provocateur Beria, the sworn enemy of the Party and people, to harm our cause.

Much of the blame for this lies also with Comrade Malenkov, who fell under the complete influence of Beria and acted as his shadow and tool. Holding a high position in the Party and state, Comrade Malenkov not only failed to restrain J. V. Stalin but made skillful use of his weaknesses and habits in the last years of his life.

On many occasions he urged him on to actions that deserve the strongest condemnation.

The great importance of the Party's work to eliminate the consequences of the cult of the individual is now clear to all.

The criticism of the cult of the individual and elimination of its consequences in ideological work have quite naturally caused intense emotional reactions and serious reflection among creative workers, and particularly among writers.

Who was most deeply and keenly affected by this? I believe, comrades, that the writers, artists, sculptors, composers and other workers in the arts were the most deeply troubled. Among the writers, those who took it most closely to heart were the comrades who stood nearest the Party and the Central Committee, and therefore to Stalin. This meant being close to the people, to all that the people did under the leadership of our party. The works of these writers truthfully and sincerely portrayed the struggle and victories of the Party and the people. Comrade Stalin was often depicted in these works. The authors of these works performed a worthy task; they wanted what was good for our party, and they struggled for lofty communist ideals together with all the people, under the Party's leadership. Of course, under the influence of the general situation in the period of the cult of the individual, works of literature and art in a number of cases gave an unobjective, one-sided view of J. V. Stalin's personality. They greatly exaggerated his merits, while the role of the people and the role of the Party did not receive merited recognition.

When the Party started to criticize the cult of the individual and Stalin's mistakes, some writers seemed to think that practically all their past creative work was wrong. Some even wondered if they should rewrite all the books they had written. It must be admitted that among the intelligentsia there were also people who did not take an active part in our cause previously and who began to vilify and smear workers in literature and the arts who had glorified the successes our people achieved under the Party's leadership. They invented and launched the abusive label of "prettifier," pinning it on all who wrote the truth about our reality, about our people's creative labor and great victories, on all who created positive images of Soviet people in works on literature and art.

Some comrades ask how we should regard the Stalin Prizes awarded to our people. I think that we must respect these prizes and be proud to wear the honorable badge of Stalin Prize Winner. If I had a Stalin Prize, I would wear this honorable badge. Mistakes were made in awarding Stalin Prizes, and some were awarded to people who did not deserve them. But these are isolated cases. With rare exceptions the workers in science, literature and the arts who received Stalin Prizes deserved them.

It must be stated frankly and clearly that the Communist Party has always supported and will continue to support writers and workers in the arts who honestly and devotedly serve their people, who together with the people rejoice in our country's achievements in building communism and who find vivid colors to reflect these achievements in works of literature and art.

III.—The Party Central Committee thinks that comradely meetings and talks with workers in literature and the arts on key issues of our ideological work are exceedingly useful and deserve every support. I was very pleased that in the recent meetings and talks in the Party Central Committee writers and artists commented frankly and without constraint on everything that bothered them. They were among friends and were correctly understood. Such forms of contact are extremely necessary for a comradely exchange of views, as a result of which mutual understanding and a common viewpoint on vital issues of our life and work are evolved.

Why does the Party pay so much attention to questions of literature and the arts? Because literature and the arts have an exceptionally important role in our party's ideological work, in the communist education of the working people. Through their work writers, artists, sculptors, composers and film and theater workers—our whole intelligentsia—actively participate in the creative work of Soviet society and faithfully serve their people. The Communist Party considers workers in literature and the arts to be its true friends and helpers and a trustworthy support in the ideological struggle. The Party is concerned about the flourishing and high ideological and artistic perfection of literature and the arts. Our people need works of literature, painting and music that reflect the grandeur of labor and that they can understand. The method of socialist realism ensures unlimited opportunities for the creation of such works. The Party relentlessly combats the infiltration into literature and art of influences of alien ideology; it combats hostile attacks on socialist culture.

The complexity and unique character of the ideological struggle in literature and the arts today consists, incidentally, in the fact that we have to defend literature and the arts not only against attacks from the outside but also against the attempts of some creative workers to push literature and the arts onto a wrong path, away from the main line of development.

The main line of development is that literature and the arts must always be inseparably linked with the people's life, must truthfully portray the wealth and variety of our socialist reality and vividly and convincingly show the Soviet people's great work of transformation, the nobility of their aims and aspirations and their lofty moral qualities. The highest social purpose of literature and the arts is to arouse the people to a struggle for new victories in the building of communism.

It must be admitted, comrades, that some of our writers and workers in the arts continue to lose their foothold and to stray from the right road. These people treat the tasks of literature and the arts erroneously and in a distorted way. They try to present matters as if the duty of literature and the arts were to find only the faults, to speak primarily of life's negative aspects, of lack of harmony, and to keep silent about all that is favorable. Yet it is the positive, the new and the progressive in life that is most important in the tempestuously developing reality of a socialist society.

Those who harbor erroneous and harmful views and sentiments have rallied against the writers and artists whose works give truthful, vivid pictures of Soviet society's progress and positive images of our contemporaries. The hack critics have ranked such writers as Comrade Gribachev and others among those scornfully labeled "prettifier."

We support writers who hold to the right position in literature by writing about the favorable aspects of life. But this does not mean that every work they produce is free of shortcomings and cannot be criticized. It is possible that in their work these comrades were at times erroneously carried away, but this does not give anyone grounds or the right to attack them or to deny the useful work they have done.

Some people will probably try to interpret this evaluation of facts and phenomena in literary life as an appeal to portray our life one-sidedly and to keep silent about shortcomings and difficulties in our reality. However, we resolutely reject such unworthy attempts in advance.

No one can accuse us Communists of fearing criticism, of trying to cover up and conceal shortcomings in work. Experience shows that fear of criticism and self-criticism is characteristic of waning classes and their political parties. As the political guide of the most advanced class, as the leader of the people building communism, the Communist Party does its great work of transformation under the banner of Marxism-Leninism, by its very nature the most revolutionary and critical theory. It never has feared any difficulties on the road to a great goal but always looks truth boldly and squarely in the eye. It serves the interests of the people, openly and mercilessly exposes and criticizes shortcomings and mistakes, and, together with the masses, outlines ways of removing shortcomings and correcting mistakes for the success of our cause.

In all its activity the Communist Party and its Central Committee sets an example in exposing and eliminating shortcomings. Remember, for example, the Party's decisions on agriculture, the reorganization of the management of industry and construction, the granting of greater powers to local agencies and development of their initiative, the reduction of the state and Party apparatus, and the improvement of the style and methods of leadership. Is not criticism of the cult of the individual and the consistent and persistent struggle to eliminate its consequences an indication of our party's high Leninist principle, courage and determination? The decisions of the 20th Party Congress and the plenary sessions of the Central Committee are imbued with the spirit of Bolshevist criticism and self-criticism and intolerance of shortcomings and mistakes. The great Lenin taught that the policy of adherence to principle is the only right policy. The Party demands from every Communist, from every worker in a Party or state agency, a high sense of responsibility for the job assigned, and it severely reprimands all who depart from the Party's political line and forget the interests of the Party and people. Neither a worker's position nor his past service does or can protect him from criticism and responsibility to the Party and people.

The whole point lies in the positions from which criticism is made and for what purpose it is made. We expose and criticize shortcomings and errors in order to remove them as obstacles on our path, to strengthen our Soviet system and the Communist Party's positions still more and to assure new successes and more rapid progress. But what happens to some writers when they undertake to criticize shortcomings? Ignorant of life, lacking the necessary political experience or ability to see what are the basic and determining factors in life, they latch onto the shortcomings and mistakes of individuals and dump them on a single pile without bothering to discriminate or interpret, frightening themselves and trying to frighten others.

The writer V. Dudintsev, in particular, put himself in such an unenviable position. His book *Not by Bread Alone,* which reactionary forces abroad are now trying to use against us, one-sidedly dragged in negative facts and tendentiously elucidated them in a manner unfriendly to us. Dudintsev's book does contain pages that are correctly and strongly written, but its general tone is basically wrong. The reader receives the impression that the author of the book is not concerned about eliminating the shortcomings he sees in our life, that he deliberately exaggerates and takes malicious delight in these shortcomings. This approach to the portrayal of reality in works of literature and art is nothing but a desire to show it in distorted form, in a crooked mirror.

It can only be regretted that some literary magazines and publishing houses failed to see this unsound and harmful tendency and to evaluate it correctly and rebuff it in time. The editors of the magazine *Novy mir* have given space to the publication of writings akin to Dudintsev's book. The editorial boards of several literary magazines and the directors of some publishing houses have proved unequal to the situation and in several instances have slipped from positions of principle. These comrades have begun to forget that the press is our chief ideological weapon. It is called upon to rout the enemies of the working class, the enemies of the working people. Just as an army cannot fight without weapons, so the Party cannot carry on its ideological work successfully without the sharp and militant weapon of the press. We cannot put the press in unreliable hands. It must be in the hands of the most faithful, most trustworthy, most politically steadfast people devoted to our cause.

Forgetfulness of this fact resulted in some press organs of the Writers' Union falling under the strong influences of individuals holding wrong positions, instead of consistently defending the line of adherence to principle in literature. They actually harbored unhealthy sentiments and tendencies. This applies in particular to the *Literaturnaya Moskva* [*Literary Moscow*] anthology, which published ideologically faulty works and articles that were severely condemned by our public and above all by writers themselves. Many writers justly noted this at the plenary session of the Board of the Writers' Union. But the members of the anthology's editorial board did not respect criticism of their mistakes. They did not respect the views of their fellow writers and evaded a straightforward and honest statement of their positions. Special mention should be made of Comrade Aliger, who still adheres to the view that the line of *Literaturnaya Moskva* was allegedly right and who came to the defense of works published in the anthology that contain ideas alien to us.

Much is being said by writers and artists about Party spirit, folk content, freedom of creative endeavor and Party guidance. These questions deserve serious attention, particularly because much that is wrong and confused and that confuses and disorients people has been said and written on these questions, preventing a correct understanding of the Party's policy on literature and the arts and of the Leninist principles of Party guidance in these major fields of ideological work.

A few remarks about Party spirit and folk content in literature and art. First of all, the concepts of Party spirit and folk content cannot be set off against each other. The strength of Soviet socialist society lies in the unity of the Communist Party and people. The Communist Party's policy, expressing the people's fundamental interests, is the vital basis of the Soviet social and state system. Therefore, it would be a great mistake to think that in our Soviet conditions it is possible to serve the people without actively carrying out the Communist Party's policy. One cannot hope to march in step with the people without sharing the Party's views and its political line. He who wants to be with the people will always be with the Party. He who stands firmly on the Party's positions will always be with the people.

Party spirit in creative work is determined not by the artist's formal membership in the Party but by his belief and ideological position. We have quite a few good writers who are not Party members but whose works are profoundly Party-minded in ideological content and political orientation and who have rightly earned the people's recognition as expressing their interests.

If struggle for the ideals of communism and for his people's happiness is the artist's goal in life and if he lives by the people's interests, thoughts and aspirations, then no matter what theme he chooses or what phenomena of life he depicts his works will accord with the interests of the people, Party and state.

This kind of creative worker chooses the path of devotion to the people freely, without coercion, in response to his own conviction and calling, at the command of his own heart and mind. For anyone who faithfully serves his people, the question of whether or not he is free in his creative work simply does not exist in a socialist society, where the people are really free, where they are the true masters of their destinies and the creators of a new life. For such a creative worker the question of his approach to the facts of reality is clear. He does not have to adapt, to force himself. The truthful presentation of life from positions of Communist Party spirit is the necessity of his soul; he adheres firmly to these positions and upholds and defends them in his creative work.

The truthful depiction in works of literature and art of the life of society, of the people, calls for both the presentation of the positive, luminous and bright sides of socialist reality, which comprise its fundamental aspect, and criticism of shortcomings, the exposure and condemnation of negative aspects that hold back our advance.

In life, in reality, there is always some bad mixed with the good; here and there we see an outcropping of weeds among the flowers. In the depiction of reality everything depends on the artist. If a writer, painter, sculptor or composer adheres to Party positions, if he serves the people and sincerely wants to help them build a new society, to clear the way in the effort to build communism, he will find an abundance of excellent models in the lives of factory workers, collective farmers and intelligentsia, in the lives of individuals and of the collectives of enterprises, collective farms and state farms; contrasting the positive and the negative, he will be able to support the positive and to show it faithfully, in bright colors. But if the author takes no joy in the achievements of his characters, he will search out only the bad, the negative, digging it out of garbage heaps, and will present it as typical of life.

We have opposed and continue to oppose, resolutely and irreconcilably, a one-sided, unfaithful, mendacious depiction of our reality in literature and art. We are against those who seek out only the negative aspects of our life and gloat over them, those who try to defame, to denigrate our Soviet way of life. We are also against those who create saccharine images that are offensive to the feelings of our people, who will neither accept nor countenance any falsehood. The Soviet people reject equally such an in effect slanderous work as Dudintsev's book *Not by Bread Alone* and such cloyingly sweet films as "Unforgettable 1919" and "Kuban Cossacks."

Unfortunately, there are among our workers in literature and the arts advocates of "creative freedom" who desire us to pass by, not to notice, not to subject to principled appraisal and not to criticize works that portray the life of Soviet society in a distorted fashion. It appears to these people that the guidance of literature and the arts by the Party and the state is oppressive. They sometimes oppose this guidance openly; more often, however, they conceal their feelings and desires behind talk of excessive tutelage, the fettering of initiative, etc.

We assert openly that such views run counter to the Leninist principles of the Party's and state's attitude to questions of literature and the arts. It will be recalled that Lenin, taking into account all the specific features of literature and the arts, time and again pointed out that the Party cannot hold itself aloof from guiding this important aspect of the spiritual life of society, and consistently abided by this principle in his political activity as leader of the Party and head of the Soviet state. V. I. Lenin pointed out that it is impossible to live in society and remain free of it. He stressed that the free literature of a socialist society will be openly linked with the working class, that it will be inspired by the interests of the working people and the ideas of socialism.

Lenin took an irreconcilable attitude toward those who deviated from fidelity to principle in questions of literature and the arts and who slid back to liberal positions with regard to ideological mistakes.

The whole history of the development of Soviet society is convincing proof that guidance by the Party and the state, their attention to artistic creation and their concern for writers, artists, sculptors and composers, has ensured outstanding successes of literature and the arts, the flowering of the socialist culture of all the peoples of the U.S.S.R. The Party's decisions on ideological questions have defined the major tasks and the basic principles of the Party's policy in the sphere of art and literature, and they retain their force to this day. One of the primary principles is that Soviet literature and art must be indissolubly linked with the policy of the Communist Party, which constitutes the vital foundation of the Soviet system. Artists and composers noted in their speeches at the recent congresses the great positive significance of these decisions.

It is impossible to deny, of course, that mistakes were made in the last years of J. V. Stalin's life, under the conditions of the cult of the individual. Here is an example: Only with great difficulty did I succeed in saving so deserving a writer as Maxim Rylsky from sharp criticism for his poem "Mother," which is imbued with deep patriotic feeling. The principal reason for the unfounded accusations against Rylsky and the attacks upon him was the fact that Stalin's name was not mentioned in the poem, which glorifies the Soviet Ukraine. And Comrade Kaganovich, who played the sycophant and did everything he could to inflate the Stalin cult, began to represent Rylsky as a Ukrainian bourgeois nationalist. He played on Stalin's weak strings without taking into account the grave consequences that might have ensued for Ukrainian—and not only Ukrainian—literature from these unfounded accusations against the esteemed Ukrainian writer-patriot Maxim Rylsky. It should be added that not literature alone might have suffered these grave consequences.

It goes without saying that we are against this kind of an approach to the appraisal of works of literature.

The Party has resolutely condemned the errors that were committed in all spheres of life, including ideological work, during the period of the cult of the individual, and it is consistently rectifying them. However, at the same time the Party vigorously opposes those who try to make use of these past errors to resist the guidance of literature and the arts by the Party and the state. Only people who do not agree with the Party's policy in this sphere can oppose the guidance of literature and the arts from such positions. Among these people are to be found, to our great sorrow, some writers who are Party members. Some of these comrades do not want to harmonize their activities with the requirements of Party discipline established by the Party Statutes; they cling to their subjectivistic interpretation of Party discipline and the duties of a Party member, camouflaging their un-Party conduct by chatter about an allegedly "creative attitude" to Party guidance. These false positions held by individuals who have drifted away from the collective, who have fallen out of step with the general formation, have evoked the just condemnation of writers —both Party members and non-Party members—at the plenary session of the Writers' Union, at a meeting of Moscow writers and in all writers' organizations of the Union and autonomous republics, territories and provinces. I gratefully second Comrade Sobolev, a non-Party writer, who spoke here and who consistently holds a principled and uncompromising position in the struggle against unhealthy moods and tendencies. I do not choose to deny that the position of the non-Party writer Comrade Sobolev on questions of Party spirit in literature is much closer to me, the Secretary of the Party Central Committee, than that of Party member Comrade Aliger, who holds to a false position and has an incorrect attitude toward criticism of her mistakes.

Certain liberally inclined people may accuse me of issuing a call to battle. Yes, we have never denied that we have been and are urging a principled ideological battle. There is a sharp conflict in the world today between two ideologies, the socialist and the bourgeois, and in this conflict there can be no neutrals.

The development of literature and art is proceeding in conditions of ideological battle against the influence of bourgeois culture, which is alien to us—against obsolete concepts and views and for the affirmation of our communist ideology.

We would not be Marxist-Leninist if we held aloof, if we remained passive and indifferent to attempts to insinuate into our literature and art bourgeois views that are alien to the spirit of the Soviet people. We must look at things soberly and take cognizance of the fact that enemies exist, and that they are trying to utilize the ideological front to weaken the forces of socialism. In such a situation our ideological weapons must be in good order and must operate unfailingly. The lesson of the Hungarian events, in which the counterrevolution used certain writers for its dirty ends, reminds us what political complacency, lack of principle and weakness of will in regard to the machinations of forces hostile to socialism may lead to. It must be clear to everyone that in the present conditions, when a sharp conflict between the forces of socialism and the forces of imperialist reaction is under way, we must keep our powder dry.

We have spoken up sharply on questions of the struggle against ideological mistakes and unhealthy moods in the course of our talks. Any other approach to these questions is unthinkable. To deal with the matter halfheartedly, not to speak up openly, would gravely damage the cause.

We want consolidation, unity of all the forces of literature and art on a principled basis, not by concessions and by deviations from the principles of Marxism-Leninism. Principled criticism and self-criticism is being developed in the interests of this consolidation. This criticism helps those who have made mistakes to realize and correct those mistakes and to stand more firmly on their feet; it heightens creative activity. In developing criticism and self-criticism it is necessary to determine carefully whether a mistake made by this or that worker is accidental or whether it reflects the system of his views, a definite line of conduct on his part, and we must also consider his attitude toward criticism. Any man can make mistakes, but it is necessary to see not only what the man did yesterday but also what he is capable of doing tomorrow, and—most important—we must help such a man realize his shortcomings and mistakes and as quickly as possible eliminate the former and rectify the latter.

For example, it is known that the public has criticized certain shortcomings in the work of our remarkable poet Comrade Tvardovsky, whose contribution to the development of Soviet literature has been widely recognized. Friendly conversations with Comrade Tvardovsky give ground for hope that this master of words will draw the necessary conclusions and will delight readers with excellent new works. At one time the public also sharply criticized the shortcomings of so prominent a writer as Comrade Panferov. We believe that this criticism was correct; Comrade Panferov himself now admits that it has been useful to him.

The aim of principled criticism is to help workers in literature and the arts in their creative endeavors, so that they may work with even greater success for the good of our people, may actively participate in the people's struggle for communism and may enrich Soviet socialist culture with their works.

Our Soviet system and the Communist Party have more than once returned people, even ones who were considered lost and beyond hope, to life and to active work. There are quite a few examples of workers in literature and the arts who have produced great works after having been subjected to criticism. Speaking of Comrade Dudintsev, I believe that he, too, with our assistance and his own desire, can find the correct path and, along with the whole fraternity of writers, work fruitfully for the good of the people, for the good of the socialist homeland.

The unions of creative artists must play an exceptionally important part in the development of literature and the arts, in the ideological training and creative life of each artist; they should become truly active, militant collectives solidly united on a principled basis. There should be real friendship in these unions; they should show a constant comradely concern for the creative growth of every writer, artist, sculptor, film worker, musician and theater worker. The collective should promptly support every good work, every manifestation of useful initiative in creative endeavor. It is extremely important to notice in time any shortcomings or mistakes on the part of a creative worker, to prevent him from sliding back from principled positions, and to give assistance and support to all who need it.

Workers in literature and the arts are active fighters for communism. Millions of people learn from their best works. This makes it incumbent upon our unions of creative workers and their Party organizations to carry out daily great ideological-upbringing work, to equip our creative personnel with a knowledge of Marxist-Leninist theory and a correct understanding of the Communist Party's policy. It is necessary that all our creative personnel should realize their large role in the struggle of all the people for communism, and their great responsibility to the people.

Our creative organizations are doing significant work toward carrying out the tasks set by the 20th Party Congress in the realm of literature and the arts. The recent plenary sessions of the Writers' Unions and the Artists' and Composers' Congresses have helped to step up this activity and to rally the creative workers. It is gratifying to note the increased activity of the Writers' Unions of our Union republics —the Ukraine, Belorussia and the republics of Central Asia, Transcaucasia and the Baltic.

There are also important shortcomings in the work of the creative organizations, however. It should be noted that laxity has been disclosed recently in the work of the Moscow branch of the Writers' Union, a major literary body. Erroneous statements were made at meetings of Moscow writers, statements than ran counter to the Party's policy in the sphere of literature and the arts. Unfortunately, these statements were not always properly refuted, nor was the Party organization of the Moscow writers always equal to the occasion. It will be recalled that the Writers' Unions of the Ukraine, Belorussia and certain other Union republics drew attention to the state of affairs in the Moscow branch of the Writers' Union and justly criticized a number of ideologically defective works and articles that were published in the *Literaturnaya Moskva* anthology.

It is impossible to tolerate such grave shortcomings in the work of the Moscow branch of the Writers' Union, which should set an example for the unions of creative workers in other cities. We hope that the writers themselves, with the aid of the Party organizations, will probe the causes of these shortcomings and take steps to correct matters.

The question of organizing a union of writers of the Russian Federation has been raised here. I believe this proposal should be supported, and that a Russian Republic Writers' Union should be formed. It is not normal that at present the writers of the Russian Federation have no union, although other Union republics have such unions. Needless to say, the Moscow branch of the Writers' Union cannot represent all the writers of the Russian Federation. And it should be remembered that the Russian Federation is a voluntary alliance of many nationalities; it contains, in addition to territories and provinces, 14 autonomous republics, seven autonomous provinces and ten national regions.

The creation of a Russian Republic Writers' Union will number itself among the important measures of the Party Central Committee and the Soviet government directed at further extending the powers of the Union republics and at enhancing the role of the Russian Federation. Besides creative ideological questions, upon which the Russian Republic Writers' Union should focus its attention, serious thought should be given to measures conducive to the growth of the writers' forces in the localities. Care should be taken to create the conditions necessary for the constant creative work of writers in the autonomous republics, territories and provinces; among other things, it is necessary to adjust the matter of royalties paid by local publishing houses and the allocation of paper quotas for printing fiction and poetry.

Our meetings and talks have been fruitful. At these meetings we have candidly expressed views on very important questions having to do with the life and activities of workers in literature and the arts.

Under the leadership of the Communist Party, the Soviet people are successfully translating into reality the decisions of the 20th Party Congress and the plans it drew up for communist construction.

We are celebrating this year the 40th anniversary of the Great October Socialist Revolution. Our people are approaching this momentous historic event with outstanding victories in all spheres of economic and cultural construction and in improving the well-being of the people. Truly immense successes have been achieved in the people's social and political life.

The historic decisions of the 20th Party Congress, which have been warmly endorsed by our people, have called forth an unprecedented upsurge of political and labor activity and of creative initiative on the part of the broadest masses and have provided the conditions for a further flowering of the people's talents. In the course of the vast creative work the communist consciousness of the working people grows, and the magnificent spiritual quality and the finest features of the character and moral makeup of Soviet man—the man of the new epoch, the builder of communism—are being revealed ever more fully.

The mighty October revolutionary wave is irrepressibly surging ahead, sweeping aside all barriers and obstacles on the road to the communist society.

The experience of history shows that our advance toward communism does not proceed along a well-trodden, smooth and level road. It is demanded of those who march in the front ranks of the builders of communism that they be able to see clearly the great goal and the prospects of reaching that goal; that they possess a profound understanding of the laws of social development and have mighty energy and an indomitable will; and that, fearing no difficulties and sparing no effort, they blaze the trail and lead millions of builders of the new society.

The 40 years' experience of socialist construction in our country demonstrates that the Soviet people, closely rallied as they are around their tried and tested leader, the Communist Party, and armed with the all-conquering revolutionary theory of Marxism-Leninism, will creditably accomplish their great historic tasks. There can be no doubt that Soviet writers, poets, artists, sculptors and musicians will continue to be worthy sons of their socialist homeland and will use all their energy and talents to glorify the heroic feats of our great people, the builders of the communist society.

1958:
Premier Khrushchev

It was in 1958 that Nikita Khrushchev became premier of the Soviet Union, that he enacted basic changes in organization of agriculture and education, that he initiated the new Berlin crisis.

From June 1957 on the prestige and authority of Premier Bulganin had declined steadily. The reasons are, of course, now clear. Bulganin had thrown in his lot with the other rivals of Khrushchev in the "anti-Party group" which tried to oust him in that month. Bulganin, like Voroshilov, had saved his position for the time by deserting "the anti-Party group" at the crucial moment and returning to the Khrushchev fold—with an abject confession of fault and error.

This, of course, saved him only for the time being. It was obvious that his political career was finished. However, for the meanwhile there was no public revelation of the fact that Bulganin had been in the opposition to Khrushchev and he retained through 1957 his office as premier. The sign of his coming resignation appeared in early 1958 in connection with the announcement of election constituencies for Kremlin leaders. Bulganin was assigned a constituency inconsistent with his further retention of his high office.

The formal eviction of Bulganin from his post took place March 27 at the meeting of the Supreme Soviet. Nikita Khrushchev himself took over the office. This meant that he held formal leadership of both the Soviet government and of the Communist Party of the Soviet Union. In this sense his formal position had become similar to that of Joseph Stalin during the latter part of his life. However, Khrushchev did not possess Stalin's title of generalissimo. And, in any case, his position was always, and remains, very different from that of

Stalin. Even possessing the title of premier he did not apparently aspire to the absolute dictatorial authority of his predecessor. His authority, from the very beginning of his leadership of the Soviet Communist Party, appeared to rest on an underpinning of genuinely collective leadership of the Party in which Khrushchev maintained a tight rein on the Party Secretariat and on the apparatus of the Central Committee and was generally able through both persuasion and adroit political maneuvering to get the Central Committee itself to go along with him and his major platforms.

It was in 1958 that Khrushchev secured the enactment of two major reforms. In the first of these, which he proposed in a speech on January 22 and which was made law by the Supreme Soviet in late February, the Machinery and Tractor Stations (M.T.S.), which throughout the entire period of collectivization of agriculture had held and operated all important agricultural machinery, were dissolved and their equipment sold to the individual collective farms. Since the M.T.S. had been as much a political device for maintaining iron-handed control over the countryside as economic organizations intended for more efficient use of machinery, this reform amounted, in one of its aspects, to a broader grant of both political and economic authority to the managements of the farms. It was one further step in Khrushchev's effort to improve the efficiency of Soviet farming.

The second major reform made law in 1958 was reorganization of the entire educational system. The changes made provided much greater emphasis on vocational training, required all secondary school students to engage in manual labor in factories and on farms while continuing their schooling, and emphasized in higher education the expansion of night-school and correspondence course education for employed young people. In general the reform made access in the form of full-time physical attendance at universities and institutes of higher education more restricted and more difficult than before. There were several reasons for the educational changes. One was the fact that with the beginning of the advent of provision of universal secondary education for Soviet young people in this period the previous system of secondary education designed primarily to prepare students for higher education was unsatisfactory since it was graduating young people unprepared for work and unable to enter higher education because the government was not prepared to provide facilities for higher education for all who desired it, not, at any rate, at that time. The political reason for the reorganization was to attempt to reduce the danger of student unrest by keeping a higher percentage of younger students in higher education away from actual full-time attendance at universities until they had completed several years of their courses through night classes and correspondence courses. The educational reforms were not popular with Soviet young people—but they were put into effect anyway.

In the field of foreign affairs in 1958 there were still being felt effects of the Hungarian revolution of 1956. Khrushchev made a trip to Hungary in April in the course of which he engaged in no little bluster and anti-Western rhetoric. On June 17 the world was shocked by the announcement of the execution of former Hungarian premier Imre Nagy. This aroused violent anti-Soviet reactions in Western countries and the United States.

At the same time there were signs indicating possibilities for improvement in the international atmosphere. Tourists from many countries disregarded international problems to pour into the Soviet Union in increasing numbers. The Soviet government had opened the country to tourists only three years previously and the fact that there was no effort by the Soviet government to cut off tourism and that, on the contrary, much was being done to expand it, showed a seemingly lasting and serious interest in this kind of cultural exchange between countries. A few Soviet tourists were even permitted to visit Western countries—but only on strictly limited and controlled tours. Despite the coolness in relations with the United States the Americans and the Russians proceeded with a cultural exchange program which, in the big events of the year, saw the Moiseyev folk dancers score a tremendous artistic triumph in the United States and in which the American pianist, Van Cliburn, became a nationally known figure in the Soviet Union.

That there still were keen limitations on cultural exchange between the West and the Soviet Union was shown by the violent official Russian reaction to the award of a Nobel Prize to Boris Pasternak. Pasternak initially accepted with appreciation. Officialdom, however, since Pasternak had published abroad his novel *Doctor Zhivago* which the government had not permitted to be published in the Soviet Union because of very frank passages depicting horrors and hardships of the Revolution and subsequent periods in a distinctly non-Communist light, considered this award to be an affront to the Soviet

Union. Vicious attacks were made on Pasternak by several leading Communist Party spokesmen. They subsided only after Pasternak had renounced the prize and begged in a plaintive letter not to be forced to leave his beloved Russia and go into exile. The most important thing about the Pasternak affair was that Pasternak, despite the storm he had stirred up, was neither shot nor imprisoned and, though subject to terrible moral pressure, was left physically untouched. The Party did take its vengeance on him somewhat later by shipping off to exile on trumped-up charges a woman whom he loved and who had inspired the portrait of the most vivid of the women characters of his epic novel.

It was near the end of 1958 that Khrushchev raised in a belligerent speech, made on November 10 in the presence of leaders of the Polish government and Communist Party, the Berlin question. Khrushchev said in blunt language that the Soviet Union intended to see to it that the status of West Berlin, which remained as an irritating enclave inside Communist-ruled territory, must be changed. This speech which created the new Berlin crisis is the tenth of this series of Khrushchev documents:

SPEECH AT FRIENDSHIP MEETING OF POLISH PEOPLE'S REPUBLIC AND THE SOVIET UNION, NOVEMBER 10, 1958 *

Dear Polish Friends,

Dear Comrades,

We have gathered here today to welcome cordially our dear guests: Wladyslaw Gomulka, First Secretary of the Central Committee of the Polish United Workers' Party (*applause*), Alexander Zawadski, member of the Political Bureau of the Central Committee of the Party and Chairman of the State Council of the Polish People's Republic (*applause*), Jozef Cyrankiewicz, member of the Political Bureau and Chairman of the Council of Ministers of the Polish People's Republic (*applause*), Jerzy Morawski, member of the Political Bureau and Secretary of the Central Committee (*applause*); representatives of the parties of the People's Unity Front—Stefan

* Russian version *Pravda,* Nov. 11, 1958. English translation from Nikita S. Khrushchev, *For Victory in Peaceful Competition with Capitalism* (New York: E. P. Dutton and Co., Inc., 1960), pp. 727–46 (translation reprinted with permission of E. P. Dutton and Co., Inc.).

Ignar, Chairman of the Chief Committee of the United Peasant Party and Vice-Chairman of the Council of Ministers (*applause*), Stanislaw Kulczynski, Chairman of the Central Committee of the Democratic Party and Vice-President of the State Council (*applause*), Edward Gierek, Secretary of the Central Committee and First Secretary of the Katowice Voivodoship Committee of the Polish United Workers' Party (*applause*), Tadeusz Galinski, Minister of Culture and Arts (*applause*), Marian Naszkowski, member of the Central Committee of the Polish United Workers' Party and Deputy Foreign Minister (*applause*), Michalina Tatarkówna, member of the Central Committee and First Secretary of the Lodz City Committee of the Polish United Workers' Party (*applause*), and Tadeusz Gede, member of the Central Committee of the Polish United Workers' Party and Polish Ambassador to the U.S.S.R.

The visit of the delegation of the Polish People's Republic to the Soviet Union, your tour of our country, dear friends, turned into a moving demonstration of fraternal Soviet-Polish friendship.

You visited Moscow, Leningrad, Tbilisi, Kiev and Minsk, and met workers and collective farmers, and people engaged in science and cultural work, Party and government workers. Everywhere you were received as true friends. During your tour of our country you were able to see for yourselves once more the sincere and profound fraternal feelings which the Soviet people have for the Polish people. (*Prolonged applause.*)

The roots of our people's friendship go far into the past. The ruling classes of Russia and Poland—the landed gentry and capitalists —tried hard to sow discord between our peoples, to incite mutual enmity among them. The tsarist policy of oppressing and subjugating Poland has left bitter memories among the Polish people. No less bitter are the memories of Ukrainians and Byelorussians of the dark years under the rule of Polish barons. In the past there was strife and misunderstanding, conflicts and clashes between our countries.

But against all barriers and obstacles, the great idea of friendship was making its way into the hearts of our peoples. It was born and grew stronger in the joint uprisings of the Polish and Russian peasants, it found expression in the creative friendship of the great poets of our peoples—Pushkin and Mickiewicz. It found expression in the utterances of Revolutionary Democrats. The working class, the most progressive, the most revolutionary class of our epoch, the consistent champion of the concepts of internationalism and brotherhood of peoples, became the true standard-bearer of this friendship. (*Applause.*)

Soviet-Polish friendship is illumined by the immortal ideas of the great leader of the working people of the world, Vladimir Ilyich Lenin, who also conducted his titanic revolutionary work on the territory of Poland, eloquently evidenced by the places associated with the memory of Lenin in Cracow and Poronino which are sacredly revered and preserved by the working people of People's Poland. (*Applause.*)

The proletarian revolutionaries of Russia and Poland always advocated the united struggle of the Polish and Russian proletariat, realizing that the independence of Poland was impossible without the freedom of Russia. Many Polish workers, peasants and soldiers took an active part in the Great October Socialist Revolution, in the struggle against the enemies of Soviet power.

A vivid personification of collaboration in the fight of the Polish and Russian working-class movement was the outstanding revolutionary, Felix Dzerzhinsky, who was one of Lenin's closest companions in arms. (*Prolonged applause.*) The Soviet people will always remember with love and admiration this great son of the Polish people who combined a passionate love for the working people with hatred for the oppressors.

The revolutionary traditions of the Polish labour movement were inherited and continued by the glorious Communist Party of Poland, the 40th anniversary of which falls due in December, this year. (*Applause.*) In the most difficult conditions of the fascist régime established by Pilsudski's supporters, the Communist Party of Poland led the struggle of the Polish workers and peasants against the exploiters, defended the principles of proletarian internationalism, educated the mass of the working people in the spirit of utmost support for the heroic struggle of the peoples of the Soviet Union.

Our Party highly appreciates the revolutionary services of the Communist Party of Poland, its selfless struggle for the victory of the great Marxist-Leninist ideas in the Polish labour movement. In the difficult years of the Second World War, the Polish Workers' Party became the continuer of the revolutionary struggle of the Communist Party of Poland. (*Applause.*) It was the leading force of the Polish working people in the struggle for the liberation of the country from the Nazi yoke, for the victory of the people's democratic system, for radical social and economic reforms in the country.

The leading role of the Polish working class has become even greater since the closing of the rift in the labour movement in the country, a fact which was of paramount significance for the further development of People's Poland. As a result of the merger of the Polish Workers' Party and the Polish Socialist Party on the basis of the ideological and organizational principles of Marxism-Leninism, a single party of the working class was formed—the Polish United Workers' Party, which rallied the people for the accomplishment of the great tasks of building a new, socialist society. (*Prolonged applause.*)

The achievements of People's Poland are great, and all her friends rejoice sincerely in them. In place of the old, economically weak bourgeois-landlord Poland which was a pawn in the hands of the big imperialist Powers, a new, truly independent state, a People's Democracy, has been established. Poland's socialist economy is growing and the well-being and cultural standards of her people are improving.

The Polish people have regained their ancient western lands and have obtained broad access to the Baltic. For the first time in history Poland has friendly states for neighbours—the Soviet Union, the Czechoslovak Republic and the German Democratic Republic. (*Applause.*)

The achievements of People's Poland are all the more significant in that they have been secured despite grave hardships. To build a socialist society is a noble, but also a difficult and complicated task. It is only natural for difficulties to arise in the process of a radical break-up of old relations and the building of a new society, in the course of socialist construction, and mistakes are bound to be made. But we Communists, as builders of a new life, should be able to see the main, the most essential, feature in every phenomenon. And the main thing in Poland's development in the years of people's power is undeniably the big achievements in the Polish people's economic and cultural life.

Friendship and fraternal co-operation have become the foundation of our relations since the establishment of the system of people's democracy in Poland. It is known that the imperialists gambled in staking their hopes on various nationalists and revisionists. They cherished the hope of setting our countries at loggerheads and wresting People's

Poland away from the socialist camp. But these insidious designs have failed ingloriously. (*Stormy applause.*)

And it could not be otherwise, comrades. The experience of the Soviet Union's relations with Poland and other socialist states offers convincing evidence that there are no issues between our countries, nor can there be any, that cannot be settled amicably. (*Applause.*)

The nearer our cherished goal, communism, the firmer becomes the co-operation of the socialist countries. With the triumph of socialist relations in the economic sphere and with the growth of communist consciousness national mistrust is being increasingly overcome and the bonds of international friendship are growing stronger. Moreover, the unity of the socialist camp is one of the basic and decisive conditions for the successful advancement of every socialist country along the road to building a new life.

Comrades, a new balance of forces has developed in the world today. The mighty socialist camp is growing and gaining in strength and nothing can arrest the peoples' advance toward socialism and communism. (*Stormy applause.*) Therefore, the attempts of the forces of reaction to prevent the building of socialism in the People's Democracies are doomed to failure.

It is high time for Messrs. Imperialists to realize that the remnants of the reactionary forces in the People's Democracies have no genuine support among the people. In all the People's Democracies the leading role of the working class has become more prominent. The labouring peasantry is in close alliance with it. The intelligentsia is working for the welfare of the people and serves them honestly.

The fact that the balance of forces in the world today is in favour of socialism reduces to hopelessness the imperialist ambitions of restoring the old order of things in the socialist countries. Only incorrigible adventurists can dream of this today. The social gains of the working people in every socialist country are guarded by the might of the entire socialist camp. (*Prolonged applause.*)

Fortunately for mankind, the course of international developments today does not depend entirely on the will of the ruling circles of the imperialist Powers. Experience shows that the international prestige of the countries of the socialist camp, and its influence on the entire flow of world history and the destinies of mankind are growing year by year. In recent years the world has time and again been spared from catastrophic explosions that threatened to touch off a new world conflagration. This has been made possible primarily by the solidarity of the socialist countries, the consistency of their peace policy, and the determination of all the peoples to uphold world peace.

Why are the political and military leaders of certain Western Powers subject to paroxysms of war hysteria? It is because big capital, the monopoly owners, need a tense international situation constantly to intensify the arms race and to enrich themselves at the expense of the working people. Therein lies the main reason for the ever new gambles which the imperialist circles, disregarding realities, undertake. They are hoping thereby to keep mankind constantly on the brink of war, to receive huge super-profits, to subjugate countries which have committed themselves to aggressive military blocs.

The imperialists have turned the German question into an abiding source of international tension. The ruling circles of West Germany are doing everything to whip up military passions against the German Democratic Republic, against the Polish People's Republic, against all the socialist countries. Speeches by Chancellor Adenauer and Defence Minister Strauss, the arming of the Bundeswehr with nuclear weapons and various military manoeuvres all bespeak a definite trend in the policy of the ruling circles of West Germany.

We wish to warn the leaders of the Federal Republic of Germany: The road followed by West Germany today is a road dangerous to peace in Europe and fatal to West Germany herself. Indeed, can realistic politicians today hope for success in a new "march to the East"? Hitler in his time also did everything to fan war hysteria, in order to prepare the ground for an attack on the Soviet Union. However, it is well known how this all ended. It is not hard to imagine the fate of those who would try to unleash new aggression against the socialist states. No speeches by Chancellor Adenauer or his Minister Strauss can change the balance of forces in favour of imperialism. To march against the East would mean marching to death for West Germany. (*Stormy applause.*)

It is high time to realize that the times when imperialists could act from "positions of strength" with impunity have gone never to return, and try as they may, the imperialists will not be able to change the balance of forces in their favour. Nor should they forget the geographical position of West Germany which—with means of warfare what they are today—would not survive a single day of modern warfare. (*Prolonged applause.*)

We do not desire another military conflict. It would be fatal to West Germany and would bring untold disaster to the peoples of other countries. The Soviet Union and the other socialist countries are doing everything to keep the adventurists who are dreaming of new wars from making a fatal step. The West German policy-makers would do well to appraise the existing situation more soberly and desist from whipping up war passions.

The Western press today says much about the Government of the Federal Republic of Germany planning to approach the Soviet Union, the United States of America, Britain and France with a proposal to call a new Four-Power meeting to settle for the Germans, and without the participation of the Germans, the question of unifying their country. But this is nothing but a continuation of the old, unrealistic policy which is contrary to common sense and devoid of legal justification. No Powers have the right to interfere in the internal affairs of the German Democratic Republic and to dictate their will to it. (*Applause.*)

We quite understand the German people's natural yearning for the restoration of their national unity. But German militarists and their American patrons are using these profound national sentiments for purposes that have nothing to do either with the reunification of Germany or with ensuring a lasting peace in Europe. West German militaristic circles are in fact following a course of deepening the cleavage of the country and preparing military adventures.

If the West German Government really wanted reunification, it would have followed the only way leading to this, the way of establishing contacts with the Government of the German Democratic Republic, the way of agreement that would suit both the German Democratic Republic and the Federal Republic of Germany.

The German question, in the sense of reunification of the two German states now in existence, can only be settled by the German people themselves along the lines of *rapprochement* between these states. The conclusion of a peace treaty with Germany is an entirely different matter which, indeed, should be settled primarily by the Four Powers which formed the anti-Hitler coalition, in co-operation with representatives of Germany. The signing of a peace treaty with

Germany would help to normalize the entire situation in Germany and in Europe generally. The Soviet Union has proposed, and is proposing, that this measure should be tackled without delay.

If one is to discuss the Four Powers' undertakings with regard to Germany, one must consider the obligations springing from the Potsdam Agreement.

Let us recall the main obligations assumed by the parties to the Potsdam Agreement with regard to their policy in Germany, what course of development for Germany was determined in Potsdam.

At that time, the members of the anti-Hitler coalition assumed clear-cut and definite obligations: to extirpate German militarism, to prevent its resurgence once and for all, to do everything to prevent Germany from ever again threatening her neighbours or world peace.

The parties to the Potsdam Agreement also recognized the necessity for putting an end to German fascism, blocking its revival in Germany, and curbing all fascist activities and propaganda.

Another important integral part of the Potsdam Agreement was the commitment to liquidate the rule of the cartels, syndicates and other monopolies in the German economy, that is, forces that had brought Hitler to power and had encouraged and financed his military ventures. Such is the substance of the agreements concluded in Potsdam in 1945.

And what do we have today, more than 13 years after the Potsdam Conference?

No one can deny that the Soviet Union, on its part, has scrupulously observed all these agreements and that they have been carried out in full in the eastern part of Germany, the German Democratic Republic. Let us see how the Potsdam Agreement is being carried out in the western part of Germany, in the Federal Republic of Germany, the responsibility for whose development rests with the three Western Powers—the United States, Britain and France.

It should be openly said that militarism, far from having been eradicated, is rearing its head ever higher in West Germany. The Powers which should have fought against the resurgence of German militarism have drawn West Germany into the aggressive military bloc of NATO that they have created. They are doing everything to promote the growth of German militarism and the establishment in West Germany of a mass army equipped with the latest weapons.

By decision of the Government of the Federal Republic of Germany, and, of course, with the approval of the NATO Powers, West Germany is building an army which the German militarists envisage as stronger than the armies of Britain and France. It is, perhaps, already stronger than the French army, in view of the fact that a substantial part of the French army is maintained outside the country in the colonies, where the liberation movement against the French colonialists is at the boiling point.

The armed forces that are being re-created in West Germany are again headed by Nazi generals and admirals. The West German army is being trained in the predatory spirit of the Nazi Wehrmacht, in the spirit of *revanche* and hatred for the Soviet Union and other peaceful states.

Moreover, the German militarists—with the blessing of the Western Powers, and primarily the United States—are receiving nuclear weapons. The Federal Republic already has American rockets which can be fitted with nuclear war-heads.

Economically, West Germany is literally grasping her West European allies by the throat. It is enough to note, for the sake of comparison, that in 1957, for instance, the Federal Republic produced 24,500,000 tons of steel as against 22,000,000 in Britain and little more than 14,000,000 in France.

West Germany is today also financially stronger than either Britain or France. Consider their gold and currency reserves, for instance. According to official figures, West Germany's reserves amounted to over $5,600 million at the end of 1957, as compared with Britain's $2,370 million and France's $775 million. All these economic resources of West Germany are being placed at the service of reviving German imperialism.

No matter which basic provisions of the Potsdam Agreement concerning the demilitarization of Germany and prevention of the resurgence of fascism we may consider, we shall inevitably arrive at the conclusion that these provisions, bearing the signatures of the United States, Britain and France, have been violated by them.

What then is left of the Potsdam Agreement?

One thing, in effect: The so-called Four-Power status of Berlin, that is, a position providing the three Western Powers—the United States, Britain and France—with the possibility of lording it in West Berlin, turning that part of the city, which is the capital of the German Democratic Republic, into a kind of state within a state and profiting by this to conduct subversive activities from West Berlin against the German Democratic Republic, the Soviet Union and the other Warsaw Treaty countries. On top of all this, they make use of the right of unrestricted communication between West Berlin and West Germany via the air space, railways, highways and waterways of the German Democratic Republic, a state which they do not even deign to recognize.

The question arises: Who stands to benefit from this situation and why have the United States, France and Britain not violated this part of the quadripartite agreement as well? The answer is clear: They have no intention of violating this part of the Potsdam Agreement. On the contrary, they cling to it, for the agreement on Berlin is advantageous to the Western Powers, and only them. The Western Powers, of course, would not be averse to perpetuating such "inter-allied" privileges for ever, even though they have long destroyed the legal basis for their presence in Berlin. (*Applause.*)

Is it not time for us to draw appropriate conclusions from the fact that the key items of the Potsdam Agreement concerning the maintenance of peace in Europe and, consequently, throughout the world, have been violated and that certain forces continue to nurture German militarism, strongly encouraging it in the direction in which it was pushed before the Second World War, that is, towards the East? Is it not time for us to reconsider our attitude to this part of the Potsdam Agreement and to repudiate it? (*Prolonged applause.*)

The time has obviously arrived for the signatories of the Potsdam Agreement to discard the remnants of the occupation régime in Berlin and thereby make it possible to create a normal situation in the capital of the German Democratic Republic. The Soviet Union, on its part, would hand over to the sovereign German Democratic Republic the functions in Berlin that are still exercised by Soviet agencies. This, I think, would be the correct thing to do. (*Applause.*)

Let the United States, France and Britain themselves build their relations with the German Democratic Republic, let them reach agreement with it themselves if they are interested in any questions concerning Berlin. As for the Soviet Union, we shall sacredly honour our obligations as an ally of the German Democratic Republic—obligations which stem from the Warsaw Treaty and which we have repeatedly reaffirmed to the German Democratic Republic. (*Prolonged applause.*)

If any forces of aggression attack the German Democratic Republic, which is a full-fledged member of the Warsaw Treaty, we shall regard this as an attack on the Soviet Union, on all the Warsaw Treaty countries. (*Stormy, prolonged applause.*) We shall then rise to the defence of the German Democratic Republic, and this will signify the defence of the vital security interests of the Soviet Union, of the entire socialist camp, and of the cause of world peace. (*Stormy, prolonged applause.*)

The Western Powers which, at one time, signed the Potsdam Agreement are today working to aggravate the international situation, to encourage the growing militarist tendencies of German revenge-seekers, that is, they support all that the Potsdam Agreement denounced. They have long since been guided by the aggressive North Atlantic Treaty and not by the Potsdam Agreement.

They have violated the Potsdam Agreement repeatedly and with impunity, while we remain faithful to it as if nothing had changed. We have every reason to free ourselves from such outlived obligations under the Potsdam Agreement which the Western Powers are clinging to, and to pursue a policy with regard to Berlin that would spring from the interests of the Warsaw Treaty.

The leaders of West Germany say that good relations between the Soviet Union and the Federal Republic of Germany can only be established if the Soviet Union ceases to support the German Democratic Republic and if it brings pressure to bear on it along lines required by the West. Bonn does not, apparently, desire good relations with the Soviet Union if it entertains such absurd hopes. If the Government of the Federal Republic really wants to have good relations with the Soviet Union it should abandon, once and for all, the hope that we shall cease to support the German Democratic Republic. (*Prolonged applause.*)

The Government of the Polish People's Republic has shown valuable initiative in proposing the establishment in Central Europe of a zone where atomic, hydrogen and rocket weapons would not be manufactured or stockpiled. This constructive proposal has been supported by the Governments of the Soviet Union, Czechoslovakia, the German Democratic Republic and other socialist and non-socialist countries which firmly stand for the preservation of peace. The ruling circles of West Germany, however, have turned down the Polish proposal and have taken to equipping the Bundeswehr with atomic and rocket weapons. German militarism today is more dangerous to the world than before. German militarists hope to swallow the German Democratic Republic and to take away from Poland her ancient western lands. They lay claims to the territory of Czechoslovakia and other socialist countries.

But they are playing with fire. The Oder-Neisse frontier is a frontier of peace. (*Prolonged applause.*) Any encroachment by German revenge-seekers on the German Democratic Republic would be regarded as an encroachment on the Oder-Neisse frontier, as a threat to the security of our peoples. (*Stormy applause.*)

The Polish people can rest assured that in the Soviet Union they have a reliable friend and ally in the struggle against German militarism and imperialist aggression. (*Stormy, prolonged applause.*)

I would like to say a few words about our relations with some of our neighbours. You have read the Soviet Government's statement to the Government of Iran, published several days ago. We made this statement because Iran is being increasingly drawn into the aggressive NATO bloc and because the threat has arisen lately of her territory being turned into an actual *place d'armes* of the American military.

We would not like to believe that the Iranian Government and the Shah of Iran personally would take this dangerous road. We hope that a sober appraisal of all the dangers involved for Iran in such a foreign policy will prevail, and that the Iranian leaders will not follow in the wake of outside forces to which the interests of Iranian security are really foreign.

It is well known that the Soviet Union has not threatened and does not threaten anyone. This applies in full to our neighbours, including Iran, whose independence we respect and shall continue to respect. We do not seek to maintain military bases on her territory and, indeed, we would not agree to this even if we were invited to have such bases on the territory of Iran.

One may ask: How, under these circumstances, should one regard the actions designed to turn Iran into an American spring-board, in particular through the conclusion of a new military treaty with the United States—the aims of which, by the way, those who press for the conclusion of the treaty make no effort to conceal? We regard it, and shall regard it, as an act hostile to our country, with all the attendant consequences.

No neighbour of the Soviet Union, whether Iran or any other

country, would place its territory at the disposal of the aggressive NATO grouping if it had the good intention of strengthening good-neighbour co-operation with the Soviet Union. If it does take such a step, it means that it will be committing an aggressive act against the U.S.S.R.

We sincerely hope that the Iranian Government will not nullify everything good done in the recent past by both countries to adjust relations between them and will not invite calamity upon its country.

Comrades, the socialist camp is a mighty stronghold of world peace. Its peace policy, the policy of friendship and co-operation, conforms to the fundamental interests of all peoples. The source of strength and power of the socialist camp is the unity and solidarity of the countries belonging to it. (*Applause.*) Any attempts to weaken and undermine this unity play into the hands of the enemies of peace and socialism.

Our enemies spare no efforts to weaken the influence of the Communist and Workers' parties among the broad masses of the working people, to undermine the international communist movement. All the attempts of imperialist reaction, however, invariably suffer shipwreck.

A most striking demonstration of the increased might of the world communist movement, of its greater unity and solidarity were the meetings of representatives of the Communist and Workers' parties held a year ago in Moscow during the celebration of the 40th anniversary of the Great October Socialist Revolution. The Declaration and the Peace Manifesto summed up in a creative way the collective experience of the Communist and Workers' parties, formulated the tasks of the communist movement in the struggle for peace, democracy and socialism at the present stage.

The most important result of the year since the November meetings has been the still greater unity of the international communist movement. Evidence of the solidarity of the world communist movement is the unanimous stand taken by all Communist and Workers' parties against present-day revisionism, which found its fullest expression in the programme of the League of Communists of Yugoslavia.

There was not a single Marxist party in the world or any sizable group within such a party which would share the anti-Marxist views set forth in the programme of the Yugoslav League of Communists or would defend the position of the Yugoslav leadership. All the revolutionary parties of the working class assessed the Yugoslav programme as revisionist and severely condemned the subversive, splitting actions of the leaders of the Yugoslav League of Communists.

I should like to stress the great significance of a number of statements by Comrade Gomulka, who pointed out that the leadership of the League of Communists of Yugoslavia, owing to its fallacious revisionist theories, is isolating Yugoslavia from the community of socialist countries and is thereby causing harm to the international labour movement, and that the attitude of the leaders of the Yugoslav League of Communists towards the camp of socialist states corresponds objectively to the wishes and aspirations of international reactionary forces, whose support for Yugoslavia is not accidental.

We fully and entirely subscribe to the assessment of Yugoslav revisionism made by Comrade Gomulka. (*Stormy applause.*)

The unanimous condemnation of revisionism by the revolutionary parties of the working class is a remarkable fact, comrades. It indicates how mature our parties have become ideologically, how great is their unity on the basis of the principles of Marxism-Leninism, what an invincible and ever-increasing force is the international communist movement. (*Stormy applause.*)

We have reiterated how highly we value the past services of the Communist Party and the people of Yugoslavia, who have made such great sacrifices in the struggle against German and Italian fascism. In that struggle our peoples fought shoulder to shoulder against a common enemy.

Unfortunately the leaders of Yugoslavia, the individuals who head the party, are backsliding from a working-class position to the position of its enemies. Therefore, one can hardly expect mutual understanding now in our relations with the League of Communists of Yugoslavia on a Party level, although we should not like to give up hope in this respect.

On a state level we shall strive to promote friendly relations with Yugoslavia, to extend trade and cultural intercourse. In the future, too, we are ready to maintain trade with Yugoslavia on a mutually profitable basis.

What does this mean? It means that we shall sell to Yugoslavia what she needs if we have such goods available for sale, and purchase from her what we need and what Yugoslavia finds it possible to sell. This is what is called trade on a mutually advantageous basis. (*Applause.*)

We stand for a broad interchange of various delegations with Yugoslavia—delegations of persons engaged in cultural activities, delegations of collective farmers, workers and others. It would be extremely beneficial, for instance, for our collective farmers to visit Yugoslavia and for Yugoslav peasants to come to our country, or for workers of the Soviet Union to be able to visit Yugoslavia and for Yugoslav workers to visit our country more often. Let the working people of our countries familiarize themselves with each other's life. Let them see that no one bears any enmity for Yugoslavia, that our peoples have only one desire—closer friendship. (*Applause.*)

After the normalization of relations with Yugoslavia, after the elimination of all extraneous elements which existed in the relations between our countries, after the clearing up of absurd accusations, quite a few positive results have been achieved both in the relations between our countries and with regard to problems of co-operation in the struggle for peace. We may note with satisfaction that on many major international issues our positions often coincide, and we hope that in the future, too, our countries will join their efforts in an active struggle for the preservation and consolidation of peace. (*Applause.*)

As for our differences on ideological problems, we shall continue to wage an irreconcilable struggle against all distortions of Marxism-Leninism. All fraternal Communist and Workers' parties are united in this. They regard revisionism as the main danger at the present stage. The struggle against revisionism is the struggle for the purity of our ideas, for the monolithic unity and solidarity of the international communist movement. (*Prolonged applause.*)

Comrades, majestic perspectives, perspectives of building a communist society are opening before us. We rejoice in the fact that the vanguard detachments of the working class, the ranks of those who are rallied under the banner of Marxism-Leninism, are multiplying. (*Prolonged applause.*)

The working class, the collective-farm peasantry, the intellectuals in the Soviet Union are confidently advancing onward to communism. (*Applause.*) The 20th Congress of the C.P.S.U. was a historic landmark on this road. Now our country is preparing for the 21st Congress of the C.P.S.U., the congress of the builders of communism. (*Applause.*) This congress will outline a programme for a further great advance in the Soviet economy, in the material and cultural standard of life of the entire Soviet people. (*Applause.*)

There is no doubt that these majestic tasks will be fulfilled with credit. The Soviet Union, within a historically short time, will overtake and forge ahead of the most highly developed capitalist countries in per capita production. This will be a great contribution to the victory of communism over capitalism, a system which is moribund. (*Stormy applause.*)

The achievements of the Soviet Union, the Chinese People's Republic, the Polish People's Republic and all the socialist countries, the radical changes in the world balance of forces in favour of socialism, instil confidence in many millions of working people in the ultimate triumph of the great ideas of Marxism-Leninism. The victorious banner of communism rises ever higher above our planet. (*Prolonged applause.*)

Allow me, on behalf of all the working people of our country, to wish the fraternal Polish people fresh successes in building a socialist Poland. (*Stormy applause.*)

Allow me to express confidence that the bonds of fraternal friendship between the peoples of the Soviet Union and the Polish People's Republic will become ever closer and stronger day by day. (*Stormy applause.*)

Long live the indestructible Soviet-Polish friendship! (*Stormy applause.*)

Long live the parties of the Polish People's Unity Front, of which the Polish United Workers' Party is the leading force! (*Stormy applause.*)

Long live the militant vanguard of the working people of the Polish People's Republic—the Polish United Workers' Party and its Central Committee headed by Comrade Gomulka! (*Stormy applause.*)

Long live the unity of the countries of the great socialist camp! (*Stormy applause.*)

Long live world peace! (*Stormy, prolonged applause. All rise.*)

1959:
Khrushchev Discovers America

During 1959 the 21st Party Congress met and approved the new Seven-Year Economic Plan, the Soviet sent rockets to the moon, and Khrushchev made his first visit to the United States.

The 21st Party Congress was convened in Moscow at the end of January. Khrushchev addressed it with his report on the proposals for the new Seven-Year Plan on January 27 and again with his concluding speech on February 5. The Seven-Year Plan was promulgated in part in order to cover up the fact that the Five-Year Plan which was to run from 1956 through 1960 had been, in certain respects, over-ambitious. But there was the additional reason for the shift from a basic five-year plan period to a longer seven-year planning period in that it gave Soviet economic planners a longer perspective in their work.

The new Seven-Year Plan served to highlight the dramatic achievements of the Soviet Union in the postwar period in increasing output of heavy industry and also, though to a markedly lesser extent, the output of light industry and agriculture. Soviet industrial and technological-scientific success was the single most important fact in Russian life in the years after World War II. It was one of the most important factors in influencing the world balance of power. Year by year the Soviet Union, both before Stalin's death and after, was steadily gaining on the United States in the effort to become the leading industrial power of the world. Take, for example, steel. In 1945 Soviet steel production was 12 million metric tons—17 per cent of American production. By 1953, it had risen to 38 million—38 per cent of that of the United States. By 1958 it was up to 55 million tons (by 1960 it would rise to 65 million tons—72 per cent of American production for that year).

The new Seven-Year Plan proposed as its basic slogan that the Soviet Union by the last year of this plan—1965—would overtake the United States in basic industrial might. Such a goal of overtaking the United States in industrial output—though not perhaps quite so soon as 1965—had already become a practical and possible goal for the Soviet government in actual fact. And the continuing economic upsurge of the country was the realistic background for the new self-assurance of the Soviet leadership manifested in so many different ways, both in word and deed, in world affairs.

In 1959 there were three outstanding Soviet "firsts" in space rocketry. On January 4 Lunik I went into orbit around the sun as the first man-made planet. On September 13 Lunik II hit the moon. In the most impressive accomplishment of all on October 4 Lunik III circled the moon and radioed back to the world photographs of the hitherto unseen other side of the moon.

In foreign affairs during 1959 Khrushchev and the Soviet government continued to keep the Berlin question in the forefront of world attention. The new Soviet position on the German question as a whole was further clarified by Khrushchev in a speech made in Leipzig on March 6—published in its full and official text by *Pravda* only somewhat later. Khrushchev in essence said in this speech that the reunification of Germany in the near future was unlikely. It seemed clear from Khrushchev's remarks that the Soviet Union looked on the division of Germany into two parts as a more or less long-term thing. This Soviet stand had, of course, broad implications for the future of Germany and of all of Europe.

On February 21 British Prime Minister Harold MacMillan arrived in Moscow for a state visit in the Soviet Union—returning Khrushchev's visit to Great Britain of 1956. The visit marked the end of the period in which the Hungarian Revolt and its aftermath had stood in the way of improvement of Russian relations with the West. In January Soviet First Deputy Premier Anastas I. Mikoyan had paid a visit to the United States and toured the country from coast to coast amidst intense public interest. The Mikoyan trip was "informal" in the sense that no formal invitation had been issued to him and that he came, so to speak, "on his own"—but, of course, with the knowledge and approval of the U.S. government. Mikoyan's visit was the curtain-raiser in the series of events which led to Khrushchev's visit to the United States in September. In the early summer of this year a large Soviet exhibit opened at the Coliseum in New York. This was one side of an exchange between the two countries which resulted in the opening of an American exhibit in Moscow at the end of July. Vice-President Nixon journeyed to Russia in order to officially open the American exhibit and to tour the Soviet Union over a period of two weeks. The outstanding event of his journey was a friendly clash and spirited debate between Nixon and Premier Khrushchev in the kitchen of the model home at the American exhibit—an event which went down into history because it had been recorded in full on television tape recorders. The Nixon visit to Russia led directly and almost immediately to the Khrushchev visit to the United States. President Eisenhower issued his invitation in August and Khrushchev arrived at Washington on September 15.

He visited Washington, New York, Los Angeles, San Francisco, Iowa, and Pittsburgh. His visit was concluded with a brief stay with the President at Camp David. He left on September 28. The Khrushchev trip to the United States provided plenty of sparks and drama and was one of the most thoroughly covered news events of the century. It represented over-all a perceptible *rapprochement* between the United States and the Soviet Union.

It was in the aftermath of the relative warmth and cordiality of the conclusion of his visit to America that Khrushchev went to Peking on September 30. Although both the Chinese Communists and Khrushchev were careful to observe an appearance of unity in the course of this visit there were sufficient small indications to point up the fact that feelings between Khrushchev and Mao Tse-tung were less than cordial.

As the eleventh item in this Khrushchev anthology there have been selected four documents arising from his trip to the United States. The first of these is his speech at the motion picture studio luncheon in Hollywood in which, in the course of an exchange with motion picture producer Spyros Skouras, Khrushchev gave a vivid scene from his uncouth youth and went on to make a plaintive complaint against the State Department and local American officials for having refused him permission on security grounds to visit Disneyland. The second of these is an American version—in the form of a stenographic report —of Khrushchev's free-for-all with American labor leaders in San

Francisco. It represents the extraordinary spectacle of one of the more voluble and outspoken statesmen of the world unable at times to get in a word edgewise in the heated discussion taking place. The third document is the Soviet version of this same meeting which illustrates, in comparison with the stenographic report, how varied the coverage of an important event can be in dependence on who is doing the reporting. The fourth document is the speech made by Khrushchev on his return to the Soviet Union on September 28 in Moscow. This gives Khrushchev's reaction to his trip:

SPEECH OF N. S. KHRUSHCHEV AT LUNCHEON HELD AT THE TWENTIETH CENTURY-FOX STUDIOS *

MR. JOHNSTON, MRS. JOHNSTON:

I am also addressing you, my dear brother Greek! (*N. S. Khrushchev turned at this point to Spyros P. Skouras, President of the Twentieth Century-Fox Film Corporation, who spoke before him.*) Yes, ladies and gentlemen, Russians have from times of old called the Greeks brothers, because the Russians took part in the war against the Turks to liberate Greece. You should also know that back in ancient times the Russians adopted the religious, Christian rites of the Greeks. So you and we are also in a way brothers in Christ. (*Animation, applause.*) You might say to me that I'm an atheist. But then I am speaking not only for myself, but also on behalf of our entire people, among whom there are both atheists and believers—Christians, Moslems and people of other religions.

Americans always begin their speeches by saying "Ladies and Gentlemen." Allow me, too, to begin that way.

Ladies and Gentlemen (*applause*),

I thank Mr. Johnston for the invitation to this meeting.

I am very glad to meet the flower of the U.S. stage and screen world represented in this hall. I think the comrades who have come with me to the United States and are accompanying me share my joy.

I must say that I had planned to speak along somewhat different lines, but Mr. Spyros Skouras here has led me off my tack. (*Laughter,*

* This speech was in part a response to the introductory remarks of Spyros P. Skouras. Russian text in *Pravda*, Sept. 22, 1959, pp. 1–2. English text, translated from this Russian text, as distributed by Soviet news and official agencies, can be found in *Khrushchev in America* (New York: Crosscurrents Press, 1960), pp. 104–14.

applause.) I hadn't meant my speech to follow the direction which Mr. Skouras laid down in his speech, for some people might have suspected me of having come here to make propaganda for our way of life and of wanting to win over all of you fine Americans to our side. By the way, I should like that. Anyone wishing to come to our country is welcome, we'll treat him to Russian pies. (*Laughter, applause.*) But since you've brought up the subject of how ordinary people work their way up, allow me to answer you.

Mr. Skouras said he had risen from the ranks. What were you in Greece? (Skouras says that he began working for hire at the age of 12.)

That naturally produces an impression, and I wish to express my respect for you. But I'm not amazed. Would you like to know what I was? I began working when I learned to walk. Till the age of 15 I tended calves, then sheep, and then the landlord's cows. I did all that before I was 15. Then I worked at a factory owned by Germans and later in coal pits owned by Frenchmen. I worked at Belgian-owned chemical plants, and now I am Prime Minister of the great Soviet state. (*Stormy applause, Voice: "We knew that."*)

KHRUSHCHEV: What if you did? I'm not ashamed of my past. All honest labor, whatever its nature, is worthy of respect. (*Applause.*) Work, as such, cannot be dirty. It's only the conscience that can be. (*Applause.*) All honest labor is worthy of respect.

SKOURAS: How many Prime Ministers are there in Russia?

KHRUSHCHEV: And how many Presidents do you have? (*Laughter, applause.*) Anyway, I'll answer you. We have the Government of the Soviet Union and I have been made Chairman of the Council of Ministers. We also have 15 Union Republics and each republic has its government. In other words, there are 15 Prime Ministers. Besides, we have Prime Ministers of the Autonomous Republics. How many do you have? (*Laughter, applause.*)

SKOURAS: We have two million presidents of companies. (*Laughter.*)

KHRUSHCHEV: We have Comrade Tikhonov here with us. Please rise. Is anyone here in America richer than this man? What is he? He was a worker, then became a metallurgical engineer. And now he is Chairman of the Dnepropetrovsk Economic Council. He is in charge of huge iron-and-steel works. He is in charge of huge chemical works. The Dnepropetrovsk Economic Council supplies more than half the iron ore mined in the Soviet Union. Isn't that enough, Mr. Skouras? (*Laughter.*)

SKOURAS: That's a monopoly!

KHRUSHCHEV: Yes, it is a monopoly, but a monopoly of the people! Comrade Tikhonov has no capital of his own. All that he manages belongs to the people. (*Applause.*) So it's no use arguing about who has greater opportunities, you or we, because you can't beat us there.

We have Professor Yemelyanov here with us. He is an atomic scientist of ours. What was he? An ex-worker, he graduated from an institute and became a metallurgical engineer. Now he is an eminent scientist in the field of atomic energy. There you have two of our presidents, and we have millions of presidents just like them.

As you see, gentlemen, you had better put aside the question of ordinary people working their way up. That's the best thing you can do. (*Animation, applause.*) I might quote the Russian saying in this regard. It says, "You cannot catch old sparrows with chaff." (*Laughter.*)

America is a fine country and its great people are a worthy people. Time was when America was admired by all peoples of the world. It has taught everyone a lesson in industrial development. It is the home of assembly-line production, which is the most progressive and efficient industrial process. After the Revolution we set out to learn from the Americans. We sent our engineers to you for training. They studied in your colleges and universities and were employed as ordinary workers at Ford's and elsewhere. The man in charge of our automobile industry today is Engineer Strokin, a Minister of the Soviet Government. He is one of our best automobile engineers. He used to work for Ford, and Ford thought highly of him; he suggested that Strokin stay and work for him. If Grandfather Ford were alive, he could have told you what his pupil is worth.

Colonel Cooper, an American engineer, was awarded the Order of the Red Banner of Labor for services as consultant for the Dnieper Hydropower Project. Hundreds of American engineers worked in our industries at the time of the First Five-Year Plan. We thank you for it and bow low before you for your help. (*Applause.*) You may be proud of our successes, just as a good teacher, or professor, is proud when his effort is rewarded by his pupil being worthy of his preceptor. We learned from you, and you need not be ashamed of your pupils, you should be proud of them, because now we want to catch up with you. (*Animation, applause.*) It follows that our people are bright pupils, not dunces. (*Laughter, applause.*) In the First Five-Year Plan years, when you helped us build our first tractor plant, it took us two years to get it going properly, because we had no experience. When Ford helped us build the Gorky Automobile Plant, we ruined quite a few machines before learning to make automobiles. But now we, your ex-pupils, have sent a rocket into outer space and a Soviet pennant has now reached the moon. (*Stormy applause.*) Not bad pupils, are we? (*Animation, applause.*) Yet there are still some people in your country who keep harping that people in the Soviet Union are little short of slaves. But what sort of slave system is that? How could a slave system have assured such unprecedented progress in science and art as we have made in our country?

The reason why Roman civilization, as well as Greek civilization, declined, esteemed Mr. Skouras, was that it was a civilization built on slave labor, which shackled man's energy, will and freedom. Science and the arts can attain full bloom only if there is the fullest freedom of the individual and of society. (*Applause.*)

You and we have different ideas on this matter. You say that profit, or business as you call it, is the prime mover of people's energy, of their intellect and initiative. We say a different thing: The prime mover is man's conscience, his awareness of the fact that he is free and working for himself, for his kin, for the society in which he lives, that the means of production belong to society and not to some individual who grows rich by exploiting other people's labor.

You are against our concept and we are against yours. Well, what's to be done about it? Carry on under capitalism, with your corporations and whatever else you have. Don't seek salvation for "God's lost sheep"—the Soviet people, who have chosen the path of socialist development. You'll only gain by it if we come a cropper and return to the fold of capitalism. Why should you worry if you think we are on the wrong path? (*Laughter.*) You have done your civic duty. You have told us that we are following a path which you think leads us to a pitfall. That will do, thank you for warning us. But I say to you that I see no pitfall ahead but a clear vista, the future happiness of mankind. Some of you may believe that I don't understand certain simple things. That is their affair, of course. But I, too, am entitled to tell such people that they have not yet risen to an understanding of the new that is communist construction.

Where are we to seek a way out of the present situation? Shall we settle the matter in a free-for-all? That, indeed, is how disputes were settled in the past. But formerly things were much simpler; people would come to grips and tear out handfuls of each other's hair, beard and whiskers, and then new beards and new whiskers would grow in their place. But now you know that if a new rough-and-tumble ensued, there would be nothing left to grow; as we say in Russia, "It's too late to cry over lost hair after your head is cut off." (*Laughter, applause.*)

That is why, ladies and gentlemen, we say: Let us live in peace. (*Stormy applause.*) Let time judge who is right and who is wrong. Time is the best judge. This is our attitude. I have come to you so that we may achieve a better understanding of each other, so that you may get a better idea of what our people are like. I am not a delegate sent to conduct diplomatic negotiations, I am the guest of your President, the guest of your great country. And that is why I want to discuss things in a way that will enable us to find reasonable solutions and settle controversial issues with the object of banishing war and establishing peace and friendship between the peoples of our countries and between all peoples. (*Stormy applause.*)

I think that the argument with my brother Greek on this matter is over and that each retains his own opinion. I respect your opinion, so you, too, leave mine alone. (*Animation.*) Carry on under capitalism, "and God help you," as the saying goes. (*Laughter, applause.*) And we, for our part, will carry on under socialism and build communism. At the moment you are ahead of us in the economic field, we still have to put in a great deal of work and sweat to catch up with you. Very good, we will put our backs to it but we will catch and pass you, and forge ahead. I am convinced of that. You may laugh at it for the moment, but you'd do better to wait till we pass you and say, "Good-bye, Messrs. Capitalists, our train is moving on." (*Animation.*) By the way, a group of U.S. economists who studied our country's potentialities in the competition with your country have estimated that in production the Soviet Union will overtake the United States by 1970. I repeat, it isn't I who say so but American economists. If you like, I will let you read their report. That is, if you haven't read it yet. I must say that nowadays I read less fiction and fewer political books, because I have to read mostly statements made by U.S. Senators, economists and journalists. (*Laughter.*)

Ladies and gentlemen, I had not meant to make a political speech here. It was Mr. Skouras who introduced class complications from the outset. (*Laughter.*) I did not want that, I wanted to say nice things to you. I wanted to tell you we were very happy to meet you. In the Soviet Union, you know, we have the deepest respect and affection for intellectuals. And you are not only intellectuals, but toilers of the most refined, I might say the most delicate, of arts—subtle artistry. That being so, you require gentle treatment, loving care and warmth, like orchids, which need the right humidity, light and warmth. In our country, we cannot think of making any progress without producing an intelligentsia of our own, without developing our culture in every way. There would be no point in building a new society without that.

I recall certain incidents of our Civil War, my meetings and conversations with intellectuals of the former, czarist Russia. I was in the Red Army when we beat the White Guards and drove them into the Black Sea. My unit was stationed in the Kuban region, and I was quartered in the house of an educated family. The landlady was a graduate of the St. Petersburg Institute for young ladies of gentle birth. As for me, I suppose I still smelled of coal when I was living in her house. There were other educated people in that house—a lawyer, engineer, teacher and musician. We Red Army men mixed with them. When they met me, a Communist, they saw that, far from eating human flesh, I was starving, to put it plainly. Sometimes I even had no bread, but I never tried to take any away from them or, indeed, ask for anything. They came to respect me. The mistress of the house saw that we Bolsheviks were not at all the sort of people our enemies made us out to be. Members of the old intelligentsia convinced themselves more and more that Communists were honest people who sought no personal gain and dedicated themselves to the common weal. We were still unpolished, uneducated workers at that time, but we wanted to receive an education, to learn to govern the state, to build a new society, and we devoted all our energy to it. I remember the landlady asking me: "Tell me, what do you know about ballet? You're a simple miner, aren't you?" To tell the truth, I didn't really know anything about ballet at that time, because I hadn't seen any ballet then and, moreover, had never seen a ballerina. (*Laughter.*) I had no idea what it was all about, so to speak. (*Laughter.*) But I said to her, "Just wait, we're going to have everything, ballet too." Frankly speaking, if I had been asked at that time just what we were going to have, I might not quite have known what to say, but I was certain that there was a better life ahead. It was Lenin's Party that had instilled this certainty in our hearts.

And now I wish to ask you what country has the most highly developed ballet. Would it be your country? No. Why, you don't even have a state opera and ballet theater. Your theaters subsist solely on the hand-outs of wealthy people. But in our country it is the state that appropriates funds for the development of art. The whole world recognizes that Soviet ballet is the most extensively developed. We are proud of it. When our ballet company toured the United States, you rewarded it with well-deserved applause and praise. And what about our dramatic theater, what about our stagecraft? I won't brag but will merely ask you to consult your conscience and tell me whether our theater is on the decline or on the rise. And what about our movies? You and we have different tastes. But it is a fact, isn't it, that our films win prizes at international festivals. They are awarded to our films by impartial people who know their business. One of the prizes at a recent world festival went to the screen version of *The Fate of a Man,* a story by M. A. Sholokhov, the outstanding writer, who is here with us. The film is a masterpiece.

We also give our intelligentsia substantial material support. At any rate, they don't have to go to the doctor to be treated for undernourishment; in fact, they often seek medical advice against excessive weight. (*Laughter.*) That isn't a bad indication. Professor Markov here, who is a prominent doctor, will bear me out. (*Applause.*)

Our art workers receive not only the remuneration that they earn. The best of them are also decorated or awarded Lenin Prizes. That is a token of the deep respect in which they are held by our people and government. Come and see our country, and speak to our art workers! And what about literature? We are proud of it. Meet Mikhail Alexandrovich Sholokhov, a Don Cossack. He has brought fame to our country by writing *And Quiet Flows the Don, Virgin Soil Upturned* and other excellent works.

Now I will answer a question put by my Greek friend. By the way, Mr. Skouras, I hope you are not offended that I take this liberty in speaking to you? It is just to show my good feelings for you. If you are offended in any way, I'm willing to apologize and to take no more liberties.

SKOURAS: I am honored to have the Premier of a great nation argue with me.

KHRUSHCHEV: I am not arguing, I am simply discussing matters with you. I am the guest and cannot argue with my host. (*Laughter, applause.*) Besides, it was you who started the argument, if that is what you call it. (*Laughter, applause.*) You referred here to the aid extended to Soviet people after the Civil War, during the terrible famine of 1921–1922, when ARA, the American Relief Administration, was set up to aid the starving population. The committee was headed by Herbert Hoover. We remember that well, and we thank you.

But I feel I must raise a "but" on this score. The "but" is that our people remember not only the fact that America helped us through ARA and that as a result thousands of people were saved from starvation in the Volga Region. They also remember that in the hard time after the October Revolution, U.S. troops led by their generals landed on Soviet soil to help the White Guards fight our Soviet system. And they were not the only ones to land. The Japanese landed too, the French landed in Odessa and the Germans advanced as far as the Soviet Caucasus. The armed forces of bourgeois Poland seized Kiev. The British, too, landed their forces to fight us. Many European capitalist countries, as well as the United States and Japan, sent their troops into an offensive against the young Soviet state in an effort to strangle our Revolution.

You can imagine what our plight was at that time. We were ruined by the First World War and then by the Civil War. Our mines lay idle and our factories were at a standstill. We were starving, we had nothing to wear and we went barefoot. But what happened? In spite of all these terrific difficulties, we beat your troops, pushed all invaders into the sea and defeated the White Guards.

Why do I recall all this? For the simple reason that if you and your allies had not landed troops at that time, we would have made short shrift of the White Guards and would have had no Civil War, no ruin and no famine. And you wouldn't have had to help Soviet people through ARA, whose work you have just mentioned.

But even so, even in these circumstances, we thank the Americans for the help they gave us.

Your armed intervention in Russia was the most unpleasant thing that ever occurred in the relations between our two countries, for we had never waged war against America until then; our troops have never set foot on American soil, while your troops have set foot on Soviet soil. You see how it is, ladies and gentlemen. Please excuse me for these comments. I assure you that I had planned to make a very short and unemotional speech. But I cannot be silent when someone treads on my pet corn, even if he does so after putting a pad on it. I cannot put up with it. I want to be a worthy partner who gives a worthy explanation in defense of his country, his people, his state and our ideology.

In conclusion, I want to express once more my heartfelt thanks for the invitation to visit your country, and to say that my companions and I are pleased with our stay in America. But, on the other hand, I cannot help voicing my disappointment, voicing some surprise, at a certain circumstance.

We have always regarded the United States as a strong, well-organized state whose people have a highly-developed culture. Here we are now, in your city, where you have the cream of the artistic world —film stars, as you say in your country. Also living here are industrial workers, ordinary Americans, people of a vast variety of trades. We should have liked to meet them, to see how they live, and how they work and rest. Now just think of it, I, a Soviet man, the Prime Minister of the Soviet Union, have come to you as a guest; when I was on my way here, an itinerary was drawn up for me and a program of what I could see here and what places I could visit. It was planned, among other things, that I would visit Disneyland. But I have just been told that I cannot go to Disneyland. (*Laughter.*) Why not? I asked. Is it by any chance because you now have rocket-launching pads there? (*Laughter.*) "No," they tell me, "you can't go there because"—just listen to this!—"the American authorities cannot guarantee your safety if you go there."

What is it? Has cholera or plague broken out there that I might catch? (*Laughter.*) Or has Disneyland been seized by bandits who might destroy me? But your policemen are such strong men, they could lift a bull by the horns. Surely they could deal effectively with bandits! Then I said I should like to go to Disneyland just the same and see how Americans spend their leisure. (*Applause.*) "Do as you like," they answered me, "but in that case we cannot guarantee your safety." What was I to do—go and commit suicide? (*Laughter.*) This is the situation I, your guest, find myself in! It is more than I can understand. I won't know how to explain it to my people. Come to our country if you like, we will go with anyone, you may walk in our streets and parks, and I guarantee that a foreign guest will hear nothing from Soviet people but words of respect and welcome. What am I to say to the organizers of my U.S. tour? I thought you had a well-organized household. Putting me in a closed car and stewing me in the sun is not the right way to guarantee my safety. I thought I could walk freely in your country and meet Americans. But I am told it's impossible. This development causes me bitter regret and I cannot but express my disappointment.

You might say, "What a restless guest." But I keep to the Russian maxim, "Break bread with me, but speak your mind." And that should in no way affect our friendly relations.

Please forgive me for speaking somewhat vehemently or heatedly. But the temperature here is to blame for it, to some extent. (*Laughter.*) Besides, Mr. Skouras had warmed me up to it. (*Laughter, applause.*) Please forgive me if I have said anything not quite pleasing to your ear, if I have let slip anything that has jarred you a little. The sentiment that guided me in speaking here before you was one of friendship and respect for you, for your people and for your President, Mr. Eisenhower.

Thank you for your attention. Thank you, dear friends, thank you, Mr. Johnston. (*Stormy, prolonged applause.*)

SUMMARY OF MEETING OF AMERICAN LABOR LEADERS WITH PRIME MINISTER NIKITA KHRUSHCHEV, OF THE USSR, MARK HOPKINS HOTEL, SAN FRANCISCO, SEPTEMBER 20, 1959 *

PARTICIPANTS

USA

Walter P. Reuther, President, United Automobile, Aircraft & Agricultural Implement Workers of America AFL-CIO, and Vice-President AFL-CIO.

USSR

Nikita Khrushchev, Chairman of the Council of Ministers of the Union of Soviet Socialist Republics.

* The accuracy of this account, distributed by the American labor leaders present at the meeting with Khrushchev, and evidently representing a stenographic or taped transcript, was disputed by the Russians (see the following document in this collection). This transcript was published in the *New York Times,* Sept. 22, 1959.

USA

James B. Carey, President, International Union of Electrical, Radio and Machine Workers AFL-CIO, and Vice-President AFL-CIO.

Joseph Curran, President, National Maritime Union of America AFL-CIO, and Vice-President AFL-CIO.

Karl Feller, President, International Union of United Brewery, Flour, Cereal, Soft Drink & Distillery Workers AFL-CIO, and Vice-President AFL-CIO.

O. A. Knight, President, Oil, Chemical & Atomic Workers International Union AFL-CIO, and Vice-President AFL-CIO.

Paul Phillips, President, United Papermakers & Paperworkers AFL-CIO, and Vice-President AFL-CIO.

Emil Rieve, President Emeritus, Textile Workers Union of America AFL-CIO, and Vice-President AFL-CIO.

Les Finnegan, Executive Assistant to President Carey.

George L. P. Weaver, Assistant to President Carey.

Victor Reuther, Assistant to President Reuther.

USSR

Andrei Gromyko, Foreign Minister of the USSR.

Mikhail A. Menshikov, Soviet Ambassador to the United States.

Alexei Adzhubei, Editor of *Izvestia.*

G. A. Zhukov, Minister for Culture and Foreign Exchanges.

N. A. Tikhonov, Chairman, Ukrainian Regional Economic Council.

P. A. Satyukov, Editor of *Pravda.*

Mikhail Sholokhov, Author.

Mr. Sukhodrev, Translator.

Chairman Khrushchev and his party appeared in the Golden Empire Room exactly at 8 P.M., as previously arranged.

As the group went to the dining table, President Reuther pointed out to Mr. Khrushchev that it had been discovered that the table legs fell precisely at the center of the oval, therefore he had shifted Mr. Khrushchev slightly to the right.

REUTHER: Even though I have shifted you to the right, Mr. Chairman, I assure you there is no political significance in it.

KHRUSHCHEV (laughing): No matter how much you move me, I will still hold to a basic Communist position. Everything is fluid and everything progresses toward Communism.

CURRAN: Has this part of your journey been fairly restful?

KHRUSHCHEV: What do you think?

CAREY: We are impressed by the statements you are said to have made at the Lincoln Memorial in Washington. We are afraid, however, that you may have seen too many bankers and businessmen.

KHRUSHCHEV: That is because you didn't want to meet me. (*Laughter.*)

REUTHER: Tell the Chairman we are happy he is going to the Garst farm. He must understand that here we eat corn as well as feed it to cattle. When I and my brother were in the Soviet Union in 1934 we went down the Volga to the Donbas and to Yalta and Batum and to Baku. I'd like to tell this little story. We know you have made great progress in terms of food since we were there in the early 1930's. In the stores there was always one kind of canned goods we could readily buy. Amerikanski Corn, because the Russians did not cat corn. When we got to Baku we bought four cans of the corn, took it home and found it was pork and beans. The cans were so old the labels had worn off. We went back and asked for eight more cans, specifying we preferred ones without labels. The man at the store said it was the same with the paper or without the paper, so we got eight without the labels. We again found they were all pork and beans, and as a result we lived like capitalists for a while. I bet they still don't eat corn to any extent in Russia.

KHRUSHCHEV: Not much. Some of our northerners can't conceive of eating corn. Some tried to eat it raw and found it impossible.

REUTHER: In Iowa you'll see big corn and we hope you will be able to use our techniques to raise more food and therefore raise living standards.

KHRUSHCHEV: That is so, and we thank you. But we want you to know we are at no lower level than the U.S. on corn growing.

REUTHER: Your major problem is with meat?

KHRUSHCHEV: Our hybrid corn is no worse than yours. Garst knows that. What we need is to extend the growing of corn, now we are extending limits up to the farthest north. We now want to devote one-third of the land of those northern areas to corn.

CAREY (laughing): By the way, this chicken is corn-fed.

KHRUSHCHEV: I once said that to take away corn from Americans would be to starve them to death.

CAREY: No, not that, but certainly it's one of our most important grains. President Curran, here, of the Maritime Union, knows that. He raises cattle and knows the importance of corn.

REUTHER: I worked in the technical division of the Gorki Auto Plant . . . I trained Russians to do what I did in Detroit. I worked 18 months and then made an 18,000-mile tour from one end of Russia to another. So I saw Soviet Russia during that period quite clearly.

KHRUSHCHEV (inquired about an engineer at Gorki who had worked at Ford, now a USSR minister).

REUTHER: What is the production in the Gorki Auto Plant these days?

KHRUSHCHEV: I don't think I could even suggest any figure.

CURRAN: In 1945, when I went through the Gorki Plant, they were making chiefly trucks then. I sailed to your country in the early 1930's, bringing Ford Motor equipment and other materials to Russia.

KHRUSHCHEV: I remember in 1922 a group of U.S. workers came to the mines where they worked with their own tools. Fine men. A lot left when they saw the conditions.

REUTHER: I grew up in West Virginia, in a coal mine country and came to know mines, and I have been into mines all over the world. I paid special attention to the mines in the Donbas.

KHRUSHCHEV: The Donbas mines are the most difficult for workers.

REUTHER: Like the most difficult mines for the British workers that extend out under the seas. One thing we must do, most of all in the future, is to harness the atom for peace and get all of the miners out of the earth.

KHRUSHCHEV: Our scientists tell me we are approaching that. They want to produce coal by utilizing the hydrogen atom.

REUTHER: This is a venture in which we would favor a mutual effort to pool the abilities and scientific knowledge of all nations.

KHRUSHCHEV: A very noble goal.

CAREY: We are familiar with the speech that the Chairman made at the United Nations and your splendid comments at the Lincoln Memorial. We are familiar with the eloquent speech you delivered to the U.N. General Assembly on disarmament. We are also familiar with the history of the past efforts to get agreement on effective control procedures, which we of labor consider to be at the heart of the disarmament problem. Will you tell us what specific implementation you have in mind with respect to enforcement of any disarmament agreement?

KHRUSHCHEV: What is it you have difficulty understanding?

CAREY: It appears now that 25 per cent of Soviet production goes for military purposes, and 8 per cent to 10 per cent of U.S. production goes to military services. All nations of the world are spending now about $100 billion a year for military purposes. Of this, the U.S. spends about $40 billion a year, and the Soviet Union spends about $40 billion. The rest of the world spends about $20 billion. Certainly with disarmament a large percentage of this could be devoted to development of underprivileged nations and areas.

REUTHER: I think we can all agree that the most pressing problem is how we can preserve the peace. We all understand that the United States and the Soviet Union have produced the kind of weapons that make war inconceivable, that make war now a question simply of human survival. The question today becomes, what will we do in a practical sense. The only war America wants to fight is war against poverty, hunger, ignorance, and disease. It's the only war mankind can win. The Chairman has said repeatedly that he believes in no interference in the internal affairs of the United States and the kind of government we prefer to live under, and we share that feeling about the kind of government the Russians may prefer to live under. We think the people of Russia have a right to choose their own government and all other people should have the same right. Therefore, as we see it, the cold war is not an attempt to change each other's systems of government, but to influence those that are uncommitted. Therefore, I want to ask the Chairman, is the Soviet Union prepared to contribute to the ending of the cold war by joining the United States and other countries through the United Nations in a co-operative effort to aid the underprivileged nations to abolish poverty and ignorance?

KHRUSHCHEV (talking very quietly and into his napkin): In our proposal, which I submitted on behalf of the USSR, it is made clear that the outlays on armaments would be greatly reduced and a certain percentage of the reduction switched from the amount saved to the underprivileged countries.

REUTHER (reminds Khrushchev of a proposal Reuther submitted to the President of the U.S. in 1950 and passed a copy to him): It seems to me that if we wait for disarmament to start we lose great opportunities. Our proposal would create the better climate in which disarmament could be carried forward, faster and more effectively.

KHRUSHCHEV: I am not familiar with your program so at this moment I cannot comment on it. But we are not waiting for disarmament to render this economic aid to needy nations. (Editor of *Izvestia* interjects.) We already render such aid through the United Nations and through the various funds, medical and food funds, and we have bilateral agreements to aid underprivileged countries. For example, we have contributed our designs and our equipment to chemical and pharmaceutical plants in India. (He continued to cite the Arab countries, Indonesia, Ethiopia, and others who received Soviet aid. He placed emphasis especially on the thousands of students who are brought to Russia as part of the aid program.)

CAREY: Let us go back for a moment. When there is such a tremendously high percentage of the national incomes of both countries spent on military preparations, doesn't it become more and more demanding that we find a formula of control and inspection? Your country is spending $40 billion a year on the military, our country is spending $40 billion a year. If there were a completely safe inspection and control system how much more aid could we provide to the underprivileged countries of the world?

KHRUSHCHEV: We agree. And that's why we submitted our proposals.

REUTHER: There's no value in this, just going around the barn, as we seem to be now. I am familiar with the steel plant in India and the other enterprises. When you do it, it's part of the cold war. When we do it, you charge it's capitalist imperialism. Why can't we do it together? Through the UN?—do it together for their benefit, not for our separate advantage.

KHRUSHCHEV: We don't agree.

REUTHER: Why not?

KHRUSHCHEV: America has now surrounded us with military bases, alliances such as NATO and SEATO, and by these means the United States wants to obtain world domination. In the United Nations we are always outvoted. Thus it would be up to the United States to decide how the money would be used.

REUTHER: How about a U.N. Commission with equal representation? Equal representation of Russia and the United States and U.S. friends and Soviet friends.

KHRUSHCHEV: That would already be progress, but it won't be accepted.

REUTHER: Why not expose the two positions to public air? That's what we do with unreasonable employers.

KHRUSHCHEV: So long as we are surrounded by U.S. bases, we can have no agreement on this.

REUTHER: Why can't we work together to fight poverty and hunger with the U.S. entitled to no advantage, and the USSR entitled to no advantage?

KHRUSHCHEV: But we do take part in these programs.

REUTHER: You do it unilaterally, and that's the basis for the charge that you are penetrating economically and subverting politically.

KHRUSHCHEV: When the U.S. sends arms and creates bases, what kind of penetration is that?

REUTHER: But what we are proposing here is an equal commission with equal control. After all, most of the people who are hungry are workers and peasants.

KHRUSHCHEV: Unilateral bread has no smell. If it has a socialist smell, it is a pleasant smell.

REUTHER: If it's politically motivated, it's not a pleasant smell.

KHRUSHCHEV: We've sent to Yemen thousands of pounds of wheat. That's not a Socialist country.

KHRUSHCHEV: A few words more on the preceding subject, one more motive in my United Nations speech. The United States exploits the wealth of other countries, under-developed countries, for profits. England and France do the same. They exploit the wealth of countries that need aid. We do not exploit any country—we only engage in trade.

REUTHER: You exploit the workers of East Germany.

KHRUSHCHEV: Where did you dream that up?

REUTHER: If you don't exploit them, why should 3,000,000 of them cross the border into West Germany?

KHRUSHCHEV: You are hopelessly sick with capitalist fever.

(Several voices interchanging across table.)

REUTHER: The workers in West Germany are free . . .

KHRUSHCHEV: We are free, too.

REUTHER: Do you have credentials to speak for the workers of the world?

KHRUSHCHEV: Do you have credentials to poke your nose into East Germany?

CAREY: This is part of our difficulty: The fear of the Chairman that the United States actually wants to dominate the world.

KHRUSHCHEV: Not just wants—striving!

CAREY: And the other way around, there is the fear in the United States, based on much evidence, that the Soviet Union wants to dominate the world.

KHRUSHCHEV: The Soviet ruble does not kowtow to the American dollar. (At this point, Khrushchev raised his voice loudly and vehemently.) You have been spoiled by everyone bowing down, by everyone cringing and crawling . . .

CAREY: It is a privilege having this sort of discussion. We have been given reason to wonder whether the Chairman's U.N. speech was chiefly for propaganda purposes. I want to re-emphasize that unless we can find some way to implement the Chairman's disarmament proposals then we might have to start hunting all over again. A reduction in the $40 billion military budget of the Soviet Union and our $40 billion budget, that reduction could be devoted to helping underprivileged nations as the Chairman cited as the most desirable objective.

KHRUSHCHEV: It is not $40 billion, but $25 billion, and that's no small sum either. I, as a former miner, have to say that I pity you as representing the working class, but your thinking is not of the working class. When Hearst says it, I am not offended. But when a representative of the workers says it, it is different.

REUTHER: The key is universal inspection and control, and to stop hydrogen bomb testing. We expect the same conditions as you expect. We believe that neither nation should be treated as a second-class power. Why can't you agree?

KHRUSHCHEV: Why are you so familiar with the Dulles arguments and not with the Khrushchev proposals?

CAREY: Dulles is dead.

KHRUSHCHEV: We say what we are saying because we have already clarified these issues.

REUTHER: You will not agree to universal inspection and control?

KHRUSHCHEV: Have you been asleep all the time? That is what we are for. I am sure you haven't read my speech.

CAREY: Yes, we have read your speech, and other propaganda. But we failed to find the basis for implementing the proposals.

KNIGHT: (Again raised the self-determination question.)

KHRUSHCHEV (interrupting): I've never liked fleas when they jumped all over . . .

REUTHER: We would prefer not to jump all over. We would prefer to exhaust one question at a time, but it's all a matter of time. Tell the Chairman we will go slower if he has the time.

VICTOR REUTHER: The Chairman has said he wants to talk to workers, and these are workers' representatives.

REUTHER: How much time will the Chairman be willing to give?

CAREY: We want to be considerate of our guest but . . .

KHRUSHCHEV: Ten o'clock, another hour. Disarmament is the question of questions, and if you misunderstand this there is almost no way out. What the Americans propose is control first, and then disarmament. What does this mean? Nothing! Let us station our bases in Mexico and Canada, then maybe you will have an understanding. (There was a fast two or three minute interchange across the table. At one point Khrushchev, talking to Curran, exclaimed, "How can you open your mouth like that and represent the workers?") Do you want a discussion, or is this a bazaar? (At this point Khrushchev became quite excited and pounded the table.)

CAREY: Here is the question on disarmament (passing it across the table) as I have phrased it. We fear there is lack of attention being given by you and your colleagues to the whole question of inspection and control.

KHRUSHCHEV: I would like to tell you, gentlemen, so long as America continues to manifest a high-handed attitude toward other people there can be no agreement.

CURRAN: We ought to talk sense here, and we're not talking sense yet. I don't want to be confused with statesmen, I am a worker speaking for workers and I'm pretty sure the rest of the guys here do.

RIEVE (Raised the question of Socialism versus Communism, and particularly public ownership under capitalism, pointing out that social ownership is compatible with the highest forms of political democracy as practiced in Scandinavia.)

KHRUSHCHEV: There is a different understanding between us. Capitalist countries can own production and it doesn't make them Socialists.

REUTHER: It is more than a matter of degree. We think that the country in the free world nearest to Democratic Socialism is Israel. Yet the Russian attitude toward Israel has been most unfriendly.

KHRUSHCHEV: We don't have an instrument that could measure the socialism there. (He tossed his head almost disdainfully here.)

REUTHER: You haven't been there, I have been there, and I have seen how Histadrut, the magnificent Israeli labor movement, which owns 60 per cent of the production, supports the nation, and aids its progress.

CURRAN: I appreciate the Chairman's fatigue . . .

(Here came a heated interchange with Khrushchev, for the most part apparently, over the interpretation of fatigue.)

REUTHER: Mr. Chairman, you are agitated again. You don't even understand a friendly question. Curran was inquiring about your weariness after a tough schedule.

CURRAN: Please accept my apologies. I was asking about your tiredness from your journey. (Curran, returning to issues under consideration, mentioned his sailings to Russia in 1945.) Curran's question was: "Specifically, will workers be permitted to exercise freedom to secure redress of their grievances by the only test of industrial democracy, the right to strike, the right collectively to withhold their labor power?" When will workers be able to negotiate agreements in Russia, including the right to strike?

KHRUSHCHEV: I quite understand you, but you do not understand anything of the workings of the Socialist system. I do not want to offend you—you just do not know, you have not been there. You measure everything by U.S. standards. What I like about you is that you do have a class sense, that feeling. Yes, they do have those rights. (Presumably this refers to the right to negotiate agreements and strike.) I understand your question. The working class does have the juridical right to strike. Does the worker have the right to exercise the right to strike? Yes. Have there been strikes since the October Revolution? Yes, I spoke at some of the strike meetings. Are there strikes now? No. Because workers and unions and the government have one thought, because in what other country would the government announce that wages would be raised and the working day reduced without pressure . . . In capitalist countries they would need to fight for this.

KHRUSHCHEV: I would think that if our disarmament proposals were accepted—we are now planning a six-hour day in 1964—we could immediately reduce it to a six-hour day and raise wages. Our workers are all organized in unions and they are learned and they know the economic conditions and the economic possibilities in our country.

CURRAN: But in spite of that, knowing economic conditions and possibilities, do they have the right to strike?

KHRUSHCHEV: Juridically, yes.

REUTHER: I grew up in a working-class home in West Virginia . . . (interruption by Khrushchev, with hand-waving.)

REUTHER: Is he afraid of my questions?

KHRUSHCHEV: I am not afraid of the devil and you're a man.

REUTHER: I worked with the anti-Hitler underground in Germany before going to Russia. What bothers me about your social system is not that you're not making economic progress for the workers and peasants. You're making tremendous technical progress. And I know all about your rationale of workers not striking against themselves. But the Chairman himself exposed—in his exposure of Stalin's crimes—the cult and power of an individual. How could the worker in that period get justice if he could not strike or publicly protest?

KHRUSHCHEV: His trade union.

REUTHER: The union is an extension of government, the Soviet Government. Does a union ever disagree with the government? Can you give us one single example in which one of your unions ever disagreed with government policy?

KHRUSHCHEV: Why poke your nose into our business?

REUTHER: Freedom is everybody's business—you are always expressing a concern for the workers of Asia—there is a thing called international labor solidarity. When I was in Russia I was a member of a union, and it was what we would call a company union.

(Fast and frequently indignant interchanges between the Chairman and the labor side of the table, too fast to be recorded.)

REUTHER: Every time we push a sharp question, the Chairman gets angry.

KHRUSHCHEV (getting red in face, and just slightly loud): And what we call what you represent—capitalist lackeys.

REUTHER: Every time I ask a question he has no answer for, he gets angry.

KNIGHT: Mr. Chairman, since it took me so long to get the floor, I want to exercise my democratic rights and ask two questions. Mr. Chairman, you have made repeated statements regarding self-determination and the freedom of people from outside interference. We agree with you on both of these principles. However, we cannot understand, since you say you favor the right of the German people both East and West to decide for themselves on unification, how do you visualize the German people making this decision since you continue to oppose a free and democratic vote by the German people on this issue. My second question is, in view of your statements favoring self-determination and noninterference in the internal affairs of other nations and your statements supporting peaceful co-existence, how do you reconcile these statements with the harsh military suppression of the Hungarian Freedom Fighters by the Soviet military powers.

KHRUSHCHEV: The capitalists have certainly trained some very good cadres. May I just voice my thoughts aloud? Do you know anything about Germany? Have you ever been there? The German Democratic Republic is based on the most democratic foundations. There is no private ownership of the means of production.

KNIGHT: If it is on the most democratic foundations, then they should not be afraid of a democratic election.

REUTHER: In Eastern Germany there is only a one-party system. (Interchange of 10 voices.)

KNIGHT: Why do you oppose a democratic vote for reunification of Germany?

KHRUSHCHEV: It depends not on me but on the two Germanys.

KNIGHT: But you take a position against democratic reunification in your propaganda throughout the world.

KHRUSHCHEV: Tell me where I said that. Hungary has its own Constitution and laws, and is freely developing.

KNIGHT: Why did the Russians interfere in Hungary?

KHRUSHCHEV: There was no interference. There was a counterrevolution, thugs and hooligans who received arms from outside and took power in Budapest. And the government asked us for aid and we gave it, and we're proud of it. We are proud of it as a feat. There would be fascism there if we had not.

REUTHER: Was Nagy a fascist, I thought he was a Communist?

KHRUSHCHEV: Don't mix good things with dirt. (Exchanges around the table.) Have we exhausted the Hungarian question?

CAREY: We have touched on it; we have certainly not exhausted it.

PHILLIPS (Brought up the question of radio jamming of Radio Free Europe and Voice of America.)

KHRUSHCHEV: What do you prefer to have for dinner? (Looking at Phillips.) What is your favorite dish?

PHILLIPS: Probably roast beef.

KHRUSHCHEV: I, borsch. You continue to enjoy roast beef, and I, borsch.

REUTHER: But you prescribe and insist on borsch for all.

KHRUSHCHEV (rising to his feet at 10:22 P.M.): If you don't read what I have stated, what can I expect . . .

REUTHER: You advocate more trade. How come you oppose a free flow of ideas?

KHRUSHCHEV: As head of the working class I will protect workers from capitalist propaganda. (At this point, unexpectedly, Khrushchev, still on his feet, gave a burlesque demonstration of his idea of the can-can he witnessed during the Hollywood rehearsal of the forthcoming film, *Can-Can.* He turned his back to the table, bent downward, flipped his coat up and gave an imitation of the can-can.) This is a dance in which girls pull up their skirts. You're going to see that, we are not. This is what you call freedom—

freedom for the girls to show their backsides. To us it's pornography. The culture of people who want pornography. It's capitalism that makes the girls that way. (Khrushchev still on his feet while saying this.)

PHILLIPS: Does the Chairman think that the girls should be prohibited by law from showing their backsides?

KHRUSHCHEV: There should be a law prohibiting the girls from showing their backsides, a moral law.

CAREY: I may not see it, I may not want to see it . . .

KHRUSHCHEV: Your children will go to see it.

REUTHER: Perhaps it was a stupid movie—it was stupid of them to show it to you. But that has nothing to do with our question of why not a free flow of ideas between our countries?

KHRUSHCHEV: Why don't you want to trade with us? The sausage tastes the same in all countries. (Referred to the press conference statement by Zhukov today on cultural exchange.)

CAREY: I will read this press statement and I'm sure that all of our colleagues will follow it up.

SATYUKOV (Editor of *Pravda*): We printed in *Pravda* in full Reuther's statement at the unemployment conference in Washington. We didn't change a word, but at the same time the New York papers said that it was a Red scheme. We wrote back in *Pravda* there was no collusion between us and Reuther. The Voice of America didn't broadcast it. If it did, we wouldn't jam it.

REUTHER: No, you wouldn't because that report on unemployment would reflect upon us. But why didn't you and why don't you publish my May Day speech of this year in West Berlin? I invite you to publish and broadcast that speech.

KHRUSHCHEV: We only publish speeches that contribute to friendly relations between countries.

REUTHER: There were at least 600,000 workers who heard my speech in West Berlin, and I am certain that my speech was far less provocative than the May Day speakers in the Eastern sector of Berlin.

CAREY: I think the Chairman answered the question, in part, in his reply to Spyros Skouras. Actually Skouras knows little about the problems of unemployment in the United States.

REUTHER: The record of struggle of U.S. unionism stands for itself. Personally, I have been shot and beaten. I have been criticized by the reactionary press as a Moscow agent and by you as a lackey of Wall Street.

KHRUSHCHEV: Without sharp edges, I would like to ask whether we cannot find a common approach. But we think differently. We pity you.

REUTHER: We don't want your pity.

CURRAN: Maybe the word he wanted was sympathize. Pity is a bad word. We don't want his pity.

KHRUSHCHEV: We are progressing toward Communism. You want to strengthen capitalism.

REUTHER: We are interested in how best to advance the interests of the workers under freedom. We disagree on how best to advance the interests of the workers.

KHRUSHCHEV: You have your point of view; we have ours. They are irreconcilable.

REUTHER: Why can't we believe in our system of individual freedom without your feeling it is a necessity to say we are betraying the workers?

KHRUSHCHEV: We did not come to this meeting to aggravate our relations, they are bad enough as they are. Let's not raise questions that disunite us. Let us join our efforts for peace. Let us not be hot-headed. Questions like Hungary are pin-pricks. What good do they do? Suppose we raised the question of Guatemala.

REUTHER: We criticized the situation in Guatemala but the most important fact is that no one in Russia could or did criticize your intervention in Hungary.

CAREY: We are making some progress, however, when we can have meetings like this. This is more pointed than any discussion we have had in recent years. If this kind of discussion is continued it holds some hope for the future.

FELLER: Mr. Chairman, I cannot understand since the Communist Party proclaims itself to be the liberator of the working class, yet we see mass exodus of workers in other countries following the Communist seizure of power. You have the example of 3,000,000 workers fleeing from East Germany to West Berlin, and about 3,000,000 fleeing from North Korea to South Korea, and as mentioned a moment ago, 300 or so thousands of Hungarians braved arrest and death in escaping to freedom. Mr. Khrushchev, can you tell us of a single instance where, following Communist seizure of power, there has been a mass influx of workers from surrounding non-Communist countries into the Communist country. If the Communist Party is the liberator of the working class, why don't we see this phenomena?

KHRUSHCHEV: Is that all? Think it over. Drink your beer. Perhaps that will help you to find the answer to your question.

FELLER: That certainly is no answer and apparently nothing will make you understand why millions want to escape from Communism.

KHRUSHCHEV: I've told you, I'm not even afraid of the devil.

CAREY: Wall Street says Reuther is a representative of the devil.

REUTHER: Wall Street says I am an agent of Moscow, and Moscow says I am an agent of Wall Street.

WEAVER: I would like to pose this question, Mr. Chairman. In fact, one of the problems as I see it and which you just referred to—for example, Hungary as a "pin-prick"—is how do we establish a basis of trust which must precede understanding. Recently I served as a labor representative at a conference of the World Association of United Nations, in Geneva. At this conference, the USSR and the United States delegations agreed on a resolution attempting to diminish the tensions of the cold war. However, at the same time the friends of the Soviet Union from the Eastern European countries were raising the kind of provocative questions you just referred to, that do not lead to understanding. How do we arrive at a basis of understanding with this kind of attitude? For our people the questions that have been raised here with you this evening must be answered.

KHRUSHCHEV: It is true that there are many issues on which we differ. Let us have more contacts. We may not solve all the issues at once but through contacts we can begin to settle the little issues which will lead to more progress. Let us not aggravate our relations. It is only our opponents who will benefit. Do you want to see a change in the social order of our country? No! We don't want to see a change in the social order of your country. I confess I myself have never been a trade union functionary. But why shouldn't you gentlemen visit us? You won't become Communists.

CAREY: We've been there; we've seen your country, time and again. I've been there three times, our other colleagues have been there.

REUTHER: It is important that the Chairman understand that changes are occurring here in the United States and that we have people as dedicated to advancing the working class as there could be anywhere else (throwing across the table to Khrushchev U.S. wage rates). How can he say these people are wage slaves exploited by capitalism, making this kind of wages in America? How can he say that they have nothing to lose but their chains?

KHRUSHCHEV: We say what we do in retaliation for what you say about us. Take, for example, Meany's speeches. I read most of them. They sound like Dulles—they sound like Dulles.

REUTHER: We have our disagreements and we recall you had some disagreements with Molotov. However, when we have disagreements, no one is exiled.

CAREY: We thank the Chairman. I suggest our guest of honor has been quite generous with his time. We thank you for joining us, and may our two great countries work together for peace and the good of all mankind.

(The meeting ended at 11:03 P.M.)

MEETING WITH U.S. TRADE-UNION LEADERS *

N. S. Khrushchev, Chairman of the Council of Ministers of the USSR, met with a group of U.S. trade-union leaders in San Francisco on September 20. The meeting took place on the initiative of some leaders of the American Federation of Labor-Congress of Industrial Organizations (AFL-CIO).

The Americans present at the meeting were James B. Carey, Vice-President of the AFL-CIO (President of the International Union of Electrical, Radio and Machine Workers); Walter P. Reuther, Vice-President of the AFL-CIO (President of the United Automobile, Aircraft and Agricultural Implement Workers); O. A. Knight (President of the International Union of Oil, Chemical and Atomic Workers); Karl F. Feller (President of the United Brewery Workers); Emil Rieve (Chairman of the Executive Council of the Textile Workers Union); Joseph Curran (President of the National Maritime Union); Paul L. Phillips (President of the United Papermakers and

* Russian version *Pravda,* Sept. 25, 1959, pp. 1–2. English translation as distributed by Soviet news and official agencies, carried in *Khrushchev in America* (New York: Crosscurrents Press, 1960), pp. 125–40.

Paperworkers); George L. P. Weaver (Union of Electrical Workers) and Victor G. Reuther (United Automobile, Aircraft and Agricultural Implement Workers).

Some questions about the international situation and Soviet-American relations were brought up during the discussion, which lasted over three hours and occasionally became sharp.

The U.S. press carried numerous contradictory reports of the meeting.

The source of information on what happened at the meeting was a news conference which the U.S. union leaders called late in the evening, immediately after parting with N. S. Khrushchev. It appears from the press reports that Walter Reuther, Vice-President of the AFL-CIO, made extraordinary statements at the news conference, about the remarks of the head of the Soviet Government, attributing to him things which he had not said or done. The news conference, according to the *San Francisco Examiner,* ended in chaos. According to the same newspaper, two of the union leaders present at the meeting—Rieve, President of the Textile Workers Union, and Curran, President of the National Maritime Union, told reporters that a considerable part of Reuther's statements about what had happened was a lot of nonsense.

On September 22 the *New York Times* published what it considered to be a complete transcript of the discussion. That transcript shows, however, that those who made it reported the discussion arbitrarily. They were apparently afraid to convey to the reader the actual statements made by the head of the Soviet Government.

To set the record straight, the Press Group of the Chairman of the Council of Ministers of the USSR published the following account of the discussion in question, the main points of which have been withheld from the public or distorted in the tendentious accounts given by some U.S. newspapers:

At the very beginning of the discussion, James Carey and Walter Reuther said that they and their colleagues were greatly interested in a frank exchange of views on major international problems of a pressing character. Carey stressed that they were interested in the new Soviet proposals for general and complete disarmament submitted by N. S. Khrushchev to the United Nations. He said that the American workers were concerned about the fact that enormous sums are being spent on armaments. Reuther, for his part, said that the most urgent problem was that of how to preserve peace. Carey and others asked N. S. Khrushchev to tell them about the new Soviet disarmament proposals. But, in effect, they did not wait to hear the reply and went on to ask other questions—in particular, about economic aid to underdeveloped countries.

Answering these questions, N. S. Khrushchev pointed out that the proposals for general and complete disarmament submitted by the Soviet Government to the UN, which envisage the allocation of a certain percentage of the funds saved on arms reduction, could be instrumental in aiding underdeveloped countries.

"But we aren't waiting till an agreement is reached on disarmament," N. S. Khrushchev said. "We are giving the underdeveloped countries substantial economic aid right now. On the one hand, we help them through the UN with funds, medical supplies and food. On the other hand, we help them on a bilateral basis. In India we are helping the government to build a steel mill, chemical and machine-building plants, and pharmaceutical factories. We grant the Indian Government credits; provide it with blueprints for industrial plants; send our specialists to help the Indians; and train engineers, technicians and skilled workers for plants under construction. We also render large-scale assistance to the Arab countries and countries in Africa. It is well known that the Soviet Union is extending friendly assistance to Cambodia, Burma, Ceylon, Yemen, Ethiopia and other countries."

Reuther interrupted N. S. Khrushchev and tried to discredit the Soviet Union's policy of assistance to economically underdeveloped countries. He went so far as to accuse the Soviet Union of using aid to underdeveloped countries for selfish purposes, for purposes of the cold war.

In repulsing that attack, N. S. Khrushchev said: "You are shooting your shafts in the wrong direction. The Soviet Union has never exploited anyone, nor is it exploiting anyone now. It helps underdeveloped countries as a friend, without any political strings attached. For example, we shipped thousands of tons of grain to Yemen. Yet its system is not socialist. It is a kingdom. Do you call that aid for selfish purposes? Just what selfish aims do we achieve thereby? We don't make any profit on that. We act as friends. But look at what the imperialists are doing. The U.S. monopolies are exploiting the riches of the underdeveloped countries and making big profits.

Britain, France and other capitalist countries are doing likewise. Why cannot those countries expand their help to the underdeveloped countries out of the profits they derive in that way? The Soviet Government has put forward and submitted to the UN a proposal to that effect. The Soviet Union trades with all countries on a basis of mutual advantage."

Unable to counter N. S. Khrushchev's arguments in any way, Reuther suddenly shouted: "You are exploiting the people of East Germany!" This statement drew smiles even from Reuther's colleagues.

N. S. Khrushchev said:

"Where did you see that dream? Calm yourself, you have the shivers. Who empowered you to speak on behalf of the German people? Why do you keep trying to speak for other peoples? You are pampered by the fact that many countries depend on the United States and are compelled to seek your aid. But the socialist countries stand firmly on their own feet. We don't take off our hats to you. The Soviet ruble has never bowed, is not bowing now and will never bow to the dollar."

The disarmament problem came up next. Reuther and some other trade-union leaders repeated the assertions of the commercial press to the effect that the Soviet plan for general and complete disarmament had been put forward merely for propaganda purposes and that the USSR spent as much on armaments as the USA, that is, 40 billion dollars a year.

"First of all," N. S. Khrushchev replied, "calculated in your currency, we spend 25 billion on defense and not 40 billion. In the second place, your statement that the Soviet proposals are propaganda makes me, a former miner, feel sorry for you. They say you were born in a working-class environment, but you talk like a spokesman for the capitalists. I can understand it when Hearst prints things like that. But when an American trade-union leader repeats them, I think bitterly of how thoroughly the monopolists have corrupted you!"

However, Reuther continued to repeat the allegations of reactionary propaganda, which distort the Soviet proposals. Among other things, he asserted that the Soviet disarmament plan did not envisage the establishment of control.

"Why is it," N. S. Khrushchev said, "that you know Dulles' arguments so well and are so ignorant of the Soviet stand? We are for all-embracing control, but how should it be organized? The United States proposes setting up control first and talking of disarmament afterward. At a time when the U.S. has encircled us with its military bases, control without disarmament can only mean one thing—military reconnaissance. What we propose, however, is to organize control by stages, accordingly as disarmament is carried out."

"But we propose organizing an equal measure of control for the USA and the Soviet Union," Reuther said.

"No, you don't, because those aren't equal terms," N. S. Khrushchev replied. "U.S. military bases surround our frontiers, while we have no bases on the American continent. How would you feel if there were Soviet military bases in Mexico and Canada?"

"Who is keeping you from having them?" said Victor Reuther, brother of the Vice-President of the AFL-CIO. "Set them up."

(This observation, provocative in effect, brought indignant protests from the entire assembly.)

"How can you, a spokesman for the working class, bring yourself to talk like that!" N. S. Khrushchev said to Victor Reuther.

Walter Reuther made a clumsy attempt to change the subject, saying that it was late and that the Prime Minister was "tired."

N. S. Khrushchev said that it was impossible to discuss things by jumping from one question to another like fleas. "Is it an earnest discussion you want or is it something else?" he asked. "You sidestepped one question, then another, and are now jumping to a third. Disarmament is the question of questions. We want you to get us right, so I must set out our stand in detail."

Nevertheless, Walter Reuther hastened to give the floor to Rieve for fresh questions. The latter raised several questions—about the role of state ownership in the capitalist and socialist countries, about democracy and dictatorship, control of the press and radio, exchange of information, and so on. He, too, repeated the attacks which hostile propaganda usually makes on the Soviet Union and the other socialist countries.

It was obvious from the manner in which Rieve put his questions that he had an exceedingly vague, and in many cases false, notion of Soviet realities.

Walter Reuther, who watched his colleague put questions according to the notes that lay in front of him, prompted Rieve to be sure to inquire about the one-party system. But Rieve ignored that.

N. S. Khrushchev said that the questions raised by Rieve were elementary and that in the Soviet Union they were studied in political study groups of the elementary type.

Then Walter Reuther, in an obvious effort to give the discussion a sharper turn, put an additional question. "Does the system of state ownership necessitate dictatorship which rules out democracy?" he asked.

While, in answering Rieve, N. S. Khrushchev described the difference between state ownership in the socialist countries, where the means of production belong to the entire people, and state ownership in the capitalist countries, where nationalization of the means of production leaves them in the hands of the bourgeoisie, the ruling class, Mr. Reuther suddenly said that "the highest degree of socialism has been achieved in Israel," where, so he said, 60 per cent of industry belongs to the trade unions.

Asked who in that case was in power in Israel, Mr. Reuther failed to give a direct reply.

N. S. Khrushchev explained that the fundamental issue in characterizing a particular social system is that of state power, of whom it belongs to—whether the working class, working people in general, or the exploiting classes. If state power is held by the people, the means of production are socialist, public property. Not so when nationalization of the means of production is carried out under conditions where power belongs to the capitalists. N. S. Khrushchev said that the Communists are proponents of the dictatorship of the working class and that the tasks of socialist construction can only be effectively carried out if state power passes into the hands of the working people. Working-class dictatorship, far from ruling out democracy, provides every condition for the development of genuine democracy. It is in itself the highest form of democracy.

Walter Reuther said again that the Prime Minister was probably "tired" and that they must hurry and ask other questions. This brought the following sarcastic comment from N. S. Khrushchev: "Will you have strength enough to vie with me? I'm in good form. I will not tire of fighting for the working-class cause as long as I live. Let us have a business-like talk if you want it. Our time isn't limited."

Joseph Curran, President of the National Maritime Union, said he wanted to ask what he called a question from everyday life. "I was in the Soviet Union in the thirties," he said, "when we delivered equipment purchased by you. We are pleased with the technical progress you have made. I should like to know whether the collective bargaining system will develop as technology makes progress in your industry, and whether the workers will have the right to strike. How do trade unions defend the interests of the working people?"

"I see what you mean," N. S. Khrushchev said. "I'm glad that you have the class instinct in dealing with questions of trade-union activity. But it seems that you have no idea at all of conditions in a socialist state, of the position of the working class there or of the role of the trade unions. You measure everything with the yardstick you are accustomed to in the United States."

Seeing that Curran took an interest in the explanation which the head of the Soviet Government was giving, Victor Reuther began talking about the "personality cult."

Curran cut him short. "Why do you butt in?" he said.

N. S. Khrushchev went on, speaking to Curran:

"I like your question because it is so forthright, and I will give you a forthright answer. We had strikes in the first few years after the October Revolution. I myself used to go to the striking workers to talk to them. Nowadays our workers do not strike. Why? You'll find the answer to that question if you recall certain facts. In what capitalist country would the government draw up plans to raise working-class living standards without the workers exerting pressure on it? It is more than one can imagine that in the capitalist countries wages would be raised while the working day was reduced, without the workers striking to achieve it. But in the Soviet Union this matter is being handled as a priority task. The government, the workers and the trade unions are cooperating closely in the matter of increasing wages further while reducing working hours. All we need is to lay the economic groundwork for it. Speaking tentatively, I think that if our proposal for general and complete disarmament were accepted, we could begin the transition to a six-hour working day and higher wages much earlier than 1964, the year envisaged in the seven-year plan. Soviet workers are always abreast of their country's economic development and know well whether or not there are, at any given moment, practical possibilities for a further rise in wages."

Curran thanked N. S. Khrushchev for his answer.

Walter Reuther made a fresh attempt to sharpen the discussion by alleging that the Soviet trade unions were "an extension of the government," and wanted to know why the Soviet trade unions did not come out against the Party. Some of the unionists asked for the floor but Reuther would not listen, and tried to speak for all of them.

"You are like a nightingale," N. S. Khrushchev said, smiling. "It closes its eyes when it sings, and sees nothing and hears nobody but itself." The audience burst out laughing and Mr. Reuther flushed. Nevertheless, he kept harping on his point, posing as a defender of Soviet workers.

"Why do you stick your nose into other people's plans?" N. S. Khrushchev asked. "The Soviet workers settle their problems by themselves, and get along without outside interference. There will be no real talk as long as you keep trying to lecture others."

"There is such a thing as international working-class solidarity," Reuther declared pompously.

"You dare talk about international solidarity after you've split the World Federation of Trade Unions and opposed your trade unions to those of most countries of the world," N. S. Khrushchev replied.

Reuther made no answer. He hastened to pass to another question as he did each time that he had nothing to say, and gave the floor to Knight.

Knight asked two questions. He casually raised the question of so-called free elections in Germany. His utterances on the so-called "Hungarian question" were in the same vein.

"Do you know anything about the German Democratic Republic?" N. S. Khrushchev asked him. "Have you ever been there? I have been there more than once and I can tell you that the German Democratic Republic is built on a most democratic foundation. All matters there are decided by a democratically elected government. Private ownership of the means of production has been abolished there and state power belongs to the working people. The working class of the German Democratic Republic is headed by the Socialist Unity Party of Germany, a party devoted to the interests of the working class. There are also other democratic parties there. As regards elections in Germany, that is an internal affair of the Germans themselves, as I have said repeatedly. Let them do as they decide between themselves. No one has a right to interfere in their internal affairs."

N. S. Khrushchev then firmly repelled attempts to pull the so-called Hungarian question out of the bag again.

During the discussion of this question Mr. Reuther unwittingly betrayed shocking ignorance. He began to "defend" Comrade Janos Kadar as if Kadar were a bourgeois nationalist. It was not until his colleagues burst out laughing, intimating that he meant Imre Nagy, that Reuther began to correct himself awkwardly.

Commenting on Reuther's attitude in "defending" the Hungarian people, N. S. Khrushchev said:

"The Hungarian People's Republic has its own Constitution, its legislation and its lawful government, elected by democratic procedure. It is developing freely, and has made considerable progress in socialist construction. What happened in Hungary in 1956? There was a revolt of anti-popular elements there, who were dissatisfied with the working people's rule. The Hungarian counterrevolution, instigated by international reactionary forces, sought to overthrow the socialist system. In doing so, the conspirators used arms received from the West. They acted on instructions also coming from the West. Having seized power in Budapest for a few days, the counterrevolutionaries began to commit outrages, to shoot and otherwise exterminate honest people. At that crucial moment, the Hungarian Revolutionary Government headed by Janos Kadar asked for our aid. We complied with that request, and we are proud of it. If we had not come to the aid of the people's government headed by Janos Kadar, the fascists might have seized power in Hungary. By rendering the Hungarian people fraternal assistance in their struggle against the fascist rebels, we did our international duty."

Phillips proposed passing to a fresh subject, and echoed the claims repeatedly made by capitalist spokesmen in interviews with N. S. Khrushchev in the United States regarding unhampered circulation of reactionary literature and anti-Soviet information in the USSR.

"What is your favorite dish?" N. S. Khrushchev asked Phillips.

"Roast beef," Phillips replied.

"And I prefer borsch," N. S. Khrushchev said. "You don't eat it, but I'm very fond of it. You are for capitalism and I am for socialism. Why am I not answering your question in greater detail? For the simple reason that I have been asked that question many times here and have answered it each time. It seems that you don't like my reply and wish to hear something different. But there's nothing to be done about it—you and we have different notions of freedom. When we were in Hollywood they danced the cancan for us. The girls who dance it have to pull up their skirts and show their backsides. They are good honest actresses but have to perform that dance. They are compelled to adapt themselves to the tastes of depraved people. People in your country will go to see it, but Soviet people would scorn such a spectacle. It is pornographic. It is the culture of surfeited and depraved people. Showing that sort of films is called freedom in this country. Such 'freedom' doesn't suit us. You seem to like the 'freedom' of looking at backsides. But we prefer the freedom to think, to exercise our mental faculties, the freedom of creative progress."

"Do you want such films to be banned?" Phillips asked.

"I think there should be such a law," N. S. Khrushchev replied, "a moral law."

"I'm free to see or not to see such films," Carey said.

"But your children see things like that!"

"I have no children."

"But other people have. Good children, who live on earth," N. S. Khrushchev remarked. "And you and we should protect them from bad influences spread under the guise of 'free cultural exchange.' "

Some of the unionists then contended that the Soviet Union was reluctant for some reason to expand Soviet-American cultural relations. N. S. Khrushchev refuted that false assertion. He stressed that in reality it was the American side which was stalling, and suggested that G. A. Zhukov, Chairman of the State Committee for Cultural Relations, who was present, be asked to inform them on the matter. But the U.S. trade-union leaders avoided that.

"We'll read about it in the papers," one of them said.

Speaking of exchanges of information, N. S. Khrushchev pointed out that Soviet people are for exchanging truthful information, such as would make for a durable peace and closer relations between peoples. P. A. Satyukov, Editor-in-Chief of *Pravda,* who was present at the discussion, pointed out that *Pravda* had published in full the speeches made at the Washington conference on unemployment called by U.S. trade unions, without changing a single word in them, while the American newspapers for some reason had not carried them, describing them as "Red propaganda."

"You and we have different views regarding exchanges of information and a number of other matters," N. S. Khrushchev said. "But that doesn't mean we cannot find a common language on problems that are of interest to the peoples of our countries. We say to you: 'Rise higher, try to take a broader view of events. Don't look at things from the tower you've built for yourselves. Come to our country, see how Soviet workers live and work, how our trade unions function, how they defend the workers' interests. You and we approach things differently; we are advancing to communism along the path we have chosen, while you want to bolster capitalism.' In other words, our attitudes are different. Let us recognize this indisputable fact. But couldn't we try and find common grounds for businesslike cooperation? We think we could. The whole working class needs such cooperation in the struggle for its fundamental interests, for peace.

"We did not come to this meeting to aggravate relations—they are bad enough as it is," N. S. Khrushchev remarked. "If we fling accusations at each other, it won't do the working class any good. Let's be reasonable, let's not bring up questions which separate us. Let's pool our efforts in the struggle for world peace."

But Feller asked another question in the cold war spirit. Reading from a sheet, he repeated the false propaganda that the workers are oppressed in the socialist countries and have to escape abroad.

A. I. Adzhubei, Editor-in-Chief of *Izvestia,* who was also present, pointed out that Feller was repeating word for word what was printed in that day's *New York Times.*

"Think of what you are doing," N. S. Khrushchev said. "You would repeat articles published in the bourgeois press, and I should answer you. Start reading the proletarian press and then you will see what's what sooner."

N. S. Khrushchev observed that Weaver, a Negro present at the discussion, had made several attempts to ask a question but that Reuther persisted in ignoring him for some reason.

"This isn't a democratic way of holding a discussion," N. S. Khrushchev said. "Let the black man speak. It's a shame, really. You still have places in this country which Negroes aren't allowed to enter."

Weaver said that the U.S. trade unions were fighting against racial discrimination and that they accorded him the honor of representing the U.S. labor movement at some international conferences. Two weeks ago, he said, he had attended a conference of the World Federation of United Nations Associations in Geneva.

At the conference, Weaver noted with satisfaction, the U.S. and Soviet delegations had cooperated closely. They had drafted a joint resolution aimed at ending the cold war, and it had been carried. Weaver pointed out, however, that the U.S. delegation and the delegations of the socialist countries had differed on many points and had had sharp clashes over them.

He asked N. S. Khrushchev how a start should be made and how common ground could be found for cooperation. "It's important for our people to have answers to the questions asked here tonight," Weaver said.

"I know that your trade unions are doing a good deal for the Negroes to become equal citizens of the USA," N. S. Khrushchev replied. "As regards the questions on which there is no agreement between your trade unions and those of the socialist countries, you know that you and we differ in our approach to many social phenomena, and appraise them differently.

"In our opinion, trade unions should have more frequent contacts. Everything cannot be settled overnight, of course. But should cooperation between trade unions begin to develop and strengthen on specific points, if only minor ones to begin with, the two countries will in the end come to join efforts. You cannot gain an understanding of the attitude of our trade unions overnight, just as our trade unionists cannot gain overnight an understanding of all that you have. That is why both you and we should take a good look at each other, examine each other's activities and get to know them better. We may have disputes and disagreements. But if you and we want to promote peace and improve the living conditions of workers, of working people, why aggravate relations? After all, that would benefit none but our common enemies.

"Do you want our socialist system changed? I hope not. We, for our part, don't want to interfere in your internal affairs and will not do it—won't try to bring about a change in the system you have. We have said in the past and say now: 'Let us be more tolerant toward each other. Though we differ with you on many questions, we have a common cause for the sake of which we should join our efforts. It is the struggle for peace. The peoples want peace, and are fighting for it.'

"As for specific questions of the trade-union movement, I must admit that I've never worked in that field and am no expert, but we have experienced trade unionists. Why don't you contact them? They will not try to make Communists out of you and I think that you, too, will not make supporters of capitalism out of them. But an exchange of views between you and them would, no doubt, be useful."

James Carey, Vice-President of the AFL-CIO, who spoke at the close of the discussion, thanked N. S. Khrushchev for the meeting.

"Thank you," he said, "for giving us so much of your time. Good-bye and good luck. Let's work together for peace, for the good of man."

The meeting ended in a friendly atmosphere. In parting, the union leaders thanked the head of the Soviet Government again and again for the meeting.

In view of the foregoing, it was really surprising that a news conference was held right after the meeting, at which Mr. Reuther did not hesitate—in the opinion of the Soviet press group—grossly to distort the substance of the discussion and attack the man whom he and his colleagues had just received as a guest of honor. Mr. Reuther went so far as to allege that N. S. Khrushchev had in the course of the discussion "pounded the table and shouted, 'I am the dictator of the working class.' "

This sort of statement is plainly intended for people who have no idea whatever of the Soviet Union or its leaders. It is not mere chance that many bourgeois correspondents asked N. S. Khrushchev to comment on the utterly incredible statement which Mr. Reuther had made about the meeting.

"I don't know whether Mr. Reuther actually said that or whether it was attributed to him by unscrupulous journalists," N. S. Khrushchev replied. "Did he really say that?"

Journalists who had attended the news conference confirmed that Mr. Reuther had made the statement in question. Then N. S. Khrushchev said:

"If Mr. Reuther made such a statement, he acted dishonestly. It's a lie. I cannot respect a man who resorts to such methods. In our interview, we spoke of the dictatorship of the working class and not any personal dictatorship. Marxism-Leninism maintains that when power passes into the hands of the working class, it has to establish a dictatorship of its own to suppress the resistance of the overthrown exploiting classes. The forms of working-class dictatorship may vary in different countries. If the deposed class puts up no resistance to the new that is born in the course of the historical development of society, as a result of revolution, the working class has no need to use forcible means of suppression. But if the exploiters try to turn back the wheel of history, to prevent the people from taking power, if they try to strangle the revolution, then the working class, working people in general, must, in the name of their vital interests, use means of suppression to maintain their social gains and to defend the vital interests of the working masses, of the entire people."

N. S. Khrushchev stressed that as it advances to communism the Soviet Union is carrying out more and more extensive measures leading to the withering away of the state. "We have already carried out a number of far-reaching measures in that field," he said. "We are reducing our armed forces and militia, and cutting the number of state security workers. An increasing number of functions involved in the maintenance of law and order and in state administration are being transferred to public organizations."

What is the outcome of the interview between the U.S. union leaders and the head of the Soviet Government?

The very fact that the interview took place suggests that the political situation in the USA is taking a turn for the better. However strong anti-Soviet sentiment may be with some U.S. trade-union leaders, the growing urge of the American people for better U.S.-Soviet relations and for a durable peace is gaining the upper hand.

It will be recalled that so far the U.S. trade-union leadership has persisted in avoiding all contacts with the Soviet Union. Many speeches made by Meany, President of the AFL-CIO, hardly differed in substance from speeches made by reactionary-minded leaders of U.S. imperialism. Speaking at a trade-union congress in San Francisco as recently as September 21, 1959, Meany violently attacked the Soviet Union and the Soviet Government in the cold war spirit. This attitude of Meany's and his associates' is at variance with the sentiments of ordinary Americans, who want a durable peace and friendly relations between the USA and the Soviet Union.

This must have been the reason why the group of AFL-CIO leaders found it necessary to invite N. S. Khrushchev, head of the

Soviet Government, to an interview to discuss some important problems of international life and Soviet-American relations.

It is reasonable to believe that that interview may serve as a good start and will help pave the way for the necessary contacts between American and Soviet trade unions.

Those contacts are indispensable and could be most fruitful in the struggle for the common cause of promoting universal peace.

As regards those who persist, trying to stay on the cold war bandwagon, they are merely exposing their true colors before the eyes of the working people of the world.

The vital interests of the working class call for unity in the struggle for peace. "Though we differ with you on many questions," N. S. Khrushchev said in his conversation with the U.S. trade unionists, "we have a common cause for the sake of which we should join our efforts. It is the struggle for peace."

It is deplorable that reactionary U.S. trade-union leaders are trying to aggravate matters at a time when there are signs of better relations between the Soviet Union and the United States, and of a more wholesome international climate.

No matter how hard reactionary-minded U.S. trade-union leaders try to conceal the appeal to unity voiced by the head of the Soviet Government or to distort his statements, the truth will triumph. One indication of this is the fact that Americans received the head of the Soviet Government with great warmth everywhere, all along the route of his U.S. tour. That warm welcome is a genuine expression of the American people's urge for peace and friendship with the Soviet people.

SPEECH BY N. S. KHRUSHCHEV, MOSCOW, SEPT. 28, 1959 *

DEAR COMRADES:

We have just stepped off the plane which made a nonstop flight from Washington to Moscow. (*Applause.*) We have come straight here to this meeting, dear Muscovites, in order to share our impressions with you and to tell you about the results of our stay in

* Russian text in *Pravda,* Sept. 29, 1959, pp. 2–3. English translation as distributed by Soviet news and official agencies, can be found also in *Khrushchev in America* (New York: Crosscurrents Press, 1960), pp. 217–31.

the United States of America, which we visited at the invitation of President Dwight D. Eisenhower.

In accepting that invitation, we were prompted by the consideration that the international situation and the relations between our states—our two Great Powers, the Soviet Union and the United States—have for a long time been strained. To preserve such a state of affairs would mean to preserve a situation in which there may be all kinds of surprises fraught with grave consequences for our peoples and for the peoples of the whole world. That is why the more far-sighted statesmen in a number of countries have come to realize the need to make some effort to put an end to the cold war, to remove the tension in international relations, clear the atmosphere and create more or less normal relations between states. The peoples could then live and look to the future without fear. The Twentieth Century is one in which human intellect and talent have attained the greatest heights. In our day, the dreams mankind cherished for ages, dreams expressed in fairy-tales which seemed sheer fantasy, are being translated into reality by man's own hands. How, then, in this age of flourishing human genius that is fathoming nature's secrets and harnessing her mighty forces, can one reconcile oneself to the preservation of the primitive relations between men that existed when men were no more than beasts?

If such relations in the remote past may be explained by the fact that man was still at the initial stage of his development and little different from animals, then today, when man has reached such heights of scientific knowledge and is step by step subduing the forces of nature, compelling them to serve the needs of society—today there can be no justification for preserving the kind of relations that existed among primitive men.

Our time can and must become the time of the triumph of great ideals, the time of peace and progress. (*Prolonged applause.*)

The Soviet Government has long since perceived this. And that is why we have repeatedly proposed to the Great Powers to organize a meeting of the heads of government in order to exchange views on urgent international issues. When we made these proposals, we believed in the power of human reason. We believed that, with a rational approach, representatives of different political views, of states with different social systems, could in the interests of peace, find a common language in order to arrive at correct solutions to the problems agitating all humanity today. In our age of tremendous technological progress, in circumstances where there exist states with different social systems, international problems can be successfully solved only on the basis of the principles of peaceful coexistence. There is no other way. Those who say that they do not understand what peaceful coexistence is, and are afraid of it, are wittingly or unwittingly helping to further the cold war which is bound to spread unless we intervene and stop it. It will reach a point of such intensity that a spark may at any moment set off a world conflagration. In that war much will perish. It will be too late to discuss what peaceful coexistence means when such terrible means of destruction as atomic and hydrogen bombs, and ballistic missiles, which practically cannot be intercepted and can carry nuclear weapons to any point on the globe, go into action. Not to reckon with this, means to close one's eyes and stop one's ears, to hide one's head in the sand as the ostrich does at the approach of danger. If we humans imitate the ostrich and hide our head in the sand, then, I ask you, what is the use of having a head if it is incapable of averting the danger to life? (*Prolonged applause.*)

No, we must show human reason, we must have faith in the human intellect, faith in the possibility of achieving agreement with statesmen of different countries and in combining efforts to mobilize people for the task of averting the threat of war. We must have the courage and determination to act in defiance of those who persist in continuing the cold war. We must stop it from spreading, melt the ice and normalize international relations.

From this lofty rostrum, before you Muscovites, before my whole people, my government and Party, I must say that President Eisenhower displayed wise statesmanship in appraising the present world situation, displayed courage and determination. (*Stormy applause.*) Notwithstanding the complex situation prevailing in the United States, the President, a man who enjoys the absolute confidence of his people, proposed an exchange of visits between the heads of government of our two countries. We give him due credit for this important initiative aimed at strengthening the cause of peace. (*Prolonged applause.*) In taking this step, he was confident that we would accept the hand he proffered us, inasmuch as we have repeatedly addressed both

President Eisenhower and other heads of government to that effect. And the President was not mistaken. (*Applause.*)

Dear comrades, it gives me great satisfaction to report to you that we have fulfilled part of our arrangement with President Eisenhower concerning the exchange of visits. At the President's kind invitation we have visited the United States of America, where we have had some important meetings and talks.

I would like to share with you my impressions of that visit and to tell you briefly of its results. I believe it will be best to tell you exactly what happened. The more candid our account, the better it will be for strengthening relations between the peoples of our two countries. (*Applause.*) It would not be true if I were to say that our tour of some American cities, and our meetings and talks with many Americans have ironed out all the controversial issues. Only a politically blind man could expect that whatever he says will be done.

No, in order to settle such important questions, one visit, one trip is not enough. Much effort is required. It will take many more meetings before complete mutual understanding is achieved, before we reach the goal which our Party, our people and our Soviet Government have always pursued—to ensure peaceful coexistence between states with different social systems, and to safeguard the security of the peoples on the basis of noninterference in internal affairs.

I would like to tell you how we felt when we first set foot on American soil.

Frankly speaking, my own feelings were somewhat mixed. The reason for this was that as soon as the first reports of the coming exchange of visits appeared, many press organs and some United States spokesmen launched a propaganda campaign against my coming to the United States. The atmospheric conditions they created did not warm me, although the temperature in the United States is much higher than in Moscow. They wanted to meet me with a cold shower. I was particularly disappointed when, in the plane en route from Moscow to Washington, I read a speech by Vice-President Nixon timed to coincide with my arrival. He chose an audience which could hardly be suspected of being bellicose. He was addressing an association of dentists. (*Animation.*) However, Mr. Nixon's speech was far from medicinal in content. (*Laughter.*) He, so to speak, added a chill to the toothache. One would think he was afraid of the atmosphere really turning warmer, of the cold war really ending. I cannot understand why this was necessary.

However, when we arrived in Washington we were accorded a reception worthy of our great country, our great people. (*Prolonged, stormy applause.*) We must give due credit to President Eisenhower for having done everything appropriate for a meeting at such a level. (*Applause.*) You probably read the newspaper reports about the reception in the U.S. capital and the President's speech on that occasion. I shall not repeat all that. It was a warm reception.

Shortly after our arrival in Washington, the President received us at the White House. The Vice-President, Mr. Nixon, and the Secretary of State, Mr. Herter, were present. I am a rather restless, straightforward sort of person, and although it may not have been altogether diplomatic of me, I asked at our very first meeting why the Vice-President had to make such a speech on the eve of my visit, not to mention the unfriendly statements and articles by people of lesser rank.

The President said he had not read Nixon's speech. I told him he need not bother to read it, since it was already past history. (*Applause.*)

This is a little detail that gives some idea of the preparations made to meet the visitor from overseas. (*Animation.*)

Here is another. You Muscovites, and not only you, but all Soviet people—Russians, Ukrainians, Byelorussians, Uzbeks, Georgians, Kazakhs, Armenians—all our peoples alike, always give a guest a proper welcome. No matter what country he may come from, whatever his political views, once he is our guest we put our bread and salt on the table and show him not only formal, but sincere respect. (*Applause.*) Here is what I witnessed on my first day there, in the United States: As we drove with the President through the streets lined with crowds, I noticed that here and there someone would raise his hand and wave, but the next moment the hand would drop abruptly as though it had touched a live wire. (*Laughter.*)

I could not understand it at first. And so I decided to look more closely at the faces of the people lining the route. I began to nod to them in greeting, and many of them nodded in response. Now what was the trouble?

Later I was told that ten minutes before we drove through with the President to the White House, an automobile had passed along the route carrying a poster inscribed to the effect that the guest should be met with dignity and politeness, but without applause or greetings. (*Animation.*)

Afterwards I asked Mr. Lodge, the President's personal representative accompanying me on my tour of the United States, whether this was true, and was told that a car with such a poster had indeed passed along the route, but whose car it was no one seemed to know. (*Laughter.*) It was said to have broken through the police guard. When I was given this explanation by official spokesmen, I told them I could not imagine how the police, who were guarding me so well, could have failed to notice a car carrying a poster of that sort. (*Animation.*)

I am convinced that the President knew nothing of all this and that it was all done without the knowledge not only of the President but of the others who organized our reception. But, as the saying goes, you cannot take a word out of a song.

From the moment we set foot on American soil I was so well guarded that it was quite impossible for me to come into contact with rank-and-file Americans. Police protection developed into a sort of house arrest. (*Animation.*) I was driven around in a closed car, so that I could catch glimpses of the people who came to greet us only through the window. And the people greeted me, even though they could not always see me.

I am far from suggesting that all the friendly feelings expressed by the American people were addressed to me personally or even to our communist ideology. By their greetings, the Americans were telling us that they, like ourselves, stand for peace and friendship between our peoples. (*Stormy applause.*)

I shall not give you a detailed account of all our meetings with the Americans. You have do doubt read about them in the papers. We spent some time in Washington, then in New York, where I had the honor to submit on behalf of the Soviet Government from the rostrum of the United Nations a plan for general and complete disarmament. (*Stormy applause.*)

From New York we went to the West Coast of the United States, to Los Angeles and San Francisco, and from there to the state of Iowa, and to Pittsburgh, the big industrial center of Pennsylvania. And, finally, we returned to Washington. It was quite an extensive tour. We visited various parts of the United States, and met all sorts of people. We had many very good meetings and frank talks. But there were meetings of a different nature, too.

During the first half of our tour, we could not help noticing that one and the same story was repeated each time. Speakers claimed that I had once said that we would "bury the capitalists." At first I patiently explained what I had actually said, that we would "bury capitalism" in the sense that socialism would inevitably replace that moribund social system, just as in its time capitalism had replaced feudalism. But as time went on, I saw that the people who persisted in repeating this sort of question did not really need any explanations. They were pursuing a definite purpose, namely, to use the communist bogey to frighten people who have only the vaguest notion of what communism is.

At a reception in Los Angeles, at which the Mayor, who is no worse than other mayors though perhaps less diplomatic, again began to speak in this spirit, I felt compelled to speak my mind.

I said to them: Do you intend to make an unfriendly demonstration in every city and at every gathering? Very well, if that is how you are going to receive me, then, as the Russian proverb says, "From the stranger's gate, the road home is straight." (*Applause.*) If you are not yet ripe for talks, if you haven't yet realized the need of ending the cold war and fear its termination, if you want to go on with it, we can wait. The wind isn't blowing in our faces either. We have the patience to wait, and the wisdom. Our country is getting along fine. Our people have more than once shown wisdom, strength and determination, and such capacity to surmount difficulties that they can stand up for their country and for the cause of peace. (*Prolonged applause.*) They will be able to give a fitting answer if the aggressive forces should try to probe us with their bayonets. (*Applause.*)

I was obliged to start diplomatic negotiations on this score. I asked Comrade Gromyko, our Minister of Foreign Affairs, to go and tell Mr. Lodge, the President's representative accompanying me, that unless the matter was rectified I could not continue my tour and would be obliged to return to Washington, and thence to Moscow.

All this evidently had its effect. Mr. Lodge conveyed to me through Gromyko that he advised me to continue with the program and to go on to San Francisco and other cities, and that the local authorities would see to it that this would not happen again.

I must tell you that the talks through Comrade Gromyko took place at night, and when I woke up in the morning everything had indeed changed. When we left Los Angeles for San Francisco, the "handcuffs," figuratively speaking, were removed and I was able to get out of the train and talk to people. (*Applause.*) People shook my hand and I theirs, and they applauded and smiled, exactly as you Muscovites do when you meet a guest, because you are glad to see him and wish to do your best to make him feel that he is welcome. (*Applause.*)

When we arrived in San Francisco, the sun was shining, it was a beautiful day, like our own summer day. The climate of this wonderful city was quite different, the sun's rays warmed us, but warmer still to us was the cordial, unconstrained reception we were given. (*Applause.*)

We are very grateful to Mr. Christopher, the Mayor of San Francisco, to Mr. Brown, Governor of California, to the people of San Francisco, to all those who showed an understanding of our visit—a visit of peace and friendship between our nations, between the peoples of all countries. (*Applause.*)

We were given every opportunity to meet and talk to ordinary people. True, the physical possibilities were limited, but that was due to the brevity of our visit. To tell the truth, my suspicions concerning the ill intentions of the local authorities were dispelled. We at once established good contact with the inhabitants of that large and beautiful city.

I want to make special mention of my meeting with the longshoremen. Mr. Bridges, the leader of the Pacific Longshoremen's Union, invited me and my companions to come and talk to the workers. That was a most cordial meeting. Among the longshoremen, simple and sincere folk, I felt as if I were among our Soviet workers. (*Applause.*) The greetings I conveyed to them on behalf of Soviet workers were met with enthusiasm, and they asked me, in turn, to convey their hearty greetings. (*Stormy applause.*)

I also recall our visit to the computer plant in San Jose, near San Francisco. The manager of the plant, Mr. Watson, and the employees gave us a warm welcome, and acquainted us in detail with the complex production processes. The explanations were given in Russian—a mark of consideration which it is particularly pleasant to note. The plant itself, the layout, and the organization of production, made a good impression.

I observed that one of the men who was showing us around the plant spoke Russian with a Ukrainian accent and I asked him in Ukrainian:

"What is your name?"

"Marchenko," he replied.

"Glad to meet you," I said. "Are your parents living?"

"Yes," he answered.

"Give my regards to them."

He thanked me.

But our stay in hospitable San Francisco came to an end, and we had to continue our journey by plane to another American city, Des Moines, in the state of Iowa. Des Moines is one of the principal agricultural centers of the United States.

After a cordial reception by the Governor of the state, the Mayor of the city, and representatives of the business community and public leaders, we drove out to the corn fields so dear to my heart. (*Animation, applause.*) I must say that the Americans know how to grow corn. It is planted everywhere in squares and the fields are in good condition. True, there too, in the fields of the leading corn expert himself, my old acquaintance Garst, I found a few shortcomings. (*Laughter, applause.*) His corn was crowded in clusters, and I drew his attention to that fact—in a friendly way, of course.

We were shown great hospitality by our host, Mr. Garst, who arranged an interesting meeting for us with the farmers. We met Adlai Stevenson there—the prominent Democratic Party leader who had come from Chicago, and we had a most frank and friendly talk with him.

I recall this episode. When we visited the local college, one of the young people gave me a copy of the students' newspaper. It contained a long article in which, I was told, the students welcomed our arrival. The article, however, said that the students would meet us without enthusiasm or cheers. Yet those very students in whose name the article had been written—those lively, eager young people—showed exactly the same sort of enthusiasm as our own youth. They shouted, and applauded, and expressed their feelings most vociferously. I heard them shout: "Tovarishch Khrushchev!" "Nikita!" and other simple, friendly words. (*Animation, applause.*)

I must also tell you about the warm welcome we were given by the inhabitants of Pittsburgh—one of the biggest industrial centers of America, the city of steel-makers and machine-builders. They showed us great friendliness and respect. I even felt a trifle awkward as I drove from the airfield. We arrived in Pittsburgh at midnight. It was a dark night, yet all along the road people stood beside cars and I saw their smiles and heard their words of welcome.

In Pittsburgh we visited the Mesta Company's machine plant. We felt that the plant management had done their best to show us the plant and to enable us to acquaint ourselves with working conditions. We went through the plant and talked with the workers. I would like to mention one detail: When we first arrived we were greeted, but with restraint. However, the longer we were with the workers, the warmer the atmosphere grew. The workers enthusiastically expressed their respect for us representatives of the Soviet state and Soviet people.

I also remember the meeting I had with Pittsburgh businessmen and intellectuals at the local university. There was the usual dinner and speeches, but speeches which seemed to me to display a more realistic understanding of the need for amicable relations between our countries.

Hearing me speak now, some people may be thinking: Khrushchev is speaking only of the friendly meetings, he says nothing about the hostile demonstrations. No, I do not intend to hush up the fact that there were instances of hostility and unfriendliness towards us. Yes, there were such instances. I must tell you that just as the American newspapermen accompanied me throughout my tour of the United States, so did some fascist-minded refugees from different countries, who went with us from town to town, parading a few miserable posters. We also saw grim and morose American faces.

There was a great deal that was good, but one must not forget the bad either. The little worm, or rather the great big worm, is still alive and is liable to show its vitality in the future.

Why do I speak of this? Is it in order to cool relations between the Soviet Union and the United States? No. I mention this because it is necessary to know the truth, because you must see not only one side, the pleasant side, but also the other, the backstage side which should not be hidden. In America there are forces which are operating against us, which are against lessening tension and for preserving the cold war. To close one's eyes to this fact would be to display weakness in combating these evil forces, these evil spirits. No, they must be dragged out into the open, exposed and publicly flogged, they must be roasted like devils in a frying pan. (*Laughter, prolonged applause.*) Let those who wish to continue the cold war fume. No ordinary people anywhere in the world, no sensible human being will support them. (*Applause.*)

Our visit to Pittsburgh rounded out our tour of the United States.

In winding up my account of our tour I should like to express our sincere thanks to the mayors of the towns and the governors of the states we visited, to the representatives of the business world and to the intellectuals, to the personnel of the factories and universities, to workers and farmers, and to all the representatives of public organizations. I particularly want to express my appreciation of all that was done for us by the Mayor of New York, Mr. Wagner; the Mayor of San Francisco, Mr. Christopher; the Mayor of Pittsburgh, Mr. Gallagher; the Governor of Pennsylvania, Mr. David Lawrence; the Chancellor of the University of Pittsburgh, Mr. Litchfield; the President of Iowa State College of Agriculture and Mechanical Arts, James Hilton; the representatives of the business world Eric Johnston, Robert Dowling, Cyrus Eaton, Thomas Watson, Frank Mesta, Roswell Garst; and others. (*Applause.*)

The numerous gifts we received were a splendid token of respect for our country and for its great people. The Mayors of New York and Pittsburgh presented us with a medallion of New York and the key of Pittsburgh.

I said, by the way, that I was accepting the key as a symbol of trust. "And you can rest assured," I said, "I promise you, that this key will never be used without the hosts' permission." (*Prolonged applause.*)

International Harvester Company presented us with a film dealing with the mechanization of corn production; President Eisenhower gave a pedigree heifer from his private farm; Admiral Strauss, a steer and a heifer; and farmer Coolidge, a pedigree hog. Many other gifts were presented, for which we are grateful and appreciative. (*Applause.*)

I would like to say that the American press, radio and television gave extensive, and on the whole correct, objective coverage of our visit to the United States. There were, of course, some unfriendly attacks on the part of individual journalists, but it was not they who set the tone in the American press.

My comrades and I were accompanied on our tour of the United States by the President's personal representative, Mr. Lodge; Mr. Buchanan, Chief of the Protocol Division of the State Department; Mr. Thompson, U.S. Ambassador to the USSR; their wives; and other officials. I would like to thank them all, and especially Mr. Lodge. He did his best to create the necessary conditions for us on our tour and to acquaint us with the life of the great American people. (*Applause.*)

I remarked in jest to Mr. Lodge that if he, a representative of the capitalist world, and I, a representative of the working class and the Communist Party of the Soviet Union, were to be cast away on a desert island, we would probably find a common language and would be able to coexist peacefully. (*Animation, prolonged applause.*) Why could not states with different social systems coexist? Our countries are also on an island, as it were; after all, with modern means of communication which have brought continents closer together, our earth indeed seems like a small island, and we ought to realize that. And once the need for coexistence is realized, it is necessary to pursue a peaceful policy, to live in friendship and not to brandish weapons but to destroy them. (*Applause.*)

Comrades, on September 25 I met the President again in the White House and together we flew by helicopter to Camp David, his country residence. We spent September 25, 26 and 27 there. We held frank and friendly talks, set forth the positions of our governments on vital international issues and also on questions of improving Soviet-American relations. Mr. Herter, the U.S. Secretary of State, and Comrade Gromyko, the USSR Foreign Minister, as well as other comrades in my party took part in these meetings and talks and did useful work.

The principal result of our exchange of opinions is given in the joint communiqué which has been published today in the press. There can be no doubt that this document will be received with satisfaction by all who are interested in strengthening peace. (*Prolonged applause.*)

It should be borne in mind, however, that naturally the President and I could not at one sitting clear away all the accretions of the cold war that have piled up in the course of many years. It will take time to sweep away that rubbish and, not only to sweep it away, but to grind it to dust. Certain things that divide us are still too fresh. It is sometimes difficult for some leaders to discard old positions, old views, old definitions.

But I can tell you in all frankness, dear comrades, that as a result of my talks and discussions of concrete questions with the U.S. President, I have gained the impression that he sincerely wishes to see the end of the cold war, to create normal relations between our countries and to help improve relations among all countries. (*Stormy applause.*) Peace today is indivisible, it cannot be secured by the efforts of two or three countries alone. Hence it is necessary that all nations, all states participate in the fight for peace.

The President and I exchanged views on the question of disarmament. He stated that the Government of the United States was studying our proposal and that the United States, like ourselves, wants total, controlled disarmament.

It would seem that there are, at present, no reasons for delaying settlement of this question. But, on the other hand, disarmament is too serious a question for one to expect one's partners to settle it hastily, right off the bat. It must, of course, be studied with a view to finding a solution that would really create confidence and ensure disarmament and the peaceful coexistence of states.

So let us not be hasty in our judgement, let us be patient and give the statesmen time to study our proposals. But we will not be idle, we shall continue to urge the need for complete and general disarmament. (*Applause.*) We regard our proposals as a basis for agreement. We are prepared to discuss any amendments to our documents, to our proposals. We are prepared to discuss any other proposals that may be made if they are directed towards the same aims as those we pursue.

The President and I also exchanged views on the German question, on the question of concluding a peace treaty. We tried to show him, and I believe we succeeded, that our proposals for a peace treaty had been incorrectly interpreted in the West. Some people had sought to whip up undue passions by claiming that this was an ultimatum, and so on. Those who did so were clearly prompted by a desire to prolong the cold war. They went so far as to declare that our proposals for a peace treaty with Germany were little short of a declaration of war. To think that anyone could distort the peaceful stand of the Soviet Union in such a fashion!

We also exchanged views on holding a meeting of heads of government. We both outlined the positions of our governments and agreed that such a meeting is necessary and useful.

We exchanged opinions on the date of President Eisenhower's return visit to the Soviet Union. At first the President intended to come to the USSR in the latter part of October. However, he asked me what time of the year was best for touring our country. That made me think. We Muscovites like Moscow at all seasons of the year. But, like all people, we find spring, the season of joy when nature awakens to life, pleasantest. And so I said that it would perhaps be best if he came later in May or early in June. And it would be good if the President would bring along his wife, his son and daughter-in-law, and his grandchildren. We would also be glad to see the President's brother, who has been to our country with Mr. Nixon.

The President was kind enough to invite me to his farm. He showed me his corn—I couldn't very well visit the President without having a look at his corn, could I? (*Animation.*) He showed me his calves and his steers. Fine animals. True, I must say that the Eisenhower farm is rather small for the President of such a huge and wealthy state. It is not a rich farm and the soil is not very good. But the President said that he wants to work to improve the land and thereby leave behind a good memory of himself.

At the farm I met the President's grandchildren and had a conference with them. (*Laughter.*) I asked them if they would like to go to Russia. And all of them, from the youngest to the eldest, declared that they wanted to go to Russia, to Moscow. The eldest grandson is eleven, the youngest granddaughter is three or four. I won their support. I remarked jokingly to the President that it was easier to agree on a return visit with his grandchildren than with himself (*laughter, applause*), because his grandchildren have a good environment, whereas he evidently has some obstacles to contend with which prevent him from realizing his wishes as and when he wants to. (*Applause.*)

I would like to tell you, dear comrades, that I have no doubt that the President is prepared to exert his efforts and his will to bring about agreement between our countries, to create friendly relations between our two peoples and to settle pressing problems in the interest of a durable peace. (*Applause.*)

At the same time, it is my impression that there are forces in America which are not operating in the same direction as the President. These forces stand for continuing the cold war and the arms race. Whether these forces are great or small, influential or uninfluential, whether the forces backing the President—and he has the support of the absolute majority of the American people—can win, are questions I would not be too hasty to answer.

Time is a good counsellor, or as the Russians say: "The morning is wiser than the evening." That is a wise dictum. Let us wait until morning, the more so since we have arrived by plane at the end of the day and it is now evening as I speak here. And perhaps more than one morning will pass before we will be able to tell for sure. But we shall not sit with our arms folded and wait for the dawn, wait to see which way the arrow of international relations will point.

We, for our part, will do everything we can to ensure that the barometer points not to "storms" or even to "change," but to "fair." (*Prolonged applause.*)

I am confident, comrades, that in the present circumstances, when the forces of peace have grown immeasurably, when the socialist camp numbers nearly one billion people and possesses enormous productive capacities, when the Soviet Union has such vast achievements in industry and agriculture, science, engineering and culture—we can do a great deal for peace.

In our actions we base ourselves on reason, on truth, on the support of the whole people. Moreover, we rely on our mighty potential. And those who wish to preserve the cold war with a view sooner or later to turning it into a hot war had best know that in our time only a madman can start war, who himself will perish in its flames. (*Applause.*)

The peoples must strait-jacket such madmen. We believe that statesmanship, that human reason will triumph. (*Applause.*) In the splendid words of Pushkin, "Let reason triumph! May darkness be banished!" (*Prolonged applause.*)

Dear comrade Muscovites! We are boundlessly happy to be home again, to see the dear faces of Soviet people. (*Applause.*)

Long live the great Soviet people who are successfully building communism under the leadership of the glorious Party of Lenin! (*Prolonged applause.*)

Long live Soviet-American friendship! (*Prolonged applause.*)

Long live friendship among all the peoples of the world! (*Stormy, prolonged applause. All rise.*)

1960:
The U-2

For 1960 there were scheduled a summit meeting in Paris, an Eisenhower visit to the Soviet Union, relaxation of international tension, and a new opportunity to make progress toward peaceful settlement of difficult international problems such as Berlin, disarmament, etc. In actual fact it turned out to be the year of the U-2 incident, of the Soviet torpedoing of the summit meeting and cancellation of the Eisenhower visit, of consequently heightened international tension between the Soviet Union and the United States, and of Nikita Khrushchev's second and less auspicious visit to the United States. It was also the year of the behind-the-scenes split between the Soviet Union and Communist Albania and increasingly bad feeling—also behind the scenes—between the Soviet Union and Communist China.

On May 1, just a little over two weeks before the summit conference was scheduled to open on May 16 in Paris, a United States reconnaissance plane, a U-2, operated by the American C.I.A. employee, Francis Gary Powers, was shot down deep in Soviet territory near the Urals city of Sverdlovsk. As it subsequently became apparent, Powers himself had parachuted safely to the ground and had been captured. His plane was not completely destroyed by whatever weapon was used to bring it down—the Soviets claimed it was an anti-aircraft rocket. The result was that the Soviet government had in its possession a living witness and also airplane reconnaissance equipment which could demonstrate that a United States intelligence agency had been engaged in sending planes over the Soviet Union.

The result, as might have been expected, was an explosive outburst of rage from Moscow. As it happened, the U-2 incident was dropped into an inflammatory situation in internal Soviet Communist Party politics which was part of a larger picture of dissension within the international communist movement.

Premier Khrushchev had staked much on his efforts at a *rapprochement* with the United States. There were no few conservative Communists in the Soviet Union who frowned on the Russian leader's trip to capitalist America, on his friendly declarations made during and after his journey, on his invitation to President Eisenhower to visit the Soviet Union. These conservative elements within Russia were being urged to take up arms against the Khrushchev leadership by an old Bolshevik, former premier and former foreign minister, V. M. Molotov, who continued to be in opposition to the Khrushchev line of policy. This Russian opposition to Khrushchev found its principal support outside the Soviet Union in the leadership of the Chinese Communist Party and that of little Albania.

Khrushchev was being accused of appeasement of the "imperialists," and the U-2 incident was bound to be fuel for opposition flames.

In this situation Khrushchev reacted violently. By bluster and threats he endeavored to render ineffective the argument that he was "appeasing" the "imperialists." The fact that the United States government and the United States President did not disavow the U-2 mission but instead defended it and asserted, in fact, American rights to overfly Soviet territory for reconnaissance purposes made the situation even more difficult for Khrushchev than it had been already. Consequently, when he went to Paris in the middle of May for the summit conference, he made a condition of Soviet attendance at the conference that President Eisenhower should apologize for the U-2 flight and disavow intentions of any further such flights in Soviet air-space. When the President refused, Khrushchev then proceeded to break up the summit conference before it started and went home to Moscow after having made some intensely bitter and violent remarks. He issued a threat to use Soviet rocket weapons against any bases from which further reconnaissance flights might be carried out over the Soviet Union. The United States government replied with threats to retaliate against the Soviet Union itself in the event of any rocket attacks on the territory of allies of the United States. All of this added up to a series of threats and counterthreats which ended whatever improved atmosphere there had previously been in Soviet and American relations. Khrushchev also, of course, canceled the Eisenhower trip to the Soviet Union which had been scheduled for June.

Threats over the U-2 incident were followed by threats over the Berlin situation. It was in this atmosphere that Khrushchev decided to attend the United Nations General Assembly session opening in September. Khrushchev came to the United States where he naturally got a reception which was less than cordial. He was not received by the President. He was confined to the New York area. He used the forum of the General Assembly to make speeches on such issues as disarmament and colonialism that were not calculated to earn him much goodwill in the West. The high point of his visit was reached when he used a shoe to thump on the table in the General Assembly —a widely publicized incident which outraged the sensibilities of many Westerners.

Following the General Assembly session Khrushchev returned to the Soviet Union where he met in November 1960 with representatives of eighty-one Communist and Workers' parties to discuss the international situation and attempt to maintain unity of the international Communist movement. At this meeting the differences between the leadership of the Soviet Communist Party and that of the Chinese Communist Party became more acute and were apparently a principal issue. In terms of ideology the principal issue between the parties was that of the "inevitability of war." The Chinese Communists took a much more militant attitude than that of the Soviet Communists. The Chinese held in general to the Leninist-Stalinist thesis that war is inevitable so long as "imperialism" (imperialism defined in Leninist terms as the last stage of development of capitalism) continues to exist. The Russians on the contrary held to the Khrushchev thesis that the Soviet Union and the "socialist camp" have now grown so powerful that they can prevent the outbreak of a new World War and that in fact it is necessary to prevent the outbreak of a new World War. Behind this question of theory lies the hard fact that the Soviet Union has now become a "have" nation with a vested interest in preservation of all that it has built in forty years of socialist construction, while Communist China is still a "have-not" nation immersed in poverty and even starvation. This issue is more than a matter of theory, obviously, for it is a question which permeates all matters of practical policy of all countries. To put it bluntly: If a new World War *is* really inevitable then the only thing of importance to the government of a nation believing this is to prepare for it on an all-out basis. Going further: If the government of either of the two most powerful nations of the world—the Soviet Union and the United States—should actually come to believe in the real inevitability of a new World War then a new World War would in fact really become inevitable. So that was the issue.

For the sake of maintaining an outward appearance of unity, however, the Chinese and the Russians managed to work out a formula which, though largely representing the Soviet view, also was reluctantly acceptable to Peking. A lengthy declaration was issued by the eighty-one parties on December 5.

Hardly had the party representatives left Moscow, however, than it became apparent that the Chinese-Soviet differences had not been overcome and that, in fact, bad feeling between the two parties had been aggravated. For the time being both sides refrained from open direct attacks on each other and continued on occasion to pay lip service to "monolithic unity" of the "world Soviet camp." However, by this time, though it had not yet become publicly known, relations between the Soviet Communist Party and that of little Albania had virtually ceased. This was an augury, since the Chinese Communists were backing the Albanians, of more difficulties to come in the year ahead.

As the twelfth item in this collection of Khrushchev documents, there have been selected here three press conferences dealing with the U-2 incident and the related question of the summit conference—May 11 in Moscow, May 18 in Paris, and June 3 in Moscow:

N. S. KHRUSHCHEV'S INFORMAL NEWS CONFERENCE AT EXHIBITION OF DOWNED PLANE, MAY 11, 1960 *

On May 11, following the press conference held by Foreign Minister Andrei Gromyko, Soviet and foreign members of the press were invited to examine the exhibition of the fragments of the American-owned plane.

During their visit to the exhibition the correspondents met Nikita Khrushchev who, having examined the wreckage of the plane and

* Russian text *Pravda,* May 13, 1960, pp. 1–2. English text from Press Department, Soviet Embassy in Washington, No. 228, May 13, 1960.

talked to experts, was preparing to leave. The newspapermen surrounded Khrushchev and a conversation ensued.

The newspapermen expressed satisfaction with having been given an opportunity to examine the plane fragments and the equipment and special apparatus it carried.

"I see that you are satisfied with the press conference," Nikita Khrushchev said. "You must have got the answers to all your questions. I have already said that we intend to take to the Security Council the question of the aggressive intrusion of an American plane within the confines of our country.

"If the Security Council—on which, apparently, pressure will be exerted by the United States—does not take the right decision, we shall raise the matter in the United Nations General Assembly. Such aggressive actions by the United States of America are a highly dangerous thing.

"This danger is enhanced by the fact that in his statement of May 10 the United States Secretary of State Mr. Herter not only sought to justify this act of aggression, but said also that the U.S. Government intended to continue such flights. This is an open threat to peace. We will shoot down such planes, and we will strike at the bases from which these planes will be sent to our country. You understand that if such aggressive actions continue, this might lead to war."

QUESTION (one of the correspondents): May I ask you a question?

KHRUSHCHEV: Even two if you like.

QUESTION: You have probably noticed a placard among the fragments of the plane urging assistance to the pilot. What do you think its authors meant?

KHRUSHCHEV: We assisted the pilot when he flew into our territory and gave him due welcome. If there are other such uninvited guests, we shall receive them just as "hospitably" as this one. We shall try him, try him severely as a spy.

QUESTION: How could all this affect the summit meeting?

KHRUSHCHEV: Let those who sent this spy plane think this question over. Though they should have thought about the consequences beforehand. After all, an aggression has been committed against our country. And we shall continue routing all the aggressors who dare raise a hand against us. You see how accurately our rocketeers shot down the plane without setting it on fire! The pilot is alive, the instrumentation intact; in other words, the material evidence is here for everyone to see. These are very skillful actions of our rocketeers. We are very grateful to them for this.

QUESTION: Will this plane incident influence Soviet public opinion when Mr. Eisenhower comes to Moscow?

KHRUSHCHEV: I would not like to be in Mr. Eisenhower's place. I would not like to be asked the questions which might be put to him when he comes to the Soviet Union! I can only say: The Soviet people and our public are very polite, so there will be no excesses, but questions will be asked, of course.

I would put it this way: One person, namely Mr. Herter, has helped the President particularly in this respect.

At his press conference Herter made an outrageous statement! Far from feeling guilty and ashamed of aggressive actions, he justifies them and says that this will continue in the future. Only countries in a state of war can act in this way. We are not in a state of war with America. These aggressive actions and Herter's statement are impudence, sheer impudence!

Herter's statement has made us doubt the correctness of our earlier conclusions that the President, the American Government, did not know about the flights. Herter's statement says that this intelligence plan was endorsed by the government.

Obviously the Americans were compelled to say this because otherwise they would have had to bring Allen Dulles to account. Dulles, in turn, would have exposed the government by saying that he carried out a plan approved by it and consequently endorsed by the head of the government. I proceed from the statement that was made by Herter.

There was a time—I remember it from my young days—when many criminals and other suspicious elements roamed the world. These people resorted to the following trick: A bandit with a small boy would hide under a bridge and wait for someone to cross it.

Then the bandit would send the boy to the passer-by and the boy would say: "Hello, mister, give me back my watch." The natural answer would be: "What's that? Now run along!" Then the boy would insist: "But look, mister, this watch is mine. Why don't you give me back my watch?" Then the armed bandit would appear, as though attracted by the noise of the argument, and tell the passer-by: "Why do you bully the boy? Give him back his watch and hand over your coat, too!"

The United States wants to live according to this law. But we are not defenseless passers-by. Our country is a strong and mighty state which can test its strength against it. If the United States has not experienced a real war on its territory, has not experienced air raids, and if it wishes to unleash a war, we shall be compelled to fire rockets which will explode on the aggressor's territory in the very first minutes of war.

I say this because I have read Herter's statement saying: "We are compelled to fly; it is the fault of the Soviet Union itself, because it does not give us access to its secrets which we simply must know. This is why, if you please, we undertake such flights. After all, the President has said that the skies should be open—this is why we fly and shall go on flying, shall go on opening the skies." How can an official representative of a state speak in this way about another nation! We do not live according to the laws of the United States. We have our own laws and this is why we shall make everyone on our territory respect these laws—and the violators will be thrashed!

I liked the article in the British newspaper *Daily Worker,* whose theme was as follows: If we accept the philosophy which some people in the United States want to instill in the public, it will be something like this—it is not the burglar that is guilty, but the owner of the house he broke into because he locked it, thereby compelling the burglar to break in.

But this is a philosophy of thieves and bandits!

I think that if world public opinion correctly realizes all the gravity of the situation and approaches this aggressive act of the United States policy with due responsibility, if everyone unanimously condemns this act, and if the United States Government no longer uses such methods with regard to other states, this will be a good, refreshing, so to say, ozonizing tendency in international relations.

Reading American press reports these days, I see that except for a few gangsters of the pen who are whitewashing this action, the absolute majority of people writing in the American press, including those who are notorious for their past lack of objectivity, are indignant about this incident, regard it as perfidy with regard to the Soviet Union.

This is a good sign. If you newsmen inform the public correctly, this incident, like every other incident, will finally be "digested." After all, gentlemen, we must live in peace, and not only in peace but also in friendship.

QUESTION: Can one remain optimistic about the United States policy?

KHRUSHCHEV: I consider myself to be an incorrigible optimist. I regard the provocative flight of the American intelligence plane over our country not as a preparation for war, but as a probing. They have now "probed" us, and we boxed the nose of the "probers."

Some United States officials are making a big noise now. Let them! The Soviet Union is not Guatemala. They cannot send troops here. We have the means to cool down bandits, should they wish to use their brazen methods against us. If they behave in this way, they will get this calmative.

QUESTION: Mr. Khrushchev, has your estimate of President Eisenhower, which you gave upon your return from the United States, changed?

KHRUSHCHEV: Well, the statement issued by the U.S. Department of State in connection with the intelligence plane naturally alters my belief that the United States President had nothing to do with this affair. I did not know that such an intelligence plan existed in the United States and that it included a program of reconnoitering flights over the Soviet territory. It follows from the statement of the Department of State, which was approved by the President, that flights of American intelligence planes over our country are not the whim of some irresponsible officer, but realization of a plan prepared by Allen Dulles, head of the Central Intelligence Agency, a department under the jurisdiction of the United States President.

Mr. Herter admitted that the United States President had issued directives to collect various intelligence information by all possible means.

These directives served as the basis for working out and carrying through programs which included, as Herter says, extensive aerial surveillance both peripheral and by penetration. I ask you to note this —by penetration—that is, by reconnaissance, spying flights over the territory of a state with which normal relations are maintained. And this plan was approved by the President. Incredible! Should I say after this: "What nice people you are!" To do this is to have no self-respect.

I would say that Mr. Herter has taken off all the evils and removed all the paint which was used to camouflage, embellish, and make up, as it were, the policy of the United States imperialists. Now, through his statement, he has revealed the bestial, fear-inspiring face of imperialism. So what? It turns out that this face inspires fear no longer. Such actions of the United States militarists are prompted not by the heroism of their masterminds, but by cowardice. Danger comes not from one who has his nerves at his command and relies on his powers and possibilities, but from a coward who fears everything.

I often read something like this: "Khrushchev claims that capitalism will die. Isn't this the reason why reconnaissance flights over the Soviet Union are made?" But it is not I who said it. It is Marx who explained this a hundred years ago. If the Messrs. Capitalists consider that Marx is wrong, then this should console them, then there is nothing to lose one's shirt about or show the white feather."

QUESTION: Did the Turkish, Pakistani, and Norwegian authorities know about the provocative flight of the American plane?

KHRUSHCHEV: It is difficult for me to speak for those governments, but I do grant that they did not know—the Americans are not accountable to them. I do not think that even the prime ministers of the countries on whose territory American military bases are situated are permitted inside those bases. The fault of such nations as Turkey or Pakistan is that they have joined aggressive blocs. The people's saying on this score is: "One sells one's soul to the devil; before one has done so, one can be one's own master; but after, it is the devil who will have one's soul at his disposal." This is just what is happening to Turkey, Pakistan, and Norway.

I warn you, Messrs. Foreign Journalists, don't sell your souls to the devil, keep them for yourself. You would do better by applying your energies to promoting the progress of society. The communist ideas shape the most progressive and the most correct trend in the development of society. The best Americans, such as John Reed, the author of *Ten Days That Shook the World,* grasped the great meaning of these ideas. John Reed was a very clever man. Yet he was not born a Communist, but came to accept it during the October Revolution, and he died a Communist.

Some of you scribble stories against communism out of lack of wisdom and understanding. May God forgive you for this.

When I read the bourgeois journalists' stories slandering Soviet realities and communism, I get angry sometimes but, on second thought, I say to myself: "Not all the journalists are John Reeds. Indeed, they are ordinary men, hired by such publishers as Hearst, for instance, who, like spiders, seize a man and enmesh him in their web. And if such a journalist fails to supply slanders against communism, what then will Hearst, or any other publishing concern, need him for? Hearst will not keep such a correspondent for a single day."

I talked with Hearst twice. During our second conversation, I told him: "How is it that you told me one thing, and wrote another?" And he replied: "Did I sum up the interview wrongly?"

I must do him justice: He summed up the essence of the talk more or less accurately, but his commentary on it misrepresented the whole meaning of it. I told him this, but he replied: "But I am a capitalist, it is my own commentary that I give." Indeed he is a capitalist, but most of you are not capitalists, nor will you ever be. So why do you have to serve capitalism? What is the point in being capitalism's flunkies? My conviction is that all roads lead to communism. Where else can they lead to?

This is just what the American imperialists fear. That is why they get nervous and fling themselves into reckless adventures. This shows they are not sure of their own system.

The State Department of the United States says that all countries engage in spying.

But the Soviet Union never sent its planes into the United States or any other countries for reconnaissance purposes, nor does it do so. If there have been any individual instances of our planes inadvertently violating the airspace of other countries—this has happened on our frontier with Turkey and Iran—we have apologized to those countries and punished those responsible for such violations.

We want to warn those who may try to send their spies into this country to think carefully of the consequences.

QUESTION: Do you still want President Eisenhower to come to the Soviet Union?

KHRUSHCHEV: What shall I say? Take my place and say it for me.

You see for yourselves what difficulties are cropping up. I am frank with you. You know my attitude toward the President of the United States. I have often spoken about it. But my hopes have been somewhat disappointed. I am a man, and I have human feelings. I am responsible for the direction of the Soviet Government. You must understand that we Russians, the Soviet people, always go the whole hog: When we play, we play; and when we fight, we fight. So how can I now call on our people to turn out and welcome the dear guest who is coming to us? The people will say: Are you crazy? What kind of a dear guest is he who lets a plane fly to us to spy? The American militarists who sent a plane on a spying mission to this country have put me, as one responsible for the arrangement for the U.S. President's visit to the USSR, in a very difficult position.

Frankly speaking, I think the United States President understands this himself.

Supposing, before my visit to the United States, we had sent such a plane over there and they had shot it down. One can imagine the kind of welcome I would have received from Americans. They would have greeted me according to my deserts. I think everyone understands that.

One can guarantee, however, that during the President's visit there will be no excesses. Ours are courteous people, they let off steam in words and will leave it to the government to act; they will not indulge in any insulting actions. I think that American journalists and tourists are now feeling the constraint and discipline of the Soviet people. I have not heard of anyone making any insulting remark to an American. This is commendable. This speaks of the strong spirit of our people.

QUESTION: Will the flight of this plane come up at the summit?

KHRUSHCHEV: It already is the subject of worldwide discussion. Therefore I believe there is no need to put it on the agenda of the summit conference. We are allowing for the fact that I alone will represent the socialist countries at the conference while the Western powers will have three representatives there. But I do not think that two of these three approve this aggressive, dangerous act of American brass hats.

Apparently you would like to know when I intend to fly to Paris. I intend to arrive in Paris on May 14, a day or even two before the conference starts, in order to get acclimated a little. I like Paris, it's a nice city. Well, and if others do not come—I mention this because some are threatening that the conference may not take place—then it will be clear that it is not our fault that the conference did not take place. So we shall go to Paris! And if the conference does not take place? Well, we have lived without it for many years and will live for another hundred.

It is not our country alone that is interested in the conference. All the world is interested in it. The peoples of all the world want international tensions to relax, want a normalization of international relations. I believe our partners in the negotiations are interested in the conference to a no lesser extent than the Soviet Union. Therefore the conference will depend upon our partners. We are ready. I repeat, I intend to enplane for Paris on Saturday, May 14.

Some diplomats take offense and say that Khrushchev is indulging in too harsh expressions. I should like to have heard their reactions had a similar aggressive invasion been committed against their country. What do you expect of me, after all, that I should take off my hat and welcome this invasion? No, we shall meet gangsters the way they deserve. And this was a gangster, bandit raid.

Have you seen here the "air sampling instruments"? How can the authors of this lie look into our eyes after it was exposed? True, we know what kind of eyes imperialists have. As the saying goes, "Spit in their eyes and they would keep saying: 'God's dew.' "

Now you see, I did not tell the whole story deliberately at the session of the Supreme Soviet because we knew with whom we were dealing. We did not say at first that the pilot was alive, that the instruments were intact, that the plane did not explode. They believed that the pilot committed suicide, and now that he is alive the American press seriously reprimands the pilot for a breach of his instructions, for failure to commit suicide and for surrendering instead.

Some in the United States say that the pilot must be brought to trial for not following the instructions and failing to destroy himself. Well, this is bestial talk. This is the ideology of imperialism. You, gentlemen, American journalists, you read your newspapers, don't you? This is a horrible thing.

QUESTION: Did not the American chargé d'affaires ask for an interview with Powers?

KHRUSHCHEV: The Americans have sent us a note on this question and asked to be allowed to have an interview with him. But they themselves understand that this is too much. The pilot is now under investigation; he is a spy, isn't he? So how can one speak about an interview with him? He must answer before our Soviet court.

QUESTION: Does this mean that neither the Ambassador nor the chargé d'affaires will be allowed to see Powers?

KHRUSHCHEV: I did not say that. Maybe they will, maybe they will not. We shall see later. I cannot reply to this question now because the investigation is in progress.

QUESTION: Will you regard as aggressive actions flights of aircraft of Western powers to Berlin after the signing of a peace treaty with East Germany?

KHRUSHCHEV: We have already made a statement in this connection. I repeat: After the signing of a peace treaty with the German Democratic Republic (GDR), the status determined by the terms flowing from the military surrender for this territory will change.

Since that moment the occupation of West Berlin will be over, all access to Berlin which was based upon the surrender of Germany will cease. Then the German Democratic Republic will exercise full control on its territory and will also control access to West Berlin which is situated on its territory. If the German Democratic Republic comes to terms with the countries concerned and will allow them to use the airspace, the waterways, the rail, and highways, this will no longer be our business, that will be the business of the German Democratic Republic. That's her sovereign right.

Some say that the Western powers will force their way into West Berlin.

I want to make it clear. If anyone tries to force his way, our military units stationed in the GDR to safeguard peace will counter the force of the peace violators with their own force, and let some hotheads in the West ponder what would come out of that for them.

QUESTION: Considering this aircraft incident and your attitude toward President Eisenhower, wouldn't you prefer Eisenhower's visit to be put off?

KHRUSHCHEV: We shall exchange views with the President on this question when we meet in Paris. We still want to find ways to improve relations with America, we want to have normal relations with the United States. And we believe that with time Soviet-American relations should grow into friendly relations between the peoples of our countries. That would be normal and that is for what all normal people are striving and will continue to strive.

Any more questions?

VOICES: No, thank you.

KHRUSHCHEV: In conclusion I have this to say: We deal harshly with those who invade the borders of our homeland, who violate our sovereignty. But we want to live in peace and friendship with all nations. I hope you will understand our attitude when we angrily condemn such aggressive action. But we take a sober view of things and realize that even the sharpest polemics are better than war.

This is why we shall do everything to relieve this strain, shall do everything to normalize the international situation and restore good relations with the United States if, of course, the United States also contributes to this. I should ask you to take this into account and not write anything that could increase tension still further. What do you need it for? After all, you too will be in for trouble if war breaks out. War does not bring happiness to anyone.

During the past few days I have read many statements by American Senators, Congressmen, businessmen, and I believe it is a good sign that many of them deplore this action by their government.

I believe it is a good sign that people do not lose their heads, that not everyone explains the matter as Herter has done.

QUESTION: What would you like to wish the French people in connection with your trip to Paris?

KHRUSHCHEV: The French people have given me a good welcome, just as the American people, but of course I do not want to set one people off against the other. However, my visit to France was undertaken later and the impressions are therefore fresher. I am very much pleased not only with the welcome given me by the French people, but also with the talks I had with President de Gaulle. As to the people, well, all the peoples want peace. Wars are started by the governments, while the peoples' lot is to spill their blood. That is why they all want peace.

The French people also want peace. We fought against militarist Germany together with France. If war breaks out, and it can be unleashed by West Germany, Frenchmen will remember that they had a good ally in the past—the Soviet Union. This ally may come in handy again. But it is best that we prevent war and be allies in the struggle for peace.

I think it is time to end this impromptu press conference. Let me thank you, dear comrades and gentlemen, let me wish you success. Uphold the truth, the noble cause of peace, and you will earn the respect of your peoples.

N. S. KHRUSHCHEV'S PRESS CONFERENCE IN PARIS, MAY 18, 1960 *

KHRUSHCHEV: Now, gentlemen, I wish to reply to those people here who "booed" and made noise in an attempt to create an unfriendly atmosphere. I was informed that Adenauer's minions have sent here some of their agents from among the Fascists who were not completely beaten in Stalingrad. Everyone remembers a time when the Hitlerites also booed us and attacked the Soviet Union. But the Soviet people gave them such a "boo" that many of these invaders went three meters underground right away. (*Stormy applause.*)

I should like to tell the people who are booing so much here: We thrashed the Nazi invaders at Stalingrad, in the Ukraine, in Byelorussia —everywhere they intruded, and we finished them off on the land from which they had invaded us. If the surviving fascist invaders "boo" us, as Hitler's gangsters did, if they again prepare an attack on the Soviet Union and the other socialist countries, we shall give them such a boo that they will never be able to gather up their bones. (*Stormy applause, shouts "Right" and "Long live peace," and several disapproving voices.*)

Gentlemen, I should like to draw your attention to the fact that the people who do the booing understand Russian without translation. This can be seen from their shouts. These apparently are surviving Nazi plunderers who were on the territory of the Soviet Union but managed to escape. (*Animation, general applause.*)

I should like to tell you, gentlemen, that even those who boo and shout here should realize who I am. I am a representative of the great Soviet people who, under the leadership of Lenin, under the leadership of the Communist Party, accomplished the Great October Socialist Revolution; a representative of a people which has built socialism and is successfully building a communist society, advancing confidently to communism. (*Stormy applause.*)

Gentlemen, the people who boo here are people of whom the German people are ashamed. (*Applause.*)

VOICE FROM THE FLOOR: This is propaganda!

KHRUSHCHEV: Listen to him, he thinks this is "propaganda." Smart,

* Russian text *Pravda,* May 19, 1960, pp. 1–2. English text from Press Department, Soviet Embassy in Washington, No. 243, May 19, 1960.

isn't he! We have shown by all our deeds what sort of "propaganda" this is! (*Animation in the hall.*)

As to the people who are trying to trip me up by shouting, I declare that they are not representatives of the German people, but fascist bastards. These angry shouts gladden my heart, because they reveal the fury of the enemies of our sacred cause. I remember the words of the great German, August Bebel, who said that if the enemies of the working class curse you, it means you are on the correct road. (*Stormy applause.*)

If you boo me, you only inspirit me in our class struggle for the cause of the working class, in the struggle for the cause of the peoples desiring a lasting peace. (*Stormy applause.*)

Gentlemen, I shall not conceal my pleasure—I like coming to grips with the enemies of the working class. I like hearing the frenzy of these lackeys of imperialism. (*Animation, applause.*)

But they cannot do anything to stem our forward movement. Our socialist homeland, the land of socialism, is like a rock, and we shall march forward to complete victory, to a communist society. (*Stormy, prolonged applause. Shouts of approval which drown individual hostile exclamations. After that the group of booers, which received a concerted rebuff from most of those present, did not try any more to obstruct the press conference.*)

Thank you for your attention, gentlemen. Now I am ready to hear your questions and reply to them as well as I can.

STEVENSON (London *Daily Sketch*): Can you tell us, Mr. Khrushchev, whether the Soviet Union will continue the Geneva talks on the banning of nuclear tests and on disarmament?

KHRUSHCHEV: Yes, we shall continue the Geneva ban-nuclear-tests negotiations. I think that if the American imperialists now have received an eye opener in Sverdlovsk there may be a chance of concluding a treaty on this question.

But if President Eisenhower resumes the testing, as he is threatening to do, then we too will resume the tests of nuclear weapons. All the people will then see who really is guilty, who sabotages the discontinuation of this thing. I am convinced that the truth will finally prevail, the people will compel those who resist to sign the treaty. And we are ready to sign an agreement on the discontinuation of nuclear tests any time. (*Applause.*)

The note asks another question as well—about the disarmament talks. We are almost convinced that our partners in Geneva do not want disarmament. They want control over armaments without disarmament, that is, the collection of espionage information. But we shall not agree to this. We are for genuine disarmament. We want the destruction of arms and the establishment of control so that no one will arm, so that no one will threaten anyone else with war. What is happening in Geneva is merely procrastination. If this goes on, we shall be compelled to approach the United Nations. We shall say that our partners do not really want to negotiate on disarmament, and we shall ask the United Nations General Assembly to consider the matter. (*Applause.*)

CORRESPONDENT (*Connecticut Herald*): If your statement concerning the U-2 incident is true, do you not think, as a great leader of a great state—the more so since you are convinced that the truth is on your side—that it would be better to hold a meeting at the summit now, when there is less international tension, than in six or eight months' time?

KHRUSHCHEV: We are for holding a summit meeting. That is why we came to Paris. But this requires the United States government's admission that an aggressive intrusion into our country has been committed, its condemnation of this aggression, and an assurance that such actions will not be repeated and that the guilty will be punished. This would satisfy us and we could take part in the summit conference so as to find a correct solution for the urgent problems at hand.

The United States government has refused to do this. How can we take part in the summit conference when the side that has committed an aggression does not want to condemn it? You are aware that the President of the United States pointed out in his statement that overflights of the Soviet Union were the policy of the United States.

Gentlemen, you all had mothers, otherwise you would not have been born. (*Animation.*) I remember well my mother, and my father, who was a miner. Very rarely could my mother buy us some cream. But when we had cream on the table, and the cat would steal some of it, she would seize it by the scruff of the neck, give it a shaking, and poke its nose into the cream, then shake it again and poke its nose into the remaining cream once more. This was how the cat was punished for doing what it shouldn't have done. (*Animation.*)

Wouldn't it be better to take the American imperialists by the scruff of the neck, give them a good shaking, and make them know they cannot commit such acts of aggression because it means violating international law and may lead to a military catastrophe. (*Applause.*)

SCHEWE (Hamburg *Die Welt*): Do you still believe that international problems must be solved by peaceful means?

KHRUSHCHEV: Yes, I do. It is the policy of the Soviet government that all disputes be settled by negotiation and not by war. This was and remains our position.

SCHEWE: Do you still stand by your proposal for transforming West Berlin into a free city?

KHRUSHCHEV: Yes, we stand by this proposal and we see no other reasonable solution. West Berlin is in the center of the German Democratic Republic, which is a socialist country, and West Berlin is capitalistic. The occupation regime which exists in West Berlin today may become a source of great conflict. Why preserve it? Would it not be better to change the situation in West Berlin in such a way as to avoid conflict? We consider that the best solution would be the withdrawal of foreign troops from West Berlin, the creation of a free city there, the provision of such conditions for the people of the free city as would enable them to live under the system—political and social—which they consider it necessary to have, and free contact for the people of the city with the entire world.

The conflict produced by the intrusion of an American plane within the confines of the Soviet Union has further convinced us that these questions must be settled, and we shall press for this with even greater energy and determination. Tomorrow, by the way, I am flying to Berlin. There we shall have talks with Comrades Ulbricht, Grotewohl, and, in general, our friends in the German Democratic Republic.

A. ROSENBERG (West Berlin *Der Tag*): Do you intend, Mr. Chairman, to conclude a separate peace treaty in Berlin?

KHRUSHCHEV: Yes, we are planning, not to make separate peace, but to conclude a peace treaty with the German Democratic Republic, to draw a line through World War II and thereby deprive the Western powers of the right to have occupation troops in West Berlin. When we deem it necessary we shall take out our pens—the drafts have already been prepared—sit down, sign the treaty, and announce it.

I should like to add the following: By signing the peace treaty with the German Democratic Republic, we shall actually do what the United States did when it concluded the peace treaty with Japan. We fought together with the United States against Japan. But then the

United States signed a peace treaty with Japan without us. We exerted much effort to prove the necessity of signing the treaty together, but it did not take us into consideration. Today all our efforts to reach agreement and together sign a peace treaty with Germany are almost exhausted. When they are exhausted completely, we, and probably the other countries that fought against Hitler's Germany, will sign a peace treaty in the same way as the Americans did with Japan.

MICHAELS (National Broadcasting Company): Knowing of such flights, why did you not tell President Eisenhower about them during your visit to the United States?

KHRUSHCHEV: I shall reply to this question with pleasure. When we were talking in Camp David with President Eisenhower I thought: "I must tell him." I almost opened my mouth to make that statement.

We had a good talk with the President. The President turned to me and said: "Mr. Chairman, call me 'my friend' (*Animation in the hall*) and I shall address you in Russian 'moi drug.' " Like a brother he was. It was then that I wanted to tell my friend that it is not nice to overfly a friend's territory without his permission. But then I thought better of it and decided: "No, I am not going to tell him. There is something about this friend that does not invite utter frankness." And I did not raise the matter. I think I was right in my doubts, and this was confirmed when we caught the American spy, like a thief, red-handed. We say to the Americans that they act like thieves, and they say that "no, this is our policy, we have flown and will fly over your territory for purposes of reconnaissance." Now, can a summit conference be started in these conditions?

We caught the thief, we shot down the plane. At the mine where I was brought up, when a cat was caught climbing up to the pigeon loft, it was seized by the tail and thrown to the floor. This drove home the lesson better.

D. SCHORR (Columbia Broadcasting System): Since, by desire or not, you have become a factor in the American election campaign, can you say which president you would prefer to deal with? (*Laughter.*)

KHRUSHCHEV: It is difficult for me to reply to this question, but I shall try.

When I was in the United States, I talked with many Americans there—ordinary people, wealthy people, workers and farmers, statesmen. And I would say that most of the people I talked to have left me with good, even pleasant memories. They are people like people, they want to live in peace.

Naturally, we differ in our ideological views. But this is no cause for a military clash. I do not agree with the views of the people who stand on positions of capitalism, while the advocates of capitalism, who do not recognize communist ideas, disagree with me. This is a matter of conviction, and not a cause for conflict, let alone war. And it is my conviction that the vast majority of Americans are sorry for what has happened, sorry that a spy plane was sent to the Soviet Union. And not a few Americans are also indignant about this.

I admit that there may be people who have been duped. I do not know how the interpreters will translate this Russian word which very aptly expresses the gist of the matter. It may be that the aggressive circles in the United States will succeed in stirring up passions for a while, shouting that the Soviet Union has shot down an American plane. But what if our military plane appeared over America? The Americans would have shot it down, naturally, and they would have been right, in my opinion.

One must not fly over the territory of another country without permission, for if we are to act in this way, war will be inevitable.

Now about the American president I would prefer to deal with. I have preferences. There is a man with whom—if he were President—we could do business, I am convinced of this.

We remember the great American Roosevelt, who was indeed a wise statesman and worthily represented the capitalist world. He recognized the need to live in peace with our socialist country, and we co-operated wonderfully with him during the war. But he is dead and the policy of the United States has changed. But we do believe that reasonable people will come to power in the United States. Life itself will see to it, and we shall have good, friendly relations with the United States.

This is exactly what we want—the best, friendly relations with the United States. We do not have any disputes with the United States which could not be settled by peaceful means.

Of course, our social systems are different: We live under socialism and are building communism, while capitalism dominates in the United States of America. But this is an internal question of every people.

As to the Soviet people, they have proved in practice the superiority of our system over capitalism. Come to us, gentlemen. We are ready to issue visas even to those surviving Hitlerites who were raising a row here. Maybe some of them will become normal people too. Come and see what we have done with our country. Formerly it was one of the most backward states. Today the Soviet Union is economically the world's second nation, and politically and culturally the first nation of the world. As to the development of science, we also hold a worthy place—I wish to be modest about it, but everyone knows what place we hold in science. (*Applause.*)

I do not wish to interfere with the American election campaign. We must be patient and have respect for the American people. I believe they don't need my suggestion about whom to elect as President. I believe that they will themselves show wisdom and elect a worthy president. If they elect an unworthy person with whom it will be difficult to reach agreement and who will not realize the need to live in peace with all countries—both the capitalist and the socialist—well, we shall be patient again and wait for the next election. If then, too, a president is elected who will not realize the need for peaceful co-existence, we shall go on waiting patiently. Where must we hurry?

Ours is the right cause and we are following the correct road. We are steering toward communism. We shall continue along this road under our Marxist-Leninist banner. We believe that you too will sooner or later follow in our footsteps. We shall not reproach you for being behind us. On the contrary, we shall help you and share our experience in socialist construction, which benefits the peoples of all countries.

A. SMUDJE (Paris *Le Combat*): Mr. Chairman, you have agreed to come to France despite the U-2 incident and knowing the categorical stand taken by America. Undoubtedly you were convinced that France would take a reconciliatory position. Why then did you not relent despite the intentions and actions of General de Gaulle? Do you hold, nevertheless, that these actions have served the cause of peace?

KHRUSHCHEV: Why did we come? Because we thought there would be some grain of honesty in the United States representatives and they would present their apologies. The more so since we have a precedent; they apologized to Cuba when their plane raided that island and was shot down. So why not apologize to the Soviet Union when their plane intruded into its airspace and was brought down?

But we were mistaken. To Cuba, you see, they could present their apologies, but not to a socialist state. Well, that is their business. This is obviously how they were brought up. That is a question of gentlemanly conduct.

Now about the efforts of President de Gaulle of France. We greatly appreciate his efforts. I think he really did everything he could to have the meeting take place.

But nothing has come of this, as you see—through no fault of ours. If I am asked why the efforts of General de Gaulle were in vain, I shall ask the correspondent to address the question to the President of France, because it was he who talked to Eisenhower. I cannot say why his efforts remained in vain.

What may be the result of the incident? It is very unpleasant, of course. But even a war ends. After the enemy is routed, peace is concluded and after a while the belligerents begin to live peacefully. We have no war with the United States. The Americans tried to poke their nose into our affairs and we punched that nose. I think that they know now where the Soviet frontiers are! If they come again, they will receive another blow, as will the bases from where the aggressors come to Soviet territory.

This spy flight has affected the relations between the USSR and the United States. But in the end it will be necessary to overcome its consequences, to "digest" all this, as it were. It is necessary to normalize relations so that the American and the Soviet people may live in peace and, as I have already said, not only peace but friendship.

I am convinced that this is how General de Gaulle thinks. But his position was extremely difficult. The President of France may not agree with me. But I should like to say, in all fairness, that Mr. de Gaulle is a man who kept his word once he had given it.

It is necessary to condemn the aggressive actions committed by the United States of America. It is impossible to do otherwise. It cannot be said of a thief that he took a thing "as a keepsake" and simply forgot to return it. No, a thief caught in the act can only be called a thief. There can be no two opinions on the matter.

I realize, however, that the obstacle to this was that the thief turned out to be France's ally, and not only an ally but a leader in Western quarters. I should not like to go into the details. It is difficult for me to be a judge in this matter, for it concerns relations between allies.

I am telling you frankly: If an ally of ours had acted this way, we would have plucked up courage and said that this is not the way to act. But if the thing has been done, you should apologize. But these are the moral principles of communism. The capitalist countries have different moral principles, it would seem.

I should like to add a few words more. If the correspondent wants to know how all this will affect the relations between the Soviet Union and France, my reply is this: My opinion is that all this will have no impact on the relations which have been established between our country and France. I talked with General de Gaulle today and was very pleased with the interview. I felt that he wants to continue the policy of improving relations with the Soviet Union. We want this, too. We respect France, the French people and its culture, and we have great esteem for the President of the French Republic.

We are leaving France confident that the relations between our countries, far from worsening, will improve.

H. JAKOBUS (East Berlin Radio): The American press has announced that the United States Secretary of Defense Thomas Gates declared an emergency alarm to the United States Air Forces from Paris on Monday. What do you think of this?

KHRUSHCHEV: I did not hear this. If it is true, and I have no reason to question your statement, it was a provocation designed to complicate matters and, I would say, intimidate the American people and dupe them into paying greater taxes for military purposes.

Perhaps it was cowardice as well. Cowards are as dangerous as *provocateurs: Provocateurs* provoke a war, and cowards can sometimes start a war by cowardice.

I do not know Gates or what he is; let the Americans reply for him —he is an American minister. I can only reply for my friend Rodion Malinovsky, a magnificent soldier who fought like a hero with the French against German imperialism during the First World War, who fought like a hero in World War II, commanding huge armies against the Nazis and against the Japanese militarists, won many decorations, and is now the Soviet Union's minister of defense. I can reply for him. He is a true son of the Communist Party, a true son of his motherland.

MALINOVSKY: We did not order any alert!

KHRUSHCHEV: Right, he did not give any alert, and we are not going to give any. We have strong nerves. (*Applause.*) If the American imperialists wish to act by methods of intimidation, let them seek people to intimidate in other countries. We are not going to be intimidated, for we have every possibility of acting in regard to such provocations in the same way as in the case of the thieving cat who used to creep into the pigeon loft. And we are going to teach this cat a lesson if he creeps into our pigeon loft!

I admit that the imperialist circles of the United States may try to capitalize on this incident; they will perhaps increase the taxes on the population, increase military orders, and consequently siphon more money from the pockets of the ordinary people and hand it over in the form of profits to the monopolies engaged in the manufacture of armaments.

Ours is a different policy. The last session of the Supreme Soviet passed a decision to abolish taxes on factory and office workers. Not a single factory or office worker will pay taxes in the Soviet Union in 1965. This year we shall complete the transfer of all factory and office workers to a 7-hour workday and the miners to a 6-hour workday. (*At this moment the lights went out and something went wrong with the microphone.*) . . . Capitalist technology has failed us. Well, I shall have to shout so that you can hear my words! (*Animation.*)

Gentlemen, here is something else I want to say. In 1964 we shall start going over to a 6-hour workday for all factory and office workers, and to a 5-hour workday for miners. This is precisely the policy of the socialist states, and we shall not swerve from this line. No provocations will make our people abandon the road of building up a communist society. This is a correct policy, a policy of the Soviet Union, of the Soviet government, a policy of our Communist Party. (*The lights go on. Applause, animation, laughter.*)

KRAUTS (GDR *Neues Deutschland*): Mr. Chairman, why do you think Eisenhower has changed his position since your talks at Camp David? Can you explain the reason for the difference in the American President's position at Camp David and now, in Paris?

KHRUSHCHEV: My preceding answer sheds light on this question to some extent. It was said here that an Air Force alarm was sounded in the United States. This fact shows that the most reactionary forces are rearing their heads in the United States—the Pentagon and the military. They exert pressure on the President. They are precisely the people who sent the plane into our country—with the President's permission, of course. This is the explanation I can give for the changes in United States policy since our talks with President Eisenhower at Camp David.

ANDRADE (*Journal de Brazil*): Mr. Chairman, would you please reply to the following three questions: Do you intend to visit the countries of Latin America shortly? How do you assess the position of the Latin American countries in the world? Do you think that the Latin American countries could take part in the peaceful solution of urgent problems along with other countries?

KHRUSHCHEV: As to the first question—will I visit Brazil? Well, nobody has invited me there. But if I am invited to Latin America, I shall try to go there. As to the second question, I must say that we rejoice at what is happening in the Latin American countries: We feel very well the pulse of the struggle for independence in these countries, of the struggle against American imperialism. The welcome given by the Latin American peoples to Mr. Nixon during his visit there is a sufficiently clear signal.

We acclaim the Cuban people who have bravely raised the banner of struggle for their independence, for the independence of Cuba, and who want to be the masters of their land, the masters of the fruits of their labor. We are convinced that the other Latin American nations that are starting to fight for their independence will also follow this road.

We sympathize with all the peoples fighting for freedom and independence, we rejoice in their successes in this just struggle. (*Applause.*)

We are convinced that the Latin American countries will gain in strength and that their role in international relations will grow.

I must say, to my regret, that there still are countries in Latin America where the governments get money from their peoples but serve United States imperialism. But the peoples of Latin America are awakening, and we welcome with all our heart and sympathize with their movement for liberation. It is only when the peoples of Latin America really have governments which loyally serve their people that the countries of Latin America will lift their voice in world politics. This voice of the Latin American peoples will ring out with greater power in the United Nations, in all international affairs, and this will be to the benefit of all countries, to the benefit of the cause of world peace.

Gentlemen, I should be glad to continue, but my interpreters are whispering into my ear that their workday is over. (*Animation.*) They tell me that our labor code safeguards their interests. They say:

"Comrade Chairman, please end the press conference, or we shall end it ourselves without you." (*Animation.*)

I should like to express once again sincere gratitude to the French government, to President de Gaulle, to the French people, to the Parisians, and not only the Parisians for that matter—yesterday we drove with Marshal Malinovsky to the village where he fought against the Germans side by side with the French soldiers in World War I. To all the French men and women who gave us such a friendly welcome we wish to express heartfelt gratitude and the best of wishes.

I want to conclude the press conference by stressing again that the Soviet Union will continue its policy of peaceful coexistence between the two systems—the capitalist and the socialist. We will continue to pursue a policy of preserving peace so that all international disputes are settled by negotiation. But at the same time we will defend our sovereignty, the sovereignty of the peoples of the socialist countries. We will resolutely repulse all attempts at aggression against us. I think that this policy of ours will meet with the understanding and approval of all the peoples because it is the only possible correct policy. This policy does not prejudice any people or any state. On the contrary, it ensures peaceful coexistence, the peaceful development of all countries and all mankind.

Goodby! Thank you! I wish you success and I ask you to write truthfully so that your pens serve the cause of peace and friendship among the peoples.

Vive la paix! (*Stormy applause.*)

N. S. KHRUSHCHEV'S PRESS CONFERENCE, JUNE 3, 1960 *

SHAPIRO (United Press International Agency): What is your attitude toward the statement made by Marshal Malinovsky at the Communist Work Teams Conference in the Kremlin on the order issued to the commander of the rocket forces to hit at the take-off bases of aircraft if the airspace of the Soviet Union and other communist countries is violated?

KHRUSHCHEV: I ask you to understand it literally as Marshal Malinovsky, the minister of defense, had put it. He has said clearly enough that planes intruding into our airspace, enemy planes, will be

* Russian text *Pravda,* June 4, 1960, pp. 1–2. English text from Press Department, Soviet Embassy in Washington, No. 270, June 6, 1960.

shot down, and crushing blows by rocket forces will be struck at the bases from which they took off. The government issued instructions to this effect to the minister of defense, and the minister issued an order to the commander of the rocket forces.

Why did we do this? Because the leaders of the United States acknowledged and still say that they reserve the right to fly over our territory for reconnaissance purposes. They motivate this right by the necessity of safeguarding the defense of the United States, their allies —satellites.

The Soviet government raised this question in the Security Council. The Security Council did not support our proposals because its majority was made up of representatives of the allies of the United States and, I would say, that some of them used the same radical methods in violating sovereignty as the United States.

In such conditions where the Security Council did not support us and did not call the aggressor to order, the United States, did not denounce it, we had no other way out but to rely on our own strength. That is why such an order was issued and this order will be strictly fulfilled. We ask to draw serious conclusions from this. This should give food for thought especially to the leaders of those countries which surround the Soviet Union and where there are American bases. If these bases are used by the Americans against us, the Soviet Union will hit at those bases.

Had we not issued instructions to the minister of defense, had the minister of defense not issued the order, we would have thus tacitly agreed to the piratical policy proclaimed by the United States against the Soviet Union and our allies, the socialist countries.

Of course, we cannot tolerate this, the more so since we have the possibility of preventing aggression, of punishing those who resort to aggression.

N. POLYANOV (*Izvestia*): What comments can you make, Comrade Chairman of the Council of Ministers, on the statement made by Mr. White, the spokesman of the Department of State of the United States, to the effect that the United States will discharge its duties to its allies?

KHRUSHCHEV: I am familiar with this statement. The statement is not sensible but stupid. Its stupidity lies in that the United States of America shows that it stands on the old position, does not admit the aggressiveness of the flights of their aircraft over Soviet territory. They continue to insist on their right to make such spy flights they had mentioned. If there were wise men in the State Department they would speak differently. They would say that the President issued instructions that their military spy planes should no longer fly over foreign countries, they would say that such planes will now not fly and therefore the question raised in Marshal Malinovsky's speech becomes pointless, since there would be no occasion for putting into effect his statement.

But this was not said in the State Department's statement. On the contrary, it said that the United States would discharge its duties to its allies. By doing so they tell those countries where the bases are located, "Don't be afraid. If the Soviet Union smashes you, strikes a retaliatory blow with rockets, we shall attend your funeral after you have been smashed. So act more confidently and carry through." A stupid policy.

I believe that thoughtful people in those countries where American bases are located will ponder over this. They will understand that the provocative statement by Mr. White, the spokesman of the United States Department of State, has the object of fanning the cold war which might end in a hot war, and that the first blow will be felt by those countries in which military bases of the United States are located.

This statement by Mr. White confirms our belief that evidently the aggressive forces of the Pentagon as well as Mr. Herter, Mr. Nixon, Mr. Dillon, and the weak-kneed President of the United States (though this does not relieve him of the responsibility) who connives at and encourages such statements, believe that if war breaks out the allies of the United States lying close to the Soviet Union will pay the price in blood. I should like for all peoples, and we want to live in peace with all peoples, to become aware of this. The Soviet Union wants no war, but we shall not retreat in protecting the sovereignty of our homeland. The Turks, where American bases are located, arrested Menderes and he is now in prison; the new Prime Minister General Gursel declared that he will be guided by the policy of Ataturk, with whom our country established good relations still in Lenin's lifetime. We should like to see friendship between Turkey and us, between Britain and us, between France and us, and other countries.

The principal bases of the Americans lie in the United Kingdom,

France, and Italy. To put it in a nutshell, we have a General Staff, and the sites of these bases are pinpointed on a map there.

MICHAELS (National Broadcasting Company): Mr. Chairman, setting forth your plan, you said that the Soviet Union proposes that a control organization should be set up within the United Nations framework and that international police forces should also be set up within the framework of the United Nations and in accordance with the United Nations Charter. However, the United Nations Charter contains a provision on a veto. Do you think that the right to veto should also exist at the setting up of the international control organization and the establishment of the international police forces?

KHRUSHCHEV: Our proposals raise the question of disarmament and there is nothing about a revision of the United Nations Charter. We are not even thinking of submitting proposals for a revision of the Charter but, on the contrary, intend to uphold this Charter. To those who press for a revision of the United Nations Charter and the repeal of the principle of unanimity of the permanent members of the Security Council or the veto right, as this is called, I should like to explain what the veto means. In the right to veto lies the strength and the wisdom of the United Nations Charter.

The world now consists of socialist and capitalist countries. They can be regarded as two connecting vessels. At present as to the number of states the capitalist vessel is larger. But this is a temporary state of affairs. History is developing in a way which will reduce the level in the capitalist vessel while the socialist vessel will get fuller. In present conditions if issues were settled in the Security Council by an unqualified majority, the United States, on which many countries depend, would succeed in forcing through their decisions. But the Charter envisages the right to veto precisely in order to take decisions not by an unqualified majority, but to take decisions which would be acceptable to both sides. This is the only reasonable principle in international affairs; any other approach would lead to war.

What would happen if there were no right to veto and if the majority would meet and decide to make flights over the Soviet Union? Let us suppose that we had no right to veto and the United States and their allies began flights of their aircraft over Soviet territory. Would we say then that if the majority took such a decision, we are prepared to look on passively. No, we would order Minister

Malinovsky: "Keep rocketry in a state of combat readiness and shoot down the planes, defend the homeland." And that is how every self-respecting country would act, because each country has the right to defend its territory and to insist on nonintervention in its domestic affairs. That is why the right to veto makes even the stupid think, makes them search for solutions that would not aggravate relations between states, but, on the contrary, ease these relations and create conditions for peaceful coexistence.

That is what the veto means.

E. LITOSHKO (*Pravda*): Comrade Chairman, some politicians and statesmen in the West declare that a summit meeting might not be held within six to eight months as you suggested in Paris. What is your opinion?

KHRUSHCHEV: A summit meeting is needed not only by the Soviet Union but also by all thoughtful peoples on earth, and hence the date of its convening concerns all interested states. If the conference is not held within six to eight months, we of course believe that this would disappoint the peoples of all countries. But because of this the Soviet Union will not cease to exist and the problems which call for solution will also not cease to exist.

Obviously some people think that if there is no summit conference, the question of concluding a peace treaty with Germany and a solution of the problem of West Berlin arising therefrom will be postponed indefinitely. If there are such people, they are wrong.

If we see at the end of this period that the governments of the Western countries do not want to meet, do not want to solve the ripe problems, we shall agree with the socialist countries, we shall meet, shall appeal to all countries that want to sign a German peace treaty. We shall meet, discuss, and sign a peace treaty. And this will do away with the right to access to West Berlin of countries which were our allies in the war against Nazi Germany and now became the allies of our, so to speak, "esteemed friend" Adenauer, who represents the aggressive forces of militaristic Germany which we beat but did not finish off at Stalingrad. Let them embrace and kiss him, but the German Democratic Republic will not let anyone pass to West Berlin without its permission, since all rights will be fully exercised by the German Democratic Republic and it will exercise its power throughout its entire territory, that is, the territory of the German Democratic Republic, which also includes West Berlin. Only the government of the German Democratic Republic, and no one else, will have the right to issue instructions in this territory. And if someone wants to threaten with war, let him assume the responsibility for the outbreak of war.

We want no war. We want peace, we want to sign a peace treaty and to put out the cinders, which are still glowing, the cinders which were not stamped out after World War II. We want to stamp them out.

Every thoughtful man understands this, the more so since we have more than once made such proposals to the governments of the Western countries.

I should like to say a few words about the stand taken by the governments of the United Kingdom and France on this issue. Let them muster their courage and tell the truth, tell what they say to themselves and to some others. In this context I recollect a skit which I liked very much. In the early years after the Revolution there were many stupid forms, questionnaires that had to be filled out; this referred mainly to the intellectuals. One such form contained the question: "Do you believe in God?" The employee thought: If he said he believed, this might unfavorably affect his official standing. One of them, filling in the form, found a way out and replied to this question: "At home I believe in God, at the office—I do not!"

The same happens in this case when the governments of the Western countries speak of a German peace treaty and they declare: "Is it really conceivable to unite the two Germanys?" We are not interested in this. By the way, President Eisenhower also said that the United States is afraid of a stronger Germany. That is why, when they speak to all mankind, they declare, "Yes, we believe in God," and when they speak among themselves they declare, "We do not believe in God." Let them have this on their conscience; we say frankly that the question of German reunification is a matter for the Germans themselves, is a matter for the governments of the two German states. We do not intervene in this matter. But questions of peace—these are our questions. The Soviet Union fought against the German Fascists and that is why we shall press for the signing of a peace treaty. This is clear to all. And if we sign a peace treaty, the right to occupation flowing from the victory over Germany will be abolished. Peace will be established throughout the German Democratic Republic. Access to Berlin by air, water, and land without permission of the government of the German Democratic Republic will discontinue. It will be accessible to those who obtain the consent of the government of the German Democratic Republic.

Is that clear?

VOICES: Clear!

KHRUSHCHEV: I also think it is clear. And if it is not clear, we shall repeat it once again. When we conclude a peace treaty it will be still clearer.

TATU (*Le Monde*): Does it mean, as you said in reply to the first question, that the Soviet Union will hit at bases where aircraft took off with rockets carrying atomic or hydrogen weapons? And the second question. How should the states be represented on the international disarmament control commission—one representative from each state, or will the Great Powers have more representatives?

KHRUSHCHEV: What weapons will strike at bases which will be used against the Soviet Union—this is a detail which falls within the competence of Marshal Nedelin, the Commander in Chief of the Rocket Forces. And we have an adequate assortment of rockets. He will find appropriate means to hit the enemy and to discourage the *provocateurs* from attacking our country. Each country has the full possibility of avoiding such retaliation. This calls for very little: Not to allow the American aggressors to use their land for military bases against the Soviet Union. But best of all would be to liquidate these bases and then the question would no longer exist. The Soviet Union threatens no one. We only warn that we will defend ourselves against aggression by all available means.

The second question—concerning the composition of the disarmament control commission. I think this is a question whose solution depends on discussion and agreement between the countries holding talks on disarmament.

SCHEWE (*Die Welt,* Hamburg): Mr. Chairman, what is your opinion on the results of the discussion in the Security Council of the appeal by the USSR in connection with the flights of an American aircraft over Soviet territory?

KHRUSHCHEV: When the Security Council was asked to denounce, to brand with ignominy the aggression committed by the United States of America, it took instead a toothless decision. Imagine a man who felt seriously ill. He goes to the doctor, he needs immediate surgical treatment, but the doctor tells him: "Mister, or Comrade—rather 'Mister,' because our doctor will not speak like this to a patient, it is in bourgeois countries that doctors speak like this—I advise you, Mister, to drink soda water or mineral water. You may feel better afterward, or you may die."

Approximately the same decision was taken by the Security Council. This helps to safeguard peace just as much as soda water helps a man who is seriously ill. I think everyone knows that soda water is also useful, it quenches the thirst, but it does not cure the patient's serious disease.

FRANKEL (*New York Times*): Mr. Chairman, you have just said something concerning President Eisenhower's statement on the problem of Germany which we did not know before. Maybe you want to state this frankly, maybe you can tell us still something more concerning your conversations with President Eisenhower at Camp David or subsequent talks?

KHRUSHCHEV: I think it is enough for today, and when need be we can add to it.

JOHNSON (Associated Press): Mr. Chairman, replying to a question asked by the correspondent Tatu concerning the possibility of hitting a blow with hydrogen or atomic weapons at air bases, you said that the choice of the most effective means, the most effective weapons, depended on Marshal Nedelin. Does this mean that Marshal Nedelin has the right at his own initiative to issue an order to strike blows with hydrogen weapons without the preliminary decision of the Soviet government?

KHRUSHCHEV: You would like to know the procedure for commanding the Soviet Armed Forces. This is a national secret. You are an American, you always feel like sniffing the odors which you normally do not feel.

It is on this matter that your President is breaking his neck—on espionage affairs. We have a clear-cut command system: We have a government which issues instructions, orders to the minister of defense; the minister of defense issues orders to the forces; and the forces must sacredly carry out the order of the minister of defense—this means to carry out the order of the government. And I am convinced that Marshal Nedelin, a respected man, a remarkable soldier, a Hero of the Soviet Union, a splendid artilleryman, now knows more about rocketry than anyone else, he will direct it better than anyone else, and he will skillfully use it against our enemies, the enemies of peace. At friends we strike no blows.

Therefore, in order not to place such a great responsibility on Marshal Malinovsky and on Marshal Nedelin one must not make provocative spy flights over the Soviet Union. You can sleep calmly because no one threatens you, God forbid. Why should we threaten you? But do not send your war planes over the Soviet Union, do not fly over the socialist countries, respect the sovereignty of states, know their frontiers. If you do not want to know the frontiers—we shall hit, we shall teach you a lesson.

W. BURCHETT (American *National Guardian*): According to press reports, Chancellor Adenauer was the only one of the United States Allies to have approved of U-2 flights over the Soviet Union. What have you got to say on this score?

KHRUSHCHEV: Such statements can be made by one who has gone off his nut. For no sensible person can approve, in this missile and nuclear age, of the violation of national sovereignty and, consequently, of the provoking of armed conflict which can bring about a disaster for the peoples. The only man who can do so is one who fails to see what danger it spells to the same Chancellor Adenauer. Or it must be a man who stakes his all, as they say, and whose line of reasoning is something like this: "I have lived for eighty-four years, I have one foot in the grave anyhow, and after me let there be the deluge."

This cannot please the Germans, however, nor must it please the allies of West Germany. Just the reverse. A man who makes such statements should long have been strait-jacketed and put into a lunatic asylum. That would be just the place for him.

N. BELOVA (*London Observer*): Couldn't you clarify the chronological sequence of the disarmament measures you are suggesting in your new proposals? Do you suggest that all the means of delivery of the weapons of mass destruction should first be scrapped and a control organization then set up to check on the implementation of the measure, or is it your suggestion that a control organization to control the very process of arms destruction be set up first?

KHRUSHCHEV: No, it is not. What we have in mind is that if we agree on disarmament and take a decision of principle, we shall then set up a control agency so that the control agency should share in the process of destroying these armaments, because otherwise there would be no trust. One nation may have scrapped the arms, while another may be a swindler.

Therefore it is necessary for every nation to have this confidence. We shall act in good faith. We Soviet people do not act the way the American government does, for we are honest men.

They have a very peculiar kind of morality taking shape now. Perhaps there will be a whole series of novels. They do not denounce spying, but they say: "This is a dirty business, and therefore the President should not have confessed to spying because, they say, spying involves murder, poisoning, and other things. Therefore there can and must be spying and killing"—that is just what they say literally—"but one does not have to admit it."

But this is not what we think. We reject this type of morality. We are men of lofty morals and we believe that our kind of morality will come to prevail not only in the socialist lands but throughout the world as well. Communism will triumph and so will man's common sense.

In this matter, I repeat, we shall act in real earnest so that there should be equal rights and equal opportunities for controlling the process of disarmament and the destruction of the means of warfare and delivery.

GERASIMOV (TASS): Comrade Chairman. The President of the United States said that America would raise the "open skies" issue at the Assembly's next meeting. In this way the United States of America will forfeit its prestige altogether in the eyes of public opinion. What is your opinion on this matter?

KHRUSHCHEV: The President of the United States can do anything he wants in the sense of making proposals, but not more than this. Whether our government accepts this proposal or not is a different thing. We have already said that this is a nonsensical proposal. I told the President in Geneva in 1955 that that was a spying proposal and that we would never agree to it. He tried to prove his own point.

I think that when the President is no longer a president and if he chooses to work in our country, we could give him the job of an orphanage director. (I am sure he will not hurt the children.) But it is dangerous for a man like that to run a state, for he may cause so much trouble that it will be hard to get out of it. I say so because I know him. I saw the way he behaved at the Geneva conference in 1955 and I felt sorry for the President.

The British sat at the conference table opposite the Americans, while we sat opposite the French. Dulles was sitting to the President's right.

Whenever the President had to speak, Dulles handed him notes. He should have at least turned aside, for the sake of decorum, to read through the note. Instead, he took it, read it, and laid it aside. Then when the President had to speak again, he took another note which had again been prepared for him by Dulles.

We could not help wondering, comrades and gentlemen: Who is running the state and whither are we going, after all? For such a President can take God knows what kind of decisions, and his is a vast, great and powerful nation. One shuddered at the thought of what a great force was in such hands.

Foster Dulles died, but Allen Dulles lives on. But it is not Dulles who matters. Once there is a space there will be someone like Nixon or Herter to fill it.

I am now reading the reports of the questioning in the Senate Foreign Relations Committee. There is a strained situation, after all, and yet the President has chosen to go off to his golf course.

The impression one is bound to get is that such a partner is beyond control. But we cannot do anything about it. This is up to the American people. We believe that the American people will draw the right conclusion. There are some men of genius there. America has presidents she is proud of, the presidents to whom we take off our hats and bow low, I mean Lincoln and others.

These are troubled times, if I may say so, for Eisenhower's presidency is a time of trouble for the United States of America and for the rest of the world.

Russia also lived through troubled times once in the past, but then she became an organized and well-arranged state, which she is, above all, today, a good state! Isn't that right?

T. LAMBERT (*New York Herald Tribune*): In Paris you said that your attitude toward U-2 flights was due in some measure to the domestic political situation in the USSR. Couldn't you explain what you meant by that phrase?

KHRUSHCHEV: I made no statement like that in Paris, and I do not know where it has come from. I simply do not understand the question and it is therefore difficult for me to answer it. What has our domestic situation to do with the flight of the American U-2 plane? That is what we call "sewing a tail on a mare."

ALI-KHAN (Indian *New Age*): Do you believe that war is inevitable as long as imperialism exists, and has this conclusion been confirmed by the events of the past month?

KHRUSHCHEV: A fairly clear statement on this subject was made by the Twentieth Congress of the Communist Party of the Soviet Union (CPSU). We still hold this view. Nothing has changed to make us change our view that war is not inevitable. On the contrary, experience confirms this conclusion.

Y. FOKIN (News Broadcast Department of Moscow Radio): Comrade Chairman: Some American observers claim that by your statements about Eisenhower and Nixon you are seeking to influence the election campaign in the United States. What can you say in this connection?

KHRUSHCHEV: It is said that there might be such a situation in America in which the very men whom we are scolding most or, one may say, "raking over the coals" in the Soviet Union, will become the most suitable candidates for the presidency. To follow this line of reasoning, I would say I believe that the best candidate is Nixon.

But I am not going to add to what has already been said. Whom the Americans will choose is their own business, it is a matter of taste for them, and as we say tastes differ, and everyone likes what he likes.

We fared quite well when Dulles was at the head of the U.S. State Department. He did so many silly things, but every silly thing our opponent does is a power to our elbow. Therefore, if Nixon becomes the President of the United States, we will not be worse off for it, because it is not by the United States' grace that we live. We rely on our people, on our economy, and on our political views, and we are moving ahead. Whether it will be Nixon or, as the Russians say, "the devil himself," it is just the same to us. We shall still move ahead. It is better, of course, to have a clever man to deal with; I still prefer to have to deal with a clever partner, but if God does not give us one, we cannot help it. It happens sometimes that a girl looks for a clever bridegroom and chooses one who looks clever, but then she finds him empty-headed; but she has got to put up with it—she just can't help it.

The election of the President is a matter of the American people's own concern. I think the American people see their interests better than we do.

J. STEKIC (Yugoslav Broadcasting Corporation): Comrade Chairman, you said when replying to a question about the international situation in Gorky Park recently that you are an incorrigible optimist. What is your view of the present international situation and the preservation of world peace?

KHRUSHCHEV: I still hold this view. I am sure that if the people of all nations take the cause of peace into their own hands and if they check the aggressors who run amuck and those unwise leaders who allow conditions likely to produce an armed conflict to be created, I am sure the cause of peace will triumph.

On our part, we shall do everything in this direction. I think that this policy will be adhered to by all peoples and by the absolute majority of the world's population. I emphasize that the American people are also indignant over what has been done. A different view of what has happened may be held only by a small portion of the United States population which waxes fat on this business, and then the peanut politicians and those who cannot make head or tail of political disputes. But even those who feel upset because of being unable to see the reasons for the worsening of the situation will eventually find their bearings. The people will understand what the truth is and who the men really responsible for this situation are.

So I believe that if we all adhere to the positions of the struggle for peace, we shall ensure peace, I am sure of this. I should like to address the British and French correspondents. Your countries are the United States Allies in the military blocs, but both the British and the French have their own shades of meaning in evaluating the provocative intrusion of the American plane into the USSR. Neither Mr. Macmillan, nor M. de Gaulle had the courage to call a spade a spade and to condemn the aggressors, yet they did refrain from declaring their solidarity with the United States in this matter. Any intelligent person understands what this means. I should like you to get me right.

It is said that Khrushchev is speaking in violent terms against Eisenhower and others. But just see my position. I would like you to be in my shoes. How would you react if our plane flew over New York or San Francisco? What would you do if we said after that we flew, are flying and will fly there. That would be outrageous. What amazes me is that after that provocation by the United States Eisenhower still wanted to come to us. While I was still in Paris I was asked to issue a visa for the crew of the aircraft on which the United States President wanted to fly to the Soviet Union. This is a position that is difficult to understand. For no one fouls the place where one eats. This is a rudimentary thing. How then could the President, who has committed such a provocation against the Soviet Union, have come to dine with me? How would I have treated him? Anyone will see my position.

I call on all honest people: Let us pool our efforts to oppose the aggressors who are set against peaceful coexistence and are provoking a cold war so that it should become a hot war. If we do pool our efforts, peace will be assured. And it is just in this direction that the Soviet Union and the entire Soviet people are acting. It is my firm conviction that all our people, the people of all the socialist countries and all men who want peace safeguarded will join their efforts in securing peace.

SHAPIRO: Considering the tension due to the breakdown of the Paris conference, do you still find it possible for trade and cultural relations with the Western nations to develop further?

KHRUSHCHEV: We believe that however our relations with the United States may have been impaired, they will, I think, improve as time goes on. And we believe that this improvement will come about probably in a more tangible way after the elections, because the temperature in the United States always rises when the elections come, even if there is a good President in office, and there is now a special situation due to the conditions obtaining in the United States today. We are on bad terms with the United States at present. But I think we shall get on with each other better.

Now about trade. I believe that our trade relations with Britain, France, Italy, and West Germany are developing fairly well for the time being. We would like them to be better still; and I think that businessmen are interested in a further development of economic relations. On our part, we welcome this and we shall do everything to make our economic contacts firmer and closer.

Now I refer to the exchange of cultural delegations and cultural values. I do not think this process is halted here. I do not know what the United States will do. Perhaps, it will impose some sort of restrictions. We are not doing anything of the kind. All the scheduled visits of our scientists and artists are being made for the time being, and our Soviet men and women are receiving visas to the United States, too.

I think that in the future, too, it will be common sense that will prevail. We should not exploit the conflict which the aggressive forces have created, nor must we let ourselves be carried away by these aggressive forces so as to create conditions of tension which would turn the cold war into a hot war. This is a stupid kind of policy, this is an antipopular policy.

Therefore we shall do everything to improve relations between our two countries and among all nations in general. And I think that the lesson which President Eisenhower, Nixon, and Herter have taught themselves is not pleasant for them either. They have failed in an espionage affair. I think this will be a lesson for the other politicians of the United States as well as for the United States Allies.

That is why we think and we should like to hope—true, this does not depend on us alone, as this is a bilateral process—that economic, political, and cultural relations will continue improving. We stand for this and we shall stand for this.

It was a pleasure, for instance, for me to meet a group of American tourists in the Kremlin a couple of days ago. They were examining the Kremlin landmarks. I talked with them and I asked them: "How do you feel here in Moscow?"

They said: "Very well. We are treated well."

And this is right. Our treatment of the American people has always been good and will be good.

Comrades, gentlemen, I think it is dinner time for you. I must take care of your health so that you may have enough strength to fight against the aggressors and to fight for world peace.

Now after this press conference, you will get the texts of our proposals in Russian, English, and French. We ask you to study them well, think them over and support us, for you have as much interest in peace as everybody else.

I wish you luck.

Good-by.

1961:
Stalin Expelled from the Mausoleum

The year 1961 has gone down into history as the year of the Soviet spacemen. It was also the year of the heightened Berlin crisis, of the resumption of Soviet nuclear weapon testing, of the proclamation of the new Soviet Communist Party Program, and of the 22nd Party Congress.

The Russians attained their goal of being the first country to orbit a man about the earth on April 12 when Yuri Gagarin successfully landed after one orbit. On August 6 the Russian astronaut, Major Gherman Titov, repeated this feat but completed seventeen orbits in twenty-five hours in the space ship Vostok II.

Efforts by Khrushchev to meet with President Kennedy resulted in a conference of the two international leaders in Vienna on June 3 and 4. It was a meeting which produced no agreement of substance and left the two sides as far apart as ever on the Berlin question.

Renewed Soviet threats to conclude a separate peace treaty with East Germany and possibly to shut off communications between West Germany and West Berlin were met by a build-up of American armed forces in Europe and elsewhere which led to a hastily increased Soviet appropriation for defense. In the period from August 10 to 12 traffic between East Berlin and West Berlin was halted and a "wall" was erected to separate the Communist part of the city from that controlled by Western occupation forces. Despite their threats the Russians refrained from actually concluding a peace treaty with East Germany and negotiations on Berlin were continued by diplomatic representatives of both countries.

The Soviet Union announced on August 31 that it had decided to resume testing of nuclear weapons. Prior to the announcement the

Russians had prepared for a lengthy, comprehensive series of tests. Among the hydrogen weapons exploded were some which had the explosive power of up to 50 million tons of TNT. The Soviet resumption of nuclear tests brought to an end the period of several years during which neither the Soviet Union nor the United States had tested nuclear weapons in the atmosphere.

On July 30 the Soviet Communist Party published the lengthy text of a new Party Program. Not since 1919 had there been issued a new Party Program. The 1961 Program promised that the Soviet Union would enter the stage of social development known as "communism" in which all Soviet citizens would work according to their abilities and receive according to their needs by about the year 1980. The program promised big increases in production of industry and agriculture, a rapid rise in the Soviet standard of living, and the provision of numerous free and vastly increased public services. The program was the principal subject for discussion at the Party's 22nd Congress scheduled for October.

When the Congress actually convened, however, the principal issues brought out were an attack by Khrushchev on the Communist Party leadership of Albania and his simultaneous renewed attacks on the "personality cult of Stalin." At the Congress it was revealed that former Soviet Premier and Foreign Minister Molotov had been circulating to members of the Soviet Central Committee attacks on the Khrushchev policies which were evidently similar in general orientation and content to criticisms leveled at Khrushchev by the Chinese Communist Party leadership. Khrushchev did not openly attack Mao Tse-tung and the Chinese leadership at the Congress. But it seemed clear enough that his violent assault on the Albanians and "dogmatists" and "Stalinists" in the international Communist movement referred in part to Peking. The Chinese Communist delegation leader at the meeting, Chou En-lai, responded to the Khrushchev remarks on Albania by a thinly veiled criticism of the Russian leadership for washing Communist dirty linen in public. Thereupon Chou left the Soviet Congress and returned to Peking. Khrushchev and his political allies at the Congress used this platform in order to make many more revelations of the misdeeds of the Stalin regime and, pointedly enough, many of the cases cited of purges of loyal Soviet Communists by Stalin also involved Molotov. Once more Khrushchev raised, as he had done in his secret speech of February 25, 1956, the question of the "mysterious circumstances surrounding the assassination of Sergei Kirov in 1934, the event which Stalin had used as the excuse to launch the great purge of the 1930's. *This* time, however, Khrushchev discussed in public this case and the indications that Kirov was assassinated on Stalin's own orders and this speech was carried in the Soviet press. The whole course of events at the 22nd Congress indicated that Khrushchev was on the offensive against the opposition to him among Communists in and outside the Soviet Union.

The Congress ended with the adoption of a decree removing Stalin's body from the Lenin Mausoleum on Red Square. The decree was adopted after particularly spirited attacks on Stalin by selected Party spokesmen. One of these was a woman by the name of D. A. Lazurkina, a member of the Party from 1902 on who had been arrested in Leningrad in 1939 and who subsequently spent not quite twenty years in prison and concentration camps. When Lazurkina proposed that Stalin be removed from the Lenin Mausoleum, Khrushchev seconded her proposal with the hearty exclamation "Correct!"

Thereupon Lazurkina went into what must be regarded as one of the more fantastic passages of Soviet history, declaring in a fervent paragraph permeated seemingly with faith in the supernatural:

"My heart is always full of Ilyich (Lenin) and, comrades, I could survive the most difficult moment because I carry Ilyich in my heart, and consulted him on what to do. (*Applause.*) Yesterday I consulted Iyich: he was standing there before me as if he were alive, and said: it is unpleasant to be next to Stalin, who did so much harm to the Party." (*Loud, prolonged applause.*) (*Pravda,* October 31, 1961, p. 2.)

As the thirteenth and last item in this Khrushchev anthology there is included here Khrushchev's concluding speech at the 22nd Congress in which he elaborates his case against the Albanian Party and against Molotov and Stalin:

N. S. KHRUSHCHEV'S CONCLUDING SPEECH TO TWENTY-SECOND CONGRESS OF THE COMMUNIST PARTY OF THE SOVIET UNION, OCTOBER 27, 1961 *

The discussion of the Central Committee report and the report on the Program of the Communist Party of the Soviet Union (CPSU),

* Russian text *Pravda,* Oct. 27, 1961. English translation from Press Department, Soviet Embassy in Washington, No. 212, Oct. 30, 1961.

that has passed on a high political level, has ended. Many delegates to the Congress have spoken from this rostrum. What may be said of these speeches? I think you will agree with me that each speech may be described as a report, as an accounting to the Party. Everyone who ascended this rostrum spoke of the most agitating, of the most essential that has been accomplished and that is still to be accomplished. The speeches were imbued with indomitable faith in the triumph of communism.

All the speakers unanimously approved both the Central Committee's political line and practical activities, and the draft of our Party Program, a program for the building of communism. The Twenty-second Congress is a most vivid demonstration of the unity of our Leninist Party, of the fact that the entire Soviet people are closely rallied around it.

The entire content of the Twenty-second Congress has reaffirmed our Party's unwavering fidelity to the line worked out by the Twentieth Congress. It is now still more evident that the Twentieth Congress has, by removing all the after-effects of the period of the personality cult, opened a new chapter in the history of our Party and exercised a beneficial influence on the development of our country and the world communist and working-class movement as a whole.

The attention of our Congress is focused on the Party Program, the program for the building of a communist society. All the delegates to the Congress who have spoken from this rostrum approved the draft Program submitted by the Central Committee and discussed in a businesslike manner concrete practical ways of translating it into reality. They expressed firm confidence that the new Program would be successfully realized and that the Soviet people would be ready to apply their every effort in fulfilling the third Program of our Party as successfully as the first and second Programs.

It is from the devoted labor of the Soviet people that our Program derives its strength and vitality. But what joy and pride one feels, listening to the speeches of such wonderful innovators as Valentina Gaganova, Alexander Kolchik, Maria Rozhneva, Vasili Kavun, Vasili Smirnov, Alexander Gitalov, and many others. How much initiative, inventiveness, skill, and perseverance in labor is being shown by the foremost men and women in fulfilling their duty to their country, to the people. The millions of such innovators are the cream and pride of our Soviet society.

It is very important at present that the efforts of all working people at each factory, each building project, each collective and state farm be concentrated on the fulfillment and overfulfillment of the production plans.

The higher the productivity of labor, the higher the quality, the more values will we create; and the more values there will be, the more rapid will be the Soviet people's advance toward the great goal of the building of communist society.

Representatives of all the republics, of the many territories and regions of our country—Party and government officials, the foremost men and women of industry and agriculture—our wonderful beacons, as they are figuratively described, have spoken at the Congress, so have scientists, writers and artists, representatives of our glorious armed forces.

The delegates raised the key questions of communist construction. They spoke of the ways and means of building the material and technical basis of communism; of the urgent questions concerning the work of industry and the further development of agriculture; of the prospects of still greater progress in science, culture, education, art, and literature in our country; of the tasks of molding the man of the new, communist society. All these measures were deeply and thoroughly studied at the Congress. Now at the Twenty-second Congress we see still more clearly that communist construction has become the practical task of the Party, the cause of the entire Soviet people.

The delegates' speeches were highly principled, to the point, and intolerant of shortcomings. The comrades rightly concentrated attention on the need for developing to the utmost the productive forces of Soviet society; for improving planning, the organization of production, methods of economic management; and for properly utilizing the potentialities of industry and agriculture. They made proposals aimed at obtaining the maximum economic results with a minimum outlay of labor.

Important questions concerning the further improvement of the management of the national economy were raised during the discussion of the Central Committee report and the draft Program. The Congress shows that the Party unanimously approves the measures carried out in this field by the Central Committee and the government in the past few years. In particular, everybody welcomed the establishment of economic areas and of councils for the co-ordination and planning of the work of economic councils in the enlarged economic areas.

The delegates to the Congress unanimously approved the measures taken in the past few years by the Central Committee of the Party and by the government in the field of agriculture. We have heard many forceful and pithy speeches here. The proposals made at the Congress on various aspects of economic, scientific, and cultural development, and concerning the work and living conditions of the Soviet people merit every support. It is difficult even to enumerate the valuable proposals made during the discussion.

Comrade Keldysh was quite right, for example, when he stressed the need for starting the organization of joint scientific institutions in economic areas and the union republics.

Comrade Rozhneva raised the question of abolishing night shifts for women. That is a big problem. You realize that it will take time and the necessary conditions to solve it completely. The Central Committee and the government will look into the problem and do everything possible to solve it.

Comrade Gitalov has stressed rightly the need to promote, truly far and wide, the experience of the comprehensive mechanization of agricultural jobs.

There has been a number of other important proposals made during the discussion at the Congress. Implementation of these proposals will unquestionably help to successfully accomplish the tasks confronting us. The Central Committee, the Council of Ministers, and the local Party and government bodies should study these proposals closely and take the necessary measures.

Comrades, delegations of nearly all the Communist and Workers' parties of the world are attending our Congress. The speeches made from this rostrum by our dear guests and the messages of greeting the Congress has received from the fraternal parties reflect the great unity of the ranks of the world communist movement and confirm once more that all the Marxist-Leninist parties approve and support the Leninist policy of our Party. Allow me, on behalf of the Congress, of all our Party and the Soviet people, to express profound and heartfelt gratitude to the Communist and Workers' parties of the world for their high evaluation of the activities of the Communist Party of the Soviet Union and of its role in the international communist and working-class movement, for their confidence and their wishes for success in the implementation of our new Program.

May I assure you, dear foreign comrades and brothers, that the Communist Party of the Soviet Union will continue to bear aloft the great banner of Marxism-Leninism, that with added energy it will build communism where peace, labor, freedom, equality, fraternity, and happiness for all peoples will reign.

The speeches made at our Congress by the leaders of the Communist and Workers' parties of the countries of the socialist camp have shown that the fraternal parties stand unanimously by the 1957 Declaration and the 1960 Statement. The socialist camp has again demonstrated the monolithic unity of its ranks and the growth and the increased cohesion of the forces of world socialism.

The presence at the Twenty-second Congress of delegations from eighty Marxist-Leninist parties, their speeches here, reflect the powerful growth of the international communist and working-class movement, as well as the national liberation movement, and the unshakable loyalty of the Communists of all countries to the principles of proletarian internationalism bequeathed to us by Marx, Engels, and Lenin. All of us rejoice that all over the world the forces of fighters for the peoples' happiness, for peace and social progress, for communism are maturing and becoming steeled!

Allow me, comrades, on behalf of our Congress to cordially thank the representatives of the democratic national parties of the independent African states of Guinea, the Republic of Ghana, and the Mali Republic. These parties are not communist, but we are glad that they have accepted our invitation and sent their delegations to the Twenty-second Congress. Representatives of these parties are attending our Congress, they see and hear what the Communists are engaged in and what tasks they set themselves.

We ask these delegations, upon their return home, to convey to their parties and peoples the best wishes of our Congress, of the Soviet people. All the Soviet people wish the independent African states that have taken or are taking the path of independent economic and political development great success and prosperity.

Comrades, in their speeches at the Congress the delegates approved the foreign policy of the Soviet government. Discussion of the matters raised in the Central Committee's report and in the report on the Program of our Party is also taking place outside the walls of this auditorium. It is not only our friends but our opponents as well who are taking part in it. They too voice their opinion about the domestic and foreign policy of our Party and assess it from the point of view of their class.

The successes of the Soviet Union and of all the socialist countries have a great force of attraction. Like the rising sun, they illuminate the right road for other people to achieve the victory of the most just social system in the shortest historical period of time.

Being aware of this, the imperialists would have liked to retard our swift advance. It is this that explains the aggressive nature of the policy pursued by the ruling circles of the United States, Britain, France, West Germany, and the other imperialist powers. Their policy is determined not by the interests of peace and the tranquility of the people but by the interests of monopoly profits, the interests of preserving the domination of the imperialists. It is for these ends that they strive to step up the tension in international relations and obstruct the peaceful settlement of urgent international problems.

Let us take, for instance, the problem of abolishing the remnants of World War II in Europe. Any further delay in solving it is fraught with grave consequences to the cause of peace.

The Soviet Union has long since been proposing that a peace treaty be signed with Germany and the situation in West Berlin normalized on that basis, ending the occupational regime in that city. The Soviet Union wants to create conditions for peaceful coexistence in the center of Europe.

What could be more just than this aim? Do we threaten anyone? Do we want to take something from the West? We do not. After the peace treaty is signed, the relations between the European countries will be normalized and the peoples will be better able to develop good-neighbor relations.

But in reply to our peaceful proposals, the Western powers openly threaten to take up arms against us.

Today the Western powers "explain" condescendingly that the Soviet Union may—just imagine it!—conclude a peace treaty with the German Democratic Republic, but has no right to abandon commitments undertaken by the Allied victor-countries when Hitler Germany was crushed.

What commitments do they have in mind? Is it the commitment

to root out German militarism and revanchism, to which the Soviet Government is indeed applying its efforts and which the Allies assumed after the end of the Second World War? No, they do not refer to the commitments undertaken jointly by the Western Powers and ourselves in Yalta and Potsdam, and which they have long since forsaken in favor of the NATO military plans. By threatening war they want to make us perpetuate the right of the United States, Britain, and France to occupy West Berlin.

It may be asked why do they need this right now, more than sixteen years after the war ended? The Western powers pretend to need this right "to ensure the freedom" of West Berlin. But neither the Soviet Union, nor the German Democratic Republic, nor the other socialist countries have any designs upon the freedom of West Berlin.

The Western powers speak of "freedom," but what they imply by it is the occupation of West Berlin. They want to keep their armed forces and intelligence centers there, i.e., they want to continue using West Berlin in their hostile subversive activities against the German Democratic Republic; that is their real purpose, and it is for this purpose that they cling to the rights of occupation which have outlived their day. What is more, they want us to help them in this!

They want us to ensure, like traffic police, the uninterrupted transportation to West Berlin of their military freight, spies, and saboteurs for subversive acts against ourselves and our allies.

Whom do these gentlemen take us for? Do they actually believe that they can do anything they want, that they can make us act against our vital interests, against the interests of world peace and security?

It is time—high time—that they understood the simple fact that today they can negotiate with the Soviet Union, and the socialist community as a whole, only from a position of reason, not of strength. And reason and justice are on our side, not on theirs.

No sober-minded person can understand or accept the contention that the Western powers have a legal or moral right to attack us in reply to our signing a German peace treaty and to the discontinuance of the occupation regime in West Berlin. Millions of Americans, Britons, and Frenchmen, in fact all the nations involved, will bitterly denounce anyone who ventures to start a war in reply to the conclusion of a German peace treaty.

The Western powers' policy on the German question is not

prompted by the interests of peace but primarily by the interests of the militarist and revenge-seeking forces in West Germany. The chief demon who is shaping this policy is Chancellor Adenauer.

The militaristic, aggressive circles make no secret of their hatred for the Soviet state and our foreign policy of peace. Nor does that surprise us in the least. One cannot expect the imperialists ever to like our social order. No matter what sentiments they entertain toward socialism, let them abandon the hope ever to impose upon the socialist countries their capitalist order. We can tell them once again today: Do not lose your reason, gentlemen; do not seek to experience the strength and firmness of our system. It is common knowledge that our enemies more than once made such attempts in the past, and everyone knows how these attempts ended.

As was already noted in the report of the Central Committee, the Soviet government considers that if the Western powers display a readiness to settle the German problem, the question of time limits will not be so important. We shall not then insist on having the treaty signed before December 31. We are not superstitious, and we believe that both "31" and "13" can be lucky. It is not the date that matters but a businesslike and honest solution of the question. We want the Western powers to recognize the need to do away with the remnants of World War II for the sake of preserving peace on earth in the interest of all countries, in the interest of all mankind.

We are prepared to meet representatives of the Western powers, exchange opinions with them in order to prepare fruitful negotiations. But one must really prepare for negotiations and strive for agreement in order to find at the round table, with the participation of all countries concerned, a mutually acceptable solution of questions bearing on the liquidation of the remnants of World War II.

However, the Soviet Union cannot tolerate negotiations for the sake of negotiations, cannot allow representatives of the Western countries to take advantage of this in order to delay a peace settlement in Europe. If someone bases his calculations on this, let him know in advance that such calculations will not be realized. This is our position. We firmly stood, and continue to stand, on this position.

Bourgeois propaganda has of late raised a clamor around the fact that the Soviet Union has been forced to resume nuclear weapon tests. This clamor assumed a hysterical nature after it had been stated at the Congress that there would be a 50-megaton nuclear test explosion. Voices are heard alleging that these tests contradict the principles of morality.

Strange logic! When the United States of America was the first to manufacture an atom bomb, it felt juridically and morally justified in dropping it on the heads of the defenseless citizens of Hiroshima and Nagasaki. This was an act of senseless brutality without any military necessity.

Hundreds of thousands of women, children, and old folk perished in the flames of atomic explosions. And this was done merely to intimidate the peoples and make them bow before the might of the United States. Strange as it may seem, some American politicians were, and still are, proud of this mass killing.

No U.S. administration, no U.S. president since the war has admitted these to have been immoral actions. Why? Because they proceed from imperialist morality which says that everything is permitted to the strong. They considered that a monopoly of nuclear weapons would enable them to establish their domination throughout the world.

But the Soviet Union, in a short time, developed powerful thermonuclear weapons and thus ended the U.S. monopoly in this field.

When we launched our first sputniks, when Soviet ships blazed the first trails into space and Comrades Gagarin and Titov accomplished their unprecedented flights around the earth, the whole world saw that the Soviet Union was far ahead of the United States in important fields of science and technology. Even President Kennedy had to admit that the United States is faced with the arduous task of overtaking the Soviet Union in this sphere. You will observe that the word "overtaking" is now to be found in the American lexicon as well.

I have more than once said that the Soviet Union will overtake the United States in corn production. The Americans were somewhat skeptical on this score. However, it is easier to overtake in corn production than in the exploration of outer space. That is much more intricate! The facts show that the situation has considerably changed in favor of socialism.

But while the United States President speaks of the need to overtake the Soviet Union, Mr. Rusk, the United States Secretary of State, persists in calling for a policy "from positions of strength." A few days ago he said that Mr. Khrushchev must know that the United States is strong. He intimated that the Western powers mean to go on negotiating with us "from positions of strength." It looks as if the right hand does not know what the left is doing.

Some Western leaders are plainly thinking the wrong way. Anyone who wants peace to be something more than just a spell of calm or a respite between two wars should create a situation ruling out war forever.

The Soviet Union is far from seeking to dictate its will or terms to other countries. Even though we have achieved indisputable superiority in rocketry and nuclear arms, we have proposed general and complete disarmament and the destruction of nuclear weapons under the strictest international control. Moreover, the Soviet Union by unilateral action effected a considerable reduction of its armed forces, dismantled its military bases on foreign soil, and carried out a series of other measures for the same purpose.

It is common knowledge that the United States, Britain, and France, far from following the Soviet example, have of late been stepping up the arms race, increasing their armies, and holding military exercises in the vicinity of our borders. They have been openly threatening us with war over the German peace treaty.

In the face of direct threats and the danger of war, the Soviet Union was compelled to take appropriate steps to strengthen its defenses, to defend the Soviet people and the peoples of the entire great community of socialist countries.

We were confronted with the necessity of improving our thermonuclear weapons and testing new types of them. The decision which the Soviet government took on this matter in view of a serious aggravation of international tension was appreciated by all who cherish peace and refuse to shut their eyes to the dangerous intrigues of the enemies of peace.

In adopting that decision, the Soviet government realized, of course, that the reasons which made it renew the tests would not be understood immediately by all. Indeed, today even fair-minded people express concern over the consequences of the nuclear explosions that are being carried out. I have been receiving letters and telegrams from some of them. We have no grounds to question the sincerity of these people who fear that nuclear blasts may contaminate the atmosphere.

To those people we say: Dear friends, ladies and gentlemen, the peoples of the socialist countries would like nothing better than that the sky above our planet be clear and limpid. What we live and work for is to achieve a happy future for the peoples, to turn the earth into a flowering garden. We have children, grandchildren, and even great-grandchildren, just as you have. We are thinking not only of their present but of their future as well. I must say that our scientists are doing everything to reduce the harmful aftereffects of the tests to a minimum.

But we cannot refrain from carrying out those tests at a time when the United States, British, French, and West German imperialists are making preparations to destroy not only the socialist achievements but also the peoples of our countries. For they threaten not only to contaminate the atmosphere but to take the lives of millions of people.

In the face of a very real threat to our security, the Soviet people could not forego measures to increase the defense might of the Soviet Union and the socialist commonwealth as a whole. We would be poor leaders if we did not perfect all the means of defense required for the security of the Soviet state.

It is very regrettable indeed that certain fair-minded people abroad have so far been unable to see their way clear in the complicated international situation. Imperialist propaganda is taking advantage of the humane sentiments of these people to prevent us, through them, from improving the necessary means of defense and to make it easier for themselves to prepare a new war against us.

In strengthening the defenses of the Soviet Union, we act not only in our interests but also in the interests of all the peace-loving peoples, of all mankind. When the enemies of peace threaten us with force, they must and will be countered with force, and greater force too. If there is anyone today who still cannot understand this, he is certain to understand it tomorrow.

I should like to point out once again to the leaders of the United States, Britain, France, West Germany, and other countries that the most sensible thing to do is to discard the policy "from a position of strength" and the "cold war." In the sphere of international relations it is necessary to pursue the realistic policy of peaceful coexistence.

And this means that one must reckon with the hard fact that the countries of the world's socialist system are successfully developing and strengthening with every passing year on our planet next to the capitalist world. Not to see this, not to reckon with this would just be ludicrous and shortsighted in our day.

The imperialists dislike the growth and development of the socialist countries. They would like to restrict us, to teach us, like children, how we should live better on earth, for the imperialists regard Soviet power as an illegitimate child. And they cannot reconcile themselves to the fact that we have now grown up so much that we not only study but can teach a lot to others. Here, too, you see, are contradictions between the old and the new. Of course, we cannot and will not live as the imperialists want us to. And they are dissatisfied, threaten to let us have it with a twig. But if they come at us with a twig, we shall let them have it with a whole broom!

To consider the matter seriously, the most sensible thing for states with different systems would be to coexist peacefully, to establish good-neighbor relations. For a neighbor is not like a wife or a husband, who choose each other by mutual consent. Neighbors are not chosen, they do not depend on our wishes. Our country, for instance, has such a neighbor in the south as present-day Iran, whose rulers pursue a policy which is anything but good-neighborly. If it were up to us, we would apparently have selected a more pleasant neighbor. And the Iranian rulers, too, I think, would have preferred another neighbor. But it has so happened in history that our countries have found themselves next to each other, neighbors. And there is nothing to be done about this, we have to reckon with the facts. One must not interfere in the affairs of neighbors, nor allow them to interfere in one's own affairs.

I should like to speak in greater detail on such an important theoretical and political question as that of the characteristics of present-day imperialism and peaceful coexistence between states with differing social systems.

The peaceful coexistence of states with differing social and political systems is the cardinal issue of our time. The states existing in the world make up two different world systems—the socialist and the capitalist. For all the power of modern science, it is impossible to cut the globe in two and allot each of the two systems a definite area, to pull them apart, if I may say so. And this means that the coexistence of countries with differing social and political systems is a historical fact.

There is an acute struggle, a dispute, going on between the two social systems as to which provides more in the way of benefits for man. How is the dispute between these two different systems to be resolved—by way of war or through peaceful economic competition? If one does not set the task of settling disputes which arise in the relations between states by way of military conflict, then one recognizes the peaceful coexistence of states with different systems. The sociopolitical system of each state is an internal matter of its people, and the peoples must themselves settle, and do settle, this question as they see fit.

Some attack us by accusing us of simplifying or softening the appraisal of the international situation when we stress the need for peaceful coexistence in the obtaining conditions. We are told that those who lay emphasis on peaceful coexistence allegedly underestimate the essence of imperialism in some way and even contradict Lenin's appraisal of imperialism.

The classical definition of imperialism given by Vladimir Ilyich Lenin is well known. This Leninist definition of imperialism reveals the reactionary and aggressive nature of imperialism as the last stage of capitalism. Imperialism is closely connected with wars, with the struggle for the division and recarving of the world, for enslaving the peoples, for their enslavement by monopoly capital. It is capable of any adventures.

This appraisal of the essence of imperialism remains fully valid today. Our Party, far from denying this appraisal, confirms it, proceeding from this appraisal in its entire policy, in working out the strategy and tactics of the revolutionary struggle, which has been convincingly shown in the draft of our new Program. The Party, if it stands on the position of creative Marxism-Leninism, must simultaneously take into consideration the big changes in the world which have taken place since Lenin gave an analysis of imperialism.

We are going through a period in which there are two world systems in existence, in which the world system of socialism is developing rapidly, and the time is not far off when it will surpass the world capitalist system in the provision of material benefits as well. As regards science and culture, the countries of the world socialist system have already considerably surpassed the countries of capitalism in some branches. The world system of socialism is also stronger than the imperialist countries militarily.

Under these circumstances, it is impossible to claim that nothing has happened in the world in the past decades, that nothing has changed. This can only be done by people who are by-passed by life, who do not see the great changes in the balance of forces in the world arena.

Indeed, the essence of imperialism, its aggressive nature has not changed. But its opportunities are no longer the same as during the period of its undivided domination. The position is now such that imperialism cannot impose its will upon everyone and freely carry through its aggressive policy.

The invincible forces of the world socialist system, primarily of the Soviet Union, stand in the way of the imperialists' predatory designs to redivide the world and to enslave other peoples. These forces restrict the wolfish appetites of the imperialists. Hundreds of millions of people in the peaceable countries are fighting for peace. All peoples are fighting for peace. And this is the main thing. This must be understood.

To make my thought clearer, I should like to cite the following example. The tiger is a beast of prey, and remains so till his death. But it is known that the tiger never attacks an elephant. Why? Elephant meat must be just as tasty as that of any other animal, and the tiger would not apparently be averse to partaking of it. But he is afraid to attack the elephant, because the elephant is stronger than the tiger. And if some mad tiger did attack an elephant, he would certainly die; the elephant would trample him to death.

You have seen in films about Africa and Asia how kings, princes, rajahs and other notables go tiger-hunting on elephants. They do this because they know that this form of tiger-hunting is not dangerous. To pursue the comparison, it could be said that the Soviet Union, the countries of the socialist camp are now even stronger compared to the imperialists than is the elephant compared to the tiger.

About the same is the situation with imperialism: The imperialists must now, not only out of prudence but, if one may put it this way, out of the instinct of self-preservation, take into consideration that they cannot with impunity oppress, plunder, and enslave everyone. The powerful forces now barring the road to imperialism compel the imperialists to reckon with these forces. The imperialists understand that if they unleash a world war, the imperialist system, detested by the people, would inevitably perish in it.

In our time the might of the world system of socialism has grown as never before. It now already unites over one-third of mankind, and its forces are rapidly expanding; it is a great bastion of world peace. The principle of peaceful coexistence between states with differing social systems assumes a vital importance in contemporary conditions.

This is not understood only by hopeless dogmatists, who, repeating general formulas about imperialism, obstinately turn away from life. It is precisely on such positions that the last-ditcher Molotov still stands. He and his like do not understand the changes in the world situation, the new features in life; they are lagging behind events, have long since become a break, a ballast.

Comrades:

The Central Committee's report, as well as the speeches by delegates to this Congress, dealt with the erroneous stand of the leaders of the Albanian Party of Labor, who have set out to fight against the course adopted by the Twentieth Congress of our Party and to undermine the friendship with the Soviet Union and other socialist countries.

The representatives of fraternal parties who spoke here said that they share our concern over the state of affairs in the Albanian Party of Labor and emphatically condemn the dangerous actions of its leaders, which prejudice the basic interests of the Albanian people and the unity in the socialist commonwealth as a whole. The speeches made by delegates and by the representatives of fraternal parties show plainly that the Central Committee of our Party was absolutely correct in reporting to this Congress, frankly and from a principled standpoint, that the situation with regard to Soviet-Albanian relations is abnormal.

It was our duty to do so because our numerous attempts to normalize relations with the Albanian Party of Labor unfortunately yielded no results. I should like to stress that the Central Committee of our Party showed the greatest patience and did all in its power to restore good relations between our parties.

Members of the Presidium of the CPSU Central Committee made repeated attempts to meet with the Albanian leaders to discuss the controversies that had arisen as far back as August 1960. Twice we made a proposal for a meeting to the Albanian leaders, but they evaded it. They were just as obstinate in rejecting talks with us during the Moscow meeting of fraternal parties in November 1960.

When a meeting was finally arranged at the insistence of the CPSU

Central Committee, Enver Hoxha and Mehmet Shehu frustrated it and resorted to actions which can only be described as provocative. The leaders of the Albanian Party of Labor ostentatiously withdrew from the November meeting, thus showing that they refused to take account of the collective opinion of the fraternal parties. They rudely turned down our subsequent proposals for getting together, exchanging views, and removing differences, and stepped up their campaign of slanderous attacks against our Party and its Central Committee.

The leaders of the Albanian Party of Labor have no scruples about using any methods to conceal from their people the truth as to what our Party and our people are doing. Albania is the only country in the socialist community that has not published the full text of the draft Program of the CPSU. The Albanian press carried only some parts of the draft, deliberately creating a distorted picture of the activities of our Party. That fact speaks for itself. Indeed, even the opponents of communism were unable to keep silent about our Program.

We are aware why the Albanian leaders are concealing the Program of the CPSU from their Party and their people. They are scared stiff of the truth. The Party Program is sacred to us, it is our lodestar in communist construction.

Had the Albanian leaders published it in full, Albania's working people would have seen who slanders and who speaks the truth, would have seen that the entire activity of our Party and all its plans are in keeping with the vital interests of the peoples, including the interests of the friendly Albanian people.

Our great Party has more than once been a target of fierce and foul attacks on the part of overt and covert enemies of communism. But it must be said bluntly that we do not recall anyone passing, at such breakneck speed, from protestations and vows of everlasting friendship to unbridled anti-Soviet calumny the way the Albanian leaders have done.

They apparently expect in this manner to clear the ground for winning the right to receive handouts from the imperialists. The imperialists are always prepared to pay thirty pieces of silver to those who split the communist ranks. But pieces of silver have never brought anyone anything but dishonor and ignominy.

Obviously, the Central Committee of our Party could not but tell this Congress the whole truth about the pernicious stand of the leadership of the Albanian Party of Labor. Had we not done so, the Albanian leaders would have gone on making out that the Central Committee of the Soviet Communist Party was afraid of informing the Congress of the differences it had with the leadership of the Albanian Party of Labor. Our Party and the Soviet people should know about the conduct of the Albanian leaders. And let this Congress, which is entitled to speak on behalf of the entire Party, take its stand on the matter; let it pass its weighty judgement.

Our Congress emphasized the readiness there is to normalize relations with the Albanian Party of Labor on the basis of Marxist-Leninist principles. But what was the Albanian leaders' reaction? They gave vent to vociferous statements slinging mud at our Party and its Central Committee.

Comrade Chou En-Lai, the leader of the delegation of the Communist Party of China, voiced in his speech concern over the open discussion at this Congress of the issue of Albanian-Soviet relations. The main point in his statement, as we see it, was the anxiety that the present state of our relations with the Albanian Party of Labor might affect the unity of the socialist camp.

We share the anxiety expressed by our Chinese friends and appreciate their concern for greater unity. If the Chinese comrades wish to make efforts toward normalizing the relations between the Albanian Party of Labor and the fraternal parties, there is hardly anyone who can contribute to the solution of this problem more than the Communist Party of China. That would really benefit the Albanian Party of Labor and would meet the interests of the entire socialist commonwealth.

It is true, of course, that Communists should build their inter-Party relations in such a way as to leave no loophole for the enemy. Unfortunately, the Albanian leaders grossly flout this principle. They have long since been openly assailing the policy of the Twentieth Congress, thereby furnishing the bourgeois press with food for all kinds of speculation. None other than the Albanian leaders are shouting from the house tops about their special stand and their special views which are different from those of our Party and other fraternal parties. This became evident at the Fourth Congress of the Albanian Party of Labor, and has been even more so in recent times.

Why did the Albanian leaders launch a campaign against the decisions of the Twentieth Congress of our Party? What is the heresy they espy in them?

To begin with, the Albanian leaders disapprove of the resolute condemnation of the cult of Stalin's person and its harmful consequences. They disapprove of our having firmly condemned the arbitrary methods and the abuses of power which affected many innocent people, including prominent representatives of the old guard, who together with Lenin founded the world's first proletarian state. The Albanian leaders cannot speak without annoyance and rancor of the fact that we have put an end for good to a situation in which one man could settle at will the most vital questions in the life of our Party and country.

Stalin is no longer among the living, but we considered it necessary to denounce the disgraceful methods of leadership that flourished in the atmosphere of the cult of his person. Our Party does this to ensure that such practices may never recur.

One would think that the Leninist course adopted by the Twentieth Congress of the CPSU and supported by the fraternal parties should also have been backed by the leadership of the Albanian Party of Labor, since the cult of the individual is incompatible with Marxism-Leninism. What happened, however, was that the Albanian leaders raised the cult of Stalin's person on high and began a bitter struggle against the decisions of the Twentieth Congress of the CPSU in an effort to divert the socialist countries from the true course. That, of course, was no accident. All that was bad in our country at the time of the cult of the individual manifests itself in even worse form in the Albanian Party of Labor. It is no longer a secret for anyone that the Albanian leaders keep themselves in power by resorting to violence and arbitrary actions.

An abnormal, pernicious situation has long since been prevailing in the Albanian Party of Labor where each person disliked by the leadership can be subjected to brutal reprisals.

Where are now those Albanian Communists who founded the Party, fought against the Italian and German fascist invaders? Almost all of them fell victim to the bloody atrocities perpetrated by Mehmet Shehu and Enver Hoxha.

The Central Committee of the CPSU has received many letters from Albanian Communists requesting that the Albanian leaders be restrained from making short work of the finest sons and daughters of the Albanian Party of Labor. The Congress delegates can get an idea of the moral aspect of the Albanian leaders by familiarizing themselves with some of the letters.

The Albanian leaders reproach us for alleged interference in the internal affairs of the Albanian Party of Labor. I should like to explain what this so-called interference consisted of.

Several years ago the Central Committee of the CPSU interceded with the Albanian leaders for the former member of the Political Bureau of the Central Committee of the Albanian Party of Labor Liri Gega, who had been sentenced to death together with her husband. For several years that woman had served on the ruling bodies of the Albanian Party of Labor, took part in the Albanian people's struggle for liberation. In approaching the Albanian leaders at that time, we proceeded from considerations of humanity, from a desire to prevent the execution of a woman, and a pregnant one at that.

We believed, and still believe, that as a fraternal party we had the right to express our opinion on this score. For even during the most sinister times of rampant reaction, the czarist satraps, tormenting revolutionaries, did not dare to execute expectant mothers. And here, in a socialist country, a death sentence was passed upon an expectant mother, and she was executed—a display of utterly unjustified brutality.

Honest people are now being victimized in Albania only because they dared to come out in defense of Soviet-Albanian friendship, of which the Albanian leaders like to speak so pompously and bombastically.

Comrades Liri Belishova and Kocho Tashko, prominent leaders of the Albanian Party of Labor, have not only been removed from the Central Committee of the Albanian Party of Labor, but are now openly called enemies of the Party and the people. And all this for the sole reason that Liri Belishova and Kocho Tashko had the courage to voice openly and honestly their disagreement with the policy of the Albanian leaders, came out for Albania's unity with the Soviet Union and the other socialist countries.

Those who today stand for friendship with the Soviet Union, with the CPSU, are regarded as an enemy by the Albanian leaders.

How can all this be squared with the pledges and assurances given by Shehu and Hoxha about friendly sentiments for the CPSU and the Soviet Union? It is evident that all their prattling about friendship is but hypocrisy and deceit.

That is the situation prevailing in the Albanian Party of Labor, that is why the Albanian leaders are opposing the Leninist course of the Twentieth Congress of the Party. For to end the personality cult would virtually mean for Shehu, Hoxha, and others to resign their leading positions in the Party and the state. This they do not want to do. But we are confident that the time will come when the Albanian Communists and the Albanian people will have their say, and the Albanian leaders will then be held responsible for the damage they inflicted upon their country, their people, and the cause of building socialism in Albania.

Comrades, as before, our Party will continue to fight against revisionists of all stripes. Abiding unswervingly by the principles of the Declaration and the Statement by the meetings of Marxist-Leninist parties, we exposed, and will unflaggingly expose, revisionism which found expression in the program of the League of Communists of Yugoslavia. We shall also fight unremittingly against dogmatism and all other departures from Marxism-Leninism.

Comrades, the Twenty-second Congress can be justly called a congress of monolithic unity of the Leninist Party, complete unanimity and cohesion.

Our enemies are frightened by the growing unity of our ranks. They seek to speculate on the fact that our Congress paid much attention to the discussion of the harmful consequences of the personality cult and also finally exposed the anti-Party factionalist group. But vain are such attempts by the enemies of communism; they will gain nothing from this.

Marxist-Leninist parties differ from all other political parties because Communists unhesitatingly and boldly reveal and eliminate the shortcomings and flaws in their work. Criticism, even the sharpest, helps our onward movement. This is a pointer to the strength of the Communist Party—evidence of its unbending faith in its cause.

Many comrades who spoke here wrathfully denounced the subversive anti-Party activities of a group of factionists headed by Molotov, Kaganovich, and Malenkov. The entire Party, the entire people repudiated these renegades, who resisted everything new and tried to revive the pernicious methods which prevailed under the cult of the individual. They wanted to revert to the times—hard for our Party and our country—when no one was guaranteed against arbitrary reprisals. Yes, Molotov and the others wanted just that.

We resolutely reject such so-to-speak methods of leadership. We stand and will stand firmly for inner-Party affairs to be settled on the basis of Leninist standards, methods of persuasion and broad democracy.

The strongest weapon of the Party is its ideology, the great teachings of Marxism-Leninism which brought many glorious victories to the Party, to the Soviet people, and to the entire international communist movement.

Is the emergence of various opinions inside the Party in various stages of its activity, especially in turning stages, possible? It is possible. How is one to deal with those who express an opinion different from that of the others? We are in favor of applying the Leninist methods of persuasion and explanation in such cases, and not repressive measures.

I recollect such an episode from the history of our Party. On the eve of the October Revolution, in the crucial days when the fate of the Great Socialist Revolution was at stake, Zinoviev and Kamenev opposed in the press the armed rising planned by the Party and revealed to our enemies the plans of the Central Committee of the Bolshevik Party. That was treason to the Revolution.

Vladimir Ilyich Lenin exposed Zinoviev and Kamenev and demanded their expulsion from the Party. The correctness of Lenin's line of preparing for an armed uprising was borne out in full by the subsequent development of the Revolution. When Zinoviev and Kamenev later said that they had been mistaken and admitted their fault, Lenin displayed great magnanimity toward them and himself raised the question of their readmission to Party leadership.

Vladimir Ilyich Lenin firmly carried through a line of unfolding inner-Party democracy. He relied on the broad mass of communist and non-Party people.

During the years after Lenin's death the Leninist norms of Party life were grossly distorted in the atmosphere of the cult of Stalin's person. Stalin made restrictions on inner-Party and Soviet democracy a standard for inner-Party and state affairs. He flagrantly flouted the Leninist principles of leadership, committed arbitrary actions and abuses of power.

Stalin could look at a comrade sitting at the same table with him and say: "Your eyes are shifty today." Afterward it could be taken for granted that the comrade, whose eyes were supposedly shifty, fell under suspicion.

Comrade delegates, I want to tell the Congress how the anti-Party group reacted to the proposal to raise at the Twentieth Party Congress the question of abuses of power in the period of the cult of the individual.

The proposal was violently resisted by Molotov, Kaganovich, Malenkov, Voroshilov, and others. We told them, in reply to their objections, that if they resisted consideration of this question, we would ask the Congress delegates. We had no doubt that the Congress would declare itself in favor of discussing this question. Only then did they agree, and the question of the cult of the individual was reported on at the Twentieth Party Congress. But even after the Congress the factionists did not discontinue their struggle and retarded in every way the inquiry into the question of the abuse of power, fearing lest their role as accessories to the mass reprisals should come to light.

The mass reprisals began after the assassination of Kirov. Big efforts are still required to find out who really is to blame for his death. The deeper we study the materials connected with Kirov's death, the more questions arise. Noteworthy is the fact that the killer of Kirov had before been detained twice by Chekists (security men) near the Smolny, and that arms had been found on him. But he was released both times on somebody's instruction. And now this man was in the Smolny, armed, in the corridor through which Kirov usually passed. And for some reason or other, at the moment of the assassination the chief of Kirov's guard was far behind Kirov, though his instructions did not authorize him to be such a distance away.

Equally strange is the following fact. When the chief of Kirov's guard was being taken for questioning—and he was to be questioned by Stalin, Molotov, and Voroshilov—the car, as its driver said afterward, was deliberately involved in an accident by those who were taking the man to those who were to interrogate him. They said that he died as a result of the accident, even though he was actually killed by those who accompanied him.

In this way the man who guarded Kirov was killed. Later, those who killed him were shot. This was no accident, apparently, but a carefully planned crime. Who could have done this? A thorough inquiry is being made now into the circumstances of this complicated case.

It has transpired that the driver of the car in which the chief of Kirov's guard was being taken for questioning is alive. He said that an NKVD operative sat with him in his cabin during the trip. They went in a truck. (It is, of course, very strange that a truck was used to take the man for questioning, as if no other car could be found for the purpose. Evidently, everything had been planned in advance, in detail.) Two other NKVD operatives were in the back of the truck together with Kirov's chief bodyguard.

The driver continued his story. When they were driving through a street, the man sitting next to him suddenly wrested the steering wheel from his hands and directed the car straight at a house. The driver regained control of the wheel and steered the car so that it only hit the wall of the building sideways. He was told later that Kirov's chief bodyguard lost his life in this accident.

Why did he lose his life while none of the other people in the car suffered? Why were both officials of the People's Commissariat for Internal Affairs escorting Kirov's chief bodyguard shot later? This means that someone had to have them killed in order to cover up all the traces.

Many, very many circumstances of this and other similar cases are still obscure.

Comrades, it is our duty to investigate thoroughly and in every way the cases of this kind connected with abuses of power. Time will pass, we shall die—we are all mortal—but while we work we can and must clear up many things and tell the truth to the Party and the people. We are in duty bound to do everything to establish the truth now, for the more time passes after these events, the more difficult it will be to establish the truth. The dead cannot be brought back to life. But it is necessary that the truth be told about this in the history of the Party. This must be done so that such things never recur.

You can imagine how difficult it was to settle such questions when the Presidium of the Central Committee included men who had been guilty of abuses of power and mass reprisals. They put up stubborn resistance to all measures designed to expose the personality cult and subsequently launched a struggle against the Central Committee, wanted to change the composition of its leadership, to change the Leninist policy of the Party, the course of the Twentieth Congress.

Of course, they did not want to investigate such cases. You have heard Comrade Shelepin's speech. He told a great deal at the Congress but, of course, by no means everything which is now known. Thousands of absolutely innocent people perished, and each person is a whole story. Many Party leaders, statesmen, and military leaders lost their lives.

Those people on the Presidium of the Central Committee who were responsible for the violations of legality, for mass reprisals, naturally resisted in every way the exposure of arbitrary actions committed in the period of the cult of the individual. They then started a factional anti-Party struggle against the leadership of the Central Committee and, above all, concentrated their fire on me as first secretary of the Central Committee, as I had to raise these questions by virtue of my duties. I had to take these blows aimed at me and reply to them.

The members of the factional anti-Party group wanted to seize the leadership of the Party and the country, to remove those comrades who exposed the criminal actions committed in the period of the cult of the individual. The anti-Party group wanted to make Molotov the leader. Then, of course, there would have been no exposures of these abuses of power.

After the Twentieth Congress, which stigmatized the personality cult, the anti-Party group tried hard to stop further exposures. Molotov said that great causes included something bad and something good. He tried to justify the actions taken in the period of the personality cult and foretold that such actions were possible, that their repetition in the future was possible. That was the line of the anti-Party factionalist group. This was not just a fallacy. It was a deliberate, criminal, adventurist position. They wanted to push the Party, the country from the Leninist path, wanted to revert to the policy and methods of leadership of the personality cult period.

But they miscalculated. The Central Committee, our entire Party, the entire Soviet people gave a resolute rebuff to the anti-Party group, exposed and routed the factionalists.

It was with a feeling of pain that many prominent Party leaders and statesmen, who perished innocently, were remembered here.

Victims of reprisals were such eminent military leaders as Tukhachevsky, Yakir, Uborevich, Kork, Yegorov, Eideman, and others. They were merited army men, especially Tukhachevsky, Yakir, and Uborevich. They were prominent soldiers. Blyukher and other prominent military leaders were victimized later.

A rather curious report leaked out in the foreign press to the effect that Hitler, preparing the attack on our country, launched a forged document through his intelligence service stating that Comrades Yakir, Tukhachevsky, and others were agents of the German General Staff. This supposedly secret "document" fell into the hands of Czechoslovakia's President Beneš, who, evidently guided by kind intentions, forwarded it to Stalin. Yakir, Tukhachevsky, and other comrades were arrested and then liquidated.

Many excellent commanders and political workers in the Red Army were liquidated. There are comrades among the delegates here—I do not want to give their names so as not to cause them pain—who spent many years in prison. They were "persuaded," persuaded by certain ways that they were German or British or some other spies. And some of them "confessed." Even when they were told that the charges of espionage against them were withdrawn, they themselves insisted on their earlier depositions, as they felt that it would be better to abide by their false statements in order to have done with torture, to die more quickly.

That is the meaning of the personality cult! That is the meaning of the actions of Molotov and others who wanted to revive the pernicious methods of the personality cult period. It is to this that the anti-Party group wanted the Party to revert; that is precisely why the struggle against them was so bitter and hard. Everyone understood the meaning of all this.

I was well acquainted with Comrade Yakir. I also knew Tukhachevsky, but not as well as Yakir. This year, during a conference at Alma-Ata, I was approached by his son, who works in Kazakhstan. He asked me about his father. What could I tell him? When we investigated this case in the Presidium of the Central Committee and were told that neither Tukhachevsky nor Yakir nor Uborevich had perpetrated any crimes against the Party or the state, we asked Molotov, Kaganovich and Voroshilov:

—Are you in favor of rehabilitating them?

—Yes, we are in favor, they replied.

—But you yourselves executed these people, we said with indignation. When did you act in good faith, then or now?

They did not reply to this question. And they won't. You have heard what they wrote in letters to Stalin. What then can they say?

In his speech at the Congress, Comrade Shelepin told how the best representatives of the Communist Party in the Red Army were liquidated. He quoted Comrade Yakir's letter to Stalin, read out the resolutions in that letter. It should be said that Yakir had been in good standing with Stalin at one time.

I can add that before the execution Yakir exclaimed: "Long live the Party, long live Stalin!"

He trusted the Party, he trusted Stalin so much that he could not even think that this act of lawlessness was committed knowingly. He believed that some enemies had gotten into the organs of the NKVD.

When Stalin was told how Yakir held himself during the execution, Stalin cursed him.

Or take Sergo Ordjonikidze. I attended his funeral. I believed what was said then, that he had died suddenly, because we knew him to have a weak heart. It was much later, already after the war, that I learned accidentally that he had committed suicide. Sergo's brother had been arrested and shot. Comrade Ordjonikidze saw that he could no longer work with Stalin, even though he had earlier been one of his closest friends. And Ordjonikidze held a high post in the Party.

He was known and appreciated by Lenin, but a situation took shape in which Ordjonikidze could no longer work normally, and in order not to clash with Stalin, not to share the responsibility for his abuses of power, he resolved to commit suicide.

Alyosha Svanidze, the brother of Stalin's first wife, who was less known among broad circles of our Party, also had a tragic fate. He was a veteran Bolshevik, but Beria, by means of all kinds of machinations, presented matters as though Svanidze had been planted near Stalin by German intelligence, though he was Stalin's closest friend. Svanidze was executed. Before the execution he was told Stalin's words—that he would be pardoned if he asked for it. When Svanidze was told of Stalin's words, he asked: What pardon shall I ask? For I have not committed any crime. He was shot. After Svanidze's death Stalin said: Look, how proud he was; he died, but did not ask for a pardon. And Stalin did not think that Svanidze was, above all, an honest man.

Thus perished many absolutely innocent people.

This is what the cult of the individual means. This is why we cannot tolerate abuses of power even in the slightest.

Comrades, the Presidium of the Congress has received letters from veteran Bolsheviks who write that outstanding leaders of the Party and the state, such true Leninists as Comrades Chubar, Kossior, Rudzutak, Postyshev, Eiche, Voznesensky, Kuznetsov and others, perished innocently in the period of the cult of the individual. They propose to honor the memory of prominent Party leaders and statesmen who fell victim to unwarranted reprisals in the period of the cult of the individual.

We think that this proposal is a right one. It would be expedient to instruct the Central Committee which will be elected by the Twenty-second Congress to settle this question affirmatively. Perhaps we should erect a monument in Moscow to perpetuate the memory of comrades who fell victim to arbitrary rule.

In the conditions of the personality cult the Party was deprived of a normal life. The men who had usurped power became unaccountable to the Party, they were beyond its control. Therein lies the main danger of the personality cult.

It is necessary that a situation should always exist in the Party in which each leader renders account to the Party, its bodies, that the Party could remove any leader when it deems it necessary.

Now, after the Twentieth Congress, the Leninist principles of Party affairs and collective leadership have been restored. The new Program and the Rules of the Party consolidate the provisions which restore the Leninist norms of Party life and exclude the possibility of a revival of the personality cult.

The Twentieth Congress of our Party denounced the cult of the individual, restored justice, and demanded elimination of the distortions committed. The Central Committee of the Party took resolute measures to prevent any return to arbitrariness and lawlessness. The anti-Party group of Molotov, Kaganovich, Malenkov, and others resisted these measures in every way.

The factionists made an attempt to seize leadership and divert the Party from the Leninist path. They were preparing to do away with those who were upholding the course mapped out by the Twentieth Congress. When the anti-Party group was routed, its members believed that they would be dealt with as they themselves had dealt with people in the times of the cult of the individual and as they wanted to deal with those who stood for restoring the Leninist standards of Party life.

I also had a significant conversation with Kaganovich. This was on the second day after the close of the June Plenary Meeting of the Central Committee which expelled the anti-Party group from the Central Committee. Kaganovich called me up and said:

—Comrade Khrushchev, I have known you for many years. I beg you not to allow them to deal with me as they dealt with people under Stalin.

And Kaganovich knew how they dealt at that time because he himself had taken part in these killings.

I replied to him:

—Comrade Kaganovich, your words confirm once again what methods you wanted to use to attain your vile ends. You wanted the country to revert to the order which existed under the personality cult. You wanted to kill people. You measure others, too, by your yardstick. But you are mistaken. We firmly apply and will continue to apply Leninist principles. You will be given a job, I told Kaganovich, you will be able to work and live calmly if you work honestly like all Soviet people.

Such was the talk I had with Kaganovich. It shows that when the factionists failed they thought that they would be dealt with as they wanted to deal with the Party cadres had they succeeded in realizing their insidious plans. But we Communists-Leninists cannot take to the road of abusing power. We stand firmly on Party, Leninist positions; we believe in the strength and unity of our Party, in the people's solid support of the Party.

Many delegates spoke indignantly here about members of the anti-Party group, cited instances of their criminal actions. This indignation is understandable and justified.

I want to say a few words about Comrade Voroshilov. He came up to me several times, spoke of his feelings. I understand how he feels, of course. But we are politicians—we cannot be guided by sentiment only. There are different sentiments. And they can be deceptive. Here at the Congress, Voroshilov hears criticism of himself and looks very downcast. But you should have seen him at the time when the anti-Party group rose up against the Party. Voroshilov was active then—in full regalia, as it were—and all but on a charger.

The anti-Party group used Comrade Voroshilov in its struggle against the Central Committee. It was no accident that the factionists delegated him to meet the members of the Central Committee who pressed for a plenary meeting of the Central Committee.

The anti-Party group expected that by his authority Voroshilov could influence the members of the Central Committee, shake their determination in the struggle against the anti-Party group. The anti-Party group also appointed Bulganin to meet with the members of the

Central Committee as Voroshilov's aide. But Bulganin had no such authority as Voroshilov. They pinned great hopes on Voroshilov as one of the oldest Party leaders. But this did not help the factionists either.

The question arises: How did Comrade Voroshilov find this group? Some comrades know the unpleasant personal relations between Voroshilov and Molotov; Voroshilov and Kaganovich; between Malenkov and Voroshilov.

And yet, despite these relations, they joined forces. Why, on what basis? Because after the Twentieth Congress they feared a further exposure of their unlawful actions in the period of the cult of the individual, feared that they would have to account to the Party. For it is known now that all the abuses of the period were made not only with their support but with their active participation. Fear of responsibility, striving to revive the order which existed in the period of the cult of the individual—this is what united the members of the anti-Party group despite their personal antagonisms.

Comrade Voroshilov committed grave mistakes, but I think, comrades, that another approach is necessary toward him than to the other active members of the anti-Party group, such as Molotov, Kaganovich, and Malenkov. It must be said that in the process of sharp struggle against the factionists early in the work of the June Plenary Meeting of the Central Committee, when Comrade Voroshilov saw the monolithic unity of the Central Committee's members in the struggle against the anti-Party group, he evidently felt that he had gone too far. Voroshilov realized that he had sided with those who were fighting the Party, and he denounced the actions of the anti-Party group, acknowledged his mistakes. Thus he helped to a certain extent the Central Committee. One cannot, comrades, underestimate such a step on his part because this was support for the Party at that time.

The name of Kliment Yefremovich Voroshilov is widely known among the people. This is why his participation in the anti-Party group, along with Molotov, Kaganovich, Malenkov, and others, strengthened the group, as it were, made some impression on people not versed in politics. By leaving the group, Comrade Voroshilov helped the Central Committee in its struggle against the factionists. Let us reply in kind to this good deed and ease his position.

Comrade Voroshilov has been sharply criticized; this criticism has been correct because he has made great mistakes and Communists cannot forget them. But I consider that we should approach Comrade

Voroshilov with attention and generosity. I believe that he is sincere in condemning his actions and in his repentance.

Kliment Yefremovich Voroshilov has lived a long life, has done much good for our Party and the people. I should like to say that when the Central Committee discussed Comrade Voroshilov's request to be relieved of his duties as president of the Presidium of the Supreme Soviet because of his state of health, the members of the Central Committee, notwithstanding his mistakes, warmly spoke of him. In recognition of his services to the Party and the state the Presidium of the Supreme Soviet conferred the title of Hero of Socialist Labor upon Kliment Yefremovich Voroshilov in May 1960.

I think that Kliment Yefremovich will actively fight together with us for the cause of our Party.

Comrades, the Twenty-second Congress has forcefully reaffirmed that the course set by the Twentieth Party Congress, the course of restoring and further developing the Leninist standards of Party and state life, enhancing the directing role of the Party, the creative activity of the masses, is the only correct course. The Twenty-second Congress consolidates this beneficial course. The Party's Program and Rules, the decisions of the Congress set forth new guarantees against any recurrence of the cult of the individual. The role of the Party as the great inspiring and organizing force in the building of communism is being further enhanced.

I should also like to say a few words about the following. In many speeches at the Congress, and not infrequently in our press, a special emphasis in discussing the activities of the Central Committee of our Party is laid on my person, my role is stressed in carrying out the most important measures of the Party and the government.

I understand the kind sentiments guiding these comrades. May I, however, emphasize with utmost vigor that everything said about me should be addressed to the Central Committee of our Leninist Party, the Presidium of the Central Committee. Not a single big measure, not a single responsible speech took place on anyone's personal instructions that was not the result of collective discussion, collective decision. This concluding speech too was examined and endorsed by the leading collective.

In collective leadership, in the collective solution of all fundamental problems lies our great strength, comrades.

However gifted this or that leader may be, however hard he may work, a real solid success cannot be achieved without the support of the collective, without the most active participation of the entire Party, of broad popular masses in implementing the planned measures. We must all understand this well and bear this constantly in mind.

Communist leaders are made strong by the activity of the masses they lead. If they correctly understand and express the interests of the Party, the interests of the people, if they fight for these interests without sparing their strength, energy, their very lives, if they are inseparable from the Party in all matters, big and small, as the Party is inseparable from the people—such leaders will always have the support of the Party and the people. And the course for which such a leader fights will triumph inevitably.

Of course, one must have qualities necessary for the struggle for the Party's cause, for the vital interests of the people, because our ideological opponents, our enemies, first and foremost, concentrate their fire on those leaders who, welding an *aktiv* around the directing bodies—and through this *aktiv,* the entire people—are managing matters along the true Leninist road.

Here at the Congress, for instance, much was said about the frantic energy of the anti-Party factionists Molotov, Kaganovich, Malenkov, and others against the Leninist Central Committee of the Party and and against myself personally. Opposing the Party line laid down at the Twentieth Congress, the splitters concentrated the main fire upon Khrushchev, who is objectionable to them. Why against Khrushchev? Because by the will of the Party Khrushchev was appointed to the post of first secretary of the Central Committee. The factionists grossly miscalculated. The Party routed them both ideologically and organizationally.

The Central Committee of our Party displayed an extremely high level of political maturity and a truly Leninist understanding of the situation. It is indicative that literally not a single member of the Central Committee, or alternate member of the Central Committee, not one member of the Auditing Commission supported the wretched handful of splitters.

While coming out resolutely against all the abominable phenomena of the cult of the individual, Marxists-Leninists have always recognized and will recognize the authority of leaders.

But it would be wrong to put this or that leader apart, by himself, to separate him somehow from the ruling collective, to extoll him inordinately. This is contrary to the principles of Marxism-Leninism. You all know how strongly Marx, Engels, and Lenin came out against those who lauded their merits. And yet the great role of the founders of scientific communism, Marx, Engels, and Lenin, and their great services to the working class, to all mankind, simply cannot be overestimated.

Both self-praise and special accentuation, inordinate magnification of the role of individual leaders are deeply alien to genuine Marxist-Leninists. It is simply insulting to them when someone importunately tries to separate them, isolate them from the directing nucleus of comrades.

We Communists highly value and support the authority of correct and mature leadership. We must safeguard the authority of leaders recognized by the Party and the people. But every leader must also be aware of the other side of the matter—never pride himself on his position, remember that in holding this or that post a man merely fulfills the will of the Party, the will of the people, who never lose control over him even if they have endowed him with the greatest of power. The leader who forgets this pays dearly for such mistakes. I'd say—pays during his lifetime or, if the people do not forgive him, even after his death, as happened with the denunciation of the cult of the person of Stalin. A man who forgets that he must carry out the will of the Party, the will of the people, cannot, properly speaking, be called a real leader. We mustn't have such "leaders" either in the Party or in the state machinery.

By virtue of many reasons great power is concentrated in the hands of a man holding some leading post. A leader promoted to his position by the Party and the people should not abuse his power. The reports to the Congress already dealt with measures which we have enacted and will enact to prevent any revival of the ugly phenomena of the cult of the individual. But one thing cannot be stipulated by any charter items—the collective of leaders should well realize that it is impermissible to allow a situation where any, even the most deserving, person could cease to reckon with the views of those who promoted him to his position.

One cannot, comrades, simply cannot permit the appearance and development of such things where the deserved authority of some individual may assume such forms that this individual will take it into his head that everything is permitted him, that he no longer needs the collective. In this case he may cease to heed the voice of other comrades, promoted like him to leadership, may start suppressing them. Our great teacher, V. I. Lenin, came out resolutely against this, and our Party has paid too high a price for not heeding his wise counsel.

Let us then be worthy disciples of Lenin in this important question too.

Comrades, a struggle has been going on for over a century between two ideologies—the ideology of the working class, expressed in the Marxist theory of scientific communism, and the ideology of the exploiting classes, the bourgeois ideology.

With the appearance of the teachings of Marx and Engels, the working class, as the most revolutionary class, received a mighty ideological weapon in the struggle for its liberation, for a revolutionary transformation of society, for the dictatorship of the proletariat.

At first the ideas of scientific communism were understood only by the more progressive intelligentsia and the advanced part of the working class. The way of the development of revolutionary consciousness was not an easy one. The spread and assimilation of new ideas were connected with considerable difficulties, as these ideas called for revolutionary struggle, for the destruction of the capitalist system, a system of brutal exploitation.

That struggle called for sacrifices and privations. It called for exploits in the name of the future which was to be built on the ruins of capitalism. It was a call to grim revolutionary class struggle, and this struggle required courageous men who had developed in themselves a hatred of the exploiting system and were confident of the inevitable victory of the working class. This road was taken by the best of the best, the revolutionaries of the revolutionaries, and they won, overcoming tremendous difficulties.

It was a great fortune for the working class of our country that leadership of its revolutionary struggle was assumed over half a century ago by a Party established by Vladimir Ilyich Lenin. At the Second Congress, the Party adopted its first Program, drafted with Lenin's active participation. The main task set in the Program was to overthrow the power of capitalists and landlords and establish the power of the working class, the laboring people.

In October 1917, the working people of Russia, under the banner of the great ideas of Marxism, accomplished a socialist revolution and took power into their hands.

But in winning power the working people inherited a war-ravaged economy. It had to overcome great difficulties and privations, make great sacrifices. It was necessary to repulse the interventionists, crush the internal counterrevolution, build up an industry, put the ravaged and neglected agriculture back on its feet, restore the transport, organize trade, overcome economic dislocation and starvation. A clear realization of the need for working devotedly in the name of the morrow, in the name of the future, was required of the working class.

It was an extremely complex, difficult but noble task. And it could only be accomplished by people prepared to make sacrifices today in order to build a better future for their children and grandchildren.

After the establishment of the dictatorship of the proletariat, our Party adopted a second Program—the program of building socialism. Its creator was Lenin. The great result of the fulfillment of the second Program was the complete and final victory of socialism in our country which became a country of mighty industry, large-scale agriculture, advanced science and culture.

And now, comrades, we have entered the third stage of the great struggle. We are adopting a third Program of the Leninist Party—the Program of communist construction. How far we have traveled, how different the present conditions are from those in which the second, let alone the first, Party Program was adopted.

The socialist economy has become so strong, so vigorous that from the summits we have reached we can issue an open challenge of peaceful economic competition to the most powerful capitalist country—the United States of America.

The struggle between two ideologies is now entirely different in character from what it was at the dawn of Marxism. The ideas of scientific socialism have taken hold of the masses and have become a great material force. They have been put into effect; the material and technical basis of a new society is being created by the efforts of the peoples. From the purely ideological sphere the struggle has now spread to the sphere of material production.

The noble ideas of communism are now fought for not only by the most progressive part of the society but by all the peoples of our country and the other socialist countries. The Soviet Union is now literally and figuratively storming the sky and, putting the ideas of communism into effect, demonstrates the superiority of the socialist system over capitalism.

Socialism is now more than an idea for whose realization the Party has rallied the working people. Socialism has become a reality. We say: Take a look at the Soviet Union, the socialist countries, and you shall see what the working class, the working people, is capable of when it holds the power and implements the ideas of scientific communism. Look what it has achieved in a historically brief period! Its successes, its example exert a great influence on the masses of the working people, on all the peoples of the world.

Socialism is no longer a thing of the future; it is already giving great material and spiritual benefits to the peoples which have taken to the road of building a new life. The example of the socialist countries is becoming increasingly attractive to the working people of all countries. The ideas of communism are spreading wider and deeper, arousing hundreds of millions of people to history-making creative endeavors.

The mighty and ever accelerating movement to communism will sweep away all that is an obstacle on the way to the cherished goal—the building of the most just society on earth. This is not a struggle of some against others in order to legalize their rule over them, it is a struggle against oppression, against slavery, against exploitation, a struggle for the happiness of all. We firmly believe that the time will come when the children, the grandchildren of those who today do not understand and do not accept communism will live under communism.

Comrades, the tasks which the Twenty-second Congress is setting for the Party and the people are truly grandiose. Great efforts by the entire Party, by the entire people will be required to put this majestic Program into effect. But we have everything necessary to fulfill this Program.

The task now is to direct all our efforts, all the ebullient, inexhaustible energy of the people, without losing a day, to accomplishing the practical tasks of communist construction.

The Program has been unanimously approved by the Congress. The thing now is to get down, with all the passion typical of Communists, to putting it into effect.

Our Congress is magnificent proof of the readiness and resolution of the Party, of the entire Soviet people to achieve the great aim of building communism in our country. And there is no doubt that communism will be built in the Soviet Union—such is the will of the Party, the will of the people!

Upon the completion of the Twenty-second Congress the delegates will leave for all parts of our great motherland. They will be armed with the Program of building a communist society. Our aims are clear and the roads are mapped. It is not in the distant future but today that we are getting down to the practical implementation of the Program.

Comrades, never have our forces, the forces of world socialism, been so mighty as they are today. The new Program is opening up the brightest, the most thrilling vistas before the Party and the people. The sun of communism is rising over our country. We shall do everything to bring closer by dedicated work the day when this sun will shine on all the boundless expanses of our magnificent motherland! Let us devote all our strength, all Bolshevist energy to the triumph of communism!

Under the leadership of the glorious Leninist Party, onward to the victory of communism! *

* On October 31, 1961, *Pravda* published the following decree of the 22nd Party Congress:

Decree of the 22nd Congress of the Communist Party of the Soviet Union on the Mausoleum of Vladimir Ilich LENIN.

The 22nd Congress of the Communist Party of the Soviet Union decrees:
1. The mausoleum on Red Square at the Kremlin wall, created to make eternal the memory of Vladimir Ilich LENIN—the deathless founder of the Communist Party and the Soviet State, the leader and teacher of the workers of the whole world—is to be named in the future: The Mausoleum of Vladimir Ilich LENIN.
2. The further retention in the mausoleum of the sarcophagus with the bier of J. V. Stalin shall be recognized as inappropriate since the serious violations by Stalin of Lenin's precepts, abuse of power, mass repressions against honorable Soviet people, and other activities in the period of the personality cult make it impossible to leave the oier with his body in the mausoleum of V. I. Lenin.

Appendix:
Official Soviet Encyclopedia Biography of Nikita Sergeyevich Khrushchev *

Khrushchev, Nikita Sergeyevich (born April 17, 1894)—outstanding figure of Communist Party and Soviet state, loyal disciple of V. I. Lenin, member of Party Central Committee Presidium and First Secretary of Party Central Committee. Member of Presidium of U.S.S.R. Supreme Soviet.

N. S. Khrushchev was born in the family of a miner in the village of Kalinovka in Kursk Gubernia. From his early years he worked as a hired shepherd and later as a machinist at factories and mines in the Donets Basin. N. S. Khrushchev joined the Communist Party in 1918. He took an active part in the Civil War on the Southern Front. After the Civil War he worked in a Donets Basin mine, and later studied in the workers' faculty of the Donets Basin Industrial Institute. N. S. Khrushchev engaged in active Party work in the regiment, the mine and the workers' faculty and was repeatedly elected secretary of the Party cell. After finishing the workers' faculty N. S. Khrushchev held responsible Party posts in the Donets Basin and later in Kiev. In 1929 he enrolled at the J. V. Stalin Industrial Academy in Moscow, where he was elected secretary of the Party committee. From January 1931, N. S. Khrushchev was Secretary of the Bauman Borough Party Committee, then of the Krasnaya Presnya Borough Party Committee, in Moscow. Between 1932 and 1934, N. S. Khrushchev served as Second Secretary of the Moscow City Party Committee, and then as First Secretary of the Moscow City Party Committee and Second Secretary of the Moscow Province Party Committee; in 1935 he was elected First Secretary of the Moscow Province and City Party Committees, where he worked until 1938. During these years N. S. Khrushchev did a great deal of organizational work in carrying out the plans

* *Bolshaya Sovietskaya Entsiklopedia,* Vol. XLVI, 2d Ed. This volume published in 1957, pp. 390–91. English translation copyrighted by *The Current Digest of the Soviet Press,* IX, No. 42, p. 10.

of the Party and government for the socialist reconstruction of Moscow, for municipal improvement of the capital and for improving the living conditions of workers and employees.

In January 1938, N. S. Khrushchev was elected First Secretary of the Ukraine Communist Party Central Committee; from March to December, 1947, he was Chairman of the Ukraine Republic Council of Ministers, and he was re-elected First Secretary of the Ukraine Communist Party Central Committee in December 1947, where he worked until December 1949. As the leader of the Ukraine Party organization for 12 years, N. S. Khrushchev played an outstanding role in rallying the Communists of the Ukraine for the solution of tasks in developing the national economy and culture and for improving the working people's well-being.

During the Great Patriotic War, 1941–1945, N. S. Khrushchev served with the army in the field, did important work at the fronts and was a member of the Military Council of the Kiev Special Military District, the Southwest Sector of Operations, the Stalingrad, Southern and First Ukrainian Fronts. N. S. Khrushchev took active part in the defense of Stalingrad and in preparations for the rout of the fascist German troops at Stalingrad.

Simultaneously with his work at the fronts, N. S. Khrushchev, as Secretary of the Ukraine Communist Party Central Committee, did much work in organizing the nationwide partisan movement in the Ukraine against the fascist German invaders.

In the postwar period N. S. Khrushchev has done important work in organizing the struggle to restore and further develop the national economy.

From December 1949, through March 1953, N. S. Khrushchev was Secretary of the Party Central Committee and First Secretary of the Moscow Province Party Committee.

N. S. Khrushchev has been a member of the Party Central Committee since 1934. In 1938 he was elected a candidate [alternate] member of the Politburo of the Party Central Committee, and in 1939, after the 18th Party Congress, a member of the Politburo of the Party Central Committee. At the 19th Party Congress (1952) N. S. Khrushchev delivered the report "Changes in the Statutes of the All-Union Communist Party (of Bolsheviks)." He was elected a member of the Party Central Committee at the Congress, and a member of the Presidium of the Party Central Committee and Secretary of the Party Central Committee at a plenary session of the Central Committee. The March 1953 joint plenary session of the Party Central Committee, the U.S.S.R. Council of Ministers and the Presidium of the U.S.S.R. Supreme Soviet deemed it necessary that N. S. Khrushchev concentrate on work in the Party Central Committee, and in view of this he was relieved of the duties of First Secretary of the Moscow Province Party Committee.

In September 1953, a plenary session of the Party Central Committee elected N. S. Khrushchev First Secretary of the Party Central Committee.

At the 20th Party Congress (1956), on Feb. 14, N. S. Khrushchev delivered the report of the Party Central Committee and on Feb. 25, at a closed session of the Congress, he delivered the report "On the Cult of the Individual and Its Consequences." He was elected a member of the Party Central Committee at the 20th Party Congress and a member of the Presidium of the Party Central Committee and First Secretary of the Party Central Committee at a plenary session of the Central Committee.

N. S. Khrushchev is Chairman of the Party Central Committee's Bureau for the Russian Republic.

N. S. Khrushchev's trips, together with other leading figures of the U.S.S.R., to the Chinese People's Republic, the Polish People's Republic, Yugoslavia, India, Burma, Afghanistan, Great Britain and other countries and his participation in the four-power conference of heads of state in Geneva [July 1955] were important landmarks on the road toward strengthening peace and friendship among peoples.

For his great services in guiding economic work and for successful fulfillment of Party and government assignments during the Great Patriotic War, N. S. Khrushchev has been awarded three Orders of Lenin, Orders of Suvorov First and Second Class, the Order of Kutuzov First Class, the Order of the Patriotic War First Class, the Order of the Red Banner of Labor and three medals.

By a decree of the Presidium of the U.S.S.R. Supreme Soviet dated April 16, 1954, N. S. Khrushchev was awarded the title Hero of Socialist Labor and presented with the Order of Lenin and the gold Hammer and Sickle Medal on his 60th birthday, for outstanding services to the Communist Party and the Soviet people.

Index